Hellships Down

Hellships Down
*Allied POWs and the Sinking
of the* Rakuyo Maru *and* Kachidoki Maru

MICHAEL STURMA

McFarland & Company, Inc., Publishers
Jefferson, North Carolina

This book has undergone peer review.

LIBRARY OF CONGRESS CATALOGUING-IN-PUBLICATION DATA

Names: Sturma, Michael, 1950– author.
Title: Hellships down : Allied POWs and the sinking of the Rakuyo Maru and Kachidoki Maru / Michael Sturma.
Other titles: Allied POWs and the sinking of the Rakuyo Maru and Kachidoki Maru
Description: Jefferson, North Carolina : McFarland & Company, Inc., Publishers, 2021. | Includes bibliographical references and index.
Identifiers: LCCN 2021006106 | ISBN 9781476682426 (paperback : acid free paper) ∞ ISBN 9781476642192 (ebook)
Subjects: LCSH: World War, 1939–1945—Prisoners and prisons, Japanese. | Bancroft, Arthur, 1921–2013. | Richards, Rowley. | World War, 1939–1945—Prisoners and prisons, Japanese. | World War, 1939–1945—Atrocities—Japan. | Prisoners of war—Transportation—Pacific Ocean. | World War, 1939–1945—Naval operations, Japanese. | World War, 1939–1945—Naval operations, American. | World War, 1939–1945—Search and rescue operations—Pacific Ocean. | Rakuyō Maru (Ship)—History. | Kachidoki Maru (Ship)—History.
Classification: LCC D805.J3 S78 2021 | DDC 940.54/72520922—dc23
LC record available at https://lccn.loc.gov/2021006106

BRITISH LIBRARY CATALOGUING DATA ARE AVAILABLE

ISBN (print) 978-1-4766-8242-6
ISBN (ebook) 978-1-4766-4219-2

© 2021 Michael Sturma. All rights reserved

No part of this book may be reproduced or transmitted in any form or by any means, electronic or mechanical, including photocopying or recording, or by any information storage and retrieval system, without permission in writing from the publisher.

Front cover image: *Rakuyo Maru* survivors rescued by *USS Sealion*, September 1944 (National Archives)

Printed in the United States of America

*McFarland & Company, Inc., Publishers
Box 611, Jefferson, North Carolina 28640
www.mcfarlandpub.com*

To Susan and Wes Witt
For their courage in adversity

Acknowledgments

I am grateful for the assistance of staff at the Australian War Memorial, the Australian National Archives at Canberra and Melbourne, the National Archives of Singapore, the Singapore National Library, and the Geoffrey Bolton Library at Murdoch University.

Assistance afforded from an Australian Army History Grant and an Australia-Japan Foundation Grant is gratefully acknowledged. The latter grant facilitated a visit of Tokyo in 2017 where I was generously hosted by the National Institute of Defense Studies. I am especially indebted to Hiroyuki Shindo, Senior Research Fellow at the National Institute of Defense Studies in Tokyo, for his insights and assistance with relevant Japanese-language documents.

My thanks to the team at McFarland, and especially Charlie Perdue, for their confidence in the project and encouragement. The project also benefited from the comments of two anonymous peer reviewers. Both reviewers were generous in recognizing the original manuscript's strengths while astute in making constructive suggestions.

My long-time friend Dr. Ian Chambers provided invaluable editorial and technical advice. Colleagues, both in the History Program and in kindred disciplines at Murdoch University, have provided a supportive environment to work in. Special thanks to Mike Durey, Arjun Subrahmanyan, Dean Aszkielowicz, Sandra Wilson, Andrew Webster, Jan Gothard, Helen Brash, Lenore Layman, Gary Wickham, Jo Goodie, Barbara Evers, Malcolm Tull, Ranald Taylor, Rikki Kersten, Jim Trotter, Takeshi Moriyama, Dave Palmer, Sue Boorer, Diane Lee, Mark Jennings, Yohei Okamoto and Leonie Stickland. As always, my wife Ying has been a source of continuous support.

Table of Contents

Acknowledgments	vi
Preface	1
Introduction	3

Part I. Convoy HI-72

1. Deadly Jungles, Dangerous Waters	8
2. Ambush	17
3. Under Siege	24
4. A New Dawn	31
5. The Mercy of Wolves	38
6. Another Convoy and More Survivors	45
7. To Saipan, to Japan	53
8. Post-Mortem	63

Part II. Aftermath

9. Going Home	72
10. Repercussions	81
11. POWs in Japan	90
12. Liberation	97
13. Americans	104
14. Friendly Fire	112
15. Adjustment	120

Part III. Crimes at Sea

16. Retribution … 130
17. *Raishin Maru* … 137
18. *Sanuki Maru* … 147
19. *Yoizuki* Incident … 154
20. Hellships in Context … 165

Epilogue … 173
Chapter Notes … 181
Bibliography … 213
Index … 227

Preface

The Japanese ships used to transport Allied prisoners during the Second World War were generally known as "hellships." These were often antiquated freighters, but even when relatively new ships transported POWs they usually became hellish through gross overcrowding, lack of toilet facilities, shortages of food and water. Many prisoners of war remember these ships as their worst experiences of Japanese captivity.

Historians have documented the cruel conditions on Japanese transport ships, including Gregory Michno in *Death on the Hellships: Prisoners at Sea in the Pacific War* and Raymond Lamont-Brown in *Ships from Hell: Japanese War Crimes on the High Seas*. There remains, however, scope for additional research and reappraisal. Having spent two decades researching and writing on U.S. submarines in World War II, I was personally drawn to the tragic stories of hellships sunk by Allied submarines. Just how many hellships were sunk by "friendly fire" was not fully appreciated until after the war ended, and even now the definitive number remains uncertain.

Many writers blame this situation on the Japanese for carrying POWs on unmarked ships. However, there was nothing in the Geneva Convention compelling combatants to mark ships carrying prisoners of war. The Allies were as guilty as the Japanese for transporting prisoners on unmarked ships. Despite the efforts of the International Red Cross to broker an agreement for the safe passage of ships carrying prisoners, both the Axis and Allied powers feared such a system would reveal convoy routes or be used to surreptitiously move troops and materials. In the European and Mediterranean theaters transporting POWs on unmarked ships had similarly tragic consequences. In one notorious incident the British ship *Laconia*, carrying about 1,800 Italian prisoners, was torpedoed by a German U-boat on 12 September 1942. Even as the U-boat mounted rescue efforts under the display of a large red cross, American planes attacked it. Nearly three-quarters of the Italian prisoners perished along with civilian passengers.

Submarines in the Pacific took a much higher toll on the lives of prisoners of war than in Europe. By some estimates, about one-third of all

Allied POW deaths under the Japanese occurred at sea. The focus of this book is one of the most-deadly attacks on Allied POWs, when a wolfpack of American submarines destroyed the Japanese convoy HI-72 in September 1944. Among the submarines' victims were two ships carrying Australian and British prisoners of war. The fate of convoy HI-72 serves to exemplify the wider war at sea in the Pacific. It illustrates the fatal ordeal experienced by many Allied prisoners, but also the quirks of fate that could contribute to individual survival. The story of the prisoner survivors also exemplifies the enduring effects of war. The hellship experience did not simply end with the war but lingered on in the lives of families who mourned relatives left with no proper grave sites, and many former prisoners of the Japanese who suffered lasting trauma.

Introduction

On 6 September 1944, convoy HI-72 departed Singapore for Japan. Six days later a wolfpack of three American submarines attacked and destroyed the convoy. In this case, the victims included about 2,000 Australian and British prisoners of war transported on the ships *Rakuyo Maru* and *Kachidoki Maru*. Men who had already survived the notorious Thai-Burma railway faced another life and death struggle at sea.

Historians often represent the naval war as a relatively "clean" conflict, more about statistics of ships which were sunk rather than lives lost. Furthermore, the war at sea frequently appears one-dimensional, concentrating mainly on the attackers rather than those attacked, so that there is little sense of the experience of those aboard doomed vessels. In the case of *Rakuyo Maru* and *Kachidoki Maru*, the attackers and attacked were mainly on the same side. The firsthand accounts of the survivors bring home the brutality of the submarine war and the terror experienced by thousands of Allied prisoners of war transported on Japanese ships during the Second World War.

At its heart, this is a story of survival. This book details the extraordinary rescue of some of the prisoners by the same submarines that attacked convoy HI-72, and the fate of those who fell back into Japanese hands. Admiral Chester Nimitz, commander of the U.S. Pacific Fleet, reportedly described the rescue as "One of the most sensational stories of the war."[1] Nevertheless, the story remains obscure compared to that of USS *Indianapolis*, torpedoed by a Japanese submarine near the end of the war on 30 July 1945. In a post-war environment in which remarkable survival tales abounded, the fate of convoy HI-72 remained relatively unknown. In the case of *Indianapolis*, rescue efforts began four days after the sinking; from the cruiser's crew of 1,196 men there were 321 survivors.[2] An even smaller proportion of Allied POWs survived *Rakuyo Maru*, 295 from 1,300, and some of them persevered at sea for an even longer period than did those from the *Indianapolis*.

Parts of the *Rakuyo Maru* story have been told before. Joan and Clay

Blair published the most authoritative account of the episode in 1979 with their book *Return from the River Kwai*.[3] Masters of oral history, they based their book mainly on interviews conducted with former-prisoner survivors. Inevitably, a reliance on personal memories raises questions of reliability and verifiability. One can, however, compare and reconcile oral testimony with other forms of evidence whenever possible. Since the Blairs published their book forty years ago, more sources have become available; more wartime memoirs are published, while archival records and the work of independent scholars have become more accessible with the advent of the Internet. The website Combined Fleet, for example, provides details on the movements of many Japanese ships previously shrouded in obscurity. My study also puts more emphasis on the official sources, in part tracking the government responses to the unexpected recovery of Allied POWs at a crucial juncture of the war.

Most importantly, I have broadened and lengthened the conventional narrative. First, I consider not only the two prisoner transports *Rakuyo Maru* and *Kachidoki Maru*, but the convoy in which they sailed. The study situates convoy HI-72 in the context of Pacific maritime warfare and, when possible, includes a Japanese perspective on events. Whereas most wartime stories end with the war, I have looked at the consequences of the episode in longer frame, extending the standard narrative beyond the rescue of Allied POWs to consider the implications of their survival and its continuing reverberations after World War II ended. Part of this constitutes what historian Michael McKernan calls the "hidden history" of veterans' adjustment in the post-war years.[4]

From one perspective, *Rakuyo Maru* and *Kachidoki Maru* serve as exemplars of the hellship experience. From early in the war, the Japanese began the practice of shipping prisoners of war for forced labor. Contrary to the Geneva Convention, POWs were used to directly support the Japanese war effort through projects like the Thai-Burma railway and the building of airfields at Sandakan on Borneo.

The dispersal of Allied POWs by sea not only served Japanese labor needs but acted as a form of propaganda. The employment of the prisoners as virtual slaves throughout Southeast Asia was intended in part to undermine the mystique of European colonial rule. As explained by Japan's minister for war, General Seishiro Itagaki, "It is our purpose by interning American and British prisoners of war in Korea to make Koreans realize positively the true might of our empire as well as to contribute to psychological propaganda work for stamping out any ideas of the worship of Europe and America which the greater part of Korea still retains deep down."[5]

When Allied prisoners were transported for labor in Southeast Asia, there was often a ritual march through towns to reinforce their new status among the locals. George Patterson recalls that after he and his fellow prisoners reached port at Takao, Formosa, on 29 August 1942, they were marched around town so that the civilian population could witness the POWs' "humiliation."[6] In another example, after *Fukkai Maru* landed 1,100 prisoners at Pusan, Korea, they were marched around the streets in columns of four headed by a Japanese officer on horseback. As described by one POW, "The march went on all day under a hot sun with only two halts in the playgrounds of two schools where the children were allowed to come close up to the prisoners and jeer and spit at them."[7] The prisoners were next entrained to Seoul, where they underwent another lengthy march before entering their detention camp.

Part of this book examines Australia's attempts at retribution after the war. Although the Allies initiated no war crime prosecutions in relation to *Rakuyo Maru* or *Kachidoki Maru*, this book details the only two Australian prosecutions involving hellships. One was the infamous *Raishin Maru* which took seventy days to travel from Singapore to Moji, Japan, one of the longest journeys at sea endured by POWs in the Pacific War. The only other Australian prosecution involving a hellship centered on the *Sanuki Maru*. This case challenges some of the popular stereotypes of hellships, yet in many respects it conformed with other war crime trials. In a final twist, the book also examines a case where Australia became embroiled in its own post-war "hellship" controversy. Fierce debate erupted over the conditions on board the Japanese destroyer *Yoizuki* after it departed Sydney in March 1946 with over a thousand former prisoners and internees for repatriation to Asia.

In relating the *Rakuyo Maru* story, I focus particularly on two survivors: Arthur Bancroft and Charles "Rowley" Richards. Bancroft, rescued by an American submarine, returned to Australia in late 1944 before the war was over. Remarkably, he survived not only the loss of *Rakuyo Maru*, but the loss of HMAS *Perth* two years earlier. The Japanese rescued Richards, a medical doctor and the most senior Australian officer to survive *Rakuyo Maru*. He continued his captivity in Japan until the end of the war. Apart from the intrinsic interest of their respective careers, both men left considerable evidence documenting their lives that helps flesh out their stories of survival.

Several major themes emerge from this study. Overall, the fate of convoy HI-72 exemplifies the effects of "total war." Unrestricted submarine warfare was indicative of the extreme commitment adopted to win the war, regardless of the consequences to the enemy or even one's own people. As is clear from prisoners' accounts, at times U.S. submarines created more terror than even their Japanese captors. The story highlights Australia's at times problematic relationship with its principal allies—the United States and Britain. Another theme that emerges is the degree to which Australians were divided in their attitudes toward the Japanese. Even among former prisoners of war, attitudes were more varied than generally appreciated. The *Yoizuki* incident further illustrates the range of community opinions in the immediate post-war period, both toward returned POWs and former enemies. Finally, the book seeks to underline the diversity of conditions prisoners faced on hellships. While few prisoners had anything positive to say about their experiences, the treatment they received from the Japanese was far from uniform.

Part I
Convoy HI-72

Chapter 1

Deadly Jungles, Dangerous Waters

Arthur Bancroft, born in Fremantle, Western Australia, in 1921, enlisted in the Royal Australian Navy (RAN) in 1940 at the age of nineteen. At six feet tall, his auburn hair earned him the flamboyant nickname "Blood." One of seven children in his family, Arthur already had one brother in the Second Australian Imperial Force (AIF), the all-volunteer army raised for the duration of the war. Another brother joined the Royal Australian Air Force.

In October 1941 Arthur was assigned to the light cruiser HMAS *Perth*, a ship originally commissioned in the Royal Navy in 1936 as HMS *Amphion*. The British transferred the 6,830-ton ship to the Royal Australian Navy in 1939. *Perth* saw action in the Mediterranean before returning to Australia in July 1941. As part of a move to bolster morale, the RAN began a policy of assigning men to ships that represented their home locales; Bancroft became one of the men from Western Australia to join the ship's complement.[1]

Less than six months later, *Perth*'s career ended when it sailed inadvertently into a Japanese landing force off Java. Along with USS *Houston*, the ship sank in the early hours of 1 March 1942 in what became known as the Battle of Sunda Strait. During the battle, Bancroft served as an ammunition loader for one of *Perth*'s eight 4-inch guns, at times close enough to enemy ships to see the rival sailors on deck. She was torpedoed during the battle, and water poured into *Perth* through two large holes on the starboard side and the ship began heeling over. At the same time, enemy ships closed in with shell fire. Captain Hector Waller, who assumed command of *Perth* only four months earlier, ordered his men to abandon ship, telling them it was "every man for himself" and "good luck."[2] From the deck, Bancroft last saw Waller on the bridge fastening his life jacket.

Bancroft jumped from the starboard side of the ship and swam away as *Perth* sank. He joined other sailors on a raft; they tried to make it to land but just when it looked like they might reach shore the currents swept them away. Throughout the night, Japanese warships passed them, but they were only interested in rescuing their own men. Finally, the following day, a lifeboat collected Bancroft and his companions. When an enemy destroyer took them aboard, the Japanese sailors gave the Australians cigarettes, biscuits and water. They also provided them with eye drops and some petrol to try to remove the oil from their bodies. The next morning the Japanese transferred the survivors to a troopship.[3]

Some *Perth* survivors managed to make it to land after the battle. Fred Skeels, who had served on *Perth* for two years, clambered into an abandoned Japanese lifeboat. He reached the Java shoreline about 4 a.m., and from there began walking inland until he reached a village. The villagers turned him over to the Japanese, and days later he re-joined his remaining crewmates.[4] From *Perth*'s crew of 676, Bancroft and Skeels were among the 352 survivors. Their numbers would be far smaller by the end of the war.

Held at Serang on the island of Java, Bancroft and the other prisoners were first crowded into a disused cinema and then transferred to the local jail. Bancroft described his time there as "thirty-eight days of hell."[5] Nevertheless, when the war correspondent Rohan Rivett encountered the *Perth* survivors at Serang on 13 March, he described them as "grand."[6] Even though some of the men nursed wounds and many men suffered from dysentery, they carried on without complaint. A month later, on 13 April 1942, Bancroft and his fellow prisoners were moved some sixty miles to an improved camp at Batavia (modern-day Jakarta), to the main Dutch barracks known as the Bicycle Camp. They spent almost seven months there.

On Thursday, 8 October 1942, the *Perth* survivors sailed from Batavia's port, Tanjong Priok, for Singapore. They were part of a larger contingent of nearly 800 men known as Black Force, named after their senior Australian commander, Lieutenant-Colonel C.M. Black. The group included 191 American survivors from USS *Houston* and Australian soldiers from the 2/2 Pioneer Battalion. The prisoners were crowded on to a battered and rusting 4,575-ton cargo ship named *Kenkon Maru*, although some of the Australians insisted on calling it "King Kong Maru." This was their first experience of what came to be known as a "hellship."

Originally launched in 1935, *Kenkon Maru* eventually became a victim of an American submarine in January 1943. When Bancroft and his fellows boarded the ship, the space below decks had been divided into levels with only 3 feet to 3 feet 6 inches of headroom. Each prisoner had a horizontal space of about 1 foot seven inches. Apart from visits to the latrines, the prisoners were only allowed on deck to escape the stifling holds at dawn and for an hour before dark. At least in this case, the journey was a mercifully brief 96 hours. *Kenkon Maru* arrived at Singapore on 11 October, after the death of one POW on board.[7]

After disembarking *Kenkon Maru*, Bancroft spent only a few days in Singapore, initially sent to Changi barracks and then on work parties based at the River Valley Road camp. On Wednesday, 14 October 1942, Bancroft with 1,700 other POWs boarded the 7005-ton *Maebashi Maru* for Rangoon, Burma. The Imperial Japanese Army requisitioned the ship, originally built in 1921, in October 1941 and converted it to a troop transport. The prisoners had to descend a 40-foot ladder to the hold, already crammed with the gear of Japanese soldiers who occupied the decks above. The men spent 54 hours in stifling conditions before the ship departed Keppel Harbor. By the time they arrived at Burma on 22 October, fourteen POWs died.[8] Like *Kenkon Maru*, the days of *Maebashi Maru* were numbered; less than a year later, on 30 September 1943, the submarine USS *Pogy* torpedoed the ship several hundred miles east of Palau. This time *Maebashi Maru* carried only Japanese troops instead of POWs, and nearly 1,400 soldiers lost their lives.[9]

Bancroft and his fellow prisoners became part of the workforce on the notorious Thai-Burma railway. The planned 270-mile railway stretched from Thanbyuzayat in Burma to Ban Pong in Thailand. Allied submarines largely motivated the building of the Thai-Burma railway; they made supplying Burma by sea a costly exercise. By April 1942 the Japanese committed to building a railway so that supplies could be sent overland rather than risking ships sailing nearly 2,000 miles from Bangkok to Rangoon. In theory, the idea made sense, but in practice it created a living hell for thousands of POWs and Asian laborers.

Brigadier Arthur L. Varley led the first sizeable contingent of Australians from Changi to Burma in May 1942. They sailed from Singapore with 2,000 men on board *Toyashi Maru*. For most of the fourteen-day voyage, the prisoners had to sit back to back below decks. Inspired by the voyage, at least some Australians credited Brigadier Varley with coining the descriptor "hellship" despite the term having a long history.[10]

The force initially worked on constructing airfields in southern Burma before moving to the railway base camp at Thanbyuzayat. Bancroft described Varley as "well built" and as a "good cricketer."[11] At one stage while on the Thai-Burma railway, Varley narrowly escaped death during an Allied bombing attack; the man standing next to him died instantly, while Varley escaped with a badly bruised face.[12] Beginning from March 1943, Allied air raids were one of the many risks faced by prisoners working on the railway. In June 1943, for example, two Allied bombing raids on the northern hub of the railway at Thanbyuzayat killed at least 29 prisoners and wounded another 40.[13] By one estimate, Allied bombs killed around 800 prisoners in Thailand and Burma.[14] Disease and malnutrition killed many more.

Bancroft toiled for over a year under horrific conditions on the

Thai-Burma railway where the men were not so much prisoners of war as slaves. As the single largest Japanese construction project of the war employing prisoners, nearly half of all Allied POWs worked on the railway at some time. The historian Gavan Daws describes the prisoners' treatment on the project as "the biggest POW atrocity of the Pacific war."[15] Nearly twenty percent of the prisoners employed on the Thai-Burma railway died along its jungle path, including 2,815 Australians.[16] Of the 272 *Perth* survivors who toiled on the Thai-Burma railway, 57 died before its completion.[17] Many factors contributed to the death rate, including inadequate food rations, the disruption of supply networks by the rainy season, deadly diseases, physical abuse by guards, but perhaps most of all an unrealistic determination to finish the railway ahead of schedule on 31 August 1943. Much of the prisoners' sufferings originated from Japanese engineers determined to make the deadline. The railway officially opened on 17 October 1943.[18]

Bancroft and many other sailors from HMAS *Perth* worked mainly alongside Australian soldiers from the 2/2 Pioneer Battalion, as part of what was called Williams Force after the commanding officer, Lieutenant Colonel John Williams.[19] Russell Savage was among the Australian POWs working on the railway. Born in Chelmer, Queensland, in 1920, Savage had joined the 2/10th Field Artillery before his capture by the Japanese. As described by Savage, the railway experience was one of "Bashings, brutality, indifference to illness and death, systematic starvation and deprivation, summary executions."[20] Even in these circumstances, in March 1943 the *Perth* survivors managed to hold a commemoration service for their comrades lost at sea the previous year.[21] They remained a tight-knit group, and despite incredible adversity, journalist and fellow prisoner Rohan Rivett described them as a "happy bunch."[22]

Following his work on the railway, Bancroft spent about three months at Tamarkan, Thailand; after what he had suffered through, he described it as "like a holiday camp."[23] As one of the more fit survivors of the railway, Bancroft was drafted for more forced labor in Japan. According to one report, those selected for work in Japan were to be over 5 feet three inches tall and of fair complexion.[24] Many POWs welcomed the opportunity to escape the jungle and looked forward to better conditions. Bancroft's draft travelled by train to Phnom Penh and then by river steamer to Saigon. Plans to ship the men to Japan from Saigon, however, were cancelled due to the heavy toll taken by American submarines on shipping off Indochina. After a twelve-day journey by train and cattle truck, Bancroft and his fellows returned to Phnom Penh and then to Bangkok before arriving back in Singapore on 4 July 1944.[25]

By this stage of the war, Singapore was experiencing severe shortages of food, resulting largely from submarine attacks on Japanese supply lines. Dependent on imported food, especially rice from Thailand, a lack of shipping translated into malnutrition for much of the population. Despite an accelerated ship-building program in Japan, from the second half of 1943 ships were being sunk faster than new ships could be completed.[26] The Japanese attempted to increase food production by various orders, including sending civil servants to work on garden plots. The Japanese also implemented plans to re-settle Singaporeans in Malaya, including a Chinese settlement northeast of Johore named "New Syonan." Prisoners of war and civilian internees suffered most from the lack of provisions.[27]

At Singapore, Bancroft worked on Palau Damar Laut Island, nicknamed "Jeep Island" by the POWs because of its compact size, where the Japanese tasked prisoners with building a graving dock.[28] At least one of the prisoners considered the work there even more exhausting than on the Thai-Burma railway.[29] On 3 September 1944, Bancroft and the other Australians on the island returned to the camp at River Valley Road in preparation for boarding a ship the following day.[30]

Bancroft was among 718 Australians and 599 British POWs loaded on to *Rakuyo Maru* at the Keppel Harbor wharf on 4 September. He was also one of 41 survivors from HMAS *Perth* to board the ship. The other Australians included the remnants of A Force under the command of Brigadier Arthur L. Varley. On *Rakuyo Maru*, the Japanese segregated Varley and other senior officers from their men; they were to be taken to a special camp for high-ranking officers at Karenko on Formosa.[31]

Those boarding *Rakuyo Maru* included Captain Charles Rowland Bromley "Rowley" Richards, a medical officer, born in Sydney in 1916. He was one of the forty-four Australian doctors who heroically ministered to the men on the Thai-Burma railway.[32] Both of Richards' parents were deaf, victims of rubella and diphtheria epidemics that had swept Australia. He entered Sydney University in 1934 to study medicine and joined the AIF in September 1940 to become a medical officer with the 27th Brigade of the Eighth Division. Fortuitously, given his later work in disease-ravaged POW camps, he developed a special interest in hygiene.

Richards was initially supposed to be shipped to Japan from Saigon, but after three aborted attempts to sail he was returned to Singapore. He spent the next three months on Jeep Island. Arthur Bancroft described Richards as "good looking" and estimated he was 5 feet 7 inches tall.[33] Richards' fresh-faced youthful appearance earned him the nickname "baby doctor" from the Japanese guards. Although slight in build, he stood up for the men in his charge and once sustained chipped teeth from an altercation with a guard in Singapore.[34]

Before Bancroft and his fellow prisoners embarked on *Rakuyo Maru*, their Japanese guards and other prisoners warned them about the dangers of their upcoming journey to Japan. At the River Valley Road camp they were joined by survivors from the 3,040-ton Dutch steamer SS *Van Waerwuyck*, renamed *Harugiku Maru* by the Japanese. On 25 June 1944, 720 Dutch, British and Australian prisoners boarded the ship at Belewan, the port city of Medan on Sumatra. A day later the British submarine HMS *Truculent* torpedoed the ship in the Malacca Straits and took the lives of about 200 POWs including thirteen Australians. Many of the over 500 survivors at the River Valley camp had broken bones, burns and other injuries from their ordeal.[35]

By this stage of the war, it was said that you could walk between Singapore and Japan on the periscopes of American submarines. In the South China Sea, wolfpacks of U.S. submarines ravaged Japanese convoys. Meanwhile British submarines, based at Trincomalee on Ceylon (modern-day Sri Lanka), combed the Straits of Malacca looking for victims. The British subs not only torpedoed freighters, but frequently surfaced to attack junks and sampans with their deck guns. These small craft were believed to be part of the Japanese supply network, and they paid a high price. During 1944 alone, British submarines sank nearly 300 small craft, most apparently crewed by local Chinese and Malays.[36]

Many who boarded *Rakuyo Maru* were pessimistic about their prospects of reaching Japan without being torpedoed. Bancroft left his treasured diary with a sailor mate, Edwin Clarence "Marcus" Clark, rather than risk losing it at sea. Clark avoided selection for the Japan party because of an injured foot. Brigadier Varley also divested himself of his diary, burying it at Changi. Rowley Richards, yet another diarist, buried his records at a Singapore cemetery rather than risk losing them at sea, although he secreted a summary in his stethoscope.[37]

Typical of Japanese transport ships, conditions on *Rakuyo Maru* were appalling. The men were crammed into hull spaces originally designed for only a fraction of the passengers. The space between decks had been filled in with tiered shelving to increase its capacity for human cargo, leaving prisoners little headroom or space to move. In the phrasing of one Australian, prisoners were habitually packed into the holds with less space than "a sardine in a tin, without its head or guts."[38]

Australian David Herbert, a former Melbourne butcher, thought *Rakuyo Maru* was "no better or no worse than all the other boats that were sent away."[39] There were the usual crude *benjo*, six slatted toilet boxes lashed to the rails and hanging precariously over the ship's side, which inevitably proved inadequate for men suffering dysentery and other diarrheal disorders. According to one of the prisoners, about ninety percent of the men "were suffering from various forms of bowel trouble."[40] Initially, the prisoners were forced down into the overcrowded holds, but following the prisoners' protests the Japanese later relented and allowed a certain number of the men on deck.[41]

The same day that Bancroft and his fellows boarded *Rakuyo Maru*, another group of British prisoners faced similar conditions on *Kachidoki Maru*. The one-time American passenger liner, previously known as *Wolverine State* and later as *President Harrison*, was originally built in New Jersey. At over 500-feet long and over 10,000 tons, *Kachidoki Maru* was larger than *Rakuyo Maru*. The Japanese captured the ship near Shanghai, painted it dark grey and renamed it.[42] At the Singapore docks on 4 September, the prisoners watched on as hundreds of Japanese civilians and troops, many injured, first boarded the ship. Then some 900 prisoners were forced into a single hold. Thomas Pounder described the space as "like nothing I had ever witnessed before," a suffocating combination of bodies, heat and stench.[43]

The prisoners were destined to spend two days in these stifling conditions at Keppel Harbor before getting underway. Once loaded on the transport ships *Rakuyo Maru* and *Kachidoki Maru*, the prisoners contrived ways to alleviate their suffering in the crowded holds. The most immediate was to insist on access to the toilets—the *benjo*. On *Kachidoki Maru* there were only two toilets allotted to the prisoners, but the long queues that formed at least afforded prisoners an opportunity to escape the hold and get some fresh air.[44]

The lack of provision for latrines on transport ships reflected the deteriorating conditions on Japanese transports during the war. Whereas the provision of one latrine for every ten men would be considered normal, a ship taking prisoners to Korea in 1942 had only three per 200 men. A transport in 1943 had latrines on a scale of three for 700 men.[45] Even that was generous compared to *Kachidoki Maru*. With many men suffering diarrhea and dysentery, the extreme conditions can only be imagined.

Once the convoy got underway at 6:30 a.m. on 6 September, many prisoners faced another problem—seasickness. This added to the misery in the holds. Eventually the British medical officer on *Kachidoki Maru* persuaded the guards to allow the sick men on deck and to leave the hold hatch cover open.[46] On *Rakuyo Maru*, food was in short supply, while a shortage of fresh water proved an even graver problem. The Japanese allowed the prisoners to fill their water bottles only every other day, even though some of their guards were seen taking fresh-water baths.[47] Alfred Allbury felt continually hungry and thirsty, but still believed that life on board once at sea was "in many ways pleasanter than life ashore."[48]

Miserable as the conditions were on transports like *Rakuyo Maru*, at least some POWs took solace that the narrow deck spaces they occupied were originally fitted out to carry Japanese troops.⁴⁹ Indeed, at times prisoners and Japanese troops were transported together on the same ships in shared misery. When the 11,409-ton *Aki Maru* sailed from Batavia in December 1942, POWs shared the crowded hold with Japanese soldiers. As described by a Dutch prisoner in his diary: "Everything too low to stand straight up. Cramped sleeping places. Japanese soldiers were in the same situation. No angry mood. Food the same for everybody: rice, three times a day."⁵⁰

The Japanese designated convoys between Singapore and Japan with the prefix "HI"; *Rakuyo Maru* and *Kachidoki Maru* became part of convoy HI-72. In addition to the two ships carrying prisoners of war, the convoy included the freighters *Asaka Maru* and *Nankai Maru*, and two tankers named *Zuiho Maru* and *Shincho Maru*. Another cargo ship, *Kimikawa Maru*, left the convoy shortly after it departed Keppel Harbor with engine trouble. Given that the ship had already survived two submarine torpedo attacks, the crew probably felt relieved to return to port. *Kimikawa Maru*'s 273 passengers and cargo of bauxite and aviation fuel were destined to remain in Singapore for the time being. This proved only a temporary reprieve, however. The following month, on 23 October, *Kimikawa Maru* sank after departing Manila with a slow convoy heading for Takao, Formosa. The USS *Sawfish* fired four torpedoes into the ship's port side; *Kimikawa Maru* sank in less than three minutes taking down 105 passengers and crew.⁵¹

Four escorts protected convoy HI-72: the destroyer *Shikinami* and three *kaibokan* or sea defense ships (*Hirado, Kurahashi* and *Mikura*). *Mikura*, commanded by Oda Takasuke, and *Kurahashi*, under Lieutenant-Commander Niki, arrived at Singapore on the afternoon of 1 September.⁵² Originally intended to protect fishing boats in the northern Pacific, the *kaibokan* proved well suited for rough seas and were increasingly adapted to combatting submarines.⁵³ One thing the prisoners shared with their Japanese guards and crew was a fear of submarines, so these escorts provided some comfort. Roy Cornford, on *Rakuyo Maru*, believed that the convoy had enough escorts to discourage any attack.⁵⁴

Once out of the sight of land, however, many prisoners began to feel anxious about the prospect of attack from an unseen enemy. Their fears were well-justified. Unknown to the prisoners, only a day after convoy HI-72 departed Singapore, the submarine USS *Paddle* sank another Japanese transport carrying POWs. The *Shinyo Maru* departed Mindanao Island in the Philippines on 3 September carrying 750 American prisoners of war. On 7 September, *Paddle* torpedoed the ship off the Zamboanga Peninsula, resulting in the loss of 667 of the prisoners.⁵⁵

On 11 September, seven ships of convoy MAMO-73 from Manila made a rendezvous with convoy HI-72 about 100 miles northeast of the Paracel Islands. "MAMO" was the designation given to convoys travelling from Manila to Moji, Japan. The merging of convoys from different ports was common at this stage of the war. Three additional transport ships joined HI-72: *Kagu Maru*, *Gokoku Maru* and *Kibitsu Maru*. Four escorts protected these ships, but three of these quickly returned to the Philippines once the convoys merged. The same day, the convoy lost its land-based air cover of circling seaplanes.[56]

Taking a zigzag course to discourage submarine attack, the combined convoy headed north across the South China Sea at 10.5 knots. Typical of Japanese convoys, the merchant ships travelled in two columns with the escorts ranging up and down their flanks. This still left considerable gaps in the convoy's screen. In the Atlantic, the sheer size of Allied convoys and numerous columns offered the most valuable ships some protection in the center from marauding U-boats.[57] The relatively small size of Japanese convoys meant that valuable targets, like oil tankers, were just as exposed as the other ships. Given the limited number of escorts available, increasing limitations on fuel consumption and the necessity of keeping in contact with the merchant ships in their care, Japanese escorts mainly adopted a defensive approach, only reacting after a submarine was sighted rather than aggressively seeking them out before they could attack.[58] Convoy HI-72's vulnerability soon became all too apparent.

Chapter 2

Ambush

As well known by the Japanese, the South China Sea teemed with American submarines. The sea was a massive area covering some 1,400,000 square miles, but it appeared increasingly difficult to evade American forces. By 1944, U.S. submarines typically travelled in groups of three officially known as "coordinated attack groups," although most submariners preferred the descriptor "wolfpack." One of these wolfpacks laid in wait for convoy HI-72. On the night of 9–10 September 1944, the Operations Officer at Pearl Harbor, Richard Voge, directed a pack including *Growler*, *Sealion II* and *Pampanito* to intercept the convoy. As later described by *Sealion*'s commander, Eli Reich, the message about a convoy from Singapore was "in great detail."[1] Two other U.S. submarines in the area, *Queenfish* and *Barb*, served as backup operating to the east.[2]

The overall commander of the wolfpack, Ben Oakley, assumed command of USS *Growler* in April 1944. As standard practice, the pack received an alliterative nickname in his honor, in this case "Ben's Busters." On 5 September 1944, *Sealion* made a brief stop at the island of Saipan to refuel and top up its torpedoes before departing two days later. On 6 September, the commander of USS *Pampanito*, Paul Edward "Pete" Summers, celebrated his thirty-first birthday. He was among the youngest to command a U.S. submarine at the time.

Shortly after 1 a.m. on Tuesday, 12 September, USS *Growler* established radar contact with a convoy about fifteen miles away. Less than an hour later, running on the surface under a sky blotched with dark rain clouds, the submarine had the convoy's starboard column in its sights. Plans quickly changed, however, when *Growler*'s crew spotted an escort bearing down on them. The submarine fired three bow torpedoes at the oncoming ship, then swung hard port to avoid a collision path with its target. As *Growler* accelerated, men on deck observed the first torpedo hit, exploding amidships "in a large ball of yellow flame and black smoke."[3]

Growler's skipper, Ben Oakley, later noted in his patrol report that the explosion brought a "Great sigh of relief." Contrary to his report, however, they had not sunk a 2,300-ton Japanese destroyer as he imagined, but a considerably smaller ship. The *Hirado*, launched on 30 June 1943, was not a destroyer but an *Etoforo*-class *kaibokan* or sea defense ship of 860 tons.[4]

Although the ship was smaller than *Growler*'s crew believed, they had nevertheless scored a significant blow against the convoy. Among those on board *Hirado* was Rear Admiral Sadamichi Kajioka, commander of the Sixth Escort Convoy Command. He took charge of the convoy's four escorts when it departed Singapore, making *Hirado* his flagship. Early in the Pacific War, Kajioka had commanded the Wake Island invasion force and garnered a reputation as "the victor of Wake Island." For the Americans, Wake Island, a U.S. territory since 1899, served as an important aircraft base and observation post on Japanese activities in the Marshall Islands. Kajioka's first assault on Wake Island on 11 December 1941 proved an abject failure. Commanding Destroyer Squadron Six from the light cruiser *Yubari*, Kajioka initially sailed too close to the atoll, bringing his force within firing range of shore batteries and aircraft. As a result, he oversaw the first loss of Japanese warships in the Pacific War. The American defenders sank the destroyers *Hayate* and *Kisaragi*; they also claimed damage on three light cruisers, two destroyers, a patrol boat and a transport. Forced to retreat, Kajioka later returned with a greatly augmented force on 23 December 1941. To his credit, after the fall of Wake Island Kajioka apparently intervened to stop the massacre of American prisoners.[5]

Kajioka later escorted an invasion force to Port Moresby but turned back after the Battle of the Coral Sea stripped him of air cover. Aged 52, he retired from service in October 1943, but was recalled to the Navy General Staff in January 1944. Kajioka died in the attack on *Hirado*, along with another 106 sailors.[6]

In the attack on *Hirado*, *Growler* exemplified several of the elements that made U.S. submarines so effective at this stage of the war. First, *Growler* and its pack mates were alerted to the intended route of the convoy by intelligence and codebreaking collectively known as "Ultra." At 3 a.m. the previous day, American submarines were informed that a convoy from Singapore was on a northeast track through the Paracel Islands to the Formosa Straits.[7] Such intelligence provided the Americans with a huge advantage.

Second, SJ surface radar enabled the Americans to detect ships and plot their movements from impressive distances. The Japanese Navy had entered the war with night-vision superiority, mainly due to the quality of their binoculars, and gained a high reputation for their night fighting in the Solomon Islands.[8] The development of SJ radar allowed the Americans to turn the tables and gain a clear advantage in night actions and in low visibility conditions.

Third, reliable torpedoes allowed *Growler* to successfully sink the oncoming ship. Whereas earlier in the war the Americans were dogged by defective torpedoes, these were greatly improved by 1944 and included new electric torpedoes that left no telltale wakes like conventional steam models. This was *Growler*'s first patrol with a full load of twenty-four Mark 18–1 torpedoes; Oakley proclaimed in his patrol report that "We were well pleased with our 'electric fish' and given our choice would prefer to carry them."[9]

At the time of *Growler*'s attack, from perhaps a half mile away, some of the Allied prisoners of war on *Rakuyo Maru* witnessed the explosion of *Hirado*. Alfred Allbury recalled seeing "a fierce, glowing torch of flame" light the dark sky.[10] Even before boarding *Rakuyo Maru* seven days earlier, Allbury was well familiar with the ship; he spent two weeks at the docks loading it with copra, rubber, tin and scrap iron before it departed Singapore. Once at sea, Allbury took some comfort in convoy HI-72's escorts, "bristling with armaments."[11] Now one of those escorts disappeared in fire and smoke.

After torpedoing *Hirado*, the submarine *Growler* lined up its stern tubes on the nearest column of the convoy. A short time later, however, *Growler* came under fire from another escort a little over one thousand yards away. The submarine went to flank speed, taking a zigzag course to evade the enemy's gunfire. Another Japanese escort joined the pursuit, but *Growler* managed to pull away. The surface speed of American submarines, approaching twenty knots, was another crucial factor in their success against Japanese shipping. The engagement left skipper Ben Oakley immensely proud of his crew, at one stage shouting to his men "you're the best Fire Control party ever seen!"[12] He also believed that in drawing off some of the convoy's escorts, he created opportunities for his pack mates on USS *Sealion* and USS *Pampanito*.

From a distance, men on USS *Sealion* had observed the explosive flash that denoted *Hirado*'s destruction. They also witnessed gunfire and tracers from the escorts that pursued *Growler*. Later a red rocket went up, the Japanese signal for a submarine attack. From its illumination, the convoy appeared to be making a course to the northwest. *Sealion* worked its way into a firing position on the convoy, but then had to abort an attack after a torpedo gyro malfunction. Soon two escorts, with deck guns blazing, began chasing *Sealion*. Skipper Eli Reich conceded in his patrol report that the situation was "too hot for comfort," but eventually *Sealion*'s superior surface speed allowed it to pull away from its pursuers.[13]

Over the next several hours, *Sealion* worked its way back to an attack position on the convoy, diving at a little after 5 a.m. to intercept it. A quarter moon afforded relatively good visibility. Twenty minutes later, *Sealion* fired six torpedoes at two overlapping ships in the convoy's right-hand column from about 2,500 yards. The torpedoes hit two ships—*Nankai Maru* and

Rakuyo Maru.[14] From some eighteen miles away, men on *Growler* observed the *Nankai Maru*'s destruction as a huge column of flame erupted.[15]

Although *Nankai Maru* and *Rakuyo Maru* were armed with guns and depth charges, they had little opportunity to use them against the attacking submarines. The Japanese escorts, though, retaliated by heavily depth-charging *Sealion*. Shortly after the submarine fired its fatal torpedoes, the soundmen on *Sealion* detected the screws of an enemy ship quickly moving in from starboard. The submarine submerged to 250 feet, and although an escort dropped six depth charges they were not particularly close. *Sealion* began edging toward periscope depth, but the sound of screws and sonar pinging drove the boat down again. The escort dropped another half-dozen depth-charges; this time they exploded close aboard.

This cat and mouse game continued for two and a half hours. Eli Reich recorded in his patrol report that "It seemed to us that the escort had picked up an oil slick at daybreak and that we were in for a rough time."[16] Finally, at a little after 8 a.m., *Sealion* managed to reach periscope depth and look at the surface; through a haze of smoke, Reich observed a burning ship well down in the water.

Although *Sealion*'s crew believed that one of the ships they torpedoed was a tanker, it was in fact the diesel-driven cargo-passenger ship *Nankai Maru*. Built and launched at Osaka in 1932, the ship had once sailed between New York, Europe and the Far East. The Imperial Japanese Navy requisitioned the ship in August 1941, and later the same year registered it as an auxiliary troop transport. In this capacity it saw action off Makassar, Midway and Guadalcanal.

More recently, *Nankai Maru* transported vital supplies to Japan. On 20–21 August 1944, the ship took on 6,500 tons of bauxite at Bintan Island south of Singapore. As a key ingredient of aluminum, bauxite was an invaluable commodity, needed for aircraft production. Japan relied on imports for over three-quarters of its bauxite supplies. Before departing Singapore with convoy HI-72, *Nankai Maru* also took on 177 tons of asphalt and a thousand gasoline drums. Once torpedoed by *Sealion*, exploding gasoline drums, as well as the detonation of depth charges carried on the ship's stern, contributed to the disaster. The sinking of *Nankai Maru* resulted in the loss of not only its cargo but 196 of the 525 passengers on board, as well as three crewmen.[17]

The human costs were much higher on *Rakuyo Maru* than *Nankai Maru*. The 9,418-ton Japanese-built passenger-cargo ship was 477 feet long and had a top speed of 15.9 knots. Its cargo from Singapore included oil drums, hemp and rubber.[18] The principal "cargo," however, was 1,318 Allied prisoners of war being shipped to Japan for forced labor. Of these, 1,051 would eventually perish at sea, along with nine crewmen.

Chapter 2. Ambush

Sealion's first torpedo hit *Rakuyo Maru* amidships, with enough force to drive the ship's bow underwater. A second torpedo then hit the ship's bow, lifting it and sending tons of water cascading over the deck. The wall of water flattened Alfred Allbury, who was standing on deck at the time.[19] Using a parlance that his fellow Western Australians could relate to, Private Harold "Harry" Bunker later described it as "like being hit by an enormous dumper on Cottesloe beach."[20] Harry Pickett, another Western Australian and a signalman with the 2/4 Machine Gun Battalion, had been sleeping under some bags on deck when explosions woke him up. As a huge wave crested over the bow of the ship, he had to scramble to avoid being washed overboard.[21]

Another prisoner on deck, John Flynn, was knocked over by the wall of water, landing head first. The fall left him bleeding from behind his left ear and probably concussed. He also suffered a deep gash to the back of his left hand; once healed a white scar served as a permanent reminder of the incident.[22] The water also swept up David Herbert, who worked in a North Essendon butcher shop in Melbourne before joining the Second AIF. The wave left him clinging for life to a steel safety wire that encircled the rigging.[23]

Some of those below deck took a similar beating. The first torpedo explosion threw one of the prisoners, Ray Wheeler, across the number two hold into a bulkhead. He suffered some deep cuts, and decades later the injury still caused him problems.[24] Miraculously, though, it appeared that no prisoners were killed in the initial torpedo attack. David Herbert believed that eight Japanese manning a gun on the ship's bow were wiped out by the wall of water, but there were no other reports of deaths.[25]

The Japanese quickly abandoned ship, leaving the prisoners to organize their own evacuation. Overall, accounts suggest that the POWs abandoned *Rakuyo Maru* in a reasonably orderly fashion, although every man had his own version of events. Given the anticipation of submarine attacks, early in the voyage those with naval or merchant marine experience were called upon to give advice on what to do if the ship sank. Plans for evacuation included getting the sick off the ship first and throwing any floatable material overboard.[26] After *Rakuyo Maru* was torpedoed, twenty-nine-year-old Captain Arthur Sumner of the Second AIF received credit for much of the order. Despite suffering injuries in the torpedo attack that left his face badly bruised and smashed his false teeth, Sumner organized men to throw over rafts and timber as they abandoned ship.[27]

As Australian POW Russell Savage suggests, it is likely that the process of abandoning ship was mainly "a case of mate helping mate."[28] For example, a former merchant seaman told David Herbert that a raft could usually be found on top of the bridge. Sure enough, they found a raft, as well as a pair of large binoculars that Herbert draped around his neck. When he jumped overboard, however, the binoculars dragged him under and he had to hack them off with a knife.[29] Alfred "Alf" Winter, from Western Australia, also nearly became a casualty when abandoning ship. When he jumped in the water, he forgot to cross his arms over his life jacket and it hit him hard in the chin. According to Winter, "I was nearly knocked out and it took me some minutes to recover."[30] He later managed to cling to a raft with eight other survivors.

Roy Cornford, who slept on *Rakuyo Maru*'s deck every night since the ship's departure from Singapore, was on deck when torpedoes hit the ship. After abandoning ship, he clung to a six-foot-by-six-foot wooden raft with seven other men. With so many men on the raft it sank under water; they were mainly kept afloat by their kapok life jackets. Cornford's group later joined up with another raft of the same size, bringing together seventeen men.[31]

Some of the men delayed leaving *Rakuyo Maru*. Russell Savage explored the ship, finding "an abundance of good food and water, whisky and medicines ... all of which could have been used to wonderful advantage on at least the sick personnel."[32] One of the British prisoners, Harry Jones, found his way to the captain's cabin, where he sampled his cigarettes and tinned food.[33] Ray Wheeler took the time to fill some water bottles. Unfortunately, he discovered later that the corks in the bottles leaked and the water became contaminated by seawater. Once in the ocean, Wheeler managed to secure a Carley float with two of his mates.[34] Kitchener Loughnan, a gunner with the 2/10 Field Regiment, also delayed leaving the ship until an officer advised him to jump overboard as the ship listed.[35]

Unable to swim and without a proper lifebelt, Arthur Hall lingered on board. He joined a group of men including Francis "Frank" McGovern, Edward Kelk, William Hubbard and Vic Duncan. Duncan, a survivor of HMAS *Perth*, would later receive high praise from his fellow prisoners for the role he took in *Rakuyo Maru*'s evacuation. He handed out lifebelts and advised men on the best way to go over the side and protect themselves from burning oil in the water.

Much of the group's efforts concentrated on freeing two lifeboats stuck in their davits that the Japanese failed to launch. They only managed to successfully launch one of the boats at about 10 a.m., and sixty of the POWs either got into it or hung from its sides.[36] At about the same time that morning, the escort *Mikura* reported by radio that *Rakuyo Maru* was adrift and that all personnel had abandoned ship. The escort requested instructions.[37]

Frank McGovern was indignant that the Japanese had left a woman on board, presumably a "comfort woman"; the prisoners took her with them once they launched the lifeboat.[38] Rowley Richards observed that the woman "sat very quietly, did not create any trouble and it was most interesting to see the chivalry of the boys who were prepared to risk their own lives to save that of a woman even though she was Japanese."[39] In fact, it is doubtful she was Japanese. Most of those women tricked or forced into prostitution came from Korea, Formosa, China, or other localities in Southeast Asia. Some of the Korean women were duped into prostitution after being promised waitress jobs in Singapore.[40] Japanese prostitutes generally serviced high-ranking officers under better conditions, whereas "comfort women" often were regarded as "military supplies."[41]

Some of the prisoners became early fatalities once in the water, either unable to swim or struck by falling wreckage. One of the Australians, Russell Savage, professed shock at how many of the British prisoners appeared unable to swim.[42] Most of the men made it to rafts or other floating debris. Alfred Allbury, who considered himself a strong swimmer, swam to a raft where his best mate already clung to a rope.[43] As dawn broke, Arthur Bancroft found himself a quarter of a mile from the still floating *Rakuyo Maru*. There were about a hundred men grouped around him, most in the water clinging to ropes around the perimeters of rafts.[44]

Chapter 3

Under Siege

Most of the prisoners had already abandoned *Rakuyo Maru* when another attack on convoy HI-72 unfolded less than two hours later. *Growler* returned to the fray, and at 6:52 a.m. fired a salvo of six torpedoes at a ship about 1,600 yards away. This time they torpedoed a genuine destroyer, the *Fubuki*-class *Shikinami*. Minutes after the attack the destroyer sank, with its depth charges exploding as it went down.[1]

Watching the confrontation from the water, Australian brothers John and Ernest Wade considered the attack miraculous, since it appeared that the submarine torpedoed the ship bow to bow.[2] From his vantage point in the sea, Alfred Allbury had also watched *Shikinami* approach, believing, or at least hoping, that it was coming to pick up survivors. The ship then appeared to disintegrate in an explosion. "Then came the concussion," Allbury recalled. "Great waves of almost unbearable pressure hammering our bodies. The walls of my stomach collapsed. My bowels emptied."[3]

Growler had ended the career of a warship active from the beginning of the Pacific War. *Shikinami*, launched in June 1929, had fired the final fatal torpedo into the cruiser USS *Houston* during the Battle of Sunda Strait. During the Guadalcanal campaign, the ship delivered reinforcements and supplies to the beleaguered Japanese troops on the island. A month before joining convoy HI-72, the destroyer ran aground on an uncharted shoal, possibly affecting its subsequent performance.[4] Those killed on *Shikinami* following *Growler*'s attack included Lieutenant Commander Tatsuhiko Takahashi, who captained the destroyer from 1 April 1944. One of the *kaibokan* escorts, *Mikura*, later managed to recover 8 officers and 120 enlisted men from the stricken destroyer.[5] In a radio message at 8 a.m., *Mikura* reported the loss of *Shikinami* and that *Nankai Maru* was burning with its stern submerged. The report added, "for the present there is apparently no danger Rakuyo Maru will sink."[6]

The sinking of *Shikinami* appeared to throw the convoy into disarray. Attempting to avoid the submarines, three of the ships (*Kagu Maru*, *Gokoku Maru* and *Kibitsu Maru*) set course independently for Hainan

Chapter 3. Under Siege

Island some 200 miles away. Another four cargo ships (*Kachidoki Maru, Asaka Maru, Shincho Maru* and *Zuiho Maru*) headed north with two escorts.⁷ *Sealion* headed north with the intention of regaining contact with the convoy. Shortly after noon, the submarine received a report from USS *Pampanito* that the convoy was moving west about 62 miles from *Sealion*'s position. Convinced that the Japanese ships would probably make a course change for the Formosa Straits, Commander Eli Reich determined to keep *Sealion* on a heading to the northeast to intercept them.⁸

Meanwhile, drama continued in the aftermath of the attack on *Rakuyo Maru*. Some of the prisoners initially experienced a sense of elation in the water. Not only had they survived the torpedo attack, but they were no longer under the direct control of the Japanese. Charlie McKechnie recalled: "We were free.... We were no longer POWs, the Japanese had abandoned us!"⁹ Many prisoners swam between rafts trying to locate friends, while others lashed groups of rafts together to stay close to one another.¹⁰ Later, as the water became choppier, the rafts were separated to avoid banging into one another.¹¹

As the day unfolded, the survivors' predicament became clearer. Alfred Allbury's raft, only six feet by six feet, had over a dozen men desperately clinging to a rope around the perimeter.¹² Many men were partially, if not fully, blinded by the oil that formed a thick slick on the water. Arthur Bancroft believed that some of the men died after swallowing oil.¹³ The concussion from *Sealion*'s depth charging, along with the explosions when *Shikinami* sank, caused some of the men in the water horrible pain. One prisoner compared the sensation to "being hit in the stomach with a sledge hammer."¹⁴

The Japanese survivors of *Rakuyo Maru* mainly huddled in lifeboats off the stricken ship. Relations with the Japanese in the water ranged from instances of cooperation to homicide. Australian prisoner Harold Ramsey found himself sharing a small life boat with a few other POWs and two Japanese officers. As described by Ramsey, "Not long after, one of the Japs stood up and just stepped over the side, wearing his sword, boots, uniform, the lot. He took a short cut, straight down."¹⁵

Some prisoners reportedly took vengeance on their former guards, drowning or beating them to death. Ray Wheeler recalled that in some cases two prisoners would hold Japanese under water until they drowned.¹⁶ Frank McGovern claimed that he saw another prisoner, "a big tough rooster" named Frank McGrath, drown a couple of Japanese.¹⁷ There were other Allied prisoners, however, who were highly skeptical of these reports. Rowley Richards later observed that "few had time to worry about the Japs—obviously some did—and I wonder how many Japs were killed by our men and how much was wishful thinking."¹⁸ Some of the prisoners looked after the Japanese survivors in their midst, in the hope that this would increase their own likelihood of being rescued.[19]

As it transpired, *Rakuyo Maru* remained afloat far longer than anyone imagined. Some of the prisoners returned to the ship to scavenge for supplies. Frank McGovern's mate, Jerry Parkes, was among those to return to *Rakuyo Maru*—it was the last time he saw him.[20] David Herbert believed he was among the last men to visit the ship, when he collected some raw rice and water.[21] Kitchener Loughnan also insisted that he was among those who returned to the ship and part of the very last group to leave it. They swam away as the ship sank and were picked up by a lifeboat that included Rowley Richards, Frank McGovern and Russell Savage.[22] When the *Rakuyo Maru* finally disappeared beneath the water Roy Cornford could observe rubber and other detritus seemingly shoot out from the holds.[23]

At 2:30 in the afternoon, Captain Hosoya, the convoy commander on *Kachidoki Maru*, delegated the escorts *Mikura* and *Kurahashi*, as well as the transport *Kagu Maru*, to carry out rescue operations. Instructions were also given that if *Rakuyo Maru* could not be towed, "will have her disposed of."[24] A message two hours later directed the ships to rescue survivors and proceed to Yulin, a base on the southern coast of Hainan Island.[25] *Mikura* received another message shortly after 6 p.m., but codebreakers could give only a garbled translation: "Unless you expect to save (Raku?)yoo Maru, destroy her. Even though (you have to forsake?) rescue of the (people?), it cannot be helped." Another version of apparently the same message transmitted a minute later, however, translated somewhat differently. "If there is no prospect of saving the Rakuyo Maru, take action to dispose of her. If _____cargo cannot be remove [sic] first, it is just regrettable."[26]

Finally, at dusk two ships began picking up survivors, but only Japanese. Any POWs who tried to board with them were knocked back in the ocean. The Japanese picked up the woman in a lifeboat with Frank McGovern and Rowley Richards, but the prisoners had to remain. The Japanese also took their water.[27] On one raft, where five prisoners had assisted two injured Japanese, the rescued pair tried to return the favor by persuading a naval officer to take the prisoners with them, but unsuccessfully.[28] Roy Cornford witnessed another instance when a Japanese officer left his water bottle with an Australian, apparently apologizing for leaving the POWs behind.[29] A Japanese officer was retrieved from Arthur Bancroft's group, but the prisoners were left behind. Bancroft may have taken solace from his memory of events after HMAS *Perth* sank in the Battle of Sunda Strait; the Japanese had only rescued their own men during the night, but they did begin to pick up Allied survivors the following day.[30] At least in retrospect, Rowley Richards considered that the Japanese picking up their own men first was "fair enough."[31]

Chapter 3. Under Siege

A radio message from *Mikura* at 7:35 in the evening reported that *Rakuyo Maru* sank at 6:20 p.m. It further reported that "Personnel" were picked up from the destroyer *Shikinami*, *Nankai Maru* and *Rakuyo Maru*. There was no specific reference to the fate of the prisoners of war.[32] According to some of the POW accounts, the Japanese shouted derisory epithets as they sailed away. Ray Wheeler recalled that a Japanese officer on one of the rescue ships pointed a pistol, saying "Goodbye, you will die."[33] Some prisoners recalled the Japanese crew of one ship giving them the "thumbs down" sign as they sailed away.[34] Others recalled groups of prisoners defiantly singing "Rule Britannia" and "There'll Always be an England."[35]

On the positive side, the rescued Japanese left their empty lifeboats afloat, which many prisoners quickly occupied. For Kevin Hyde, the lifeboats proved a godsend. He had occupied an improvised raft with another Australian and seven British POWs. By late afternoon, the raft was in danger of breaking up and they were up to their necks in water. Fortunately, in the early evening a lifeboat picked up Hyde and the other men.[36]

Rowley Richards was also among those to occupy an abandoned lifeboat, shifting from the damaged boat he originally occupied. While some of those in Richards' boat were British, the occupants of the lifeboats largely divided along national lines.[37] As Richards put it, even in captivity the British and Australians remained very much separate forces, "neither enthusiastic to interact with the other when it wasn't necessary."[38] Other Australians in Richards' lifeboat included David Herbert, army gunner Ian Angus MacDiarmid and Jim Mullins. They also picked up a fellow from the Royal Australian Air Force named "Bluey" McKay, who up until then had been swimming on his own.[39] Some of those to share the boat were sailors who survived the loss of HMAS *Perth*. Richards believed that having some experienced seamen in the lifeboat was a definite advantage; one of their first contributions was to collect all the knives from the men on board in case someone "ran amok."[40]

After their morning attacks, the American submarines continued to search for the remainder of convoy HI-72. By 8 p.m. *Growler* had surfaced and headed for a pre-arranged rendezvous with pack mates *Sealion* and *Pampanito*. After nearly an hour of trying to establish radio contact, however, *Growler*'s crew felt frustrated and departed the rendezvous area.[41] USS *Pampanito*, having traversed 600 miles pursuing the convoy toward Hainan Island, was otherwise occupied. The submarine's skipper, Pete Summers, was originally from Lexington, Tennessee, and graduated from the Naval Academy with the class of 1936. Eventually, using its SJ radar, *Pampanito* made radar contact with ships fifteen miles away. After closing the distance, the submarine mounted a night surface attack some 200 miles east of Sanya, the southernmost city on Hainan Island.[42]

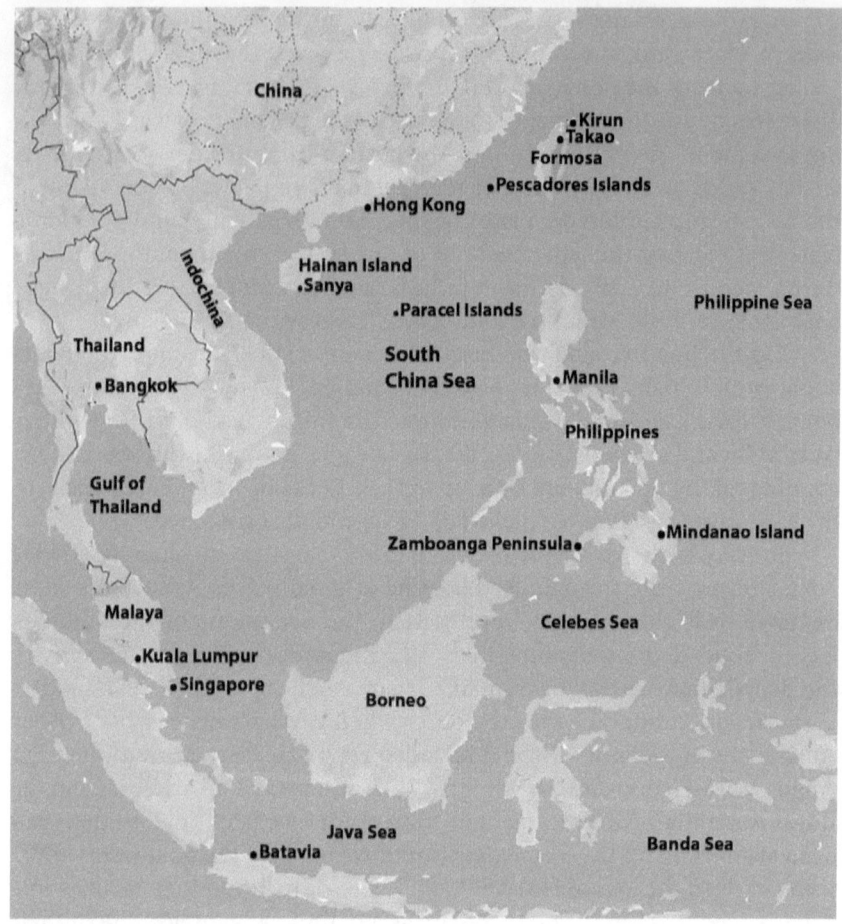

Map of South China Sea (courtesy of Ian Chambers).

As the convoy prepared to change course toward Hainan, one of *Pampanito*'s torpedoes struck *Zuiho Maru*. The 5,135-ton tanker was a new ship, launched little over a year earlier, on 30 July 1943. While under civilian operation, the tanker was chartered for specific voyages by the Imperial Japanese Army. It carried 8,000 tons of oil when it departed Singapore. At 10:40 p.m., the ship sent a distress signal; the crew then managed to evacuate without loss of life.[43]

Those on *Pampanito*'s second victim, *Kachidoki Maru*, would prove less fortunate. At 524 feet long, the ship was a former American passenger-cargo ship, SS *President Harrison*, before it fell into Japanese hands in 1941. The 10,533-ton ship was launched in 1921, and requisitioned by the U.S. Navy in 1941 to be used as a troop transport. The ship was in the East

China Sea the day of the Pearl Harbor attack, and the following day a Japanese aircraft and a mail boat, *Nagasaki Maru*, pursued it until its captain ran aground on Shaweishan Island. After the occupants abandoned ship, one of the lifeboats was swept into *President Harrison*'s still-churning propellers, killing three men and injuring many others. Men from a Japanese destroyer forced the crew back on to the ship, where they remained for the next forty days until the Nippon Salvage Company re-floated it. The ship then sailed to Shanghai, where its crew was interned in a POW camp.[44]

The Japanese initially renamed the ship *Kakko Maru*, but this later became *Kachidoki Maru*.[45] When it departed Singapore on 6 September, *Kachidoki Maru*'s cargo included 6,000 tons of bauxite. It also carried Japanese dead and wounded; in its holds were the ashes of 582 war-dead and 608 wounded Japanese soldiers. The passengers also included 487 Imperial Japanese Army troops and 950 British prisoners of war. As on *Rakuyo Maru*, the prisoners on board faced appalling conditions in the holds but managed to take advantage of any opportunities to get fresh air. Many of the men would sneak up on deck at night, where they often found the sentries sleeping, believing that the prisoners were unlikely to mount a revolt in their weakened condition.[46]

At 10:54 p.m., *Pampanito* fired three torpedoes at *Kachidoki Maru*. Lookouts on *Kachidoki Maru* spotted the torpedoes streaking toward their port side, but despite a hard evasive turn one of the torpedoes struck them, splitting seams along the waterline. *Kachidoki Maru* had already sustained some damage earlier in the day when the crew reacted to the attack on *Hirado*. Amid screams from the bridge, *Kachidoki Maru*'s crew narrowly evaded ramming another ship head on, but even a dramatic turn could not prevent a collision. *Kachidoki Maru* scraped along the length of the other ship and heeled over steeply. Below decks, bags of cement were used to try and stanch the ingress of water.[47]

At the time of *Pampanito*'s torpedo attack, Thomas Pounder, a gunner with the Royal Artillery, was on deck. He had feigned illness, confident that the Korean guards wouldn't know the difference at night. To Pounder, the torpedo hit registered only as a thud, but it quickly became evident that something was amiss. There was a muffled explosion from the rear of the ship, but among the prisoners in the forward hold there were no signs of panic. The ship's peril only became obvious after the Korean guards suddenly appeared on deck for roll call. Soon the Japanese were rushing about, launching the ship's dinghies and rafts.[48]

Chaos seemed to erupt on board, with some of the Japanese dashing about aimlessly, at times donning several life belts. With the engine room flooded, the ship stopped moving at 11:15 p.m. and the captain gave the order to abandon ship. The ship went down quickly by the stern at 11:37

p.m. The losses told their own story; while 57 Japanese passengers and crew were lost at sea, 431 of the POWs perished.[49]

Among those lost with *Kachidoki Maru* was Captain Sukehiko Hosoya of the Sixteenth Convoy Command Section. As the convoy commander, Hosoya had overall command of the convoy transports. Thomas Pounder witnessed a flash and the report of a shot from the bridge, leading him to speculate that the captain took his own life with a revolver.[50] In any case, convoy HI-72 had lost its leader in addition to the commander of the escorts who went down with *Hirado*.

Under the direction of British officers, the prisoners threw rafts into the water as the ship listed.[51] For those who managed to escape the ship to the water, the sea was mercifully calm with visibility aided by a bright quarter moon. One of those in the water was Bill Marks, a Canadian from Nova Scotia who joined the British army as a private. Like some of the POWs on *Rakuyo Maru*, Marks was shocked by their captors' lack of concern about rescuing women, in this case nurses tending the wounded Japanese on board.[52]

As the ship listed, Thomas Pounder, wearing a life jacket, jumped into the water. He felt himself being pulled straight down and unable to move, as if he were tightly wrapped in a rug. Most likely he was being dragged under by the sinking ship, and momentarily he succumbed to letting himself glide toward the bottom of the sea. But then self-preservation kicked in, and he struggled to the surface. He could see a boat in the distance, but the Japanese repelled any POWs who tried to board it. He then struck out toward a raft, reaching it just as *Kachidoki Maru* capsized. After a while, he managed to pull himself up on a large bamboo raft which held a half dozen other men. Despite witnessing the Japanese repelling prisoners, those on the raft helped a few Japanese to board during the night.[53]

One of the British prisoners to survive was John Edward Huckins, a 24-year-old from North Yorkshire who joined the Royal Artillery on 1 February 1939. He had experienced the debacle at Dunkirk and then the fall of Singapore before becoming a prisoner of the Japanese. According to Huckins, many prisoners on *Kachidoki Maru* had initially remained below, fearing they would be shot if they went up on deck. By the time he ventured up, the Japanese were gone. He put on a life vest and jumped overboard, then clung to a piece of floating timber. At dawn he could see wreckage everywhere, but still believed it "the best dawn that I have ever seen in my life."[54]

Chapter 4

A New Dawn

Wednesday, 13 September 1944

For *Rakuyo Maru* survivor Alfred Allbury, the night seemed to last an eternity. Clinging to the rope of a raft, with his eyes shut and his head resting on his hands, he drifted in and out of an exhausted stupor. With dawn, Allbury experienced a new sense of hope. But dawn also brought the realization that five of the fourteen men holding on to his raft had disappeared during the night. By mid-day, Allbury and his raft mates drifted into a group of about thirty other rafts. Many of the survivors redistributed themselves so that each raft supported about a half dozen men. Some of the men, however, were already losing their grip on reality; they claimed to see imaginary rescue ships while others began screaming and fighting. Just before dusk, Allbury believed he heard the engine of a plane, bringing another glimmer of hope. The night, punctuated by a brief rainstorm and the screams of the delirious, brought no sign of help.[1] For British survivor Wilfred Barnett, the screaming of men in the night was the worst part.[2]

Another group of survivors, including Harry Chivers, decided that instead of waiting for rescue they would strike out for the coast of China. With some makeshift oars, they began paddling, oblivious to the fact that China was hundreds of miles away.[3] The same morning an Australian warrant officer named William Smith swam over to the raft holding Arthur Bancroft and his best friend, Harry Lionel "Lofty" Nagle. Smith, who had befriended Bancroft while at Jeep Island in Singapore, sought his advice on what they should do. Knowing that Bancroft survived the sinking of HMAS *Perth*, he assumed he might have a plan. Bancroft thought that they needed to get out of the water and recommended that they swim to some timber floating about fifty yards away. His friend Lofty, however, refused to make the swim; it would be the last time Bancroft saw him. The timbers turned out to be some six-by-six-foot rafts, which they lashed together. Like Harry Chivers' group, they decided to be proactive. Bancroft believed the nearest land was the Philippines rather than China, so they started paddling with their hands in that direction.[4]

The only survivor from the Royal Australian Air Force, Noel Charles Ephraim Day, later recounted clinging to a hatch plank. Convinced that they would die, he and some others carved their names and addresses on the plank. They also added a message: "Left to perish by Japanese on September 12, 1944."[5] Meanwhile another Australian survivor, Ray Wheeler, witnessed a shark attack. He saw a badly burned Japanese man, who he presumed was the survivor of a tanker, lashed to some debris. At one point the man disappeared in a flurry of water and blood, before the debris re-floated empty. Wheeler spotted numerous shark fins in the water; when sharks approached, he and his fellows slapped the water to drive them away. In any case, there were hundreds of bodies in the water, so he believed the sharks had little incentive to come after them.[6]

Only a day after the loss of *Rakuyo Maru*, the number of men with British survivor Ernest Fieldhouse's raft was down from over twenty to seventeen. Oil covered their bodies after they drifted through an oil slick. Fieldhouse believed that the oil helped protect him from the sun during the day and provided some insulation from the cold at night. But the oil was also progressively blinding him.[7]

Those prisoners fortunate enough to secure a place in the lifeboats abandoned by the Japanese formed a separate flotilla. Rowley Richards' boat drifted in the company of three other lifeboats. At this stage, there was no sign of men going mad, and Richards' presence as a senior officer and physician almost certainly contributed to morale.[8] Those on board included sailor Victor Duncan, who served as an electrical artificer and chief petty officer on HMAS *Perth*. Born in Dundee, Scotland, Duncan enlisted in the Royal Australian Navy in 1937 at the age of 22.[9] Also on board was Private Edward William Anderson from the Eighth Division Postal Unit. The four lifeboats in Richards' group headed west in the hope of sailing to the coast of China. Another group of seven lifeboats headed north; during the day they vanished over the horizon.[10]

The latter group of lifeboats included two senior officers—Australian Brigadier Arthur Varley and the sole American among the prisoners, Colonel Harry Ripley Melton, Jr., of the U.S. Army Air Force. Melton, born in Wickliffe, Kentucky, in 1911, graduated from West Point in 1936 and was promoted to full colonel in August 1943. As commander of the 311th Fighter-Bomber Group, his P-51A Mustang was shot down while escorting B-25 bombers on a mission to bomb Mingaladon Airfield near Rangoon, Burma. He was forced to bail out of his plane northwest of Rangoon and some twenty miles east of the Bay of Bengal. Quickly captured by the Japanese, he was designated a "war criminal" and sent to Singapore.[11] Before *Rakuyo*

Chapter 4. A New Dawn

Maru sank, Melton, like Varley, was destined for confinement on Formosa with other high-ranking Allied officers.[12]

The survivors from *Kachidoki Maru* spent a miserable night in the water. Despite the prisoners in Thomas Pounder's group having helped some Japanese on to their raft, another group of Japanese forced them to exchange it for a smaller raft that had already started sinking. Perilously perched on the raft, the men spent the remainder of the night with waves washing above their waists. Pounder described it as the longest night of his life. At daybreak, he realized that his best mate had disappeared.[13]

By mid-morning Japanese ships began picking up their own people with scramble nets. In addition to the escort CD-11, which stayed at the site of the sinking, ships from Hainan (including *Niishio Maru*, *Kasuga Maru*, and SC-19) were on the scene. Several fishing trawlers also towed lifeboats and rafts for those still alive. Thomas Pounder watched a ship nearby, but it only picked up Japanese survivors. According to Pounder, there appeared to be a protracted discussion on board as to whether to recover POWs. He credited the Japanese man in charge of the prisoners, Lieutenant Tanaka, with allowing him and his fellows to board. To the prisoners, Tanaka's concern appeared out of character since he had a horrible reputation, but they reasoned he was only protecting himself since he was responsible for their transport to Japan. A small boat manned by British prisoners picked them up from the water and transported them to the ship.[14]

Once they climbed on board, Tanaka motioned Pounder and his fellows to the front of the ship. They huddled around the forward gun and were later given some rice balls and tea. To Pounder, this seemed to confirm what he had heard about the Japanese navy being superior to the army, at least in their dealings with POWs.[15] Allied sailors tended to assume a certain kinship among all navy men. Ray Parkin, a survivor of HMAS *Perth*, believed that in the case of the British-trained Japanese "there was still more sailor in them than there was enemy."[16] The ship continued to pick up survivors, before setting off through choppy seas for the remainder of the day. In the evening they came within sight of land, although the prisoners had no idea where they were. At an inlet, they were transferred off the navy ship to a merchant vessel. There was plenty of room since there were only about fifty men at this stage.[17]

Meanwhile, in the late afternoon, another warship collected Japanese and Korean survivors, before apparently debating what to do about the prisoners in the water. In this case, a Japanese officer, speaking in English through a loud speaker, informed the prisoners they would have only fifteen minutes to board the ship. About a dozen of the men were left behind.[18]

While the Japanese sea defense ship CD-11 continued picking up survivors, the other ships from convoy HI-72 had headed for sanctuary at

Sanya on Hainan Island.[19] The escort *Mikura* arrived at the port at about noon, followed about eight hours later by another escort, *Kurahashi*, with the cargo ship *Kagu Maru*. At about midnight, *Mikura* and *Kurahashi* departed Sanya to continue the search for survivors before setting course for Yulin.[20] Whereas the Japanese had left the prisoners from *Rakuyo Maru* in the water, they launched a significant rescue effort for those from *Kachidoki Maru*. Leaving aside the supposed influence of Lieutenant Tanaka, there were probably two reasons for this. First, *Kachidoki Maru* sank closer to land than *Rakuyo Maru* and second, *Kachidoki Maru* carried large numbers of Japanese passengers in addition to the prisoners.

Rowley Richards later described the Japanese decision to send out ships in search of survivors as "an extraordinary act of bravery and compassion" given the likelihood of American submarines still in the area.[21] Indeed, the U.S. submarines continued to search for the remaining ships of convoy HI-72. USS *Growler* finally made radio contact with its pack mates in the early hours of 13 September and planned a rendezvous with *Pampanito* and *Sealion* for that evening. Before this could happen, however, *Growler* received orders to head for port at Fremantle, Western Australia, leaving Eli Reich on *Sealion* as the senior skipper.[22] Reich had taken the *Sealion* north, initially believing the convoy was headed for Formosa. At one stage, they crossed the path of the still-burning tanker *Zuiho Maru*, torpedoed by *Pampanito*. Reich then elected to head west and search along the coast of Hainan. As midnight approached, *Sealion* reached the approaches of Hainan Strait and began a submerged patrol.[23]

Thursday, 14 September 1944

After two days and two nights in the water, Arthur Bancroft remained confident that the Japanese would rescue him. Counting Bancroft, there were six men in his group of survivors from *Rakuyo Maru*. The most recent addition was Ray Wheeler, who the group snagged as he drifted by on his own. Although they began drinking small amounts of sea water—rinsing their mouths and allowing a little to trickle down their throats—for the time being they avoided succumbing to the delirium that caused so many others to die.[24]

Even as the likelihood of rescue receded, Bancroft never doubted that he would survive. After all, he had already survived the sinking of HMAS *Perth*. Part of his self-confidence had been cultivated as an athlete in Western Australia, where he distinguished himself as both a footballer and cricketer.[25] Like many men during the war, Bancroft described himself as "fatalistic." In practice, this could range from a complete denial of

Chapter 4. A New Dawn

the possibility of death to an acceptance of its inevitability. At least initially, Bancroft convinced himself that nothing serious would happen to him.[26]

James Beilby's group was less fortunate. Although Beilby had been able to move from the water to sit on a raft, the water was still up to his waist. Some of the men began drinking seawater and went crazy. By evening, there were only four men left on the raft, and by the following morning the number would be down to three.[27] Whereas the men on the rafts gave the first men to die proper burials, later they simply pushed the bodies of the dead unceremoniously overboard.[28]

British prisoner Ernest Fieldhouse awoke to find there were only four men remaining with his raft from the seventeen men clinging to it the previous day. His own state of mind bordered on delirium and the oil in his eyes made him progressively blinder. But the blinder he became, the more clearly it seemed he saw things including palm trees, double-decker buses, traffic lights and, at one point, a neon sign spelling out "fish and chips."[29]

Alfred Allbury's group fell in with a large group of rafts, comprising two or three hundred men. Most of these men were Australians, many still wearing their signature slouch hats. To Allbury, they appeared well organized compared to his British compatriots. At least they had a plan, however impractical, to find some islands supposed to be in the vicinity.[30]

For some of the *Rakuyo Maru* survivors in lifeboats, salvation came suddenly that morning. According to Frank McGovern, they spotted a Japanese reconnaissance plane followed by smoke on the horizon astern of them.[31] The four lifeboats in Rowley Richards' group were strung out over a half mile when, at about 10 a.m., three Japanese ships described as frigates or corvettes came into view heading towards them. The first two ships steamed past without stopping, but then the third broke off toward their boats.[32] A radio intercept from the Japanese that morning reported the position of military personnel (originally prisoners of war embarked in *Rakuyo Maru*) "trying to escape under sail" in four boats.[33]

As recalled by David Herbert, the sight of the Japanese ship heading directly toward his lifeboat initially filled the occupants with fear. Before the ships appeared, they heard gunfire over the horizon; now they assumed they were about to be massacred. According to Herbert, the men said, "Oh well this is it, fellows, we've got this far, this is the finish."[34] To their relief, when the ship stopped it threw a scramble net over the side. Before boarding the Japanese ship, Herbert managed to retrieve one of his few remaining possessions from the lifeboat—a pocket edition of the New Testament that his mother had given him.

The men in Rowley Richards' lifeboat included George Carroll and Kitchner Loughnan. Loughnan recalled that when the Japanese ship approached their boat, they asked if the prisoners were Dutch. They replied "yes," apparently thinking they would be treated more leniently than if they said they were Australian or British.[35] This did not necessarily appear to be the case, however. According to George Carroll, one of the Japanese sailors hit him as he climbed on board, causing him to fall back into the lifeboat. He received another whack when he climbed back up.[36] Kevin Hyde also recalled that each man was hit across the buttocks with a belaying pin as they boarded.[37]

The Japanese ship next nosed alongside the lifeboat carrying Frank McGovern. He noticed the Japanese standing ready with their guns. Again, there was a scramble net down for the prisoners to climb aboard the ship.[38] Including McGovern, eight of those picked up by the Japanese were survivors of HMAS *Perth*; the others were Victor Duncan, Alf Thomas, Tommy Johnston, Hugh Campbell, Pat Major, Keith "Freddie" Mills, and Syd Matsen.[39]

In total, 136 prisoners boarded the ship CD-11. The Japanese confined the rescued men to an area in front of the twin turret guns on the ship's bow. The sailors gave them some broken biscuits soaked in brandy to eat. According to George Carroll, the ship's captain spoke English.[40] Rowley Richards credited the captain, Kimata Nagahashi, with saving his life. After Joan and Clay Blair brought out their book *Return from the River Kwai*, Richards wrote to them: "My only disappointment is that you did not give adequate recognition to the compassion—and bravery—of those Japs who risked their ships and lives to pick up the hundreds of survivors" from *Rakuyo Maru* and *Kachidoki Maru*. "In my view," he continued, "they deserve as much recognition as the sub commanders—if not more!"[41] Another rescued prisoner, Stanley Manning, offered a somewhat less dramatic interpretation of their rescue. According to Manning, the ship's crew told them that "the vessel was making for port in order to lay in fresh supplies, and that was the reason why we had been rescued, as the port was not far distant."[42]

As a reserve officer, Nagahashi was previously a civilian ship captain, called into service during the war. He served as a First Lieutenant attached to the 11th Special Base Force and had commanded the auxiliary minesweeper *Otowa Maru*. From 10 February 1944, he served as the commissioning officer of CD-11, assuming the role of captain from 15 March.[43] Although Richards later concluded that Nagahashi died in October 1944 during the Battle of Leyte Gulf, this appears erroneous.[44] Japanese naval sources indicate that he survived the sinking of CD-11 at the Battle of Ormoc Bay on 10 November 1944, after which he and his remaining crew temporarily were attached to the 31st Special Base Force headquartered in Manila. Nagahashi and his crew may have been evacuated to Takao in late November. On 19 February 1945, Nagahashi became captain of *Mokuto*, a

Chapter 4. A New Dawn

kaibokan that later sank after hitting a mine in Kanmon Straits on 4 April 1945. Again, Nagahashi survived, and within two weeks, on 23 April, Nagahashi assumed command of the No. 16 Fast Transport.[45]

The fate of the half dozen other lifeboats, that included the Australian Brigadier Arthur Varley and the American Colonel Harry Melton, remains a mystery. Many of the prisoners assumed that the gunfire they heard earlier in the morning was the killing of this group.[46] Frank McGovern, however, thought the gunfire sounded more like a naval pom-pom gun than a machine gun.[47] Without definitive evidence, a massacre appears possible but unproven. In any case, the Japanese were not the only combatants guilty of sinking lifeboats and the killing of survivors in the water.[48] The same day, when USS *Pampanito* came across some Japanese lifeboats, the crew prepared to turn their machine guns on them. The lifeboats in this case proved to be empty.[49]

In addition to the rescued prisoners in lifeboats from *Rakuyo Maru*, survivors from *Kachidoki Maru* continued to be recovered. In the end, Japanese naval craft collected 520 British POW survivors from *Kachidoki Maru*, most having spent at least twenty-four hours in the water.[50] One of them, John Huckins, had spent the night clinging to a piece of timber, drifting in and out of consciousness. Nearly blind from oil in his eyes, he experienced an intense sense of isolation and loneliness. Then, almost mysteriously, he found himself on a Japanese escort ship. The sailors gave him some water to drink and to bathe his eyes. Within a few hours, it seemed, they reached a port and transferred him to a whaling ship.[51]

Chapter 5

The Mercy of Wolves

Friday, 15 September 1944

The 136 prisoners recovered from four of the *Rakuyo Maru* lifeboats believed that they sailed for about twenty-four hours on the Japanese ship before reaching port, but their whereabouts was unclear. Some believed they were in Indochina, others that they were at Amoy, the coast of China or on Hainan Island.[1] They were in fact at Sanya on Hainan Island's southern coast.

Initially, the Japanese transferred the rescued survivors to the open deck of *Shincho Maru*, a 5,136-ton tanker constructed at Kobe in 1943. The wartime civilian shipping authority, *Senpaku Uneikai*, requisitioned the ship in December the same year. The Imperial Japanese Army in turn chartered the ship with a civilian crew. The ship departed Singapore with convoy HI-72, carrying 573 passengers in addition to its load of fuel oil.[2] On the tanker, the lifeboat survivors from *Rakuyo Maru* joined 520 British survivors from *Kachidoki Maru*.[3]

Thomas Pounder had been among the first recovered prisoners from *Kachidoki Maru* put on the tanker. Confined to the ship's deck, they tried to find ways to shelter from the burning sun. When more survivors recovered from *Kachidoki Maru* arrived, Pounder described them as in far worse shape. They suffered from exposure, with their bodies covered in thick oil. Some were nearly blind, while others were unable to stand and had to be carried.[4] Most were covered in large skin eruptions caused by their prolonged immersion in seawater and fuel oil.[5] Rowley Richards, horrified by their oil burns, later recalled, "The stench was something I'll never forget, of oil and burnt flesh."[6] There were no medical supplies, even for the approximately 1,000 Japanese survivors.[7] Another horrified prisoner from *Rakuyo Maru*, Kitchener Loughlan, claimed, "I do not think I have seen men in a worse mess."[8] He witnessed many of the British survivors trying desperately to crawl out of the heat to shade under the piping on deck. Many of them were blind from oil or had broken limbs.[9]

Chapter 5. The Mercy of Wolves

Having experienced firsthand the destructive force of torpedoes, the prisoners not surprisingly dreaded the idea of continuing their journey to Japan on the tanker.[10] Basically, it would be like riding a giant bomb. On this occasion, the prisoners' protests to the Japanese appeared to bring some results.[11] During the day, a huge ship pulled alongside the tanker. To the prisoners' relief, they transferred to the 9,574-ton *Kibitsu Maru*. Even at this stage, more survivors continued to arrive, including Japanese who crowded the upper deck while the prisoners occupied the ship's cavernous hold.

Although not a tanker, the ship still carried fuel oil that made it potentially explosive. *Kibitsu Maru* was one of three large ships that joined convoy HI-72 on the morning of 11 September, about one hundred miles northeast of the Paracel Islands, having departed Manila the previous day. Although some POWs described *Kibitsu Maru* as a converted whale factory, the Imperial Japanese Army designated it a landing craft depot ship.[12] For once, there was no shortage of space for the prisoners. They made their way below down a 20-foot ladder to the ship's expansive interior.[13]

In addition to the Australian and British POWs, *Kibitsu Maru* carried a thousand or so Japanese survivors from the wolfpack's victims. With the reorganization of convoy HI-72 at Sanya, *Kibitsu Maru* joined the faster transports in the first echelon of ships that also included *Gokoku Maru* and *Kagu Maru*, along with the escorts *Mikura*, *Etorofu*, CD-10, CD-18 and CD-26. The slower second echelon included *Shincho Maru* with a subchaser and the auxiliary net layer *Kainan Maru* as escorts.[14]

By the fourth day, those survivors from *Rakuyo Maru* still at sea clinging to rafts and to debris were dying in large numbers.[15] At dawn, Alfred Allbury and his companions awoke to find their raft alone, having parted company from the Australian flotilla during the night. Of more immediate concern than their solitude, however, they watched the dorsal fins of sharks circling their raft. They tried to drive the sharks off by throwing pieces of driftwood at them. Even after the fins disappeared, they remained afraid to dangle their legs over the side of the raft, further constricting their movements.[16]

Roy Cornford's party on two lashed-together rafts was down from seventeen to seven men. They had no water or food, apart from a bit of rain they managed to cup in their hands on the third night at sea. Cornford never witnessed any of the men in his group dying; they simply disappeared during the night. They saw bodies float past in life jackets from time to time, sometimes recognizing acquaintances.[17] By this stage, James Beilby experienced a thirst so terrible that he completely forgot about his hunger. Even though partially blinded by oil, he found the glare off the water excruciating. Some of the men around him wanted to take off their life jackets and drown themselves. Others simply fell off the raft to their deaths.[18]

One man recounted how he cut some of the flesh from his hand to catch a fish.[19] On another raft that included Australians Strachan McLaren White and Jim Lansdowne, the men noticed a school of fish following them. The fish would swim up and bite their toes in the water. This gave them the idea of luring the fish to the surface with their toes, and they managed to catch two fish this way. White and Lansdowne shared one of the fish, but it was so salty they could not finish eating it.[20]

In the afternoon, some of the survivors benefited from an amazing stroke of luck. That morning, *Sealion* and *Pampanito* held a rendezvous, with the skippers conversing through megaphones. They agreed to form a scouting line about twenty miles apart, moving east toward Luzon Strait in search of Japanese ships.[21] Shortly after 4 p.m., while patrolling on the surface some thirty miles north-west of where *Rakuyo Maru* sank, a bridge lookout on USS *Pampanito* spotted a mass of debris in the water.

As the submarine closed to investigate, some of the crew positioned themselves at the deck guns while others appeared on deck carrying small arms. They assumed that any people discovered alive would be Japanese. *Pampanito*'s skipper had ordered the gun locker opened and more or less said anyone who wanted to shoot a Jap could come on deck armed.[22] As later recalled by Gordon Hopper, one of the deck gun crew, "the captain had said we'll make a run past … one of these rafts and when I give the word, we'll shoot the men off them." Another crewman, Tony Hauptman, positioned himself on the submarine's bow with a shotgun, later explaining that "we thought they were Japs, so I was going to see if I could get all 12 of them in one shot with buckshot."[23]

USS *Pampanito*'s patrol report recorded the crew's initial reaction to seeing the survivors: "The men were covered with oil and filth and we could not make them out—black curly hair didn't look like Japs."[24] Some of the survivors subsequently came to believe that the curly hair of Harold David "Curly" Martin, an Australian private in 2/10 Ordnance Unit originally from Esperance, Western Australia, had saved their lives.[25] The men in the water shouted at the submarine, but initially they were incomprehensible to *Pampanito*'s crew. Eventually those on the submarine made out the words "Pick us up *please*."[26] Robert Bennett stood on *Pampanito*'s bullnose as they approached the survivors. Once they established that the men in the water were British and Australians, he was among the first to dive into the water, swimming to the rafts with a line. Those submariners who went into the sea risked their lives; there was no doubt that if a Japanese ship or plane appeared the submarine would make an emergency dive and leave them to their fate.

Although the survivors were exhausted, the prospect of rescue animated many. Some survivors claim that one of the Australians shouted

Chapter 5. The Mercy of Wolves

to the submariners, "You sink us and now you want to shoot us!"[27] *Pampanito*'s patrol report noted that some "came alongside with cheers for the Yanks and many a curse for the Nips."[28] Among those first pulled on to the submarine was Frank Farmer, an ex–school teacher.[29] Some of the former prisoners, however, found the rescue bewildering. Having spent days without food or water and wearing only an undershirt, Kenneth Clive Renton from Melbourne described himself as "a bit dippy." His vision was obscured by oil, but as a submarine drew near he made out a couple of men with machine guns. He professed, "I didn't care because it would have been a quicker way out."[30] But instead of being shot, he was thrown a rope.

Harry Pickett from Perth, Western Australia, recalled his rescue in similar terms. After the sinking of *Rakuyo Maru*, he had clung to a makeshift raft with ten others, but now he was the only man left. He had started to hallucinate that "the waves going by were blokes" and became agitated when they didn't answer his calls. It was growing dark before he sensed the presence of a submarine, feeling its engine vibrations before seeing it. He then heard an American voice ask, "Can you catch a rope, Buddy?"[31]

British prisoner Ernest Fieldhouse had experienced similar disorientation and loneliness during his 84 hours in the ocean. He spent days clinging to a raft, and that morning he woke aware of only his fingers curled around the raft's rope. Slowly he realized that the raft had disappeared and that his clinched fingers in fact gripped nothing. Later a body brushed against him, and he took the corpse's lifejacket. He began hallucinating until he became aware of someone shouting at him.[32]

Roy Cornford heard engine noises in the afternoon, and at one point spotted what he took to be a fishing trawler in the distance. One of the submariners, Robert Bennett, swam out to Cornford with a rope and assisted him to *Pampanito*. It was the beginning of a lifelong bond between the two men. When alongside the submarine, Cornford extended his hands to be pulled on board; he begged the submariners not to grab his arms because blisters covered them from the oil and sun. Once on the submarine's deck, he was amazed to find he could still walk.[33]

One of the British prisoners recovered by *Pampanito* was Samuel Whiley. He later recounted that he had abandoned *Rakuyo Maru* about a half hour after it was torpedoed. He swam to a raft with about five or six other men clinging to it. He didn't know the men, but he believed several were Australians. Dressed only in a pair of cloth shorts, he was pulled on board the submarine days later.[34]

Pampanito's crew quickly realized they were participating in a unique event. Despite an official ban on crew bringing private cameras on submarines, Paul Pappas, a twenty-three-year-old electrician's mate, retrieved his camera and brought it on deck. In this instance, the skipper encouraged him to take as many photos as he could. He also instructed Pappas to use the submarine's 16-mm movie camera, usually reserved to verify the sinking of enemy ships, to record the rescue.[35]

Many of the submariners were shocked by the physical condition of the recovered men. Pete Summers recorded in his patrol report that the POWs were "A pitiful sight none of us will ever forget."[36] Another *Pampanito* officer, Landon Davis, Jr., reported, "Every one of them on board had malaria, most of them had pellagra, beriberi, bad cases of scurvy, and then they had salt-water sores on them that they got when they were in the water before being recovered."[37] Not all of *Pampanito*'s crew felt emotionally equipped to deal with the rescued men's condition. One professed, "My stomach couldn't take it. It was terrible."[38]

Not long after the rescue effort began, *Pampanito* broke radio silence to summon *Sealion* for assistance. *Sealion* headed for the area at high speed, and within an hour arrived to find debris extending to the horizon, a heavy oil slick, floating dead bodies and *Pampanito* in the distance.[39] Within another ten minutes, *Sealion*'s crew began spotting men on rafts, pulling the first survivor aboard at 6:40 p.m. Skipper Eli Reich described the rescued men as "a woe-begone looking lot. Skinny, dirty with oil, bewildered!"[40]

One of the "woe-begone" men pulled on to *Sealion* was John Wilfred Turner. Turner had been in a group of three rafts with eighteen men, but

Rakuyo Maru survivors rescued by USS *Sealion*, September 1944 (National Archives and Records Administration, College Park, Maryland).

Chapter 5. The Mercy of Wolves

Crewmen on USS *Sealion* clean oil-soaked POWs recovered from *Rakuyo Maru*, September 1944 (Australian War Memorial).

only five remained alive. Most of his fellows had gone mad before drowning. He believed his optimism saved him from the same fate.[41] Another prisoner pulled from the oily sea was Tony Clive, who had served with Australia's Eighth Division Postal Unit. He had survived the infamous 105-Kilo Camp at Ankanan, Burma, considered one of the worst outposts on the Thai-Burma railway.[42]

On *Sealion*, communications officer Joseph Bates filmed part of the rescue effort; the footage with his narration was uploaded to YouTube in January 2009. As recalled by Bates, most of the prisoners were covered in bunker oil, and about half were unable to see. Some thought they were being picked up by a cruiser. Bates also recalled seeing corpses still floating in life jackets, half-eaten by fish. As crewmen jumped in the water to pull survivors to the submarine, some of the men stood shark watch armed with machine guns and rifles. Once the survivors were on deck, the crew threw away the men's filthy clothing, and in one case inadvertently threw away a man's dentures.[43] They then set to work trying to clean away the oil that clung to their bodies. Initially they used mineral spirits, but when that ran out they used hydraulic oil.[44]

The submariners continued to rescue men until after dark. USS *Pampanito* retrieved 73 survivors including 47 Australians and 26 British. *Sealion* recovered 54 men: 29 British and 25 Australians. The submarines radioed the base at Pearl Harbor and received permission to transport the survivors to Saipan, some 1,800 miles away.[45] As the submariners knew, there were still survivors left in the water when they departed the area. Reich recorded in his patrol report that "It was heartbreaking to leave so many dying men behind."[46] Some of *Sealion*'s crew felt embittered about deserting the men. Joseph Bates recalled, "This was not an orderly process. Finally, the captain just said, 'That's all,' and that was all."[47] He could still hear men calling out "over here!" as they left.[48] Even decades later, some of *Sealion*'s crew could weep at the thought of those left behind.[49]

Australian Ray Wheeler was among those left behind, left adrift as the weather began to close in.[50] James Beilby had heard the diesel engines of a submarine and at one stage put his shorts on a bamboo pole, waving this make-shift flag in a fruitless attempt to get attention.[51] Arthur Bancroft was also left behind. Tormented by the sound of diesel engines that seemed to approach and then head off in another direction, occasionally he could even glimpse a submarine over the waves moving toward his raft. He didn't care if the submarine was Japanese or German so long as it picked him up. But then it disappeared. Finally left in the darkness, Bancroft experienced his darkest hours.[52]

Chapter 6

Another Convoy and More Survivors

Saturday, 16 September 1944

For those POW survivors rescued by *Pampanito* and *Sealion*, their sudden reversal of fortunes was staggering. Not only had they evaded almost certain death, but they were now in friendly hands. As described by some of the rescued men, the American submariners cared for them almost as their mothers.[1] Tragically, some of those plucked from the sea still died. Shortly after midnight, *Sealion* lost the first of the former prisoners, a man never identified by name.[2] There was also an early fatality on USS *Pampanito*. John Campbell of the British Army had first been spotted lying motionless on a raft. One of the *Pampanito* crew swam over to him with a line; startled, Campbell sat up and tried to get off the raft. The crewman managed to settle him down, but when brought on the submarine he was semi-conscious and almost totally blind. Campbell died within a matter of hours, at 6:30 p.m.[3]

In the case of both deaths, the submariners held a burial service and committed their bodies to the deep. As later described by Eli Reich, the disposal of the bodies was done in the "classic way," with the men placed in a blanket and tied to a 4-inch shell.[4] On *Pampanito*, Campbell was buried at sea less than two hours after passing away; crewman Joseph Bates later recalled the burial as one of his most "vivid memories."[5]

For those *Rakuyo Maru* survivors still in the water, the dying continued. After drifting through thick oil during the night, Alfred Allbury could use only one eye. His mate, Ted, was even worse off, with both eyes sealed shut. After succumbing to delirium, Ted began drinking seawater and then drifted off into the darkness.[6]

Neville Thomas and the others on his raft watched as a shark circled them. As Thomas related, "We were not unduly concerned, we were past the stage of worrying about death by shark attack or drowning."[7] Arthur

Bancroft's group was also giving into pessimism; their prospects of survival quickly diminished as the seas got bigger and strong winds presaged a storm.[8] Bancroft took some comfort that at least his death "would be a clean honourable one far away from the steaming jungles of Burma and Thailand where we had seen so many of our mates suffer and die in unbelievable squalor."[9]

Unknown to these survivors, there was still the possibility of salvation. At about 3 a.m. that morning, as USS *Queenfish* prepared to dive, the submarine received a directive from Pearl Harbor to proceed to an area over 400 miles away where *Sealion* and *Pampanito* had conducted their rescue efforts. *Queenfish*'s skipper, Charles Eliot Loughlin, ordered his crew to bring all four diesel engines on line and they headed due west. Loughlin, originally from North Carolina, gained distinction as a basketball player at the Naval Academy before graduating in 1933. He began the war stationed in the Caribbean and spent two and a half frustrating years making patrols off the Panama Canal on the antiquated S-14 before assignment to the modern fleet submarine *Queenfish*, at the time still under construction.[10] Now 34 years old and commanding *Queenfish*'s first war patrol in the Pacific, Loughlin seemed determined to make up for lost time. By the end of the patrol, he received credit for sinking six ships for a total of 48,000 tons.[11] Working as part of a wolfpack with USS *Tunny* and USS *Barb* off the Philippines, *Queenfish* had only four torpedoes left. *Tunny* had already withdrawn from the pack. A Japanese aircraft flying out of the sun in the late afternoon managed to catch *Tunny* on the surface and crippled it with a bomb.[12]

The same directive to proceed to the rescue area had been sent to USS *Barb* commanded by Eugene Fluckey. *Barb* had already dived at the time *Queenfish* received the dispatch, and it would be another hour before its crew received the instructions. Fluckey had been a classmate of *Sealion*'s commander, Eli Reich, at the Naval Academy.[13] Like Loughlin, Fluckey gained his first wartime experience making patrols off the Panama Canal in outdated submarines.[14] As commander of *Barb*, he was destined to become one of only seven submariners to be awarded a Medal of Honor, America's highest combat award, during the Second World War.

While *Queenfish* and *Barb* sped toward the survivors, they encountered an unexpected but not-unwanted distraction. As Loughlin later explained, "I ran smack into a tremendous convoy."[15] He immediately sent a contact report to *Barb*, reporting a convoy of five ships with six escorts. This was music to Fluckey's ears. He was still fuming that *Barb* had received no contact reports when *Sealion*, *Growler* and *Pampanito* attacked convoy HI-72 days earlier. At least in Fluckey's view, Loughlin was "a team player."[16]

The "tremendous" convoy that *Queenfish* encountered, designated

Chapter 6. Another Convoy and More Survivors

Oil-covered survivors of *Rakuyo Maru* recovered by USS *Queenfish*, September 1944 (U.S. Navy photo).

HI-74, had departed Singapore at dawn on 11 September, five days after convoy HI-72 left port. HI-74 was better protected than its predecessor. The escort carrier *Unyo* had a dozen planes to provide air cover. In addition to the carrier, there were four escorts (CD-21, CD-19, CD-13 and CD-27) and two destroyers (*Kashii* and *Chiburi*). Other ships in the convoy included *Otowayama Maru*, *Harima Maru*, *Omuroyama Maru* and *Hakko Maru*.

After receiving a submarine alert following the 12 September attacks on convoy HI-72, convoy HI-74 moved some sixty miles east but ultimately into the path of *Queenfish* and *Barb*.[17]

The submarines were still over a hundred miles from the rescue site, and a decision had to be made as to whether to press on to the survivors or make an attack. Although Fluckey commanded *Barb*, there was also a senior officer on board, Captain Edwin Swinburne, who had overall command of the wolfpack. Aged 40, Swinburne normally played an administrative role, but his presence on *Barb* reflected a policy of allowing senior staff to make war patrols.[18] As usual, the wolfpack was assigned an alliterative nickname in his honor, in this case "Edwin's Eradicators." It fell to Swinburne to have the final say on whether the submarines continued at top speed toward the POW survivors or intercepted the convoy; he elected to attack.

Queenfish made a night surface attack on the convoy, firing its last four torpedoes. Loughlin believed that they scored one torpedo hit on a large ship, but this was never confirmed. At about the same time, *Barb* launched a four-torpedo salvo. It proved one of the most successful torpedo attacks of the war, claiming two huge prizes—the 11,777-ton tanker *Azusa Maru* and the even bigger 22,000-ton *Otaka*-class escort carrier *Unyo*. The tanker *Azusa Maru*, constructed only a year earlier, carried 100,000 barrels of oil. The ship sank slightly before midnight with all on board. Its loss was a significant blow to Japan's fuel-starved military.[19] The carrier *Unyo* represented an even greater prize. One of the *Barb* crewmen, Charles Tomczyk, recorded in his diary "Wahoo! Always wanted to hit a carrier."[20] Meanwhile, two of the convoy escorts punished *Barb* with a storm of depth charges.

The same evening, remnants of convoy HI-72 departed from Sanya on Hainan Island to resume the journey to Moji, Japan. The recovered POWs on *Kibitsu Maru* were included in the first echelon of ships, along with *Asaka Maru, Gokoku Maru, Kagu Maru*. These ships were shepherded by five escorts: CD-10, CD-18, CD-26, *Mikura* and *Etorofu*. The second echelon of the convoy departed the same night but was considerably smaller. The tanker *Shincho Maru* headed for Takao, Formosa, in the company of the sub-chaser CH-19 and the auxiliary net-layer *Kainan Maru*.[21]

On board *Kibitsu Maru* were 136 British and Australian POWs from *Rakuyo Maru*, 520 British prisoners from *Kachidoki Maru*, and roughly another one thousand Japanese survivors from the convoy's encounters with submarines.[22] Initially, at least, there were no restrictions on the prisoners' movements, and the Japanese survivors mingled with them on deck. Although they received meager amounts of food, Kevin Hyde considered the quality "quite reasonable."[23] Once they left port, however, the prisoners were confined to the hold. With only light from a couple of low-wattage

Chapter 6. Another Convoy and More Survivors 49

bulbs, the men had to make do sitting and sleeping on the naked iron deck. Their only access to the open air was to use the latrines, and with only two to six men allowed at a time, the men spent lengthy periods waiting to go topside.[24] Following an outbreak of dysentery, about a dozen prisoners died. According to prisoner Harold Ramsey, they had to use considerable persuasion before the Japanese allowed them to dispose of the corpses.[25] The bodies were wrapped in old hessian or any other material the prisoners could scrounge, before being dropped over the ship's side with "no weights, no nothing."[26]

As described by Thomas Pounder, the POW survivors all showed signs of the strain they had recently experienced. With the ship's departure, "began the torture of waiting and wondering, desperately hoping nothing would happen this time."[27] Any sudden noise in the hold was likely to jerk the men into panic and start a rush to the hatch. According to Pounder, "With nothing to occupy our minds we pondered constantly on our chances of survival in the event of another attack from Allied submarines."[28] Kitchener Loughnan later claimed, "In spite of the hell of Burma this was my worst experience."[29]

Eventually, the prisoners were allowed access to the deck and fresh air. Their diet remained Spartan, consisting of only a half-cup of water and one rice cake per day. According to George Carroll, rescued from the same lifeboat as Rowley Richards, he could barely stand by the time they arrived at Moji, Japan. He was still covered in oil and half blind.[30]

Sunday, 17 September 1944

About 1 a.m., *Barb* and *Queenfish* received renewed orders to proceed to the rescue area. After making a quick inventory on *Barb*, Fluckey believed that, while their medical supplies were limited, they might take on board as many as one hundred survivors. With the torpedo room now empty of torpedoes, the crew converted the torpedo skids into a dozen bunks in preparation. *Barb*'s executive officer and navigator, Robert McNitt, drew on an article published in the U.S. Naval Institute *Proceedings* to calculate where the survivors would have likely drifted. At about 10 a.m. the submarine began passing through wreckage, and a couple of hours later started spotting "floaters," the corpses of both Japanese and Allies. Finally, shortly before 1 p.m. in the afternoon, they spotted the first survivors on rafts. The men were so dark from the sun that many believed that they were Japanese until one shouted out "Hey, Yank!"[31] Fluckey recorded in the patrol report that they would never forget the survivors' expressions as they approached: "at first dubious, then amazed, and finally hysterically thankful."[32]

The survivor who yelled out proved to be an Australian, John "Jack" Flynn. He had clung to a one-man raft with three others, each man taking turns to sit on it. Not long before the *Barb* appeared, one of the men had drifted away after drinking seawater. Flynn had gone after him, but just as he caught up the man sank feet first with his arms outstretched.[33] Another man from Flynn's raft, Murray Thompson, was unconscious when brought on board *Barb*. Thompson was a private in the 2/2 Reserve Motor Transport Company from South Australia.[34] Other men picked up by 2:30 in the afternoon included Cecil Hutchinson, Ross Smith, Jimmy Johnson and an Australian sailor named Lloyd Munro who had survived the sinking of HMAS *Perth* in March 1942. In the next hour, the *Barb* crew recovered a British man drifting on his own, Thomas Carr, as well as two more Australians—Leo Cornelius and Robert Douglas Hampson.[35] Hampson from Perth, Western Australia, clung to a raft with one other survivor before they spotted a submarine; he recalled, "they dropped us a rope and we went up."[36]

Racing against a brewing storm, in the next hour *Barb*'s crew retrieved the Australian Neville Thams of the 2/10th Field Regiment and a British soldier, Augustus Fuller, both described by Fluckey as "half dead."[37] Thams later recalled that "We were past the stage of worrying about death."[38] To him the submarine appeared like a grey ghost. Five minutes after *Barb* rescued Thams, the crew pulled aboard a lone Australian, Jim Campbell.

As the waves grew bigger, Alfred Allbury's raft seemed at times to stand up vertically. He no longer felt any hunger and was almost beyond feeling any thirst. His death appeared inevitable. Then, as if in a dream, he recalled grasping a rope and being hauled onto a submarine. When he woke hours later, he discovered he was lying in the third tier of a bunk bed.[39]

Most of the survivors required considerable help to board the submarine. As described by Robert McNitt, "They were beyond comprehending what was happening to them."[40] Once on board, some found standing impossible. One of the *Barb* crew, Don Miller from Pittsburgh, claimed that the survivors had thighs the size of his wrist.[41] In total, *Barb* recovered ten Australians and four British survivors.[42] *Barb*'s pharmacist's mate, William Donnelly, cared for the recovered prisoners with the assistance of Ezra Davis, Joe Zamaria and Julian Kosinski.[43]

The *Queenfish* crew began spotting survivors only slightly later than *Barb*. In the rough seas, the submarine needed to be steered gingerly to avoid colliding with the survivors' fragile rafts. With the waves and wind building toward a typhoon, *Queenfish* managed to pull eighteen men out of the sea in the space of two and a half hours.[44] One of the survivors in the water, Cliff Farlow, compared the sound of *Queenfish*'s diesel engines to the sound of approaching thunder. His first recollection of the rescue was when one of the submariners said in effect, "Christ, they're bloody Australians."[45]

Chapter 6. Another Convoy and More Survivors

By this time, James Beilby from Western Australia was the only man left on his raft. That day, rough waves washed away his shorts. As the water churned around him, he recited silent prayers and sometimes worried about the presence of unseen sharks lurking beneath the surface. At about 2:30 p.m. he spotted a submarine and swam toward it until they threw him a line with a life buoy. Once on *Queenfish*, he found it hard to stay on his feet. Someone gave him a mouthful of brandy, but this seemed only to burn his mouth.[46]

Eugene Fluckey, commander of USS *Barb*, on the deck of his submarine in December 1944 (Naval History and Heritage Command, Washington, D.C.).

Ray Wheeler, a printer's apprentice before enlisting in the Army at age seventeen, was approaching his twenty-first birthday.[47] In waves twenty to thirty feet high, the six men in Wheeler's group managed to spot the submarine about a hundred yards away. Initially they assumed the submarine was German. "They're Jerries," insisted one of the men. Once on board, the pharmacist's mate looked after them. Despite a desperate thirst, they found it hard to swallow. The pharmacist's mate added a bit of brandy to some ice water and told them to hold it in their mouths. As recalled by Ray Wheeler, "you put it in your mouth and you couldn't swallow straightaway. You'd just hold it there and all of a sudden you felt this cold starting to go down your throat. It was just glorious!"[48] The submariners put Wheeler in a bunk where he slept the next twenty-four hours.

In the rising storm, Arthur Bancroft and the others in his group had lashed themselves to their raft to prevent being washed away. From his vantage point in the water, Bancroft could sometimes catch sight of a submarine, but then it would disappear behind the towering waves. Eventually the *Queenfish* crew threw him a line, and he held on to it while the other men on his raft got off. When it was his turn to board the submarine, Bancroft instinctively saluted and said, "permission to come aboard sir."[49]

This incident would become more and more embellished over time.[50]

In a 2003 interview, Bancroft conceded he was "non compos" at the time, and heard the stories later.[51] Elliot Loughlin, commanding *Queenfish* from the bridge at the time, recalled his initial encounter with Bancroft somewhat differently. According to Loughlin, "He staggered toward me, I was on the bridge, shook his fist and said, 'I knew you bloody Yankees would pick us up.'" In any case, Bancroft appeared in better condition than the other survivors, who Loughlin described as looking like the "most horrible human beings you've ever seen in your life."[52]

Even when recounting his rescue forty years after the war, Arthur Bancroft was unable to keep tears from his eyes.[53] On *Queenfish*'s deck, the Americans began the process of trying to remove the oil from him. Once taken below, they put Bancroft in a bunk in the forward torpedo room. As on the other submarines, the survivors' health became mainly the responsibility of the pharmacist's mate. As recalled by Ray Wheeler, the submariners pretty much allowed the recovered men to eat what they wanted, although they apologized for running out of fresh milk.[54] James Beilby fondly remembered eating roast chicken, strawberries and ice cream.[55] "Those wonderful people fed us with marvellous food, things we hadn't seen for years."[56] On all four of the U.S. submarines, the care received by the recovered men seemed to overwhelm them. As recounted by one Australian soldier, "The crew of the sub was wonderful to everyone on board. They would come off a four-hour shift and then start mothering us. They were better than nurses."[57]

CHAPTER 7

To Saipan, to Japan

Monday, 18 September 1944

Barb continued to look for survivors during the morning, battling storm conditions and with some of the crew suffering from seasickness. They found only corpses and empty rafts. One of the men rescued the previous day died without regaining consciousness; he was buried at sea at noon.[1] Recovered survivor Alfred Allbury described himself as in a "half-hysterical state," unable to sleep or to walk more than a few steps.[2]

On *Queenfish*, after a sound sleep, Arthur Bancroft was up and about exploring his new environment. He was struck by how white the American sailors looked, and the cleanliness of their clothes. Someone asked him what he would like to eat, and Bancroft replied "sausages," recalling his last meal on HMAS *Perth* before it sank. The pharmacist's mate intervened, pointing out that Bancroft wasn't ready for that kind of solid food. Instead, they gave Bancroft some fresh-baked bread, which he compared to eating cake.[3] He later recalled his seven days on the submarine as "a marvellous experience."[4]

To James Beilby, the Americans also appeared incredibly generous. He later recalled the submariners on *Queenfish* as "the kindest people I have ever met."[5] Some gave up their bunks to the rescued men and slept on the deck. They shared some of their clothing with him. And some seemed quite emotional when he recounted the suffering the prisoners had endured. One of the crew told him that he had a girlfriend who lived in the Perth suburb of Cottesloe in Western Australia. Remarkably, the woman had been one of Beilby's customers when he had run a garage there.[6] In some ways, time on the submarine represented a re-introduction to popular culture after so many years in captivity. Beilby was struck by the piped music played on board of singers like Bing Crosby and Frank Sinatra, including songs that he had never heard before.[7] For men who had long since lost their libido and fantasized only about food, the sexy pin-ups over some of the crew's bunks were a revelation.[8]

With the number of men on board *Pampanito* suddenly doubled, some of the recovered men were put two to a bunk, while some slept on the floor.[9] The addition of 73 survivors to the 89 crew on board strained the submarine's habitability from air quality to food supplies. Skipper Pete Summers reported that the situation could only be managed through "careful planning and supervision."[10]

USS *Pampanito*'s pharmacist's mate, Maurice "Doc" Demers, assumed the main responsibility for the men's health. Although there was some pressure during the war to include medical officers on patrols, a shortage of doctors meant that this never eventuated. The pharmacist's mates, who joined submarine crews from the 1920s, were essentially volunteers and initially received little medical training. From 1943, candidates had to undergo six weeks of classes at the Submarine School at New London, Connecticut. By 1945 the training extended to include sixteen weeks at the U.S. Naval Hospital Corps School at Norfolk, Virginia, followed by an additional eight weeks at New London. The men still needed to qualify as submariners at sea and played a variety of roles on board apart from medical duties.[11]

Demers worked nearly around the clock with the *Rakuyo Maru* survivors, and at one stage resorted to taking amphetamines to stay awake.[12] While Demers focused on the most critical cases, virtually the whole crew contributed to looking after the rescued men. The survivors' most urgent need was for water, and initially each man was given a wet cloth to suck on to regulate their intake. Gradually their diet was widened to include beef broth, tomato consume, eggnog, canned fruit, chicken soup, soft-boiled eggs and hash.[13]

On 18 September, *Pampanito* made a rendezvous with the destroyer USS *Case*. Plans to transfer the recovered POWs to *Case*, however, changed due to the rough sea conditions. Instead, the destroyer transferred some medical supplies, along with a doctor, Lieutenant-Commander G.H. Schiff, and a chief pharmacist's mate, W.A. Cumstock, to examine the survivors. Both men were from the U.S. Navy Reserve. Before returning to *Case*, the doctor instructed the submariners to feed the survivors fresh fruit and lettuce. *Pampanito*'s bemused skipper, Pete Summers, reminded the doctor that they were at the end of a war patrol without the luxuries of fresh fruit and lettuce.[14]

On *Sealion*, the survivors' health mainly became the responsibility of pharmacist's mate Roy Williams. He knew that the men had to be introduced very slowly to solid food. Even by the second day, however, he could detect a change in some of the survivors' mental attitude.[15] At around 4 p.m. on 18 September, *Case* made a rendezvous with *Sealion*, about 700 miles west of Saipan. On a relatively calm sea, the two vessels laid to. Again, Schiff and Cumstock were transferred in a small boat to the submarine to look over the survivors. *Case* then provided an escort for *Sealion* for the remainder of the journey.[16] Crewman Joseph Bates was unimpressed by the doctor, claiming he merely gave the rescued men a pat on the head. To Bates's mind, it was an "unworthy moment" for the U.S. Navy.[17]

As the rescued men made their way toward Saipan, in the late afternoon another prisoner-of-war tragedy began to unfold. Off the island of Sumatra, the British submarine HMS *Tradewind*, commanded by Stephen L.C. Maydon, sank the 5,065-ton Japanese freighter *Junyo Maru*. About 1,700 Allied POWs had been loaded on the ship at Tanjong Priok on Java before it departed on 16 September. The prisoners were mainly Dutch, but also included 14 Americans, 506 Ambonese and Menadonese. Also crammed on board were 4,320 Javanese laborers conscripted by the Japanese. The sinking claimed the lives of 1,520 Allied prisoners, while the Javanese laborers suffered the largest losses. Only 200 of the laborers survived. In total, over 5,600 POWs and Javanese laborers lost their lives in the sinking. Some writers claim that more lives were lost than in any other attack on Japanese shipping during the war.[18] Indeed, Van Waterford, himself a survivor of *Junyo Maru*, describes it as "the largest maritime disaster in world history."[19] He attributes the relative anonymity of the disaster to the fact that the main victims were Indonesian.

September 1944 proved the worst month of the war for prisoners on Japanese transports. By 1944, there was a dramatic escalation in the dangers Allied prisoners faced at sea. A U.S. assessment (based on captured documents, prisoner interrogations, survivors' statements, Japanese official reports and intercepted Japanese messages), stated Allied submarines or aircraft sank at least eight Japanese ships carrying Allied prisoners of war during 1944. According to the assessment, the ships carried a total of 9,242 Allied prisoners, of whom 5,879 were missing.[20] In September alone, five ships (*Rakuyo Maru, Kachidoki Maru, Shinyo Maru, Junyo Maru, Toyofuku Maru*) were sunk carrying Allied prisoners of war, resulting in an estimated 4,478 missing or dead.[21] So grave had the problem become that U.S. submarines received instructions to search for Allied survivors in the vicinity of any Japanese ships sunk heading for their home waters.[22]

Wednesday, 20 September 1944

Shortly before 9:30 a.m. on the morning of 20 September 1944, *Pampanito* arrived at Tanapag Harbor, Saipan, and moored next to the submarine tender USS *Fulton*.[23] Roy Cornford recalled the natural beauty of the island, as they sailed in amid the coral. The rescued men were delighted to see boxes of apples and oranges immediately brought on board, along with ice cream.[24] *Sealion* arrived an hour and a half later at a little after 11 a.m. and moored next to USS *Fulton*. At least on Saipan, the recovery of the prisoners was big news; according to *Pampanito* torpedoman Robert Bennett, the submarine's deck was soon "covered with gold braid and photographers."[25]

Until relatively recently, Saipan had been a Japanese possession. Located about 1,500 miles east of Manila Bay, Japan gained control of the island from Germany at the end of the First World War. For the Americans, the Mariana Islands offered a key to operations in the Pacific, providing a base for advances west toward the Philippines or north to Japan.[26] U.S. Marines first landed on Saipan on 15 June 1944. The island's capture proved costly for the Americans; from the invasion force of 70,000, twenty percent, or 14,000 men, became casualties. The Japanese defenders suffered an almost 95 percent death rate, losing 41,244 of their 43,683 troops. The capture of Saipan by the Americans the following month represented a huge blow to Japan's military, precipitating the resignation of Prime Minister Tojo and his cabinet.[27] At least one Japanese admiral later declared, "Our war was lost with the loss of Saipan."[28] For the first time, the Allies had penetrated Japan's so-called "Absolute National Defense Zone" and captured pre-war territory.

USS *Cavalla* became the first U.S. submarine to make port at Saipan on 2 July. Even as fighting on the island continued, *Cavalla* topped up its fuel tanks before departing the same day. An entry in *Cavalla*'s patrol report noted appreciatively that "The reception we received on arriving at Saipan, and the services while there, left us feeling damn glad we are Americans, and mighty proud to be members of the United States Navy."[29]

When USS *Cobia* entered Tanapag Harbor on 13 September, only a week before the rescued POWs arrived, there was still clear evidence of the recent battle. According to one of *Cobia*'s crew, "Saipan was pretty messy at that time, there were still dead Japs."[30] There was also a rumor going around that some crew from another submarine had gone looking for Japanese in the hills as a lark and never returned.[31] Although the battle for Saipan was declared officially over on 9 July, many Japanese hid in caves and remote places, so mopping up operations continued for over a year.[32] When some of *Barb*'s crew later tried to leave the base for a picnic, Marines stopped them.[33]

At Saipan the *Rakuyo Maru* survivors disembarked wearing the sailor outfits donated by American crewmen but were still barefoot. Landing barges were used to ferry the men to shore, where ambulances waited to transport them to the No. 140 Army General Hospital.[34] The physical improvement of many of the survivors during the brief submarine transit was remarkable. By this stage, Eli Reich described the recovered men

Chapter 7. To Saipan, to Japan

Rescued prisoners of war from *Rakuyo Maru* being transferred from USS *Pampanito* at Saipan, 1944 (National Archives of Australia, Melbourne).

on *Sealion* as "rather a sprightly bunch," and most were able to disembark under their own power.[35] Nevertheless, some still needed to be taken off the submarine on stretchers. Four men had also died on board *Sealion* since the rescue effort. The last, a British Army private named Douglas Rolph, passed away the night before and crewmen buried him at sea. In addition to Rolph, three other British soldiers died in transit—Gunner Cyril Grice from Yorkshire, Private Harry Winters from London and John Campbell.[36]

Battling storms and rough seas, *Queenfish* and *Barb* took another five days before arriving at Saipan on the morning of 25 September. They too had suffered fatalities in transit. On *Queenfish*, two of the survivors died.[37] Lieutenant John Bennett, who had supervised the rescue operation, read the burial service when they committed the men to the deep. As skipper Elliot Loughlin explained, "He knew these people and was with them every day and almost every minute for the whole time we were on the way back."[38]

As with the men on *Pampanito* and *Sealion*, the survivors rescued by *Barb* and *Queenfish* received a rousing welcome at Saipan, with hundreds of Marines and sailors on hand to greet them.[39] Each of the survivors wore khaki clothes and a white sailor hat supplied by the submariners. The crews had also chipped in to supply each man with some toiletries, cigarettes and money. Alfred Allbury emerged from *Barb* to be photographed and "news-reeled" as he put it.⁴⁰ *Barb*'s skipper, Eugene Fluckey, suspected the episode would make the news in the United States. He wrote to his family, "Between us'uns let me know if you read anything published in the newspapers about Australian and British survivors being rescued by submarines. If so, I'll have some interesting dope for you. If not, don't mention it."⁴¹

Survivor John Wilfred Turner, who arrived with *Sealion*, suffered some residual deafness from spending time in the submarine's engine room. On Saipan, he professed to being astounded because everything looked so modern. He saw American jeeps for the first time and found these toy-like vehicles running around endlessly amusing. He had to cultivate the new habit of shaving daily. Over the coming nights, there were open-air film screenings in the hospital area, re-introducing him to popular icons like Lana Turner in *Marriage is a Private Affair*.⁴² Those well enough to move about were issued a full set of U.S. Army tropical clothing, including a pith helmet.⁴³

The Western Australian contingent of rescued prisoners from *Rakuyo Maru* on Saipan, 1944. Arthur Bancroft is standing on the far right (National Archives of Australia, Melbourne).

There was still some Japanese activity on the island. Ray Wheeler claimed that from the high ground of the hospital location they could see tanks in some of the continuing mopping up operations.[44] Arthur Bancroft recalled being woken up by gunshots on his first night. Nevertheless, he relished the care he received in the hospital, especially from the nurses. A doctor noted on Bancroft's medical chart "Patient had no complaints."[45]

The survivors lived under canvas, with some of the more ill like Alfred Allbury and Alf Winter confined to their beds for days. In fact, some had difficulty adjusting to sleeping in a bed and spent their first few days sleeping on the ground.[46] As in the case of Bancroft, those restricted to bed rest considered the companionship of female nurses one of the compensations for confinement.[47] Ray Wheeler recalled that the nurses treated them as well as their own mothers, at night tucking them in and giving them a kiss goodnight.[48]

With the former prisoners offloaded, the submariners set about disinfecting their boats before resuming their patrols to Pearl Harbor. On *Pampanito*, a relief crew installed new bedding.[49] Just a day after delivering the survivors, *Sealion* set sail from Saipan at about 4 p.m., and arrived at Pearl Harbor nine days later. Some of the crew on *Sealion* subsequently developed minor infections attributed to the overcrowding, loss of sleep and irregular meals necessitated by having the survivors on board.[50] Once *Pampanito* arrived back at Pearl Harbor, each crew member was given a series of inoculations to ward off any possible diseases from the rescued POWs they had transported.[51]

In some cases, the submariners' experience with the rescued prisoners hardened their attitudes toward the Japanese. Don Miller, a torpedoman on USS *Barb*, recalling the rescued men's emaciated bodies, stated that he would "never forget the Japanese for what they did to them."[52] Another crewman, Harold Case on USS *Sealion*, professed that "The reality of it made me madder than hell at the Japs."[53] But what most of the sailors took away with them was an immense sense of pride at having contributed to the rescue of their allies.

In a form of warfare that generally lacked humanity, the rescue of survivors provided the submariners with an opportunity to exercise compassion on a meaningful scale. Gordon Hopper from *Pampanito* later recalled that "All the rest of my life I have treasured the memory of helping save lives rather than terminate them."[54] In similar terms, engineman second class William Fisk enthused that "It was great to see something that turned out good. That was my most satisfying patrol."[55] Whereas *Pampanito*'s battle flag had previously only displayed icons symbolizing its "kills," the crew added a large number "73" to the flag in tribute to the prisoners of war rescued. *Pampanito*'s crew triumphantly flew the flag when they arrived at

Pearl Harbor on 27 September, where four admirals and a host of "lower reaching officials" greeted them.[56]

Eugene Fluckey continued to search for Japanese targets even as *Barb* made its way to Saipan with its complement of rescued men. On 23 September, *Barb* received a message that there was a Japanese weather ship near the submarine's track. Fluckey tried to intercept it, but *Barb* was forced to dive by a patrol plane. While submerged, the crew took the opportunity to celebrate their recent sinking of a carrier and a tanker with a victory cake. The cake even included a few miniature rafts on top to represent the rescued survivors.[57]

As with *Pampanito*'s crew, those on *Barb* took enormous pride from their role in the rescue. As one crewman, Don Miller, put it, "Of all the things Barb did for the victory over Japan, this is the one I always have foremost in my mind."[58] Even *Barb*'s battle-hardened commander seemed to concede that there was more satisfaction from their rescue efforts than their success against the enemy: "There is little room for sentiment in submarine warfare, but the measure of saving an Allied life against sinking a Japanese ship is one that leaves no question once experienced."[59]

While the rescued prisoners convalesced on Saipan, the remnants of convoy HI-72 battled through the same storm that had hindered the submarines' progress, and some of the Japanese ships became separated. The same day that *Pampanito* and *Sealion* arrived at Saipan, 20 September, the convoy's first echelon again faced attack, this time from the air. At about 10 a.m., when off Formosa and some 30 miles south of the Pescadores Islands, a formation of U.S. Army Air Force B-24 "Liberator" heavy bombers attacked the Japanese ships. Based on the Chinese mainland, the bombers took a heavy toll. The aircraft damaged *Gokoku Maru* by a direct hit; *Asaka Maru* sustained damage, as did *Kagu Maru* from near bomb misses. The escort *Mikura* also suffered damage. As fate would have it *Kibitsu Maru*, transporting the surviving POWs, was virtually the only ship in the group not to sustain damage.[60]

Kibitsu Maru made for Kirun (present day Keelung) at the northern end of Formosa. When Australian prisoner of war Ray Parkin visited Keelung Harbor not long before on the Japanese transport *Raishin Maru*, he described it as "a vast maritime museum."[61] The harbor was full of ships of every description, some crammed with Japanese troops. The prisoners on *Kibitsu Maru*, according to Thomas Pounder, had no idea what port they were at, although someone correctly believed they were at the island of Formosa.[62] *Kibitsu Maru* waited there for *Kagu Maru* to undergo repairs at the port of Mako (present-day Makung) in the Pescadores Islands.[63]

Gokoku Maru and *Asaka Maru* were also towed to Mako for repairs. In the meantime, left without power or communications, *Mikura* drifted for days before being spotted by a Japanese aircraft. Eventually, fellow escort CD-18 towed *Mikura* to the port of Mako. As CD-18 towed *Mikura*, on 23 September another escort, CD-26, departed Takao to meet the pair. *Mikura* reached Mako a little after 8 p.m. on 25 September and remained there for repairs until it returned to duty on 6 November 1944.[64]

A day after the air attack on the first echelon of HI-72, the second echelon of the convoy also suffered an attack by American bombers. At about 2 a.m. on 21 September, *Shincho Maru* was damaged by a bomb. An escort from the nearby convoy HI-74 came to give assistance. The sea defense ship CD-21 took *Shincho Maru* in tow for Takao before returning to its convoy.[65]

On the morning of 24 September, the escort ships CD-10, CD-11 and CD-20 made a rendezvous with *Kibitsu Maru*, before arriving at Kirun, Formosa, in the early afternoon. At 1:00 p.m. the following day, *Kibitsu Maru* and *Kagu Maru*, along with the three escorts, departed for Moji, Japan.[66] As these remnants of convoy HI-72 continued their journey to Japan, more danger laid in wait. The POWs on board *Kibitsu Maru* lived in fear of another submarine attack. John Huckins succinctly described the voyage as "a nightmare."[67] Roy Whitecross recalled that during the journey he "prayed to 'whatever gods may be' that no Allied ship would sight us."[68] Harold Ramsey later recalled the trip as "the worst experience I encountered and we were all nervous wrecks by the time we eventually arrived at Moji in Japan."[69] Rowley Richards went so far as to claim, "The constant anticipation of a torpedo attack was a far more powerful tormentor than our keepers could ever hope to be."[70]

There were certainly submarines eager to put the ships in their sights. USS *Plaice* departed from Midway on the afternoon of 17 August 1944 for its second war patrol under command of Clyde Stevens, Jr. The submarine had been commissioned only eight months earlier on 12 February 1944, at Portsmouth, New Hampshire. *Plaice* made its first patrol from Pearl Harbor in June. The early part of the second patrol did not auger well. The crew had already battled their way through a typhoon and extinguished a fire in the forward engine room, before the submarine's luck appeared to change on the morning of 24 September. At 7 a.m., two huge ships emerged from the mist that so often blanketed the South China Sea. The submarine identified their targets as *Fuso*-class battleships, screened by four destroyers. *Plaice* fired a salvo of six torpedoes from the bow tubes, and then went deep to avoid an oncoming destroyer. Based on the sound of timed explosions, *Plaice*'s skipper optimistically believed he had sunk one of the battleships, but official records never confirmed any torpedo hits.[71]

Two days later, as midnight approached on 26 September, *Plaice* made another contact. Using their SJ radar, the submarine crew picked up a small convoy making a zigzag course 20,450 yards ahead. As the submarine moved in, the crew identified a large "three-island" freighter and another large transport estimated to be 565 feet long. The ships had three escorts, each estimated to be 287 feet long. One of the escorts led the column while the other two moved up and down its flanks. This was the type of situation for which *Plaice*'s crew trained, before commencing their patrol from Midway.[72] One of the ships was *Kagu Maru*; the other was *Kibitsu Maru*, which carried among other passengers the Allied POWs rescued from *Rakuyo Maru* and *Kachidoki Maru*.

In the early hours of 27 September, about 100 miles northwest of Amami Oshima island, *Plaice* reached position for a surface attack. At 1:49 a.m., the submarine fired four torpedoes from the bow tubes at an overlapping target of escort and transport. Stevens believed that the first torpedo hit the escort and that the other three hit the transport. As described in the patrol report, the transport burst into flame "illuminating the entire scene like daylight."[73] Furthermore, Stevens believed that the violence of the explosion and the color of the flame indicated that the ship was carrying gasoline.

In fact, none of the torpedoes had hit a transport. This was one of many examples during the war in which submariners making night attacks grossly misinterpreted what they were seeing. Nevertheless, the submarine had sunk one of the escorts. CD-10, commanded by Lieutenant-Commander Shiro Ichinose, a graduate of the Kobe Higher Mercantile Marine School, sank almost instantly.[74] *Plaice*'s radar indicated that the ship literally broke in half, showing up as two pips.[75] The power of the explosion and the rapidity of CD-10's sinking took a heavy toll, claiming the lives of 148 men.[76] Some of the prisoners observed the attack from the deck of *Kibitsu Maru*. In fact, the explosion was close enough to blow out the windows of *Kibitsu Maru*'s bridge.[77]

The Japanese escorts responded to the attack with depth charges, further terrifying the prisoners on *Kibitsu Maru*.[78] One of the other escorts, CD-11, looked for survivors but retrieved only eight men. The remainder of the convoy ships made a run for it independently. By the time the smoke cleared, the men on *Plaice* saw no sign of the transport, reinforcing their belief that they had sunk the ship. *Plaice* set off in pursuit of the freighter and the remaining escort, but by 3:30 a.m. Stevens conceded that they would be unable to catch the ships before dawn. He decided to give up the chase and return to the site of the sinking to look for survivors, presumably to verify the ships believed sank. The escort CD-11 was still there when *Plaice* arrived a little after 5 a.m. Once the escort left the scene over four hours later, *Plaice* did a sweep of the area looking for survivors or wreckage but found neither.[79]

Chapter 8

Post-Mortem

Kibitsu Maru, along with *Kagu Maru*, arrived at Moji on the morning of 28 September. For the Allied prisoners on board *Kibitsu Maru*, it meant a new phase in their captivity and their battle for survival. For the Japanese, also, convoy HI-72 had paid a high price. Only days before the attack on convoy HI-72, Japan's Navy Minister, Admiral Mitsuasa Yonai, proclaimed that the Imperial Navy "confidently believes there is a way to achieve sure victory." At the same time, however, he emphasized, "the destruction of enemy submarines is an urgent, vital problem to Nippon."[1] The fate of convoy HI-72 illustrated just how effective American submarines were at this stage of the war, as well as the increasing role of aircraft in disrupting Japanese supply lines. Of the ten ships which originally departed Singapore on 6 September, six were sunk on 12 September. The only transport to survive the journey unscathed was *Kibitsu Maru*.

Most of the convoy's cargo was lost, although the absence of manifests makes it impossible to calculate the full damage to Japan's war effort. At least 12,500 tons of bauxite, used to produce aluminum and vital to aircraft construction, went to the bottom of the sea. *Nankai Maru* had taken on 6,500 tons of bauxite before departing Singapore, while *Kachidoki Maru* carried another 6,000 tons. The attacks on convoy HI-72 also deprived Japan of over 12,000 tons of oil, accentuating an already critical lack of supplies.[2] It is estimated that less than one-sixth of the oil shipped from the East Indies during 1944 made it to Japan's home islands.[3]

It is difficult to calculate the loss of Japanese lives with certainty. Their losses from *Rakuyo Maru* appeared light, with perhaps a dozen crew and Army personnel killed, but a hundred sailors were lost with the destroyer *Shikinami*. Current evidence suggests that 196 of the 525 passengers on *Nankai Maru* were also lost, along with three crewmen.[4] As a major supply base, Singapore attracted personnel from many Japanese firms, so it is likely that many of the passengers lost from *Nankai Maru* were Japanese civilians.[5] The sinking of CD-10 by USS *Plaice* caused the deaths of 148 men on board.[6]

To some extent, the Japanese gradually became inured to their shipping losses. In the early phase of the war, when the number of U.S. submarines was relatively small and their torpedoes were often defective, Japan exhibited little apparent concern about the loss of merchant shipping. The losses steadily mounted, however, so that by 1944 the Japanese navy appeared accustomed to disasters on the magnitude of convoy HI-72. In the month of September 1944 alone, submarines claimed 68 Japanese ships totaling 329,000 tons.[7]

Despite a relative dearth of official records, the surviving battle action reports for two of the convoy ships, *Nankai Maru* and *Asaka Maru*, provide some insight into Japanese thinking at the time. Particularly instructive is a section on "lessons learned" included in the reports.[8] *Asaka Maru*, launched in 1937, was requisitioned by the Imperial Japanese Navy in 1940 and underwent conversion to an auxiliary armed merchant cruiser. The high-speed cargo ship *Nankai Maru*, launched in 1932, was requisitioned by the navy in 1941 and frequently used to carry invasion troops. Both ships were armed with an array of guns, and at least *Nankai Maru* carried depth charges and a hydrophone detector as anti-submarine equipment.[9]

The battle reports of the two ships attributed much of the American submarines' success to their electronic equipment, specifically radar and wireless telephones. In the case of radar, the Japanese were certainly correct in highlighting one of the Americans' principal assets at this stage of the war. SJ surface search radar was arguably the most important technical innovation of the submarine war.[10] The first SJ radar sets were trialed on USS *Haddock* in August 1942, although initially there were teething problems.[11] Following USS *Snook*'s first patrol using the equipment, skipper Charles "Chuck" Triebel described it as "temperamental and delicate."[12] The technology steadily improved, however, with submarines able to make contact on enemy ships from impressive ranges.

Once *Growler*, *Sealion* and *Pampanito* received intelligence information on the projected track of convoy HI-72, the submarines formed a scouting line roughly eight miles apart from one another.[13] The first submarine to attack the convoy, USS *Growler*, initially made radar contact from almost 30,000 yards (fifteen miles).[14] Before attacking *Kachidoki Maru*, USS *Pampanito* similarly made contact with the ship from fifteen nautical miles.[15] Without radar, it is unlikely that *Pampanito* would have sunk *Kachidoki Maru* on 12 September. When USS *Plaice* made its attack on remnants of the convoy on 27 September, the submarine used its radar to pick up the ships from over ten nautical miles (20,450 yards).[16]

Radar provided a huge advantage in making night surface attacks. The equipment included a Planned Position Indicator (PPI) which enabled submarine crews to not only track a prospective target but monitor its escorts.

Chapter 8. Post-Mortem 65

This facilitated making an escape as well as planning an attack.[17] Another innovation, the Target Bearing Transmitter (TBT), further aided making surface attacks. The device essentially allowed submariners to place binoculars in a bracket on the bridge, and easily transmit a target's bearing to the Torpedo Data Computer. *Growler* carried out its attack on *Hirado* using radar ranges and TBT bearings.[18] With the benefit of such equipment, well over half of U.S. submarine attacks in 1944 were carried out on the surface at night.[19]

The failure of the Japanese military to keep pace with American innovations in radar proved a huge liability. By a subtle irony, *Asaka Maru* had carried a naval delegation to Germany for a visit in 1941; the delegation's exposure to German technology disclosed just how far behind Japan was in appreciating radar's potential.[20] Not only had Japan been slow to recognize radar's value, but development was further stymied by the insistence of the army and navy that electronic research be carried out separately. The Japanese army began researching radar sets for ships as a protection against submarines in late 1942, but when tested in February 1943 they were found to have insufficient range.[21] The same month, experimental surface radar was fitted to the submarine I-158 under command of Mochitsura Hashimoto, but again proved disappointing. A surfaced submarine could only be detected within about 2,000 yards. According to Hashimoto, Japanese submariners longed for radar like farmers longed for rain during a long drought.[22] As late as August 1944, two weeks before convoy HI-72 departed Singapore, Admiral Matome Ugaki described Japanese radar as "far behind" the Allies in both "capacity and accuracy."[23] *Pampanito* reported that during its attack of convoy HI-72, there was no evidence of the enemy using radar.[24]

While the battle reports of *Asaka Maru* and *Nankai Maru* correctly highlighted the importance of radar to the submarines' success, it seems that they overstated the benefits of their wireless telephones. By mid–1944, short-distance very high frequency (VHF) radio telephones allowed submariners to communicate through voice contact with less danger of being detected by enemy direction finders.[25] It is clear, however, that submariners remained reluctant to use this technology. Once the *Growler-Sealion-Pampanito* wolfpack left Midway for patrol, the submarines tested their VHF radios and reported them "not very satisfactory."[26] Many submarine skippers believed that using the wireless telephones increased the danger of detection by the enemy, although even at this stage of the war many Japanese escorts lacked a radio-direction finding capability.[27] The night before attacking convoy HI-72, *Growler*, *Sealion* and *Pampanito* made a rendezvous at sea, coming to within twenty-five yards of one another. For "security," the skippers conducted a discussion through megaphones.[28] After

Growler departed the wolfpack, *Sealion* and *Pampanito* held a similar rendezvous on the morning of 15 September, again communicating through megaphones instead of radio.[29]

One reason the Japanese probably exaggerated the effectiveness of the submarines' radio telephones was the deficiencies of their own ship-to-ship communications. The poor quality of intra-convoy signals handicapped convoy ships' response to an attack. The ships relied heavily on signal blinkers, which not only increased the likelihood of being spotted by the enemy but might be missed by smaller ships in rough seas. While there was some belated success in introducing radio telephones for escort ships, merchant ships remained out of the loop. For those convoys fortunate enough to have air cover, neither merchant ships nor escort ships were able to communicate directly with the aircraft.[30] Too often, however, this was a moot point. When USS *Plaice* completed its second patrol in October 1944, skipper Clyde Stevens reported that they had been "hardly bothered" by enemy aircraft.[31]

The battle reports of *Asaka Maru* and *Nankai Maru* quite rightly identified the surface speed of the American submarines as another reason for their success in carrying out attacks. In contrast, convoy HI-72 consisted of a combination of fast and slow ships in which the slower ships acted as a drag on the faster ones. The submarines estimated that the convoy was travelling at between 9 and 10.5 knots.[32] With a top surface speed of 20 knots, the U.S. submarines were able to not only outpace most of the merchant ships but often their escorts. Many of the escorts used were *kaibokan* with a top speed of between 16 and 19.5 knots.[33]

Japan entered the war with few escort ships specifically designed for antisubmarine warfare, apart from a couple of dozen sub-chasers (*kusentei*). Without deep-water sailing capabilities, these were not well suited to lengthy voyages across the Pacific. Destroyers were potentially best suited to the task, but they were in short supply for escort duties. In practice, convoys came to rely heavily on *kaikoban*, ships of about 1,000 tons that the Allies often referred to as "frigates." Originally designed to protect fishing craft in the Kurile Islands, the Imperial Japanese Navy increasingly adapted them to convoy protection and armed them with large numbers of depth charges.[34]

While the *kaibokan* were faster than the ships they protected, they had great difficulty in keeping up with a surfaced submarine. As described above, at one stage in the pre-dawn hours of 12 September, two escorts pursued *Sealion* firing their guns. While *Sealion*'s patrol report conceded that the pursuit "was close and, for a while, too hot for comfort," the escorts gave up the chase.[35] The submarine was able to overtake the convoy again and make an attack that sank *Rakuyo Maru* and *Nankai Maru*.

Chapter 8. Post-Mortem

Another problem faced by Japanese escorts was the need for strict economy in fuel consumption. Japan had entered the war with an inadequate number of tankers, and from February 1944 tankers became priority targets for U.S. submarines.[36] By early 1945 oil supplies from Southeast Asia were virtually severed.[37] Japan's critical oil shortage meant that lengthy pursuits and prolonged submarine hunts were not encouraged. The heavy fuel consumption of Japanese destroyers was one of their deficiencies when used as escorts.[38] At the same time, a lengthy submarine hunt created opportunities for other submarines in the wolfpack to attack convoy ships. In general, Japanese escorts lacked persistence in trying to "kill" submarines, partly because of the necessity of continuing to protect the ships in their charge.

Japan began the war with not only an inadequate number of escort ships, but a lack of antisubmarine tactics and training.[39] These deficiencies persisted into 1944. On 24 March 1944, the Imperial Japanese Navy renamed its "Mine School" the "Antisubmarine Warfare School" suggesting a new appreciation of the need for antisubmarine training, but the school remained without a single *kaibokan* for instruction.[40] In July 1944 the first permanent escort group of four ships was organized, potentially improving tactical proficiency.[41] Nevertheless, as identified by the *Asaka Maru* and *Nankai Maru* battle reports, the ad hoc way in which escorts assembled and a lack of unit training continued to weaken Japan's anti-submarine capabilities. The reports recommended that escorts should be organized into fixed formations under a regular commander, and that the escorts should undergo unit training in anti-submarine tactics.

Rather than convoys trying to make their way through waters infested with submarines, the battle reports recommended a strategy to destroy as many submarines as possible.[42] Presumably, they envisioned offensive sweeps by hunter-killer groups. By this stage of the war, however, the number of U.S. submarines in the Pacific had increased dramatically. In the fifteen months from February 1943, the number of American submarines on patrol had more than doubled, from 47 to 104.[43] At the same time, the Americans had established forward bases closer to Japan's shipping lanes. Saipan, where the rescued POWs were taken, was a case in point. Before attacking convoy HI-72, *Sealion* was able to replenish its torpedoes at Saipan, rather than forced to terminate its patrol at Pearl Harbor in Hawaii or Fremantle in Western Australia.[44]

The improved performance of American torpedoes was another factor in the submarines' success. The standard weapon at the beginning of the war, the Mark 14 steam torpedo with magnetic exploder, had myriad faults that included running too deep, failing to explode or exploding prematurely.[45] Early in the war, the frequent failure of American torpedoes encouraged Japanese merchant ships to sail individually rather than in convoys. Indeed, the full implementation of convoys did not evolve until early 1944.[46]

By September 1944, U.S. submarines not only had reliable steam torpedoes, but newly-developed electric torpedoes. Eli Reich, skipper of *Sealion*, played a role in the development of the electric torpedoes while executive officer of USS *Lapon* in 1943, spending six weeks at Newport, Rhode Island, to test fire them.[47] When *Sealion* took on additional torpedoes at Saipan on 6 September, a dozen Mark 18 electrics were loaded in the aft torpedo room.[48] Described by one writer as "colorful, opinionated and ambitious," Reich continued an association with torpedoes following the war.[49] In the early 1950s he headed the torpedo research division of the Bureau of Ordnance, styling himself as "Mr. Torpedo."[50]

As with radar, the new torpedoes had some teething problems. *Sealion*'s initial load of twenty-four Mark 18 electrics taken on from the tender USS *Fulton* at Midway appeared to include many defective ones.[51] Electric torpedoes also had a shorter range and slower speed than conventional steam torpedoes. On the other hand, the electric torpedoes did not leave the telltale wake of steam torpedoes which often allowed enemy ships to avoid them. The electrics were also reputed to hold their depth more reliably.[52]

USS *Growler* carried a full load of electric Mark 18 torpedoes on patrol for the first time when it sank *Hirado* and *Shikinami*. Skipper Ben Oakley noted in the patrol report that "We were well pleased with our 'electric fish' and given our choice would prefer to carry them rather than Mark 14's or 23's."[53] USS *Plaice*'s skipper, Clyde Stevens, gave the electric torpedoes a similar thumbs-up at the end of his patrol, describing them as "highly satisfactory."[54] Stevens stated he wanted to carry a full load of electric torpedoes on his next patrol. At least in retrospect, Japanese naval personnel came to appreciate the improvements in the U.S. torpedoes. According to Admiral Tomiji Koyanagi, "We tended to deprecate American submarines and torpedoes during the early part of the war, but by late 1944 they were our greatest menace."[55]

While the battle reports of *Asaka Maru* and *Nankai Maru* recognized some of the advantages American submarines possessed and the shortcomings of their escorts, the reports' omissions are also revealing. They suggest that the Japanese navy and merchant marine were still unaware of just how heavily the odds were stacked against them. First, Japan remained oblivious to Allied signals intelligence collectively known as "Ultra." From early 1943, the Allies had cracked the Japanese Maru Code (also known as JN40) which disclosed shipping routes and schedules.[56] The submarines that attacked convoy HI-72 were specifically directed to it, alerted by an

"Ultra" received at 3:00 a.m. on 11 September that a convoy from Singapore was headed northeast through the Paracel Islands to the Formosa Straits.[57] Even before convoy HI-72 departed Singapore, code-breakers were aware of some of the ships composing it.[58]

While the battle reports appreciated the surface speed of U.S. submarines, they apparently remained unaware of their full diving capabilities. Many American submarines survived extensive depth charging because the charges were set to explode too shallow. Initially, Japanese depth charges only had depth settings of 98, 197 and 295 feet, and U.S. submarines could dive substantially deeper than this. By 1944 the depth charges could be set to explode at greater depths, up to 492 feet, but Japanese antisubmarine forces continued to have difficulty making "kills."[59]

At one stage during the 12 September attack, *Sealion* was pinned down by escorts. The crew could hear the sonar echo ranging of the escorts and counted the explosion of thirty-one depth charges. The submarine, however, remained deep enough, at times submerged over 500 feet, to avoid any damage.[60] As a newer *Balao*-class "thick-skinned" boat only commissioned in March 1944, *Sealion II* could dive deeper and take more punishment than previous classes. The diving capabilities of American submarines help to explain the gross disparity between Japanese claims and reality. A report from Tokyo confirmed that Imperial forces had destroyed at least 169 enemy submarines by the end of 1943, whereas in fact only 52 U.S. boats were lost during the entire war, to all causes.[61]

A further weakness in Japanese antisubmarine efforts was the lack of a forward-throwing weapon comparable to the Allies' multiple mortars, or "Hedgehog." Unlike depth charges, these exploded on contact rather than at a pre-set depth, and enabled ships to overcome the blind spot in sonar contact as surface ships approached a target. Japanese escorts had to rely on dropping depth charges over the side or stern after losing sonar contact. By one estimate, Japanese surface ships managed to sink only seventeen U.S. submarines in the Pacific.[62]

Despite the continuing weaknesses in Japan's anti-submarine warfare, there is nevertheless evidence that by late 1944 it was improving. Japan expanded its building of escorts; between March 1943 and May 1944, construction began on an additional 26 *kaibokan* of the *Etorofu* and *Mikura* classes.[63] As described by naval historian Mark Stille, the *Mikura*-class represented the first Japanese ship to be "maximized for ASW."[64] By the end of the war, Japan produced 169 of the ships.[65]

The importance of protecting merchant shipping was also recognized by the formation of the Grand Escort Command Headquarters in November 1943. At least in theory, if not in practice, this put the Escort Command on an equal footing with the Combined Fleet Headquarters, with both reporting to the Chief of the Naval General Staff.[66] As the Chief of the Naval General Staff, Admiral Osami Nagano, admitted, "the establishment of the Grand Escort Command at this time may be like calling a doctor only when the patient's condition has turned critical."[67]

The adoption of more cautious practices by convoys was evident when prisoners including Mick McCarthy and Neil MacPherson sailed on *Awa Maru*. They departed Singapore on 26 December 1944 as part of convoy HI-84, initially consisting of eight ships. The convoy included the escort carrier *Kaiyo*, which kept low-flying aircraft searching for submarines during daylight hours. More ships joined the convoy at Saigon, and from this stage the ships were rarely out of sight of land. The ships not only hugged the coast but spent some nights in enclosed bays for protection. Even so, a submarine attacked *Kaiyo* off Indochina on 30 December, and a torpedo narrowly missed *Awa Maru*.[68]

Although these changes proved too little, too late, they paid some dividends. During 1944, American submarine losses reached a peak of nineteen, with five submarines lost in the month of October alone.[69] USS *Growler*, which had made the first attack on convoy HI-72, disappeared the following month.[70] Ironically, just as Japan was devoting greater resources to cope with American submarines, Allied aircraft increasingly took the initiative in destroying its merchant marine. The B-24 bomber attacks on the remnants of convoy HI-72 were symptomatic of this shift, with aircraft and air-dropped mines displacing submarines as the main threat to Japanese shipping by the end of the year.[71] *Asaka Maru*, already damaged by aircraft while part of convoy HI-72, sank after a carrier plane attack on 12 October.[72] The same day, POWs on the transport *Oryoku Maru* witnessed carrier-based planes attack Keelung Harbor on Formosa.[73]

Even before the air war intensified, Japan's wartime economy had been destroyed by its lack of available shipping.[74] While submarines and aircraft continued the war of attrition on Japan's merchant shipping, the Imperial Japanese Navy suffered a massive setback with the sprawling Battle of Leyte Gulf fought in October 1944. The same day that Australian survivors from *Rakuyo Maru* arrived in Brisbane, 18 October, Allied ships commenced a bombardment of Japanese installations on Leyte in the Philippines. Days later, Japanese fleets converged on Leyte attempting to counter the American drive. Eventually the re-occupation of the Philippines by the Americans enabled land-based aircraft to join submarines in decimating shipping in the South China Sea.[75] With the benefit of hindsight, we can view the destruction of convoy HI-72 as a harbinger of Japan's devastating losses at sea.

Part II
Aftermath

CHAPTER 9

Going Home

The same day that *Kibitsu Maru* and its human cargo reached Moji, 28 September, most of the Australian survivors on Saipan began their journey home. That morning 86 Australians judged fit enough for travel were taken to the waterfront by ambulance. There a motor barge took them to the anchored Liberty ship SS *Alcon Polaris*. On board, 500 U.S. Marines headed for Guadalcanal welcomed them.[1] Another six convalescing Australians, including Roy Cornford, remained on Saipan until well enough to travel.[2] A recurrence of malaria prevented Cornford from departing with his fellow Australians, and he remained on the island for several more weeks.

Also on 28 September, through an administrative blunder, the Australian Casualty Section received notification that the rescued POWs were on their way to Pearl Harbor. Initially the plan had been to send the Australian survivors to Hawaii, an arrangement that apparently appealed to at least some of the recovered prisoners.[3] The plan quickly changed but, due to miscommunication, an officer with the Australian Prisoner of War section of the Army, Captain G.B. Massingham, departed for Hawaii to arrange for the men's interrogation and return to Australia.[4] Massingham arrived at Pearl Harbor after ninety-six hours in transit from Melbourne, only to discover that the Australians were on their way to Guadalcanal.[5] Meanwhile, the better-informed British liaison officer Captain Desmond Tufnell of the Royal Navy travelled from Pearl Harbor to Saipan for the same purpose. Despite delays to his aircraft, Tufnell arrived on Saipan on 21 September, only a day after the first rescued prisoners of war, where he interviewed the survivors.[6]

Among the Australians on board *Alcon Polaris* as it made the first leg of the journey to Australia, John Wilfred Turner helped pass the time by writing an account of his recent experiences. He sometimes stayed up writing until four in the morning. He found the food served on board impressive, especially the servings of chicken and turkey. To Turner's delight, there were movies screened on the ship. There were also group sing-alongs; the Americans appeared especially fond of singing "Waltzing Matilda."

Chapter 9. Going Home

Nevertheless, for most of the survivors the voyage was stressful. Given their recent experience, Turner recalled that the men were "very jittery."[7] On one occasion, when a general alarm went off, the survivors nearly went into a panic before realizing it was only a drill. On another occasion, when the ship's engines failed, Arthur Bancroft remembered the men spending a very tense six hours worrying that they might be torpedoed again.[8] Such anxiety among men rescued at sea was common, especially on a homeward voyage.[9]

On 3 October, *Alcon Polaris* reached the coral atoll of Eniwetok in the Marshall Islands, which had been captured from the Japanese earlier in the year. Turner described the landscape as flat and barren, with all the palm trees decapitated.[10] By this stage, the Australian Army had realized its mistake in sending Massingham to Pearl Harbor, but there still appeared to be confusion about the Australian survivors' destination.[11]

On 6 October, *Alcon Polaris* departed the Marshalls for Guadalcanal, this time escorted by a destroyer that presumably eased the anxiety of some survivors. Two days later the ship crossed the equator at midday. To the great amusement of the survivors, who were exempt from the somewhat cruel initiation rites, they witnessed the rituals of King Neptune for those crossing the line for the first time.[12] *Alcon Polaris* arrived at Guadalcanal on a Tuesday, 10 October. An American Red Cross worker there, twenty-eight-year-old Edith Monks Stark, caught sight of the Australians on a truck after their arrival. The men's emaciated bodies and their sad demeanor stayed with her long after this brief encounter. When she inquired about why men on their way home looked so sad, someone told her because their repatriation remained top secret and no one in Australia was expecting them.[13]

At Guadalcanal, Captain Massingham finally managed to catch up to the Australians. Turner described him as from the "Intelligence Department," noting that he gave the men "some interesting information as to our movements in the near future."[14] Their most-immediate move was to the 20th Station Hospital on Guadalcanal, where the men occupied mosquito-proof huts located between rows of coconut palms. By this stage, the men felt well enough to walk to the beach.[15] Each man received two 12-ounce bottles of beer a day, courtesy of the American Red Cross. To Turner's evident joy, there were also more movies screened, including comedy, with *The Impatient Years*, and film noir, with *The Mask of Dimitrios*, starring Peter Lorre. Turner was further cheered when, at the end of the week, he met a woman from South Australia named Dorothy Harvey. It turned out that they had many mutual friends in South Australia.[16]

On Saturday morning, 14 October, the Australians boarded the 3000-ton U.S. minelayer *Monadnock*, which sailed at 11 a.m. John Turner declared it the cleanest ship he had ever travelled on. He found it difficult to sleep, however. As he put it, his "nerves were pretty well strung up" and he couldn't stop thinking about home. It proved a rough voyage, until they arrived at Moreton Bay on Wednesday, 18 October. Turner described it as "a perfect spring day" and claimed that all the men had lumps in their throats as they finally viewed their homeland.[17]

Well before the ship docked, a Royal Australian Navy commander, C.R. Reid, boarded *Monadnock* from a launch as it made its way up the Brisbane River. Almost immediately, he began interviewing in the captain's cabin four men who were survivors of HMAS *Perth*. The details of HMAS *Perth*'s loss in the Battle of Sunda Strait in March 1942 remained shrouded in mystery, and this was the navy's first opportunity to get a firsthand account. Reid questioned Arthur Bancroft, Bob Collins, Darby Munro and Jack Houghton about the fate of every man in *Perth*'s company, with the interviews continuing until they reached Brisbane.[18] In fact, interviews of the *Rakuyo Maru* survivors began soon after they were pulled aboard the American submarines. On *Queenfish*, for example, skipper Elliot Loughlin questioned the men on the fate of the USS *Houston*, Japanese shipping at various harbors, and the location of enemy fuel and ammunition dumps.[19]

When *Monadnock* reached the wharf at Brisbane, there appeared to be some confusion on what protocols to follow until Captain Massingham finally took charge of the proceedings. Still wearing American uniforms, the Australians were led off the ship by the senior survivor, Warrant Officer William George Smith from Longreach, Queensland. Once disembarked, the men lined up and gave three cheers to the *Monadnock*'s captain and crew. A Colonel McCahon then instructed a band on hand to play "God Save the King." At least one Australian officer present, the Records Embarkation Officer Captain G. Kerrigan, considered this was tantamount to insulting the minelayer's American crew, especially since the band failed to follow up with their national anthem.[20] Whether anyone else was bothered by this is unknown. Certainly, John Turner appeared oblivious to any breaches of protocol, recalling only that the band played familiar tunes like "Waltzing Matilda" and "The Beer Barrel Polka."[21]

The men were addressed by no less than the Commander-in-Chief of the Australian Army, General Sir Thomas Blamey. He congratulated the men for their courage and endurance, themes that would become increasingly familiar in describing the returned prisoners of war.[22] At least privately, however, Blamey expressed an ambivalence toward prisoners of war. A year earlier, Blamey warned the Minister for the Army against "any tendency to extol them [returned prisoners] unduly or give them privileges greater than soldiers who have not surrendered."[23] Ominously, what struck Turner was that there were no civilians present.[24] James Beilby recalled

Chapter 9. Going Home 75

their arrival in Brisbane as all "hush hush," although at the time he did not understand why.[25]

A bus took the returned AIF survivors from the wharf in Brisbane to a former Catholic convent known as Stuartholme, about four miles from the city. It was perched on a hill overlooking Brisbane, and Turner described it as "a marvelous camp."[26] Predictably, the movies screened there nightly especially impressed Turner. The Army Amenities Service supplied a mobile cinema that screened newsreels as well as feature films. Other activities included tennis, table tennis and badminton.[27] James Beilby recalled the camp facilities as "wonderful," including the daily arrival of a keg of beer and with a couple of dances held during their stay.[28] At Stuartholme, the men were under the supervision of Major R.E. Steele, himself a returned prisoner of war. Steele had escaped from Borneo and managed to return to Australia via the Philippines with five others.[29]

One of the priorities at the camp was looking after the men's medical needs, including dental treatment. As later described by an official press release, the men were "attended by a picked team of Army nurses, the first Australian women most of them had seen for more than three years."[30] Most of the men suffered from worms, and Turner offered that the treatment was "pretty terrible."[31] The worst part of their stay, however, was isolation from their loved ones. A couple of days after arriving at Stuartholme, the men received their first letters from home. Turner professed he "cried like a baby."[32] For the time being, however, the army prohibited the men from contacting their families directly. James Beilby made his first contact with his parents by telegram and eventually a telephone call.[33]

The government decided that the returned Australians could keep the considerable clothing and cigarettes given to them by the Americans. At the same time, there was a sense of reclaiming the men into the Australian services. While at the camp, the army outfitted the men with Australian uniforms and equipment.[34] A news report later quoted one of the men saying: "It was good to feel that we were Australian soldiers again instead of being kicked around by the Nips."[35] Reintegration into the Australian military implied a restoration of Anzac values challenged by the men's status as prisoners of war. At the time, the experience of surrender and captivity ran counter to a carefully cultivated image of Australian soldiers' courage and sacrifice. At least some of the returned men experienced guilt over their capture, while others denied that there was anything heroic about their survival.[36]

The Australian government was in a conundrum about how much to make public about the survivors, but it made some preparations in case they decided to break the story to the media. The Australian war correspondent Thomas Farrell was on hand to draft stories about the survivors that might, or might not, be released as the government saw fit.[37] At one point, Fox Movietone prepared a newsreel of the men, in which Turner offered "a few words about the humorous side of our POW days."[38]

As it transpired, the first official announcement on the recovery of POWs from *Rakuyo Maru* came from the British War Office in London. The British government feared accusations of withholding information unless they made a public statement, and issued a press release on Monday, 16 October. The press release disclosed that prisoners of war had been rescued from a Japanese transport the previous month and expressed fears "that a number of prisoners lost their lives when the transport was torpedoed."[39] The survivors' descriptions of their treatment by the Japanese also prompted the Secretary of State for War, Sir James Grigg, to address the House of Commons on 17 October.[40]

Again, the Australians appeared to be a step behind the British and were determined to release no more information than necessary. Australia's Prime Minister, John Curtin, first learned that American submarines had rescued prisoners from a torpedoed Japanese ship in a "secret and personal" message dated 28 September. General Thomas Blamey recommended against any disclosure of the incident for the time being.[41] In early October, the government instructed Australia's chief censorship officer, Edmund Bonney, not to allow any publicity on the recovered prisoners. This was especially the case for the four men who served in the Royal Australian Navy, on the presumption that they would have valuable information about the loss of HMAS *Perth* in the Battle of Sunda Strait.[42]

Ironically, the first public report on the prisoners involved one of the HMAS *Perth* survivors. On Friday, 13 October, the *West Australian* newspaper reported on the impending return of Arthur Bancroft, after his parents received a telegram from the Royal Australian Navy. The newspaper made no mention of *Rakuyo Maru*, but simply reported Bancroft "escaped from a prisoner-of-war camp and is safe in Allied hands."[43]

The Royal Australian Navy had taken a somewhat different approach from the Army in handling the returned prisoners. Although they treated the sailors' return as "top secret," the Navy acted quickly to reunite them with their families. The RAN cabled the sailors' parents that their sons would soon be home. While the AIF survivors remained at Stuartholme, the navy men returned home after their interrogations. Arthur Bancroft flew back to Perth on a DC-3 via Melbourne and Adelaide. Instructed not to speak to anyone, he was still wearing an American uniform. Bancroft did not understand the emphasis on secrecy at the time. As it happened, though, on the aircraft to Perth he ended up seated opposite Senator Dorothy Tangney, a member of the federal parliament. Tangney had once been

Chapter 9. Going Home

his schoolteacher, but when she questioned him, he told her that he had been instructed to keep quiet about his experiences.

On arrival at the Perth airport, Tangney offered Bancroft a ride home. Unknown to Bancroft, however, the Red Cross had already contacted his parents and arranged for them to meet him. His sisters and his girlfriend, Mirla Wilkinson, were also there to greet him.[44] It was a poignant reunion. He had received his first letters in captivity from his mother and Mirla only days before he departed on *Rakuyo Maru*. He had already written Mirla, asking her "have you married a yank yet?"[45]

It was another two weeks before the Army men from Western Australia arrived home. Despite the slip up with Bancroft's name appearing in the *West Australian* newspaper, the government continued to suppress any information on the *Rakuyo Maru* survivors. An Australian War Cabinet minute dated 18 October instructed that there should be a "blanket censorship" of the incident.[46] It was almost two weeks later before Prime Minister Curtin publicly announced that ninety-two Australian POWs had been rescued following the sinking of a Japanese transport. He disclosed that eighty-six of the men had arrived back in Australia, including eighty-one men of the AIF, four men of the Royal Australian Navy and one member of the air force.[47] It would be over two more weeks, when Acting Prime Minister Francis Michael "Frank" Forde made a statement to the House of Representatives, before the government officially revealed that U.S. submarines rescued the recovered prisoners of war.[48]

By this time, all but one of the recovering men detained in hospital on Saipan had been repatriated to Australia. On 28 October, ten days after the first group of Australians reached Brisbane, five additional men initially judged unfit for travel, arrived by plane. By this time, Roy Cornford considered they had fattened up to the point where they no longer looked like former prisoners. They flew first to Los Negros in the Admiralty Islands. The weather turned bad there, so they spent about a week waiting on the island before departing for Brisbane.

In addition to Roy Cornford, the second group of returning men included George Frederick Hinchy from Glebe, Sydney, James Leo Boulter from South Melbourne, Private Murray Andrew Thompson from South Australia and Private Frederick Victor Cross from Western Australia. In Brisbane's Greenslopes Hospital, the men received treatment for a range of conditions, including hookworm. After a couple of weeks, doctors determined that Hinchy needed at least an additional week in hospital before being fit enough for transfer to a hospital in New South Wales. They judged the other men well enough to proceed on leave.[49] The same day they left hospital, the story of *Rakuyo Maru* broke in the press. Once out of hospital, Cornford received eight weeks of leave from the army. After his return from leave, army personnel interviewed him in Melbourne about his knowledge of other prisoners of war still in captivity. The army then discharged him as medically unfit on 24 May 1945, his twenty-third birthday.[50]

Reginald "Jock" Hart, the final Australian survivor repatriated, did not arrive home until late November. Flown from Saipan on an American aircraft, he arrived in Australia without fanfare or an official briefing.[51] Meanwhile, after nearly two weeks of confinement at Stuartholme, the army permitted the AIF men to return home. On 31 October, John Turner flew from Brisbane to Sydney in a Dakota transport.[52] James Beilby flew back to Western Australia, initially to see his brother at Kalgoorlie. He then returned to his parents in the Perth suburb of Claremont, before finally reuniting with his wife, who had a flat in the city.[53] Jack Houghton, a married man from Brisbane, returned home in a car. His wife was not home at the time he arrived, and when she returned she wondered why an American was loitering outside her gate. Horton was still wearing a U.S. uniform.[54]

The British survivors spent a few more days on Saipan than the first group of Australians to leave, finally departing for Hawaii on 1 October with the Liberty ship *Cape Douglas*. Two of the men not fit enough for travel, Gunner A.C. Fuller and Private A. Wyllie, remained on Saipan.[55] The other 58 survivors reached Pearl Harbor on 13 October with considerable fanfare. Admiral Chester Nimitz, commander of the Pacific Fleet, personally greeted the former prisoners and shook each man's hand. He reportedly described the rescue of the men by submarines as "One of the most sensational stories of the war."[56] Nimitz assured the survivors that if the U.S. Navy had known POWs were in the convoy, they would never have attacked it.[57] According to Alfred Allbury, at this stage the men began to realize that they were "VIPs."[58] They spent four days on Oahu relaxing and sightseeing, although instructed not to discuss their experiences as prisoners of the Japanese.

From Hawaii, the men travelled to San Francisco, then Chicago and New York. At New York, they boarded the ship *Queen Mary* for the voyage to Britain, arriving at Greenock, Scotland, on Thursday, 9 November 1944. One of the men required hospitalization on arrival in Scotland. The other 57 men reached No. 90 Reception Camp located at The Vache in Buckinghamshire at 2 a.m. on Saturday, 11 November 1944.[59]

Even before their arrival, the War Office determined that the men should be confined in camp for at least three days in order to avoid any risk of them spreading tropical diseases. The War Office also considered it imperative to interrogate the returned men as soon as possible.[60] By 11 a.m. on the same morning of their arrival, the men were introduced to four representatives from the Casualty Prisoner of War branch including Mr. G.T.H. Rogers, Mr. Perry, Miss Gebbett, and Miss Edgeworth Johnstone.

Chapter 9. Going Home

They conducted interrogations of the survivors until 5:30 p.m. the following day.[61]

A report on the interrogations emphasized the "good bearing, close comradeship, high morale and mental alertness" of the returned men. The interrogators quickly concluded that the returned prisoners "had a mass of information which in the short time available we could not hope to commit to paper."[62] Much of the questioning focused on establishing lists of men who were on *Rakuyo Maru*. In the end, the interrogators compiled 507 names out of the 599 British soldiers believed to be on board the ship.

Suddenly the VIP treatment ended, leaving some of the men feeling embittered at their homecoming. Ed Starkey commented, "We were celebrities until we disembarked in England."[63] By the end of November, 58 of the survivors were on leave, with orders to return for duty on 28 December 1944.[64] On finally arriving home at Gourock in west Scotland, Alfred Allbury reunited with his wife and family within a few hours.[65] Some of the POWs who had dreamed of their homecomings, however, probably felt disappointed by the austerity they found; rationing and shortages in Britain continued for years.[66]

In Britain, the interrogation of some of the men recovered from *Rakuyo Maru* continued into 1945. By January 1945, the survivors had returned from leave and assembled at Fenham Barracks at Newcastle-on-Tyne.[67] Four of the survivors (Sergeant Harry Jones, Corporal Eric Halfhide, Corporal Cyril Anderson and bombardier William Fuller) were selected as "those most likely to be able to supply information on the parts of Malaya and Siam where they were held by the Japanese."[68] The military considered Sergeant Jones in particular as a valuable asset. On the journey back to Britain, Jones had already put together a list of prisoners which he recalled were on *Rakuyo Maru* and a list of those who had died in Thailand.[69]

The interrogations of the four selected men were held on 31 January and 1 February 1945. The many government departments and branches represented at the interviews suggest their perceived importance. Representatives from nearly a dozen organizations participated, including the Admiralty, Air Ministry, Economic Advisor Branch and various intelligence groups. The interrogations focused mainly on details of the Thai-Burma railway. Among other tasks, the interrogators enlisted the men to give the specific location of each prisoner of war camp, so that Allied air forces could avoid bombing them.[70]

Other interrogations conducted at various locations in early 1945 focused mainly on the fates of men recorded as "missing" following the fall of Singapore. Although many of the *Rakuyo Maru* survivors were in hospital or on leave (in some cases absent without leave), twenty-five survivors were interviewed at Newcastle on 16 and 24 January 1945. The interrogators, a Miss Eccles and G.S. Jordan, obtained information on the fates of over 200 officers and men reported as missing in Malaya in 1942. The interrogation of another dozen survivors were conducted at Leeds on 8–10 February 1945. Through this process, the interviewers were able to obtain information on over a hundred men.[71] In April 1945, the "sorting and sifting" of information on those missing continued, and it was expected to be several more months before presumption of deaths could be determined.[72]

Chapter 10

Repercussions

For those Australian *Rakuyo Maru* survivors kept at Stuartholme in Brisbane, much of their time was devoted to undergoing interrogations. A War Cabinet minute on 18 October 1944 instructed Justice Sir William Webb, chief justice of Queensland, to participate in the interviews of the survivors.[1] Already in June 1943, the Australian government had commissioned Webb to write a secret report on Japanese atrocities in New Guinea. He headed a second commission to gather evidence from August to October 1944.[2] In fact, contrary to the impression given by the Cabinet minute, interviewing the former prisoners was Webb's idea. He became aware of the *Rakuyo Maru* survivors while preparing his second report on war crimes, after reading a press release from London. He immediately contacted Herbert Evatt, Minister for External Affairs, and the Department of the Army to arrange taking the rescued survivors' evidence.[3]

Although 86 Australians arrived at Brisbane, Webb interviewed only a dozen of the men from Saturday, 21 October, over four days. As explained by Webb, he limited the number of interrogations due to the men's fragile health and the other demands on their time since "each man was being urgently examined for information for use in war operations." Webb believed the evidence from the twelve men he heard gave "a fair idea of the general treatment meted out by the Japanese."[4]

The prisoners rescued from *Rakuyo Maru* mainly described the treatment of prisoners in Southeast Asia, and especially on the Thai-Burma railway. At times, however, Webb's report strayed into conjecture. When commenting on the failure of Japanese to pick up Allied prisoners from *Rakuyo Maru* after the ship sank, the report claims, "Had they [the Japanese] thought that rescue was likely, they would have machine-gunned the men on the rafts."[5] On the other hand, the report conceded that at times the Australians "came under control of humane Japanese commanders and had relatively decent conditions."[6]

For his second report, Webb heard the testimony of 112 witnesses in all. On 31 October 1944, he tendered his interim report of 104 pages.[7] Even before this, based on the evidence of the *Rakuyo Maru* survivors, Australia's Director of Prisoners of War and Internees publicly stated on 25 October 1944 that the Japanese treatment of prisoners in Thailand and Burma amounted to "one great atrocity."[8] Indeed, even from the initial interviews carried out on the American submarines that recovered the rescued prisoners, their suffering at the hands of the Japanese quickly became apparent. A report by the skipper of USS *Queenfish*, for example, noted that "the stories of Japanese atrocities are too numerous to mention."[9] Japanese mistreatment of Allied POWs was not entirely a revelation, given that over a year earlier U.S. submarines had spirited away some escaped American prisoners from the Philippines, with many debriefed in Australia. Based on their accounts, President Franklin Roosevelt, in January 1944, authorized the release of information on Japanese mistreatment of POWs. Australian newspapers reported the stories of prisoner abuse the same month.[10]

The British government, based on fragmentary reports on POWs' treatment in Thailand, had already lodged a formal protest to the Japanese through the Swiss ambassador in Tokyo on 5 July 1943. They made a second protest on 12 August 1943.[11] By early 1944, they also had some inkling of the conditions suffered by POWs on the Thai-Burma railway. The arrival of a significant number of prisoner postcards from the Far East bolstered public hopes that POWs in Japanese hands were well treated. Through its intelligence sources, however, the government knew differently. Britain's Foreign Secretary, Anthony Eden, intimated as much in the House of Commons at the end of January 1944. On 28 January 1944, he informed the parliament that he had "grave news" and told them there was reason to believe that the postcards and letters recently received from prisoners were probably dictated by the Japanese rather than reflecting the true state of affairs. At this stage, the British received reports of large numbers of men forced to work on building a railway and roads in the jungle without proper shelter, clothing, medical attention or food resulting in "some thousands of deaths."[12]

What distinguished the accounts of the *Rakuyo Maru* survivors from earlier reports is that they brought the first detailed reports by Australian prisoners of war of Japanese mistreatment. In particular, they disclosed horrific stories of the Thai-Burma railway, the 265-mile railway built between Kanchanaburi in Thailand and Thanbyuzayat on the coast of Burma. All of those rescued from *Rakuyo Maru* had worked on the railway. The construction of the railway between June 1942 and October 1943 represented the largest single Japanese use of POW labor during the war and claimed the lives of 2,646 Australians.[13]

At the time, the Australian government was uncertain how much of the information obtained from the returned prisoners it should make public. In fact, the prisoners' reports of ill-treatment by the Japanese posed a huge and unforeseen dilemma. Making the information public was likely to alarm the many Australians with loved ones in Japanese hands and more generally affect morale. The issue of censoring enemy atrocities for the sake of morale remained an on-going issue. For example, Admiral James Somerville, Britain's commander-in-chief of the Eastern Fleet, was concerned that reports of some Japanese submariners killing sailors in the water might become public, to the detriment of morale.[14] There was also the possibility that by publicizing the abuses of Australian prisoners, the Japanese might treat those still in captivity even worse.

In handling the issue of how much to make public, the Australian government became caught up in a tug of war between its two principal allies. On 11 November 1944, the British and Australian governments informed the U.S. Department of State that they planned to issue simultaneous announcements on Japanese atrocities reported by the *Rakuyo Maru* survivors. The Americans, however, reacted strongly against the idea, claiming that the release of information on Japanese mistreatment of prisoners in January 1944 had "delayed by months the possibility of negotiating an exchange of our people."[15] The Japanese response to publicity about the conditions in Japanese camps was mainly denial and counter accusations about the treatment of Japanese civilian internees in the United States. Nevertheless, Japan later became slightly more accommodating on the issues of camp inspections and Red Cross relief supplies.[16] With negotiations believed to be at a critical phase on the shipment of relief supplies for Allied POWs and camp inspections, the Americans feared that an official announcement might scuttle any chance of an agreement.

The Australians initially reacted by stating that they shared this concern, and that the matter would need to be discussed by the Australian Cabinet.[17] The British, however, took a counter position, claiming that publicizing Japanese atrocities might have a positive effect. The British Foreign Office had just received word via Swiss emissaries that the Japanese agreed to delegates of the International Red Cross visiting some POW camps previously off limits; they believed negative publicity might apply additional pressure. Before the government made a formal statement, the War Office advised that "propaganda treatment" should emphasize that Japan's treatment of prisoners "put the whole nation beyond the pale."[18] With the *Rakuyo Maru* survivors soon returning to their homes in Britain, the government also believed it would be difficult to keep their stories of abuse out of the press.[19]

In response, the U.S. Department of State suggested that negotiations with Japan over the welfare of Allied prisoners might be "less endangered" if prisoners' mistreatment were publicized by newspaper stories rather than by official declarations.[20] Again, the British saw the matter differently, arguing that stories published in the press would only lead to further questions in parliament and force an official announcement.[21] Australia's Minister for External Affairs, H.V. Evatt, conceded that an unofficial statement might be better, but also believed that any statements given directly by the *Rakuyo Maru* survivors were likely to be "much more terrible" than a statement by the government.[22] In any case, given the determination of the British government to make an official announcement, the Australians had little option but to follow suit.

The Australian statement closely paralleled that of the British, although they planned to soften it with "some paragraphs added giving Japanese credit for humane treatment in some known instances."[23] When questioned in parliament over the release of reports on prisoner mistreatment, Frank Forde as Acting Prime Minister emphasized that the government made a decision only after consultation with Britain and the United States, the War Council, the Defense Committee of chiefs of staff and representatives from the Prisoners of War Relatives' Association. At the same time, he suggested that conditions for prisoners in other areas "may be relatively better."[24] Some newspapers also tried to soften the message. The *Newcastle Morning Herald* reported, "conditions as bad as those described by Australian survivors of the recently torpedoed Japanese 'hell-ship' are not accorded to all prisoners of war."[25] One of the recovered survivors told the annual meeting of the Prisoner of War Relatives' Association at Sydney Town Hall that the camps in Burma were worse than other camps under the Japanese.[26] The British government later tried to paint a more optimistic picture as well, stating in parliament on 19 December that since the completion of the Thai-Burma railway prisoners' "conditions did improve somewhat." Nevertheless, those conditions remained "far below anything which would be regarded as reasonable for our prisoners of war in Europe."[27]

In the end, the Australian government justified releasing information on the mistreatment of prisoners on the basis that it would signal to the Japanese that they were aware of their misdeeds and that they would be held accountable for them.[28] As a cable to the Australian High Commissioner in London phrased it, by publicizing the abuses the "interests of the prisoners of war still in Japanese hands will be best served by making the Japanese aware that the world knows of their infamy."[29] In light of the *Rakuyo Maru* survivors' accounts, Justice William Webb publicly concluded in November 1944, "the Japanese almost entirely disregarded the rules of warfare concerning prisoners of war."[30] The same month, the Australian and British governments lodged a protest through Switzerland against the Japanese treatment of POWs not only on *Rakuyo Maru*, but at camps throughout Burma and Thailand.[31] A letter addressed to Japan's Minister of Foreign Affairs, Mamoru Shigemitsu, further protested the "dreadful death rate" of

Chapter 10. Repercussions

prisoners employed on the Thai-Burma railway, along with the failure of the Japanese to rescue prisoners following the sinking of *Rakuyo Maru*.[32] Based on the evidence of the *Rakuyo Maru* survivors, some believed the death rate on the railway to be at least 20 percent, an estimate that proved all too accurate.

Claims that the Japanese failed to rescue any of the prisoners from *Rakuyo Maru* proved highly contentious. Based on evidence of the recovered survivors, Frank Forde informed the Australian parliament that after a submarine torpedoed *Rakuyo Maru*, the Japanese did not display "the slightest interest in the fate of the prisoners of war."[33] The press also highlighted the Japanese abandonment of Australian POWs, leaving them to drown after rescuing their own people.[34] Only later did they discover that the Japanese did in fact pick up over one hundred of the *Rakuyo Maru* survivors from lifeboats.

At a press conference with foreign correspondents on 6 December 1944, a spokesperson for Japan's Board of Information, Mr. Iguchi, contradicted the Australian and British accounts. Iguchi not only labeled allegations of prisoner mistreatment as "slanderous," he claimed that at the time of the *Rakuyo Maru* sinking orders were "for women and children to jump off first, then the prisoners and then our soldiers were ordered to escape." Furthermore, Iguchi stated that the Japanese rescued 136 Allied POWs, many of whom were in Tokyo and Fukuoka where they were "in sound health and are deeply appreciative."[35]

Not surprisingly, given the blatant contradictions to eyewitness accounts, the Australian government received this news with extreme skepticism. Nevertheless, at least one of Iguchi's claims proved to be true; the Japanese had picked up 136 prisoners who were now in Japan. At the time, however, the Australians concluded that any survivors in addition to those rescued by American submarines were unlikely. On 11 December, the Australian Army notified the next-of-kin of those known to be on *Rakuyo Maru* that they had "probably" perished at sea.[36] On Australia Day, 26 January 1945, the Japanese broadcast "Humanity Call" gave the names of eighty Australian survivors from *Rakuyo Maru* claimed to be in their hands.[37] Finally, on 15 February, the Prime Minister publicly acknowledged receiving official notification from Japan that eighty Australian prisoners previously classified as presumed dead were apparently alive.[38]

Determining who had died in the *Rakuyo Maru* sinking proved a protracted process, especially since the government initially remained unaware of those rescued by the Japanese. Although next of kin usually received notification of deaths by telegram, on 27 October 1944 the Casualty Section decided to take a different tact in relation to those on *Rakuyo Maru*. They believed a letter could be "more sympathetically phrased" than the standard telegram, but also more definitively indicate the person's death in order "to avoid false hopes being built up." They informed relatives that those believed lost with *Rakuyo Maru* were "missing believed deceased on or after 12 Sept 1944."[39]

The evidence provided by survivors was often incomplete or misinformed. Arthur Bancroft was among those who reported to the Australian military authorities that he believed Rowley Richards died, either when *Rakuyo Maru* was torpedoed or later drowned.[40] On his eventual return to Australia from Japan, Richards discovered that no less than three soldiers from *Rakuyo Maru* visited his parents and gave varying accounts of his death. One claimed he drowned, one that he went mad from thirst and another that he died from malaria. Richards insisted this was not done with any malice but resulted from what he termed "contaminated memory."[41] In a similar case, some of the *Rakuyo Maru* survivors informed the mother of Warrant Officer M.M. Downes that he had drowned. Eventually, however, Allied occupation forces discovered him in a prison camp near Tokyo.[42]

The process of notifying next of kin continued well after the war. Investigators from the Casualty Section attempted to establish the fates of those lost, not only from *Rakuyo Maru* but other ships, in what one newspaper described as "The greatest man-hunt in Australian History."[43] For example, the widow of Reginald Gebhardt was not informed that he presumably lost his life on 12 September 1944 until 1946. Gebhardt had been a leading seaman on HMAS *Perth*; he never saw his daughter, who was born while he was in captivity.[44]

As predicted by the government, the reports of the *Rakuyo Maru* survivors caused huge consternation for those with loved ones still in Japanese hands. The *Sun* newspaper proclaimed that the returned prisoners' story would "chill the blood" and "bring deeper grief" to thousands of Australians.[45] One of those affected was Freda Dickson, whose husband Cecil, a staff sergeant of the 2/2 Pioneer Battalion, was captured on Java in March 1942. Although never sent to Japan, some of Dickson's fellow soldiers were. The survivors of *Rakuyo Maru* brought back to Brisbane included nine Australians from the 2/2 Pioneer Battalion. Of the 73 men from the 2/2 Pioneer Battalion on board *Rakuyo Maru*, 55 drowned. Of the survivors, the Japanese picked up nine. The other nine rescued by U.S. submarines included Leo Cornelius, Vic Clifford and Jack Hocking. They reported to Dickson's wife Freda something of his living conditions. When the government released reports on Japanese mistreatment of prisoners in November, she became increasingly worried about his fate.[46]

The return of the *Rakuyo Maru* survivors to their families and communities in Australia generated enormous pressure on them from those with relatives and loved ones still in Japanese hands. For families with sons, fathers, husbands and brothers still Japanese prisoners, any information about their circumstances or location could help maintain a sense of connection.[47] This was especially the case given the tight restrictions that the Japanese imposed on any communications to and from prisoners. For the most part, the attitude of the Imperial Japanese Army toward prisoners' mail appeared to be one of indifference if not passive cruelty.[48]

Whereas the Germans provided regular mail services for POWs, the Japanese severely limited the reception and sending of mail. After six months confinement at Changi, the prisoners had received no correspondence from the outside world and were allowed to write only one postcard.[49] The first letters delivered from Australia to POWs were not distributed until March 1943; most had been sent about a year earlier.[50] Stan Arneil declared 21 March 1943 as one of the most important days of his imprisonment because he received his first letter from home.[51] Not that all news from home was always welcome. Ray Parkin recounts how one man received a letter informing him that his wife died in a car accident; another prisoner received word that "his wife was being unfaithful all over the town."[52]

When the Japanese surrendered in August 1945, thousands of letters suddenly appeared; Rohan Rivett received a letter from his wife dated October 1942.[53] Lack of communication from home was one of the most difficult aspects of captivity.[54] Rivett described the habitual withholding of the prisoners' mail as "a refinement of cruelty."[55] According to one American POW, next to physical brutality, "nothing made us more bitter against the Nips than this willful withholding of our mail, without rhyme or reason."[56]

At the other end of the pipeline, families in Australia rarely received correspondence from loved ones. War historian Michael McKernan estimates that the total number of letters or postcards received from the 22,000 Australians held by the Japanese amounted to only about 500 during the first fifteen months of the war.[57] The Japanese permitted prisoners held at Changi to write letters home on only five occasions. Many of these were never mailed, while others could take many months to reach a recipient. Les Hall's family did not receive a card he had written from Changi for over two years.[58] Mail from prisoners in other parts of Southeast Asia was equally rare. When allowed to write at all, they sometimes had to include stock phrases such as "The Nipponese treat us well" and "I am very happy here."[59] The Japanese allowed Ray Wheeler, for example, to send a card home from Burma only after eighteen months of captivity. His mother received it mere weeks before he arrived home.[60] Similarly, James Beilby was only allowed to fill out a couple of cards while in captivity—he claimed that one of them was in his parents' letterbox when he finally got home.[61]

Two of the survivors from *Rakuyo Maru*, Colin Latham from Granville and Fred Brown from Parramatta, visited Les Hall's wife, mother and children, and at least could reassure them that they had seen Hall alive in January 1944.[62] In the almost total absence of information about prisoners of the Japanese, relatives had largely turned to each other for support. In Perth, a prisoner-of-war information group met fortnightly to exchange any letters received or other bits of news. Some women drew comfort through contact with other wives with missing husbands.[63]

As feared by the Australian government, insistent relatives inundated the *Rakuyo Maru* survivors with requests for information. A "Welcome Home" function for the survivors, held in Melbourne at the Cathedral Hall in Brunswick Street, Fitzroy, on 15 November, took the form of part inquisition. The program included giving the survivors lists of names from their respective units and questions about the individuals when last seen. The survivors were informed, "Songs will be sung at intervals during the questioning to give you a rest."[64] Meanwhile, on the other side of the country in Perth, Arthur Bancroft attended a tea party sponsored by the Prisoners of War Relatives' Association. Bancroft found himself confronted by hundreds of relatives with photographs of their loved ones asking, "Excuse me, but do you remember this face?"[65]

In December 1944 the POW of Japan auxiliary of the AIF Women's Association sponsored a welcome home event at the Melbourne Town Hall; the organizers requested "that all present will refrain from making any effort to personally contact soldiers who are being welcomed."[66] Concerned relatives, however, largely ignored such pleas. Les Bolger received over four hundred letters from relatives, in addition to those who turned up on his doorstep. According to Bolger, "It was very distressing to have to tell them, the ones that had died."[67] Arthur Bancroft received some one hundred letters from relatives of those on HMAS *Perth* and, despite Navy instructions not to reply, he was proud that he answered each one. He and the other sailors who survived collectively decided that if they had died, they would want their families to know the truth. Even so, not all the relatives were prepared to accept the truth.[68]

In Britain, the *Rakuyo Maru* survivors similarly received an avalanche of letters from relatives seeking information about loved ones. Already by mid–November 1944, one of the returned men had received 500 written inquiries. The men were "invited to unload such enquiries" to the Casualty Prisoner of War department, but it is unclear how far they did this or if they attempted to personally respond to letters. The main strategy of the War Office was to try to assure the public "that they can safely leave the interrogation of the returned prisoners to us in the knowledge that if there is any information available relative to their husbands, sons, etc. they will be given it."[69]

Chapter 10. Repercussions

Some survivors found themselves unable to cope emotionally with such requests.[70] One of the Pioneer Battalion survivors, Leo Cornelius, described a meeting with relatives in Melbourne as one of the "greatest difficulties of my life."[71] Meeting relatives was especially hard when he knew their loved one had died or was ill when he last saw them. Some of the survivors sought seclusion so that they did not have to face the wave of inquiring relatives. Roy Cornford found himself "besieged" with letters, photos and phone calls from anxious relatives. He helped those he could.[72] The most fortunate families received information directly from *Rakuyo Maru* survivors. Ted Buerckner, one of the 23 Australians recovered by USS *Sealion*, visited the family of his good mate Mick McCarthy. He could report to them firsthand that Mick was alive.[73]

Chapter 11

POWs in Japan

For those prisoners from *Rakuyo Maru* rescued by the Japanese, the ordeal of captivity continued unabated until Japan's surrender. They joined another estimated 35,000 Allied prisoners sent to Japan by sea from 1942, including 2,700 Australians.[1] With from 90 to 160 POW camps spread over the home islands of Honshu, Kyushu, Shikoku and Hokkaido, once in Japan their fate could vary enormously. The total number of prisoners to die in prison camps in Japan during the war was reported to be 3,432. Many are still there, with 277 Australians who died in Japanese captivity buried at the Commonwealth War Grave Commission cemetery at Yokohama.[2]

The primary purpose of sending prisoners to Japan was to provide labor, especially in mines, on the docks and in factories. The first group of Australians sent to Japan included officers from HMAS *Perth*. In April 1942, after spending about a month at Serang in Java, the Japanese selected a dozen *Perth* officers for shipment to a camp at Ofuna. These included *Perth*'s naval doctor Surgeon-Lieutenant Samuel Stening. At this infamous interrogation camp near Yokohama, prisoners were routinely tortured.[3] The first northbound prisoners dispatched from Singapore departed on *Fukkai Maru* and *England Maru* in August 1942.[4] More HMAS *Perth* survivors were sent to Japan on 26 October 1942 aboard *Tojuki Maru*. From among the 1,200 prisoners on board, 27 died before the ship reached Moji on 8 November.[5] That same month, November 1942, C Force, with 2,200 men, including 563 Australians, was sent to Japan to labor in factories, mines and shipyards.[6]

In a disaster that in some ways paralleled the later sinking of *Rakuyo Maru* and *Kachidoki Maru*, the submarine USS *Tang* sank the prisoner transport *Tamahoko Maru* on 24 June 1944.[7] Lieutenant Lance Aldworth Gibson was among the 772 prisoners that originally boarded the Japanese transport *Miyo Maru* at Singapore on 2 June. They departed in a convoy the following day. As reported by Gibson, "Naturally all were apprehensive of submarines and this feeling was accentuated when the leading corvette was torpedoed on the night of 6–7 June."[8] This attack by USS *Raton* sank the escort CD-15 and claimed the lives of 104 crewmen on board. The convoy's fortunes further waned on 15 June when it sailed into a typhoon that left *Miyo Maru* badly damaged.[9]

The convoy arrived at Takao, Formosa, on 18 June 1944. The prisoners from *Miyo Maru*, along with 500 Japanese soldiers, transferred to the larger *Tamahoko Maru* and departed two days later for Moji, Japan. Shortly before midnight on 24 June, about 40 miles southwest of Nagasaki, explosions awakened the prisoners. According to Gibson, the ship sank in less than two minutes. A survivor of HMAS *Perth*, chief engine room artificer Cedric Mellish, helped to organize the prisoners' evacuation. The following morning, only Japanese survivors were initially picked up, but 211 prisoners were later allowed to board a ship. The prisoners arrived at Nagasaki at midday, from where a truck took them to Fukuoka No. 14 Camp. From the original complement of 257 Australians on *Tamahoko Maru*, only 72 survivors landed at Nagasaki.[10]

The first prisoners drafted from among survivors of the Thai-Burma railway for shipment to Japan departed on two ships from Singapore on 4 July 1944. The force of 2,250 men included about 1,000 Australians under Captain Reginald Newton. Syd Barber, a survivor of HMAS *Perth*, was among those disembarked at Moji after the epic 70-day voyage on *Raishin Maru*.[11] Two Japanese sprayed the prisoners with DDT powder as they walked down the gangway.[12] Barber was assigned to work in a metal refinery at Seganoeski, not far from Moji. He found the camp "much better than anything we had on the Railway."[13] Ray Parkin, another HMAS *Perth* survivor who arrived on *Raishin Maru*, similarly considered conditions in Japan "a great improvement."[14] Assigned to a mining company, he was surprised to be issued not only work clothes, but bed clothes and a mattress with a cover.

Kenneth Harrison, another passenger on *Raishin Maru*, also found Japan a definite improvement by the standards of the Thai-Burma railway. Sent to Fukuoka No. 2 Camp, he believed the food was the best yet received and he appreciated the communal hot baths allowed every three days. By the standards of his previous experience, he found the sergeant-major in charge of his camp "a just and humane soldier with a definite sense of humour and fair play."[15] Harrison was put to work on ship-building at the dockyards. Don Moore, another prisoner to arrive in Japan on *Raishin Maru*, worked at the Nagasaki dockyard and integrated well with the local workers there. He quickly discovered that the civilian population was not much better off than the prisoners of war.[16] Hugh Vincent Clarke noted that on arrival at Nagasaki, the prisoners were examined by a Japanese doctor, given treatment and received two weeks rest before commencing work.[17] Lance Gibson, an Australian survivor of *Tamahoko Maru* sent to Fukuoka

No. 14 Camp, found the camp staff "fairly sympathetic though comforts and medicine were scarce."[18] He believed that a visit to the camp by a Captain Takarta from the POW Information Bureau led to some improvement in conditions there.

As Kenneth Harrison acknowledged, though, there were other camps in Japan full of horrors.[19] About 300 Australians interned at a POW camp north of Tokyo at Naoetsu (now known as Joetsu) experienced starvation, ill treatment and severe cold. Punishments at the camp included standing naked in the snow. About sixty men lost their lives due to the harsh conditions. The fact that four of the camp's commanders were subsequently sentenced to death for war crimes is indicative of the regime there.[20] Samuel Stening, who worked as a medical officer at the Oeyama POW camp, believed that the most brutal Japanese were those deemed medically unfit for more active service.[21] Some of the prisoners from *Raishin Maru* were taken to Yamawi Camp on the island of Shikoku where they worked in a copper mine owned by the Sumitomo Besahin Copper Company.[22] Thomas John Martz was one of a party of 300 put on a train for a ten-hour trip to a port, and was then ferried to Shikoku to work in the mines.[23]

The 500 Americans who arrived to work at the Omuta coal mine in August 1943 also found conditions far from hospitable. After departing Manila on 23 July 1943, they disembarked at Moji seventeen days later from the transport *Clyde Maru*, nicknamed "Benjo Maru" by the prisoners. From Moji they were taken by train to Fukuoka No. 17 Camp just east of Nagasaki, and forty miles south of the city of Fukuoka. The barracks, constructed by the Mitsui Coal Mining Company, were infested with vermin. Despite an abundance of coal, the prisoners were denied proper heating. Although issued woolen uniforms taken from British supplies in Hong Kong, the POWs were forbidden from wearing them except on rare Red Cross inspections.[24]

One former prisoner, Sergeant Harold Feiner, recalls the camp was "as tough as they came." According to Feiner, "If there was nothing else that had gone wrong, the work itself would have made it bad. We mined coal twelve hours a day, had a thirty-minute lunch break, and were given one day off every ten days."[25] Given the brutal and risky nature of the work, with little training, inadequate tools and frequent cave-ins, not surprisingly some prisoners used self-inflicted injuries to gain a temporary respite.[26] Thanks mainly to the benevolence of Baron Mitsui, a Dartmouth graduate, one bright spot was an expansion of hospital facilities at the camp.[27] In total, over 6,000 Allied POWs were employed in Japanese coal mines, making up less than two percent of mine workers.[28]

Like most prisoners sent to Japan, those recovered from *Rakuyo Maru* and *Kachidoki Maru* entered at the port of Moji on the northeast tip of the island of Kyushu.²⁹ Eight of the prisoners died during the voyage of *Kibitsu Maru* before reaching the port.³⁰ In the words of one prisoner, "by the time we reached the Port of Moji we were living on the last dregs of our resistance."³¹ Frank McGovern recalled arriving at Moji at night and finding it "a drab looking place."³² The prisoners were later off-loaded, and made to sit on the jetty in full view of the locals. The men were then marched through the streets practically naked and at one stage were confined to a courtyard over-looked by female clerical workers. Denied permission to dig latrines, the prisoners had to relieve themselves in full public view. After going through a delousing facility, they lodged in a former stable.³³

Ten of the most seriously ill from among the survivors remained at Moji for treatment, while the Japanese transported the remainder to various locales for labor. About 300 of the British POWs went to Yokohama, while fifty of the Australians went to a camp at Kawasaki, nearby.³⁴ Frank McGovern was among the group that made the 36-hour train journey to Yokohama. The blinds were drawn on the train and the prisoners instructed not to look out the windows. Once they arrived at Yokohama station, curious onlookers gathered around as the prisoners got off the train. Eventually the prisoners' guards produced some blankets for them to use. The Australians were loaded on trucks and taken to the camp at Kawasaki, where McGovern found himself designated prisoner number 158. He had to wear the number on his back.³⁵

Apart from the Australians, the other POWs at Kawasaki camp were mainly Dutch and Americans. Frank McGovern developed a friendship with Mike Palmer, an American from the U.S. Navy captured in the Aleutians. Each day at 4 a.m., McGovern and his fellows marched through the streets to a factory—Shabor Engineering Works—where his job was arc welding. The men worked until dark. Somewhat ironically, much of their work involved producing components for Japanese submarines, including fans, condenser tanks and hull plating.³⁶

At the Kawasaki camp, a twenty-foot-high bamboo fence surrounded the compound. Indeed, virtually everything in the camp appeared made from bamboo. George Carroll described the Kawasaki camp as "not too bad."³⁷ According to Carroll, there were civilian guards at their camp and military guards at the factory. McGovern described one of the Japanese soldiers in charge, a lieutenant named Watanabi, as a sadist. On the other hand, he considered that the Japanese foreman who supervised his arc welding "wasn't a bad Nip."³⁸ The ordinary Japanese they worked with also seemed OK. To McGovern, they appeared as much under the thumb of the military as the prisoners.

Across Japan, prisoners tended to find relations with the civilian population relatively amicable. Fred Lasslett, a survivor of HMAS *Perth*, eventually ended up at a camp on the island of Hokkaido. He became responsible for looking after an electric train that carried iron ore from a mine. He found the Korean guards at his barracks cruel, but his relations with the Japanese civilians were generally good. Some were in fact "very kind" to him.³⁹ Another survivor of HMAS *Perth*, Ray Parkin, worked in a coal mine near Nagasaki. He found that the mine officials took a certain paternal interest in the prisoners and that the other workers accepted them uncritically, "showing only polite curiosity and some fellow feeling."⁴⁰ Alan Whelan also worked in a mine. He claimed, "The Japs treated their own people as badly as they treated anyone else. If a Japanese mine worker was sick and couldn't work, the family were only given half rations."⁴¹

Hugh Clarke, sent to work in a shipyard at Nagasaki, recalled seeing many Japanese workers walking barefoot. "All over the dockyard were the signs of hardship being endured by Japanese civilians. Very young boys and girls worked at tasks as hard as ours—and they wore clothes no better and ate food of a similar standard."⁴² As the Allies increased pressure on Japan, the quantity and quality of food for both civilians and prisoners deteriorated. U.S. submarines successfully blockaded much of Japan's food supplies. Many Japanese city-dwellers found it necessary to periodically forage for food in the countryside.⁴³ By 1944, some prisoners sensed civilians' increasing disenchantment with the war, and at least some were prepared to assist them in pilfering. Those assigned to work on the docks particularly found opportunities to supplement their diet through pilfering food.⁴⁴

Another 290 prisoners from *Rakuyo Maru* and *Kachidoki Maru*, including 29 Australians, went to Sakata on Honshu's north-west coast. Rowley Richards was among the POWs sent there by train. At Sakata, they lodged in a deserted rice warehouse, where they slept on wooden floors and grass mats.⁴⁵ There they mainly worked on the docks or in factories for a nine-and-a-half-hour day. Kitchener Loughnan spent most of his working day stacking or loading saw timber and carting coal.⁴⁶ Similarly, Edward Kelk was mainly employed ferrying timber and lumping coal.⁴⁷ Thomas Pounder's work at Sakata involved loading and unloading trains, moving logs, coal, stones, rice, salt, cement and bags of sulfur.⁴⁸ Another survivor of *Rakuyo Maru*, David Clark, worked on the docks and at a chemical plant.⁴⁹

Their diet was sparse, containing little protein, fat or vitamins. Even so, Thomas Pounder found the food more palatable than in Malaya, although ironically a couple of prisoners died from food poisoning after eating from Red Cross parcels. There was less disease in Japan, but Pounder continued to suffer from bouts of malaria and dysentery.⁵⁰ Many prisoners, however, saw their symptoms of malaria disappear after a few months in Japan's cooler climate.⁵¹ At least medically, the prisoners at Sakata appeared better looked after than most. There were Japanese physicians, both from

Chapter 11. POWs in Japan 95

military and civilian practices, along with supplies of medicine and essential instruments.[52] Civilians helped at least some prisoners. At one stage, a 58-year-old mother showed David Clark and some other POWs how to supplement their diet with seaweed. When Clark suffered a bout of pneumonia, the same woman and her daughters helped to look after him by supplying rice and fish.[53]

Camps in the colder areas of Japan were particularly miserable. They lacked facilities for extreme weather conditions, and by some reports the 1944–45 winter was the coldest in over a half century. At the Niigata camp temperatures could drop to twenty-five degrees below zero; prisoners had to cope with no heat in their barracks.[54] At Sakata, the temperature dipped to seventeen degrees below zero.[55] Frank McGovern recalled that the prisoners wore everything they had to bed to keep warm.[56] According to Rowley Richards, eight men at Sakata died of pneumonia during its severest winter in seventy years.[57] Indeed, pneumonia was the number one killer of POWs in Japan, aggravated by inadequate heating, poor diet and widespread respiratory infections.[58] At the Fukuoka Camp No. 17, where medical officer Thomas Hewlett kept records, of the 126 men who died 48 deaths were attributed to pneumonia. Another 35 deaths were attributed to "deficiency disease," 14 to colitis, 10 to "miscellaneous diseases," 8 to injuries, 6 to tuberculosis and 5 to executions.[59]

By 1945, prisoners had to cope with not only one of Japan's worst winters in memory, but the growing threat of Allied bombing. On one occasion, while working at the docks, Thomas Pounder watched on as Allied planes bombed ships in the harbor. Then more threateningly, a plane made a strafing pass at the prisoners with its machine guns, obviously mistaking them for Japanese. At least one prisoner died in a bombing raid on Sakata.[60]

Some prisoners at Kawasaki witnessed the dramatic fire-bombing of Tokyo in March 1945. With their camp burnt, the prisoners relocated. Even so, they remained vulnerable to Allied bombing. On one occasion, 13 June 1945, their camp took a direct hit from an Allied bomber, injuring Frank McGovern and killing his best mate. McGovern believed that the bombing killed about thirty POWs, including three men from HMAS *Perth*, and wounded many other POWs. For McGovern, it was the lowest point of his captivity.[61] H.W. "Johnny" Sherwood, a British survivor of *Kachidoki Maru*, was at Fukuoka No. 25 Camp when a bomber dropped an atomic bomb on Nagasaki. He heard a rumble in the distance and saw a huge cloud rise over Nagasaki Bay, assuming bombers hit a chemical factory. Only later did he hear that a "Death Ray Bomb" had killed thousands.[62]

Allied bombing had an impact on the prisoners' relations with civilians, although the authorities generally tried to minimize contact between POWs and local populations. Especially in 1945, as Allied air raids intensified and supplies diminished even further, feelings against prisoners increased. At some camps, prisoners were beaten by their guards in the wake of American air raids. Some civilians reportedly refused to sell food supplies to POW camps.[63] Colin Finkemeyer, from Australia's Fourth Anti-Tank Regiment, recalled that when marching to work in Nakama the locals demonstrated "their hatred for us by contemptuously yelling and spitting at us. The children showed their wrath by hurling handfuls of stones at us."[64] Similarly, at Niigata civilians started abusing prisoners marching to work and sometimes shouting at them from outside their camp.[65]

On the other hand, Tom Wade, held at the Omori camp in Tokyo, noted that even after bombing raids, the local Japanese showed no open hostility to the POWs.[66] Following an Allied air raid on Kobe in June 1945, Private Roly Dean of 2/19 Battalion recorded that when the POWs helped the young and elderly victims, "a strong spirit of camaraderie developed."[67] Lance Sergeant Alex Dandie of the 2/30 Battalion concluded that most Japanese civilians were "not bad people to get on with," although he considered their guards as quite different.[68] After witnessing an incendiary air raid on Omuta, Robert Holman professed that "the screams of those women and children were shocked into my brain for life."[69]

CHAPTER 12

Liberation

What was likely the last group of prisoners to sail from Singapore for Japan departed aboard *Awa Maru* on 26 December 1944. The ship, including 600 Australians, arrived at Moji on 15 January 1945.[1] Among those who sailed on *Awa Maru*, Robert Holman described the vessel as "a large new passenger cargo ship."[2] According to Holman, at one stage a torpedo narrowly missed the ship. After arrival in Japan, Holman found himself at the Omuta camp, where he considered the guards were even crueler than those on the Thai-Burma railway.[3] Mick McCarthy and Neil MacPherson were also among those shipped to Japan on *Awa Maru*. They went to a camp at Senryu, about 40 miles north of Nagasaki, where they labored in a coal mine. At Senryu they received decent quarters and treatment. Towards the end of the war, McPherson observed, "the Japanese miners' lunch boxes contained very little more than ours." He concluded that he was probably fortunate to have the opportunity to interact with Japanese civilians and not just "the brutal military."[4]

When the Japanese surrendered on 15 August, the news circulated at varying pace to the scattered POW camps in Japan. At Fukuoka Camp No. 17, prisoners about to enter a coal mine for work were told by their guards to return to camp. When they assembled in the camp mess hall they were given Red Cross boxes! Lester Tenney, an American captured in the Philippines, decided to test the waters by refusing to salute or bow to the guards. Instead, when he waved at a guard and said "Hello," the guard smiled, bowed, and said "Hello" in English.[5]

The commandant of a camp at Hakodate did not announce the war was over until 24 August.[6] Thomas Pounder knew nothing of the atomic bombs dropped on Hiroshima and Nagasaki. When the war ended, he was suffering a bout of dysentery. He saw groups of Japanese listening to radios, and later learned they were listening to Japan's emperor.[7] Frank McGovern knew something was up after the Japanese ordered the prisoners to paint "PW" on the roof of their hut in 30-foot white letters. The guards were also now trying to fraternize with them. There was no rejoicing at that stage. The men thought instead of the prisoners who had only recently died.[8]

Prior to the surrender, many had expected a fight to the death as Japan drafted women and children into the war machine, armed to fight with only sharpened pikes. Many, if not most, prisoners assumed their own annihilation in the event of an Allied invasion. Robert Holman was among those who reported stories that the POWs were all to be killed once Japan faced defeat.[9]

As it transpired, the mass exterminations that POWs so long feared as a concomitant of the war's end never eventuated. On the contrary, with the Japanese surrender, Thomas Pounder experienced a sudden change. Now the Japanese were saluting them, and he was able to leave the camp at will.[10] Sergeant Graeme McCabe from the 100th Squadron RAF witnessed a similar *volte face*: "The Japs who had been brutal stand over merchants up to the surrender by their leaders, suddenly became docile, humble, obsequious."[11] The attitudes of Japanese guards at some camps literally transformed overnight. At a camp on the island of Shikoku, Lieutenant Ralph Sanderson recorded in his diary for 16 August that "Japs' boisterous attitudes have changed to meekness. Jap guards keep well away from us."[12]

Kenneth Harrison was among those amazed by the "almost unbelievable" lack of hostility and resentment by the Japanese once they surrendered. He concluded, "An enemy who was so often an appalling winner ... did at least prove to be the best of losers."[13] He later attributed this in part to broadcasts by General MacArthur warning the populace that POWs should not be harmed, and even more to the Emperor's expressed wishes.

With Japan's surrender, Red Cross parcels, withheld from the prisoners for months if not years, suddenly appeared. Some POWs received mail dating back to 1942. At some camps, Red Cross supplies were released that might have saved lives if handed over earlier. At Naoetsu camp on the west coast of Honshu, the prisoners received Red Cross parcels that had been at the camp since 1943. There were also boots and clothing that could have helped them survive Japan's brutal winters.[14] The large amount of Red Cross supplies found stockpiled naturally incensed many prisoners. At least some Japanese excused this hording, claiming that they expected the war to continue years longer or reasoning that the food would be needed in case of an Allied invasion.[15]

For their part, prisoners who had fantasized of reprisals against their captors for years largely lost their appetite for revenge. According to one Australian POW, Colin Gooch, "No one thought of taking spite out on the Japanese. You need quite a lot of energy for spite."[16] Kitchener Loughnan stated, "We were too weak to do much, and not only that, there were about 40,000 troops in our district—they did not take the surrendering too easily.

Besides, we just wanted to go home."[17] Frank Hole from the 2/20 Battalion also commented on the lack of retribution against their guards. "I think we had all reached the stage of exhaustion where even the effort of revenge was beyond us. Also we were a couple a hundred miles from Tokyo and nobody knew how we were going to make contact with the American Forces."[18] Kenneth Harrison attributed the lack of revenge partly to pity, reasoning that the prisoners were "going back to so much" while "leaving them with so little."[19]

Once Allied food drops to POW camps began, many prisoners were inclined to share their booty with civilians. American B-29 bombers based in the Marianas made some 900 flights over prison camps in Japan to drop food and supplies.[20] George Carroll and Bill Mayne shared some food with their former factory foreman who had treated them reasonably well.[21] Claude Roediger, who worked in a Japanese mine, felt no ill will toward his former co-workers once Japan surrendered. In his view, they were "just common ordinary folk," and they shared many of the supplies that began arriving.[22] At Sakata, David Clark claimed that after the American air drops of food and clothing, they gave much away as presents.[23] At the Nakarma camp where Kenneth Harrison was held, the airdrops of food and cigarettes attracted Japanese civilians to the camp looking for jobs. The POWs happily employed some of the locals to wash and clean. As Harrison put it, "the wheel had come full circle."[24]

Like news of the surrender, the actual liberation of prisoners took place at a variable pace. As recalled by Frank McGovern, about a week after surrender, they went to Tokyo Bay by bus. The prisoners then boarded the American hospital ship USS *Benevolence*. As described by one prisoner, "never was such kindness, gentleness and understanding displayed as by the officers, nurses, doctors and men of that magnificent American vessel."[25] Once on board, the returning men showered and dressed in American uniforms.[26] Since stories of the prisoners' mistreatment had circulated widely, they tended to be "fussed over" on the hospital ships. Some POWs found the sudden attentions of nurses unnerving; self-conscious about their appearance, they feared they looked sub-human to the women.[27]

After about a week, Frank McGovern sailed on the British escort carrier HMS *Speaker* to Manila, which became a major clearinghouse for returning POWs.[28] By the end of October 1945, some 31,617 American former prisoners were processed there.[29] Most of the Australians were routed through Manila as well. Ken Iskov, a member of the Australian Army, worked there as a cook and described the condition of the men arriving as "frightful."[30] At Manila, prisoners of all nationalities were under American command, and well looked after by the U.S. Army and Red Cross. In the words of George Carroll, the Americans treated them "real good."[31]

At least some of the former prisoners, however, felt greater ambivalence toward the Americans. For Ray Parkin, conditioned by years of frugality and subsistence living, the Americans appeared profligate. "Yanks were there, oh chuck everything away, we've got everything, we'll give you the world, and all the rest of it, you know and they had petrol on everything burning it up and we had things we wanted to save."[32] At the time, Parkin seemed to have more in common with the Japanese villagers he had worked with than the Americans he encountered.

For Robert Holman at Omuta camp, liberation came on 2 September, the same day Japan signed the instruments of surrender on the USS *Missouri*. A car full of officers representing the various Allies arrived at the camp. It was not until 15 September, however, that the prisoners departed from the camp, transported by train from Omuta to Nagasaki where a dockside center processed some 9,000 former POWs.[33] At Nagasaki, they boarded the American aircraft carrier USS *Cape Gloucester*, and that evening watched the film *It Happened One Night* on the flight deck. They sailed to Okinawa, commonly used as a staging point for liberated POWs before transport to Manila. Mick McCarthy, a survivor of the Thai-Burma railway and labor in a Japanese coalmine, arrived at Okinawa on a Tuesday, 18 September 1945. He encountered Rowley Richards there, and heard firsthand the story of the ill-fated *Rakuyo Maru*.[34] In the meantime, Holman transferred to the Liberty ship SS *Hiram Bingham* at Okinawa and headed to Manila by sea.

For prisoners in Sakata, the Japanese organized a train to take them to Sendai on the east coast. Rowley Richards, Thomas Pounder and their fellow prisoners walked to the railway station and boarded the train for Sendai on 12 September, exactly twelve months after the sinking of *Rakuyo Maru* and *Kackidoki Maru*. Among those departing, David Clark later recalled, "I can still see the platform of the station with many of the workers waving and crying. It was very sad. In a way I was sorry to leave."[35] At Sendai, the prisoners transferred to the hospital reception ship USS *Rescue*. On the ship the men went through lengthy processing that included disposing of their clothing, given a hot bath, sprayed and deloused, medically examined and issued new clothing. Kitchener Loughnan recalled the Americans looking after them as "marvelous."[36] The sailors allowed them to send messages to their families from the ship's radio room. For some families, having believed their loved ones were missing or dead, the news came as blessed relief.

Loughnan next transferred to the hospital ship *Benevolence*, where doctors diagnosed him as possibly having TB. Separated from his friends, including Rowley Richards, he ended up in a TB ward on a Dutch ship at Yokohama. Eventually he arrived at Okinawa, and then took an eight-hour

Chapter 12. Liberation 101

Australian survivors of the Sakata prisoner of war camp, October 1945. Rowley Richards is in the front row, third from the left (Australian War Memorial).

flight to Clark Field in the Philippines. At Manila, he met up again with Rowley Richards.[37] Meanwhile, the other prisoners from Sakata were ferried to a British destroyer, HMS *Wakeful*, anchored offshore. For the first time, they learned that U.S. submarines had rescued some of the *Rakuyo Maru* survivors. Also for the first time since their captivity, they ate sliced white bread. They were flown to Okinawa and then to Manila, where they stayed at least a week in a convalescent hospital. The Australians had sent some nurses to Manila to help look after the men. At Manila, authorities allowed the ex-prisoners to record a radio message to family and friends for broadcast in Australia by the ABC.[38]

From Manila, Frank McGovern took a Liberator aircraft to Darwin, arriving after an eleven-hour flight that included engine trouble. From there he flew to Mascot in Sydney. It appears the press was waiting to interview him, as were representatives from the navy and army. A navy truck took McGovern to the Balmoral Naval Depot where he met up with his parents for a "terrific" reunion.[39] He had received only two letters from home during his captivity, so there was much to catch up on.

McGovern proved among the more fortunate. Many Australians resented the time spent in Manila waiting for transport to Australia by sea. By the third week of September, most of the prisoners had been evacuated from Japan. At the end of the month, however, less than 400 Australians had made the trip from Manila to home. At last, on 4 October, some 1,500 Australians departed on the Royal Navy aircraft carriers HMS *Formidable* and HMS *Speaker*, made available for getting them home by Admiral Bruce Fraser as commander of the British Pacific Fleet.[40]

On HMS *Formidable*, Kitchener Loughnan and other former prisoners occupied stretchers in the aircraft hangars, looked after by nurses and Red Cross girls. Entertainment on board included movies screened at one end of the hangar, while vaudeville shows took place at the other end. There were ice-cream and soft drink stands in between. Loughnan pronounced the arrangement as "heaven."[41] Mick McCarthy also travelled to Sydney by HMS *Formidable*, arriving on Saturday, 13 October 1945. He then went to Ingleburn Army Camp by double-decker bus, where his family and friends met him.[42]

Ray Parkin, a survivor of HMAS *Perth*, initially departed Japan from Osaka on the U.S. Navy hospital ship *Consolation*. He was "processed" by the Americans at Manila and then travelled to Sydney on the escort carrier HMS *Speaker*, one of 660 Australian ex–POWs on board. His ship berthed in Sydney on the morning of 14 October 1945. After a night in a depot at the suburb of Cremorne, he travelled to Melbourne by train to reunite with his wife and two children after nearly four years without contact.[43] Kenneth Harrison was also among those to sail on the escort carrier *Speaker* from Manila. The tumultuous welcome the ship received on reaching Sydney greatly impressed him.[44]

Not all POWs were happy with the organization of their departures home. Stan Arneil felt incensed by the delays in getting the prisoners supplies and described his trip home as a "disgrace to Australia." They received no mail and no more than a couple of bottles of beer, which Arneil attributed to a "bumbling Army Administration."[45] He boarded a ship on 22 September and arrived at Darwin on 1 October, where there was still no promised mail or beer. He arrived in Sydney on 9 October.[46] George Carroll flew from Tokyo to Okinawa, where he spent nearly a month before proceeding to Manila. He did not reach Sydney until November 1945.[47]

Others returning to Australia became temporarily stranded en route. John Lane found himself in a recovery camp in the Philippines, a few miles outside Manila, with thousands of other former prisoners. While there, he wrote some stories for the *West Australian* newspaper about Japan. Weeks later, he finally got transport to Sydney on HMS *Formidable*.[48] Cecil Dickson was among the last POWs to leave for Australia. From Bangkok, he and a party of 75 were transported to Singapore, where they boarded the waiting motor vessel *Circassia*. The ship, converted from a passenger liner to a landing ship in 1943, carried not only POWs, but combat troops and civilians.[49]

Tragically, some POWs did not survive the journey home. On a flight from Okinawa to the Philippines on 10 September 1945, twenty prisoners including five Australians died after their B-24 Liberator crashed. Among those killed was Sergeant Bert James, leaving a widow and six-year-old son. His son, Clive James, would later become a well-known writer and television personality in Australia and Britain.[50]

For those who did make it home, many faced new challenges in trying to resume relationships with loved ones and leave behind the trauma of captivity. On his return to Britain, Tom Wade immediately faced the decision of either leaving the army or signing on for another year. He chose the former, at which point the army severed any responsibility. "I never received one talk, one leaflet, one pamphlet, any guidance or advice on how to return to civilian life in much-altered Britain after three years and seven months of prison camp and over five years of army service."[51] Many prisoners returning to Australia faced similar dilemmas. Some no longer knew their home addresses, whether they still had wives or what awaited them.[52]

In general, the Allied military authorities underestimated the psychological damage many prisoners suffered from captivity. The psychiatrist on Lord Mountbatten's command staff in Southeast Asia, T.F. Rodger, reported to London that "British Prisoners of War recovered from Japanese hands showed fewer psychiatric symptoms and much more stable and satisfactory reaction to their captivity than POWs from German hands."[53] Such misplaced optimism resulted in large part because of the poor physical state of prisoners recovered from the Japanese, which tended to overshadow any mental and emotional problems. At least for the time being, the Allies focused on treating the effects of disease and malnutrition rather than mental disorders. At least some former prisoners, keen to get on with their lives, downplayed any mental or physical symptoms fearing that military doctors might delay their discharge or keep them hospitalized for a long period.[54]

Chapter 13

Americans

Although most American prisoners of war were concentrated in the Philippines, there was some interaction with other nationalities in Singapore, Java, Manchuria and Japan. While imprisoned at Bicycle Camp on Java, American and Australian prisoners shared a certain amount of mutual admiration. One American described the Australians as "the most resourceful individuals that we met anywhere." Another American soldier perhaps gave them the ultimate accolade, declaring that "If I ever had to go to war again—God forbid—I'd rather be with some Australians than anybody I know in the world."[1] It seems the two nationalities shared not only a mutual contempt for the Japanese, but also a suspicion of the British who were often characterized as arrogant and lacking sufficient concern with hygiene. As explained by one American POW, "The Australian people have this warmth of fellowship, and warmth of attitude, whereas the British is always a Britisher to the last degree."[2]

The Americans were a relatively small presence on the Thai-Burma railway. For the most part, they got on well with the Australians, although at times their insistence on the superiority of all things American could grow tiresome. The war correspondent Rohan Rivett recounts an incident in which an American called out to a group of Australian POWs, "Cheer up, boys, it won't be long now. Uncle Sam'll be here soon." One of the Australians immediately replied, "What! Is he a prisoner too?"[3] Rivett concluded that despite a good deal of chiding and argument, relations with the Americans were good.[4]

The sinking of *Rakuyo Maru* and *Kachidoki Maru* by American submarines might have challenged Australian and British relations with the U.S., but instead turned into a triumph of propaganda. Ignoring the issue of Allied submarines sinking Japanese ships carrying prisoners of war, both the British and Australian governments focused on the U.S. Navy's efforts to rescue *Rakuyo Maru* survivors. The War Office in Britain advised that press releases give "prominence to the rescue of the survivors by American naval vessels and the overwhelming kindness of the care they received at the hands of the American naval authorities everywhere as typical examples of the brotherhood in arms which exists between the United States and the British Empire."[5] In a statement to the House of Commons, the British Secretary of State for War, Sir James Grigg, expressed "admiration for the way in which the United States submarine crews risked their own safety to rescue these men from the sea" and "very deep gratitude" for their care.[6]

The Australian government went a step further, sending the U.S. submarine crews involved in the rescue of prisoners from *Rakuyo Maru* a letter of appreciation. The letter noted that their actions "touched the Australian people profoundly and the Australian Government would like the American Government to know of the deep gratitude which it feels for the kindnesses shown, which go far beyond the requirements of duty, and contrast strongly with the barbarous treatment from which the prisoners have been recovered."[7] American diplomatic staff in Canberra also reported receiving "numerous vocal expressions of appreciation."[8]

Japan had tried to capitalize on the loss of nearly a thousand POWs on *Lisbon Maru* after an American submarine sank the ship in October 1942. The same month, Radio Tokyo began a series of short talks by the survivors.[9] Japan followed a similar strategy after the loss of *Rakuyo Maru*. Japan's spokesperson for the Board of Information, Mr. Iguchi, attempted to underline the apparent irony of the Allied reactions. In a radio broadcast he stated that while Australian and British ministers "thank the American submarine which after all first sank the ship and rescued a few prisoners," the Japanese "saved 136 Anglo-Australian prisoners even at the sacrifice of a number of Japanese women and children and Japanese soldiers."[10] Such claims, however, gained no traction with the Australian press or public, and certainly not with the rescued POWs themselves. Indeed, despite the tremendous fear that submarines generated among Allied prisoners of war, they seemed to accept being sunk as simply a contingency of war. A survivor of *Lisbon Maru*, Robin Poulter, commented that among the 200 survivors in his regiment "I never heard any man complain of the submarine that sank us, in fact they all agreed it was the right thing to do."[11]

The kindness and generosity of the American submariners became the dominant theme of the rescued prisoners' accounts. An Australian government report on the episode concluded that the survivors "cannot find adequate words of praise" for the men who assisted them.[12] Harry Chivers, one of the Australians rescued by USS *Pampanito*, claimed that his first words after being pulled on the submarine were "Thank god for the Americans!" Jack Pearson, recovered by USS *Queenfish*, recalled that once on board the song "God bless America" played over and over in his head.[13] In the first book written by a returned Australian prisoner of war, Arthur Bancroft claimed that they "could find no words of praise fitting enough for our gallant ally, who succoured us. Their unselfish devotion to stricken comrades should tend to strengthen the bond of friendship which exists between the fighting men of both Australia and America."[14] Far from creating any apparent animus between allies, the *Rakuyo Maru* story reinforced the image of America as a nation of extraordinary benevolence and resources.

A visit to Fremantle by USS *Pampanito* in December 1944 reinforced the close relations between the American submariners and the rescued Australians. With about one quarter of American submarine patrols in the Pacific emanating from Fremantle, the port served as an important hub in the war at sea. After completing its fourth war patrol, *Pampanito* moored in Fremantle Harbor near noon on 31 December 1944. Surprisingly, given the top-secret nature of submarine activities, a handful of Western Australians waited to greet *Pampanito*'s crew. Six of the 47 Australians rescued from the *Rakuyo Maru* by *Pampanito* were now back in their home state, and eager to reciprocate some of the goodwill they received on the submarine.

At this stage, Mike Fenno had replaced Pete Summers as *Pampanito*'s skipper. Most of the crew, though, had been on board when the former prisoners were pulled from the sea. The survivors who greeted them, wearing the same dungarees they were given on board *Pampanito*, included Alfred John "Jack" Cocking, Harry Pickett and Walter Victor "Wally" Winter. These men had all served with the 4th Machine Gun Battalion of the Second Australian Imperial Force. Raised from men across Western Australia, the battalion of 860 soldiers departed Fremantle for Singapore only weeks before the island fell to the Japanese. Almost a third of the battalion were killed or wounded before being captured.[15]

As related by *Pampanito*'s crew, they received a tumultuous welcome in Western Australia from the survivors. This was especially the case for pharmacist's mate Maurice "Doc" Demers who had almost continuously tended the men. "They hugged and kissed me! They took us to their homes. We met their families. *They* hugged and kissed us. They gave us parties. Everything you wanted. Food. Drink. Dance. Whatever. The whole town was ours. It was an emotional experience, hard to describe."[16] The submariners received frequent visits from the survivors at the Cottesloe Beach Hotel where they stayed during their leave, while other survivors visited the submarine with their families.[17] Some of the *Rakuyo Maru* survivors also hosted men from other U.S. submarines, apparently feeling a special kinship. Marshall Roberts from USS *Cobia* recalled one of the men hanging out with his crew while they were in port.[18]

USS *Pampanito* sailed from Fremantle on 23 January 1945 for its next war patrol. Many of the submarine crew and survivors of *Rakuyo Maru*, however, continued to keep in touch long afterward. Jack Cocking kept

Chapter 13. Americans

a treasured small notebook with the names of *Pampanito*'s crew.[19] Frank Farmer made a habit of calling Robert Bennett at his home in Mason City, Iowa, each year on 15 September to say, "Thank you for another year of my life."[20] Roy Cornford continued to correspond with several submariners from *Pampanito*. He attended a reunion in San Francisco commemorating the fiftieth anniversary of the rescue, even appearing on television. According to Cornford, while in the U.S. "they treated us like lords" with a series of banquets and expense-paid activities. There was another reunion in 2003, marking the sixtieth anniversary of *Pampanito*'s launch. Another reunion commemorating the sixtieth year since the rescue was scheduled for the following year in San Francisco.[21]

The restored USS *Pampanito*, which opened to the public at Fisherman's Wharf in San Francisco from March 1982, remains the most tangible reminder of those bonds. In January 1986, the U.S. government recognized *Pampanito* as a National Historic Landmark. In July 1990, the Australian government presented the submarine with a plaque that commemorated its role in the rescue of Australian servicemen.[22] The submarine has thus become in part a memorial to the alliance between Australia and the United States. Like all commemorations, however, *Pampanito*'s status depends on selective memory. The submarine's role in the deaths of hundreds of British prisoners on *Kachidoki Maru* has been largely erased from its history.

To some extent, the close relations formed between Australian soldiers and the American submariners who recovered them served as an antidote to the many growing weary of the heavy U.S. presence in Australia by 1944. In a 2003 interview, Roy Cornford observed that "Some people are down on Americans but I wouldn't be alive if it wasn't for the Americans."[23] Despite the uniform appreciation of *Rakuyo Maru* survivors rescued by the American submariners, the attitudes of Allied POWs generally were far more ambivalent. For many prisoners, the prospect of submarine attack created unbridled terror. The British as well as the Americans contributed to the slaughter at sea. For example, two of the survivors of HMAS *Perth*, Cedric Bell Mellish and David Bowie Ferguson, died after a British submarine sank their Japanese transport ship *Eiko Maru*.[24]

Apart from those rescued by U.S. submarines, prisoners who survived the war tended to focus their gratitude on things other than the Americans. Some survivors adopted rituals of their own as symbols of thanks giving. Frank McGovern, a Catholic, credited his faith with helping him through his years as a prisoner. Each 15 August he put a bunch of flowers on the church altar, along with a note thanking God for his intercession.[25]

Representations of the *Rakuyo Maru* and *Kachidoki Maru* disasters, both at the time and since, often emphasize the culpability of the Japanese for not marking the ships as carrying prisoners.[26] As described by Rowley

Richards, the only marking on *Rakuyo Maru* was a Rising Sun flag, "a Bullseye for every Allied submarine."[27] In reality, there was no provision under the Geneva Convention requiring ships conveying prisoners to be marked. The only belligerent ships protected from attack were hospital ships or ships granted safe passage to perform specific missions agreed to by the combatants. As noted in the Preface, despite efforts by the International Red Cross to implement a system of safe passage for ships carrying prisoners, these were rejected by the Allied and Axis powers. Both sides feared the other might take advantage of revealed convoy routes or use ships designated for POWs to carry arms and troops.[28]

On the other hand, in many instances the Japanese certainly were responsible for increasing the number of deaths once an Allied submarine attacked a transport. In some cases, Japanese commanders and ship officers ordered the killing of prisoners or failed to mount rescue operations for POW survivors. The *Lisbon Maru* carried nearly two thousand British prisoners of war captured following the fall of Hong Kong, in addition to 800 Japanese troops, when torpedoed by USS *Grouper* on 1 October 1942. Although the ship took 25 hours to sink, the Japanese locked the prisoners in the holds rather than helping them to safety. Those prisoners who managed to escape *Lisbon Maru* were shot at with small arms, rifles and machine guns, or in some cases run over by boats.

For the most part, the 828 POWs who died were victims of Japanese actions rather than the actual sinking of their ship. The 1,066 prisoners who survived owed their lives mainly to Chinese fishers who used their sampans to rescue them. Indeed, it was only after Chinese fishers began picking up prisoners that the Japanese mounted their own rescue efforts. At least one survivor, Royal Scots bandsman Denis Morley, did credit the Japanese with giving him a cigarette and a bowl of tea once they picked him up. The captain of *Lisbon Maru*, Kyoda Shigeru, was later tried as a war criminal for locking the prisoners in the holds and received a sentence of seven years imprisonment.[29]

Another atrocity took place after *Oryoku Maru* was hit by an Allied bomb. Japanese guards fired at prisoners trying to escape from the holds, and other survivors were shot in the water.[30] In yet another incident, after USS *Paddle* torpedoed the 2,600-ton *Shinyo Maru* off the west coast of Mindanao in the Philippines on 7 September 1944, the Japanese fired on POWs climbing from the holds and in the water. The ship sank in only ten minutes, taking down most of the prisoners on board. While launches picked up Japanese survivors, the POWs who managed to escape the ship were shot at or beaten with oars. Japanese planes also strafed prisoners attempting to reach shore. With the assistance of friendly Filipinos some of the prisoners reached shore on the island of Mindanao, but only 81 of the 750 American prisoners aboard *Shinyo Maru* survived.[31]

Chapter 13. Americans

In a case somewhat analogous to *Rakuyo Maru*, Allied submarines featured not only in the deaths of prisoners aboard *Shinyo Maru*, but the later rescue of some survivors. The American POWs assisted by Filipinos were later evacuated from Mindanao by the oversized submarine USS *Narwhal*. For months, *Narwhal* had spearheaded the delivery of supplies to guerrillas in the Philippines from Australia, often picking up refugees for the return voyage. On the night of 29 September 1944, the 81 survivors from *Shinyo Maru* gratefully boarded USS *Narwhal* for their escape.[32]

As already described, in the case of *Rakuyo Maru* the failure of the Japanese to pick up survivors in a timely fashion resulted in mass deaths. In similar scenes, after a submarine sank *Arisan Maru* on 24 October 1944 with 1,783 American prisoners on board, the Japanese prevented the prisoners from boarding rescue ships. Prisoners attempting to board ships were pushed away with poles while Japanese destroyers deliberately pulled away from prisoners trying to reach them. Only five POWs survived the ordeal.[33]

Survivors of *Junyo Maru* also faced Japanese reluctance to mount rescue operations on behalf of prisoners. One of the survivors, RAF member Rouse Voisey, recalled that prisoners attempting to board an escort ship after the sinking were beaten away. This was initially understandable to Voisey, since the number of survivors might have swamped the relatively small vessel. But it was only after forty hours that he was eventually recovered, and then put in a filthy local jail at Padang, Sumatra.[34]

The Japanese were further culpable for the dilatory way that they reported the losses of prisoners of war on transport ships. It was only in November 1944, for example, that the Japanese government reported through the International Red Cross at Bern, Switzerland, the loss of Australians on a ship sunk in June. According to the Japanese report, 184 Australians were lost in the incident, while 72 survivors reached camps in Japan.[35] Obtaining information from the Japanese War Prisoners Information Bureau proved habitually difficult. It took until the end of November 1947 for the compilation of lists of prisoners who died during transport on the ships *Oryoku Maru*, *Enoura Maru* and *Brazil Maru*.[36]

Michno claims that although submarine commanders had no idea that they were attacking ships carrying prisoners of war, the U.S. Navy did. Through the efforts of codebreakers, according to Michno, the navy were aware of the human cargoes on Japanese transport ships.[37] The work of Lee A. Gladwin, however, casts serious doubt on Michno's claim. First, the skills of those deciphering Japanese communications, while of critical importance to the war effort, are sometimes overstated. For example, the day before USS *Paddle* sank *Shinyo Maru*, American cryptographers intercepted a message that the ship was transporting "750 troops." Over three months later, translators realized that the message in fact referred to "750 Ps/W."[38]

Intercepts were often incomplete, garbled or made no mention of POWs. Decoding and translation of radio messages intercepted from convoy HI-72 frequently included gaps and ambiguities. The first reference to prisoners of war in the messages came only two days after submarines attacked the convoy.[39] Most importantly, Gladwin's research indicates that the intercepts generally used by the Joint Intelligence Center Pacific Ocean Area (JICPOA) at Pearl Harbor were from the Japanese Water Transport Code that contained no information concerning the transportation of POWs.[40] According to Lamont-Brown's research as well, while codebreakers at Pearl Harbor knew the movements of convoys, they lacked intelligence on what the ships carried.[41]

In at least one instance, American prisoners attempted to get word through Filipino guerrillas to the U.S. Navy not to attack their convoy. On 25 August 1944, 1,035 survivors of the Bataan Death March boarded *Noto Maru* at Manila. The ship departed 27 August as part of convoy MAMO-02. The attempt to warn off American submarines apparently failed, since on 29 August two torpedoes narrowly missed *Noto Maru* during an attack. Following stops at Takao and Keelung, Formosa, the ship arrived safely at Moji, Japan, on the morning of 4 September. There were no POW deaths reported. Eventually, on 2 November 1944, a U.S. Liberator heavy bomber ended the ship's career at Ormoc Bay, Leyte, in the Philippines.[42]

Some prisoners transported on hellships professed the hope that an Allied submarine would sink their ship and end their suffering. One prisoner transported on *Noto Maru* recalled that during an attack on their convoy: "Believe it or not I hoped to hell we got hit. Kill us all, Blow [sic] us sky high."[43] A survivor of *Kachidoki Maru*, Bill Marks, similarly claimed that many prisoners welcomed the thought of being torpedoed. "Even if they had to follow their comrades to Davy Jones's locker, it would be better than the worse-than-animal-like existence."[44] Arthur Bancroft considered death at sea "a clean and honourable one far away from the steaming jungles of Burma and Thailand."[45] But these were the retrospective thoughts of men who ultimately survived torpedo attacks and the war.

Whether knowingly or unwittingly, Allied submarines clearly added to the terror and mental anguish of many prisoners of war. Andrew Aquila conveys some of that anguish; as a 26-year-old, he was among some 1,600 American prisoners on *Nissyo Maru* in convoy HI-68. As the convoy made its way from the Philippines toward Formosa in the early hours of 26 July 1944, three U.S. submarines began an attack. After two freighters in the convoy were sunk, "Men really started to panic." The chaos only increased after a nearby ship carrying gasoline, *Otoriyama Maru*, exploded in flames and quickly sank. According to Aquila, "I've never seen so much horror. I remember fingering my ring and just closing my eyes. I was so scared at that point that I felt numb. It was almost like hovering over everything and watching the whole thing from above. We were expecting to be hit any second."[46] Australian prisoner of war Kenneth Harrison concluded, "submarine warfare, whether waged by friend or foe, is a cruel and monstrous God-cursed thing."[47]

Chapter 14

Friendly Fire

The numbers of prisoners killed by Allied attacks (aircraft as well as submarines) on Japanese shipping remains open to debate. Van Waterford, himself a hellship survivor, claims that over 22,000 POWs, or over a third of all of those transported by sea, lost their lives.[1] Raymond Lamont-Brown estimates the death toll of prisoners of war on transports to be around 21,000. Although his estimate is comparable to Waterford's, he suggests the death rate was considerably lower at 16.5 percent of all those transported by sea.[2] Gregory Michno, author of the most thorough study of the topic, calculates that 21,039 Allied prisoners died on hellship voyages.[3] He indicates that of these, "Only 1540 deaths can be attributable to disease, starvation, thirst, suffocation, suicides, beatings and murder—deaths that ultimately stemmed from intolerable treatment."[4] This leaves roughly 20,000 Allied prisoners on transports who were killed by "friendly fire."

These numbers appear overstated, however, since in some cases Michno's figures include Asian laborers as well as Allied prisoners of war lost in attacks. Most notably they include about 4,000 Javanese laborers who died when *Junyo Maru* was torpedoed by the British submarine HMS *Tradewind* on 17 September 1944, precipitating one of the worst maritime disasters of the Second World War.[5] Also included in Michno's estimates are approximately 3,000 Javanese laborers who lost their lives following the sinking of *Tango Maru* by USS *Rasher* on 25 February 1944 and over 1,200 laborers aboard *Koshu Maru* who died following an attack by USS *Ray* in August 1944.[6] In short, Michno's figures appear considerably inflated by the inclusion of non–European civilians.

Hugh Clarke more modestly estimates that 10,853 prisoners were lost at sea, including 1,515 Australians.[7] Brian MacArthur makes a similar estimate, claiming that there were 10,800 deaths from among the 50,000 prisoners transported by sea. He suggests that one in three of those who died on Japanese ships were killed by friendly fire but adds the sobering claim that over twice as many Americans died from the sinking of the *Arisan Maru* after it was torpedoed by a U.S. submarine than from the Bataan Death March.[8]

Chapter 14. Friendly Fire

At the end of hostilities, the Japanese government advised the International Red Cross in Bern that some 1,600 British prisoners were missing due to the sinking of Japanese ships. This was clearly an underestimate and, as noted at the time, subject to "many discrepancies."[9] In November 1945, Douglas MacArthur's headquarters in Tokyo requested the Japanese government to provide a report on all vessels sunk carrying Allied prisoners of war and lists of all those killed.[10] Information supplied by the Japanese, however, remained far from complete.

A postwar summary by Allied Forces put the number of Japanese ships sunk while carrying prisoners of war at fourteen, with a total of 10,154 dead and missing Allied POWs.[11] The British also identified fourteen sunk Japanese transports that carried prisoners of war. The total number of prisoners dead and missing from these ships, including British, Australians, Dutch and Americans, was 12,163.[12] According to these statistics, four of the ships (*Rakuyo Maru, Kachidoki Maru, Nighimei Maru, Toyofuku Maru*) were sailing from Singapore when sunk and together resulted in the deaths of 2,660 Allied prisoners of war.

Table 1: Japanese Transports Carrying Allied POWs Sunk by Allied Submarines and Aircraft

	Total Dead	Australian Dead
Montevideo Maru, 1 July 1942	1054	1054
Lisbon Maru, 2 October 1942	839	
Nighimei Maru, 15 January 1943	139	
Suez Maru, 29 November 1943	548	
Tamahoko Maru, 24 June 1944	560	184
Harugiku Maru, 26 June 1944 aka SS *Van Waerwuyck*	177	14
Shinyo Maru, 7 September 1944	750	
Rakuyo Maru, 12 September 1944	1179	543
Kachidoki Maru, 12 September 1944	435	
Junyo Maru, 18 September 1944	1477	4
Toyofuku Maru, 21 September 1944 aka *Hofuku Maru*	907	

	Total Dead	Australian Dead
Arisan Maru, 24 October 1944	1773	
Oryoku Maru, 15 December 1944		
Enoura Maru, 9 January 1945	1002	
Total	12,163	1799

Source: Lists of missing and dead from 14 sunk Japanese transports carrying British POW, WO 361/1741, NAS; Summary enclosed in Allied Land Forces SEA to Under Secretary of State for War, London, 19 March 1946, Record Group 407, entry Ai-1069, box 146, NARA. Note that the number of POWs killed is combined for *Oryoku Maru* and *Enoura Maru*, and that the figures occasionally include small numbers of personnel designated "Other."

These figures are by no means comprehensive and must be used cautiously. There are at times discrepancies between sources on the number of fatalities resulting from Allied attacks. Apart from the fourteen ships officially acknowledged, numerous other ships attacked by the Allies carried a small number of prisoners. For example, the escort carrier *Chuyo*, sunk by the submarine USS *Sailfish* on 4 December 1943 after departing from the Japanese base at Truk, carried twenty-one American prisoners. The destroyer *Yamagumo* recovered the men following the sinking of the submarine USS *Sculpin* a couple of weeks earlier. The American survivors were taken to Truk for interrogation, and twenty-one men from this group were put on *Chuyo* bound for Japan. From among the over 1,200 passengers and crew on board *Chuyo*, there were only 161 survivors, including one American prisoner.[13]

In another instance, Allied forces sank *Kokai Maru* on 21 February 1944 after it departed Rabaul. All passengers were lost, including seventeen POWs and ten internees who were most likely Australians. Submarines torpedoed two other ships, *Ken-yo Maru* and *Nippon Maru*, on 14 January 1944 after they departed Rabaul. These ships also possibly carried prisoners of war. *Kuramasan Maru* was sunk on 2 November 1944 after departing from Makassar with three Australians known to be on board. In another case, two American aviators were known to be aboard the submarine *I-365*, sunk by USS *Scabbardfish* after it departed Truk on 16 November 1944.[14] It is likely that a small number of prisoners were sunk on numerous other Japanese ships that may never come to light.

The British and American compilations of prisoners killed by friendly fire did not include non–Caucasian victims, but it is worth remembering that large numbers of non–Europeans were transported by hellships. By late 1942, the Japanese were transporting Chinese POWs for forced labor overseas. In December 1942, 130 Chinese prisoners boarded the 5,289-ton

Chapter 14. Friendly Fire

Panama Maru at Shanghai for Truk to work on construction gangs.[15] As discussed at greater length in a subsequent chapter, the 5,000-ton *Thames Maru* sailed from Singapore on 5 May 1943 with 2,000 Indians and 150 Indonesian POWs sent to the Palau Islands for forced labor. In fact, the *Thames Maru* figured in the first war crime trial prosecuted by the British in Southeast Asia.[16]

U.S. submarines sank at least two transports carrying Indian POWs. On 21 January 1944, USS *Seahorse* commanded by Slade Cutter torpedoed the ship *Ikoma Maru* travelling in convoy from Palau to Hollandia. Of the 611 prisoners of war on board, 418 went down with the ship.[17] A year earlier, on 26 January 1943, USS *Wahoo* sank the Japanese transport ship *Buyo Maru* about 250 miles north of New Guinea. In an incident that became one of the most notorious of the naval war, *Wahoo*'s commander, Dudley "Mush" Morton, surfaced the submarine and ordered his crew to fire on survivors. Unknown at the time, most of those killed were Indian prisoners of war. From among the 491 POWs on board, 195 died.[18]

As discussed in the previous chapter, the death rates of POWs following Allied submarine and aircraft attacks was often exacerbated by Japanese neglect of rescue operations, and in some cases direct actions to kill survivors. For example, after torpedoes from HMS *Truculent* split the transport ship *Harugiku Maru* in two, the Japanese captain rendered little assistance to the prisoners on board. It was only three days after the attack that efforts were made to rescue POWs, who were subsequently sent to the River Valley Road camp in Singapore.[19]

As in the case of *Rakuyo Maru*, there were some remarkable stories of survival following Allied attacks. On 24 October 1944, USS *Snook* sank the 6,886-ton *Arisan Maru* east of Hong Kong as it travelled from Manila to Japan. Three of the eight POWs who survived the sinking were later recaptured by the Japanese and detained at a camp in Formosa. The other five American survivors managed to occupy a life raft and rig it with sails. They sailed 300 miles in rough seas to the China coast where they were picked up and assisted by Chinese fishermen in a junk.[20]

It is likely that Michno understates the many prisoners who died at sea as victims of disease and appalling conditions as opposed to Allied attacks. On some ships deaths from ill-treatment confusingly intertwine with those caused by Allied submarines or aircraft. This is the case for *Oryoku Maru*, a ship originally built at Nagasaki in 1937 and requisitioned by the Imperial Japanese Army in 1943. On 13 December 1944, 1,650 prisoners of war boarded the 15,000-ton former luxury liner at Manila along with about 2,000 Japanese troops and civilians. Many of the Japanese civilians were merchant seamen who had been left stranded in the Philippines after their ships were sunk.

One of the prisoners, American artillery officer Lieutenant Melvin Rosen, left a vivid description of those crammed in the holds. "There was no place to lie down; some people couldn't even sit down, and everybody had diarrhea. The floorboards were full of human waste and vomit, and the stench was unbearable. The temperature was over 100 degrees, and people started going mad that first night, screaming for water and air."[21] As described by another prisoner, Captain Marion Lawton, "Claustrophobia and total darkness created a terrible, terrible feeling."[22] Even before the ship departed Manila's Pier 7 the following day, it appears thirty prisoners confined to the aft hold died from suffocation. Prisoners' cries for water were ignored by their guards and many men went berserk.

On 14 December, *Oryoku Maru* departed in a convoy of five merchant ships. The same day, waves of carrier planes from USS *Hornet* attacked the convoy and scored hits on *Oryoku Maru*. The ship beached at Olongapo to make repairs; by late evening the Japanese passengers were offloaded along with the dead. The prisoners had to endure another night of horror crammed in the holds as many men lost their minds and more died. Beginning at dawn on Sunday, 15 December, the carrier planes from *Hornet* resumed their attacks on *Oryoku Maru*. A direct bomb hit on the ship's aft hold killed over a hundred POWs. More prisoners died in the ensuing fire and chaos on board.[23]

On 27 December 1944 about a thousand of the prisoners who survived *Oryuko Maru* were transferred to *Enoura Maru*, while another 235 boarded *Brazil Maru*.[24] John M. Wright was among the 1,074 American prisoners taken aboard *Enoura Maru*. He noted that the ship's previous cargo was cavalry horses, and that considerable evidence of their presence remained in the holds.[25] *Brazil Maru*, at 5,860 tons, was the smaller of the two ships. The Imperial Japanese Army requisitioned the ship, originally built in 1919, to serve as a troop transport from October 1941. The two prison transports departed Lingayen Gulf with a nine-ship convoy. Travelling at about ten knots by day, the ships spent much of the nights anchored attempting to avoid attack.[26]

At least some of the prisoners on *Enoura Maru* believed a U.S. submarine attempted to torpedo the ship on the night of 30 December.[27] In fact, this is confirmed by post-war records. At about 9 p.m. USS *Razorback* narrowly missed *Enoura Maru* with its torpedoes.[28] On New Year's Day 1945, *Enoura Maru* anchored at Takao, Formosa. While the convoy spent days anchored there the weather became colder, adding to the suffering of the poorly clothed prisoners.

On the morning of 9 January, *Enoura Maru* again came under attack, this time from the air. A U.S. dive bomber made a direct hit on the ship while it sat anchored in shallow water. The bomb strike killed over half of the five hundred men in the ship's forward hold. The Japanese kept the survivors confined to the hold for the next three days, finally sending down a cargo net for them to load with the dead.[29]

On the afternoon of 13 January 1945, prisoners from the disabled *Enoura Maru* were transferred to the smaller *Brazil Maru*. On the following day, *Brazil Maru* departed Takao Harbor in a convoy of about dozen ships. As described by one prisoner, the next two weeks were "an eternity of horror."[30] Many of the men who survived the Allied attacks on *Oryoku Maru* and *Enoura Maru* died on *Brazil Maru*. The prisoners were given little water and only one food ration a day. As they sailed north, the increasing cold and ice storms added to the prisoners' misery, with some dying of pneumonia or freezing to death. Prisoner deaths on board continued at a rate of about twenty men a day, and then escalated to an average of about thirty a day.[31]

The ship's progress slowed further on 20 January when *Brazil Maru* took another torpedoed freighter in tow. The prisoners wondered how much longer they could elude the American submarines known to be prowling the waters. At least some hoped that a direct torpedo hit might end their sufferings. As the ship approached closer to Japan, the prisoners were no longer allowed to bury their dead comrades at sea. Instead they had to stack the bodies in the hold, until the pile reached five feet high.[32]

Brazil Maru arrived at Moji, Japan, at 3 a.m. on 30 January, having lost over half of its prisoners due to abuse and disease. From among the over 1,600 American prisoners originally embarked on *Oryuko Maru* 47 days earlier, the number remaining was only about 500.[33] Many of these would soon die in Japan. *Brazil Maru* proved to be the last hellship to arrive from the Philippines. In one of the many flukes of war, American soldiers and Filipino guerrillas liberated the Cabanatuan prison camp from which most of the prisoners came the same day the ship arrived in Japan.[34]

Prisoners from Singapore on the small steamer *Dai Ichi Maru*, a ship originally built in Glasgow in 1903, were shipped to Japan via Saigon. Even by the standards of hellships, the sanitary facilities were appalling. As described by one of the prisoners, British gunner Peter Barton, "there were no toilets, there were buckets, but they'd be filled in seconds and you'd be splashed and you actually waded in urine and dysentery and phew, it stank!"[35] The dead were jettisoned at sea, while of the 600 prisoners who arrived to work in coke plants and cement quarries in Japan, only 250 survived.[36] During a relatively brief voyage from Formosa to Moji, nineteen men died on board *Hakusan Maru*. The prisoners were only allowed outside the ship's hold for ten minutes in the morning and ten minutes at night.[37]

The aging freighter *Singapore Maru* sailed from Java in late October

1942, stopping at Singapore during its five-week passage to Japan. Within a few days of the ship departing Singapore, dysentery broke out, aggravated by overcrowding, lack of sanitary facilities, lack of medicine and food. From among approximately 1,100 British, Australian and Dutch prisoners on board, nearly a quarter (240 men) died during the voyage or shortly after arriving in Japan on 24 November. The sick remained on board *Singapore Maru* for two days after it docked at Moji until an American medical officer, Lieutenant Commander T.I. Moe, was summoned from a nearby POW camp to evacuate them. According to Moe's account, he found "the filth and stench of bloody mucous, pus, and feces which covered living spaces, effects, mess gear and the persons themselves, surpassed description."[38] After the war, four defendants including *Singapore Maru*'s captain, the ship's commandant, the POW draft conducting officer and a guard were charged with the prisoners' ill-treatment.[39]

War crime trials will be discussed in greater detail in subsequent chapters, but for now it can be noted that many of these revealed the extent to which prisoner deaths resulted directly from disease and abuse. The physical abuse of prisoners on *Maros Maru* (also known as *Haruyoshi Maru*) along with the withholding of food, resulted in the prosecution of one Korean guard at Singapore in October 1946. Kioshi (aka Kilo) Kaneoka, nicknamed "Cyclops" by the men under his supervision, was charged with ill-treatment of prisoners resulting in deaths at Ambon Island, Moluccas and at sea. In one incident on *Maros Maru*, Kaneoka allegedly beat a prisoner who crawled on deck to get water, resulting in the man's death the following morning. The ship departed Ambon on 17 September 1944 with about 500 British and Dutch POWs, and only arrived at Surabaya 68 days later. The prisoners spent much of the voyage anchored off Makassar while the ship underwent repairs. At one stage about eight prisoners were dying every day. The Japanese transferred an additional 142 POWs to *Maros Maru* after the prisoners' original transport was set on fire by an American bomber. From among the over 600 prisoners on board, 306 men died during the voyage. A British court sentenced Kaneoka to death by hanging at Changi Jail.[40]

As detailed in another war crimes trial prosecuted by the British in Singapore, 98 British and Dutch prisoners died from disease aboard *Hofuku Maru* after it departed Singapore on 4 July 1944. Most of those who died perished while the ship remained at Manila for fifty days undergoing repairs and awaiting a convoy to depart with. Not long after it departed Manila, American torpedo bombers sank *Hofuku Maru* on the morning of 21 September 1944. The ship went down in only a few minutes and, in a familiar scenario, the Japanese escorts initially rescued only their own people. The prisoners of war aboard had to wait another eight hours before a flotilla of coastal vessels arrived to pick them up. All but 280 prisoners on board were lost. A Japanese sergeant-major, Kitaichi Jotani, was executed at Changi Jail in May 1947 for his role in mistreating the prisoners.[41]

Many, if not most, Japanese vessels employed transporting prisoners eventually ended their careers at the hands of Allied submarines. The following are only some examples of former hellships sunk by submarines while *not* carrying POWs. The 5,859-ton *Ume Maru*, built at Kawasaki in 1919, carried about 1,500 Australians from Singapore to Borneo in July 1942. USS *Seahorse*, commanded by Slade Cutter, subsequently sank the ship in the early hours of 2 November 1943.[42] *Tottori Maru*, built in 1913, shipped about 2,000 POWs from Manila to Pusan and Moji in November 1942 to work in chemical plants and steel works. The USS *Hammerhead* torpedoed the ship in the Gulf of Thailand on 15 May 1945.[43] *Clyde Maru* had already been damaged by a torpedo from USS *Sawfish* before it transported prisoners of war in 1943. The ship's career ended in another torpedo attack by USS *Picuda* on 29 January 1945. In this case the victims were not prisoners of war, but over a thousand Japanese soldiers aboard.[44] USS *Tarpon* sank the ship *Tatsuta Maru* on 8 February 1943, only a month after it delivered POWs to Japan. Nearly 1,500 troops, passengers and crew went down with the ship.[45]

The numbers of former hellships sunk by submarines further illustrates just how effective the Allied submarine offensive was in eliminating Japan's merchant fleet. The odds were very high that anyone on a Japanese ship, whether Japanese or Allied prisoner of war, would be attacked. Most Japanese escorts shared the fate of their transport ships. *Kurahashi*, one of the escorts with convoy HI-72, was a relative rarity in surviving the war. The Allied occupation forces later assigned the ship mine-sweeping duties.[46]

CHAPTER 15

Adjustment

Arthur Bancroft was typical of many other returning prisoners of war of various nationalities who moved quickly to wed the woman who had waited for him.[1] Within a couple of weeks of his return to Australia, Bancroft became engaged to his longtime girlfriend, twenty-one-year-old Mirla Wilkinson. They married early in 1945, on the Saturday afternoon of 10 March, at St Andrews Church in the Perth suburb of Subiaco.[2]

With Bancroft having assumed a certain celebrity status as a survivor of both HMAS *Perth* and *Rakuyo Maru*, he and Mirla were formally presented to the Governor-General and Duchess of Gloucester when they visited the Leeuwin Naval Depot in Western Australia the following month. A full-page photo of Bancroft shaking hands with the Duke, with Mirla at his side, featured in Perth's *Sunday Times*.[3] The couple was also presented with a wedding present from the Prisoner of War Relatives' Association. The gift, a chair, was inscribed "Presented to Arthur Bancroft on the occasion of his marriage, 10/3/45, from relatives and friends of the crew of the H.M.A.S. Perth."[4] The romantic and "happy-ending" element of Bancroft's return to Australia no doubt added to its newsworthiness at a time of continuing anxiety over the fate of the other prisoners of the Japanese.

While married life suited him, Bancroft soon became disenchanted with the Navy, concluding that they did not know how to deal with returned POWs. After a period of leave, Bancroft returned to Flinders Naval Depot in Victoria. For his first assignment, he was given a pick and shovel, and told to ballast a depot rail line. Because of the secrecy surrounding his POW experience, no one knew about his history on the Thai-Burma railway. Bancroft refused to work and, following the intervention of a liaison officer, the navy sent him to a convalescent home in Melbourne to begin a "rehabilitation course" from 20 November 1944. Initially, the other sailors at the home were told not to talk to Bancroft because he might be mentally unbalanced. He encountered similar problems with a doctor due to the secrecy around his background. When he sought medical advice about his stomach problems, he found the doctor dismissive. A medical report dated 1 June 1945 recorded Bancroft as having an "anxiety state" and the navy approved his discharge the following month on 25 July.[5]

The returning survivors and the military shared a mutual ambivalence. James Beilby sensed that the Army did not really know what to do with them.[6] The government announced in late November 1944 that given "the extraordinary privations the men have suffered," the *Rakuyo Maru* survivors received two months leave and the option of discharge from their respective services once that expired. If medically fit, they could elect to remain in the armed forces for assignment to "an appropriate unit."[7] In general, however, the military remained committed to the idea that returned prisoners should be treated no differently than other soldiers. They feared that former POWs might assume they were especially entitled, or even encourage the idea that surrender was preferable to fighting.[8] Australia's Repatriation Commission instructed that former prisoners "should not be encouraged to regard himself as a palpably abnormal person, with a spirit scarred, a mind warped or a body weakened by his experiences."[9]

In contrast to the military, the civilian population appeared to have few reservations in welcoming home the former prisoners as exemplars of a special breed if not heroes. In Brisbane, for example, the Lord Mayor hosted a special luncheon for the *Rakuyo Maru* survivors and their next of kin. The mayor told them, "We admire the pluck with which you have carried on."[10] At Brisbane's annual Anzac Day parade in April 1945, thirteen of the survivors marched under a banner proclaiming "prisoners of war." According to Brisbane's *Courier-Mail*, "they received the greatest ovation given to any unit in the march."[11]

Nevertheless, ideas that the returning prisoners were somehow mentally unstable persisted and appeared widespread. Frank McGovern, although returning to Australia many months after Bancroft, found similar attitudes towards POWs. He believed people had been warned not to talk to him and other former prisoners about the war, for fear they "might just go off the deep end or something."[12] As another contemporary put it, "There was a school of thought that the men should not be reminded of their experiences."[13] Many experts warned their families not to let them discuss their time as prisoners.[14] In Britain at least, ex-prisoners' next-of-kin were issued official pamphlets with instructions to this effect.[15]

Frank McGovern received a medical discharge from the navy about March 1946. He then returned to his old job working for the Water Board. Like many other returned POWs, McGovern had a feeling that the world had passed him by during his three and a half years in captivity. In his words, "We were just out of kilter with things."[16]

Rakuyo Maru survivor Roy Cornford initially went back to his old job at the steel works in Wollongong, New South Wales. When he came back to

Australia, he did not really want to talk about his wartime experiences. He was trying to forget, even to the point that he showed little interest in news about the continuing war. He got treatment intermittently for "nerves," but received no counseling. He joined the Ex-Prisoner of War Association. He later applied to do an army rehabilitation course and started working as a painter. Eventually he built up his own painting business before retiring at the age of fifty-five to undertake charity work. In the meantime, he had married a nurse and had three children.[17]

James Beilby initially spent some time after his return making speeches to promote war bonds. Like Cornford, he was determined to put the past behind him and focus on his new life. He returned to run a garage that he operated before joining the army. Although he told himself there was no point brooding over the past, on at least one occasion he experienced what he called a "spasm of great sorrow" over the many friends he had lost. On the other hand, he believed that his war experience had "toughened" him up and broadened his mind.[18]

Ray Wheeler managed to see his family in Melbourne only after doctors pronounced him fit enough to return home. He celebrated his twenty-first birthday on 27 October 1944. He had lost half of his body weight while a prisoner, and when he arrived in Melbourne by train only his younger brother recognized him. After an extended leave, the army gave him the option of an immediate discharge. He chose to remain in the service and found himself assigned to guard Japanese prisoners at Murchison prison camp. From Wheeler's perspective, Australia treated the Japanese POWs with "kid gloves." He did have a chance to get some of his own back. On one occasion, for example, he forced some Japanese to salute a magpie. After leaving the service, Wheeler ran the *Western Port News* for a while, but he later became a "Totally and Permanently Incapacitated" pensioner (TPI). Like some other survivors of *Rakuyo Maru*, he remained active in the Returned and Services League of Australia. He served as a long-term president of the Frankston RSL, and at one stage became president of the Prisoners of War Association in Victoria.[19]

Fred Skeels, another HMAS *Perth* survivor, was down to 99 pounds when the war ended. As Skeels described his homecoming, "It took quite a while to settle down." He often sought out the company of other former prisoners. "Each day you'd go into town and meet cobbers ... it wasn't that you wanted to talk about what had happened, it was that you didn't know what to talk about at home."[20] Decades later, he still professed a dislike of crowds and noise that he attributed to his time as a prisoner of war.

Rowley Richards resumed his work at St Vincent's Hospital in Sydney as a resident medical officer in early 1946. In the evenings, he worked on his war diary, trying to fill in missing sections. When *Rakuyo Maru* sank, he lost a summary of the diary secreted in his stethoscope. Eventually, in February 1947, the War Graves Commission managed to return to him a six-page summary that he had buried while in Singapore.[21] He kept in close touch with other former prisoners, initially through informal reunions and later through his unit's 2/15th Field Regiment Association formed on the eve of Anzac Day 1946. Richards became president of the association and remained in that office for decades. He focused their energy on raising funds for distressed comrades and the families of those who died.[22]

Some prisoners described their return home in terms of a rebirth. Others, perhaps most, found the transition difficult. With little or no communication with their families or loved ones during captivity, some discovered their wives had moved on to new relationships. An article published in May 1945 reported that of the fifteen married men among the *Rakuyo Maru* survivors, one had divorced and another four had divorces pending. In the same article, the honorary secretary of the Prisoner of War Relatives' Association, Sydney Smith, criticized the government's lack of support for the men in transitioning back into "normal" life.[23] The recovered survivors had to not only recalibrate their personal lives, but adjust to a changed popular culture.[24] Robert Holman ends his memoir on captivity with the observation that "We had returned with a different set of values and we would never quite fit into civilian society in our lifetime."[25]

For most prisoners who survived the war, their experience once home was at odds with the idealized life they dreamed of while in captivity. As one army psychiatrist put it, the men's "high pitch of exaggerated optimism and false hope" about the lives they left behind were often quickly dashed.[26] Many returning POWs experienced a sense of unrest and isolation. Some missed the comradeship that helped them survive captivity, and sought out the company of other former prisoners.[27] Arthur Bancroft confessed that at the war's end he felt lonely—lonely for the mates he had grown so close to as a prisoner.[28] James Beilby, who like Bancroft returned to Perth, thought it was wonderful being back with his wife, but he still missed the company of the men from his captivity.[29] Even as his ship departed Singapore for home in 1945, Russell Braddon began to miss his comrades.[30] Many men sought solace with other former prisoners, mates, who shared a common ground. Former prisoners and their relatives formed associations to maintain a sense of comradeship and afford mutual support. Colonel Edward "Weary" Dunlop headed an association in Melbourne and Lieutenant Colonel Williams headed another in Sydney.[31]

Most of the returned Australians were reluctant to share their experiences as prisoners of war, at least outside the tight circle of other former prisoners. As recalled by David Herbert, the military advised him not to discuss his experiences with relatives since it would only upset them. They advised him to focus on getting on with his life. Herbert attempted to do just that. He returned briefly to work as a butcher and then went into the upholstery business before marrying in April 1948.[32]

Many returned prisoners were intent on trying to rebuild their lives and, as far as possible, forget about their sufferings in captivity.[33] Lieutenant Ronald George Williams, a survivor of the notorious *Raishin Maru* hell-ship, stated in an affidavit for the War Crimes Tribunal on 26 November 1946: "Since my return to Australia I have purposely mislaid any date I had compiled, as official records had been made, and I was desirous of breaking any link with the past."[34] Some prisoners suspected that if they related what they had endured, no one would believe them. Some may have remained silent through a sense of shame for surrender or guilt for surviving when so many died.[35] A day after the surrender at Singapore, Alec Hodgson of the Royal Australian Engineers recorded in his diary a "feeling of utter disgust and shame, never saw a Jap, never fired a shot and there are thousands like us."[36]

Sailors whose ships were lost in battle were in a different category. Unlike those who may have felt embarrassed by surrender, Arthur Bancroft believed he had done his duty. "We on the *Perth* had gone down against a superior force with all guns blazing; a lot of those blokes [at Changi], even though they outnumbered the Japs, had put their hands up without firing a shot."[37] Bancroft turned his hand to writing a book on his experiences soon after his return to Australia, and became the first returned POW to publish his story. Even before the war ended, he published *The Mikado's Guests*, co-authored with naval veteran Rowland Roberts.

As with many former prisoners who eventually published memoirs, Bancroft began his writing with a diary kept while in captivity. At the end of a day's work, while others sat around chatting, Bancroft would scribble his diary.[38] Despite the Japanese prohibition on such activities, Bancroft used scraps of paper and stolen pencils to keep a record, initially as a way of dealing with incarceration. According to the book's Foreword, written by Commodore John Augustus Collins, Bancroft's account was "not a grim tale of atrocities in concentration camps but a cheerful story of how spirit and determination made the best of things."[39] Collins overstated the "cheerful" aspect of the book; as described by another reviewer, the story was above all "a monument to Japanese disregard for human life." Nevertheless, the same reviewer believed that Bancroft's book "high-lighted amusing incidents and the courage and sense of humour of the prisoners."[40] The book certainly has elements of what historian Stephen Garton classifies as "comedic adventure," but there is also a fair amount of horror.[41]

It is likely that Bancroft understated the story of Japanese atrocities for at least two reasons. First, a degree of self-censorship at the time he wrote

Chapter 15. Adjustment   125

was needed since thousands of Australians still had relatives and loved ones in Japanese hands. Secondly, his emphasis on the prisoners' courage and sense of humor helped meld the experience of captivity with those values traditionally associated with the Australian military. On the face of it, surrender sat uneasily with Australia's celebration of fighting prowess in previous conflicts. The prisoner of war story did not obviously fit into the Australian literary view of warfare.[42] Bancroft's emphasis on traditional Anzac attributes such as mateship and a sense of humor served to link the POWs with their forbearers.[43] Bancroft, as the first ex-POW to publish a book on Japanese captivity, helped set a precedent for representing the prisoners as exemplars of national traits and making them appear less as victims. He thus began a process, which would gain momentum in later decades, of assimilating the prisoners into Australia's national war mythology.[44]

Although his book never achieved the popularity of subsequent works such as Russell Braddon's *The Naked Island* or Rohan Rivett's *Behind Bamboo*, Bancroft contributed to what developed as a specific genre of war writing. In *The Mikado's Guests*, the most elaborate example of the Australians' spirit and humor is a chapter titled "The Melbourne Cup" which recounts how the prisoners ingeniously celebrated the famed horse race while on the Thai-Burma railway.[45] Bancroft also related the incident in a 1982 interview with historian Tim Bowden, describing how innovative the Australians had been in simulating the 1943 Cup with costumes, hobby-horses and a skilled race-caller. It was the type of thing that helped to maintain morale and, according to Bancroft, even the Japanese found "magnificent."[46]

Apart from Bancroft's book, it would be decades before any of the other *Rakuyo Maru* survivors published their memoirs. When they finally appeared, these accounts were written by men who had continued as slave laborers in Japan after their rescue. In contrast to Bancroft's sudden reversal of fortune, their extended captivity may help to explain why it took them so long to process their experiences. Rowley Richards recalled that following the war, "My shutters came down and I resolved that when I returned to Australia, I wouldn't try to describe, in specific terms, the enormity of our experiences."[47] If reluctant to share his experiences with others, however, he began writing a meticulous diary while details were still fresh in his mind.[48] Russell Savage was aged 74 when he published his recollections, *A Guest of the Emperor*, in 1995. Savage professed that he only felt capable of writing the memoir once the "fires of hatred" had receded. Much of the material for the book came from the statements he prepared in 1948 for the Tokyo War Crimes Tribunal.[49]

In the case of Rowley Richards, he contemplated publishing a book by 1979. This was the year that Clay and Joan Blair published their book

Return from the River Kwai, and as one of their interviewees Richards took a keen interest in the book's reception. Writing to the couple in September 1979, Richards told them, "As for my book, I feel it may be wise to wait and see whether yours will create a demand or whether it will kill it."[50] By the following year, Richards appeared to conclude the latter was true. He wrote that the response to their book "has been one of horror rather than 'What a good book' etc. You made your point—almost too well."[51] Richards' confidence may also have been shaken by Clay Blair's critique of his interview after he sought his advice on writing. He told Richards, "Your mind runs to statistics and facts rather than human interest.... You have real difficulty, it would appear, in describing people."[52]

An executive of *Reader's Digest* in Sydney later encouraged Richards to write a book and teamed him up with Marcia McEwan. The co-authored work, titled *The Survival Factor*, appeared in 1989.[53] Richards was 89 years old before he published his more personal memoir, *A Doctor's War*, in 2005. The memoirs of Richards and Savage represented part of a broader renaissance of POW literature that began to flourish from the 1980s.[54]

Concurrently, the recognition from 1980 of Post-Traumatic Stress Disorder (PTSD) as a legitimate psychological condition by the American Psychiatric Association heralded a new era and a flood of discourse on survivors of war. As defined by the American Psychiatric Association, PTSD was "a response, sometimes delayed, to an overwhelming event or events" which might manifest in a wide variety of ways.[55] Few could doubt that the events experienced by prisoners of the Japanese were "overwhelming." Rowley Richards concluded that every prisoner of war, including himself, suffered from PTSD.[56]

As argued by Didier Fassin and Richard Rechtman, the diagnosis of PTSD removed the stigma and negative connotations often attached to those defeated or captured in war. Whereas the psychological damage of war frequently was attributed to personal weakness, PTSD shifted the discussion to victims of trauma.[57] Public awareness of PTSD came largely through discussion of Vietnam War veterans, which in turn inspired a reassessment of the broader experience of war.[58]

Prisoners of war became obvious candidates for investigations of trauma. According to one study in the 1980s, about half of the ex-POWs who had been held by the Japanese continued to suffer anxiety resulting from their wartime experiences.[59] Another study estimated that some forty years after the Second World War, about one-third of the men who experienced Japanese captivity showed symptoms of PTSD.[60] Some former prisoners recorded their memoirs following the prompting of psychiatrists, as a way to ease their continued psychological suffering, often manifested in recurrent nightmares, anxiety, depression and other disorders.[61]

Chapter 15. Adjustment

The death rates of former POWs were considerably higher than that for other veterans, although the disparity apparently narrowed after age forty.[62] Some prisoners of the Japanese continued to suffer from tropical diseases decades after their repatriation.[63] An Australian study published in 1986 comparing the medical records of former prisoners of the Japanese with combat veterans of the Pacific War over the forty years since the war ended, found little difference in their physical health other than a higher incidence of duodenal ulcers among the POWs. In terms of mental health, however, the former POWs showed a significantly higher incidence of clinical depression and anxiety disorders.[64] An extensive follow-up study in 1992 found that rates of post-traumatic stress disorder, depression and anxiety were higher among POWs in the Pacific theater compared to those captured in Europe. Typical mental health effects suffered by former POWs include apathy, dependence, irritability and anxiety.[65]

As Gerald Linderman suggests, it seems that Vietnam veterans' outspokenness about their postwar struggles allowed World War II veterans to acknowledge their experiences in similar terms.[66] As noted by Christina Twomey, the popular perception of former POWs as traumatized victims reinvigorated public interest.[67] The language of "trauma" had already made its way into an interview of Arthur Bancroft by historian Tim Bowden in 1982. Bowden referred to Bancroft's account of the loss of HMAS *Perth* as a "sudden traumatic" event. In the same interview, Bancroft referred to the treatment he and other prisoners received from the Japanese as "traumas." Recalling in the interview the moment he realized he would be rescued by an American submarine after days at sea, Bancroft broke down crying.[68]

Similarly, when Arthur Bancroft published a new narrative of his wartime experiences in 2010, written with John Harman, these developments appeared to have left their mark. Following an interview of Bancroft by Tara Brown on the popular TV show *60 Minutes* in 2008, Penguin recognized his story as having commercial potential. The publisher put Bancroft in touch with Western Australian writer John Harman, who conducted interviews with Bancroft and his wife over a number of months.[69] In the book *Arthur's War*, Bancroft explains that once he became a prisoner following the loss of HMAS *Perth*, he "suffered a shock to the system which, nowadays, I suppose they'd call a trauma."[70] Characteristic of that trauma is the reliving of the events over and over. Bancroft relates that although writing sixty-eight years after the loss of HMAS *Perth*, he thought about it every day. He further relates that "Back then we didn't have counselling for blokes like me coming back from POW camps."[71]

In contrast to his earlier accounts, Bancroft discloses in *Arthur's War* an element of survivor's guilt. The emergence of survivor's guilt as a clinical condition from the 1960s is closely associated with literature on the

Holocaust, but it became linked with other traumatic situations including the Vietnam War.[72] In Bancroft's case, part of the trauma he experienced and re-lived was the loss of his best mate, Harry "Lofty" Nagle. It will be recalled that following the sinking of *Rakuyo Maru*, Bancroft separated from his friend after joining another group of survivors. In *Arthur's War*, he professes, "Swimming away from a mate is the hardest thing I've ever had to do."[73] When Bancroft reached Saipan, he desperately searched for Nagle, and "felt weighed down with a tremendous guilt" when he could not find him.[74] Worse was to come. When he related the circumstances of his death to Nagle's mother, she blamed him for leaving him alone. According to Bancroft, "The loss and sadness has stayed with me always."[75]

In short, the emotional and psychological costs of his experiences at war are far more evident in *Arthur's War* than his original book, *The Mikado's Guests*. As some writers have pointed out, life narratives are under constant revision, and thus tell us something about changing cultural priorities and values.[76] In his later years, Bancroft challenged some of his earlier representations, perhaps most of all, the notion that participants of war could return home relatively unscathed.

Part III

Crimes at Sea

CHAPTER 16

Retribution

While the impulse for revenge by prisoners of war in Japan was mainly constrained in the immediate aftermath of the surrender, many later hoped for the prosecution of their tormentors for war crimes. The International Military Tribunal of the Far East (IMTFE) became the main vehicle of retribution against the Japanese for their mistreatment of POWs. The president of the tribunal, the Australian judge William Webb, had already carried out investigations into atrocities against Australian soldiers during 1943 and 1944, resulting in a 400-page report.[1] In line with critics of the IMTFE as "victor's justice," Webb appeared far from an impartial adjudicator.

In addition to the trials held in Tokyo, the Allies established fifty-one courts across the Asia Pacific to conduct trials of accused war criminals. A total of 5,700 individuals faced 2,244 trials at these national courts.[2] Australia's war crime trials convened under the authority of an Act of Parliament, the War Crimes Act 1945. The Australian War Crimes Section worked closely with British war crimes investigators in Singapore and Dutch investigators in Java.[3]

The desire for retribution among prisoners of war was by no means universal; not all former prisoners were interested in getting involved in the war crime trial process. Frank McGovern resisted the authorities who wanted him to go to Singapore to give evidence.[4] The iconic Australian physician Edward "Weary" Dunlop also refused the opportunity to attend the war crime trials.[5] While medical doctors became important spokesmen, they frequently seemed to be more philosophical and forgiving of Japanese mistreatment than other prisoners who have left a record of their feelings. Perhaps this stemmed in part from a belief that they were better off than most of those in captivity because they carried on doing what they were trained to do. As Rowley Richards put it, "I was one of the lucky ones because I was doing my own job."[6]

Albert Coates, a senior surgeon with the Eighth Australian Division, described the sudden outbursts of rage POWs suffered from their captors, but he also allowed that the Japanese exhibited the same behavior toward their own men. Having experienced firsthand the misery of being transported on a Japanese hellship, in his case *England Maru*, Coates noted that Japanese troops sailed under similar conditions. On some matters, Coates praised the Japanese, as when they allowed POWs to retain their own kit and showed respect for the dead.[7] Although Coates, at the request of the Australian army, testified at the Tokyo War Crime Trials in 1946, some contemporaries criticized his attitude toward postwar Japan as too "soft."[8] At a service commemorating the fall of Singapore held in 1953, Coates took the opportunity to call for an end of bitterness toward Japan.[9]

Although Australia aspired to prosecute all war criminals, this proved unrealistic in practice. From 30 November 1945 to 9 April 1951, Australian military courts conducted 296 trials involving 924 defendants, which convened in Singapore, Hong Kong, Labuan, Wewak, Morotai, Rabaul, Manus and Darwin. The conviction rate was seventy percent. Of those tried, 148 received sentences of death and another 496 received sentences of imprisonment.[10] The need for interpreters considerably slowed down the pace of the trials and became a point of criticism for the trials' detractors, since arguably the courts received a less than nuanced account of what defendants and witnesses said. Despite the language problems, however, the average war crime trial lasted only about two days.[11]

Among the Australian war crimes trials, 23 were held in Singapore between 26 June 1946 and 29 April 1947. The British conducted another 17 cases in Singapore that included Australians as victims.[12] In these cases, as stipulated by Allied Land Forces South East Asia, an Australian observer was invited to attend the trials.[13] All but five of the trials conducted by the Australian Military Court in Singapore related to the Thai-Burma railway. The Australian War Crimes personnel, along with their British counterparts, used Goodwood Park Hotel on Scotts Road, formerly occupied by the Japanese high command, as their base. The buildings became Southeast Asia's main center for the identification and apprehension of war crime suspects.[14]

Despite media reports that all Japanese connected with sea transport were placed on the lists of war crime suspects, the numbers brought to trial proved relatively small. Prosecutions were hindered by Japanese instructions to destroy incriminating evidence and allowing those who mistreated prisoners to flee.[15] While eager to prosecute suspected war criminals, Australia lacked the resources of their Allies to carry through on this in a timely manner. In part, a lack of court space in Singapore slowed the pace of trials. The First Australian War Crimes Section in Singapore also came under pressure from the British to conclude their trials in a timely fashion. The British enlisted them to be more selective in choosing cases for prosecution, and to focus on defendants likely to be sentenced to death or to over seven-years imprisonment.[16]

Scene at a Japanese War Crimes Trial in Singapore, 1947 (Tham Siew Yen Collection, National Archives of Singapore).

War crime investigators interviewed Rowley Richards at length when he was processed at the end of the war in Manila, during his stop over on his way back to Australia. Richards' testimony, as the only officer to survive *Rakuyo Maru*'s sinking, carried a special weight. In addition, Richards later provided an affidavit to war crime investigators in January 1948 on the sinking of *Rakuyo Maru* and its aftermath.[17] Affidavits were taken as well from many other Australian *Rakuyo Maru* survivors during 1948 including James Bassett, Raymond Burridge, Owen Curtis, Ross Dunbar, Arthur Hall, Kevin Hyde, William Hubbard, Edward Kelk, Kitchener Loughnan, Stanley Joseph Manning, Keith Martin, Harold George Ramsey, Russell Savage and Herbert John Wall. Given the timing of the affidavits, they may have been linked to the arrest of six former Japanese generals in mid–1948, who were to be tried for the ill treatment of the estimated 17,000 to 30,000 Allied POWs shipped to Japan. Found guilty by a U.S. military court, the generals received sentences of imprisonment ranging from 1 to 24 years hard labor.[18]

Nevertheless, no war crime prosecutions resulted directly from the *Rakuyo Maru* episode. The identification of suspects presented a problem. Often former prisoners could identify their guards only by nicknames such as "Bludger Bill," "Blood Pressure," or "Liver Lips."[19] Proof of an accused's identity often depended on the use of photographs, a process that frequently raised problems when the prosecution relied on affidavits rather than witnesses in a court room who could personally identify alleged offenders.[20]

The one Japanese person most *Rakuyo Maru* survivors could identify was Lieutenant Yamada, who had accompanied some of the men in Burma, Saigon and Singapore. Yamada was described as about 35 years old, 5 feet 4 inches tall, with a heavy build and dark complexion. Russell Savage, who at one stage acted as Yamada's batman at Saigon, recalled him as a womanizer: "frequently I had to ask two or three girls to leave his bed so that I could make it up."[21] Generally, prisoners remembered Yamada as one of the more reasonable Japanese officers. Kitchener Loughnan described him as "quietly spoken and mannered" and his conduct as "quite reasonable."[22] Based on interrogation of the survivors, a secret Australian report on Japanese camp commandants and guards described Yamada as one "who worked wholeheartedly for the welfare of our men."[23]

The most significant violation of the rules of war was the failure of the Japanese to rescue prisoners following the loss of *Rakuyo Maru*. Attributing responsibility for this to specific individuals, however, would be extremely difficult and may explain why no prosecutions resulted. As it transpired, only one of the Australian trials prosecuted at Singapore involved a hellship and war crimes on the high seas. These charges stemmed from the voyage of *Raishin Maru*, a ship better known to prisoners as "Byoki Maru" or sick ship.[24] The only other hellship trial prosecuted by the Australians was held at Hong Kong and involved *Sanuki Maru*. A detailed account of these trials is provided in subsequent chapters.

The first war crime trial prosecuted by the British in Southeast Asia began in Singapore on 21 January 1946 and involved a hellship. Perhaps surprisingly, the victims in the case were not British POWs but some 2,000 Indians and 150 Indonesian POWs sent to the Palau Islands for forced labor. The Indians were soldiers of the 2/12 Frontier Force Regiment and the First Battalion of the Hyderabad Infantry of the Indian States Forces, captured at Singapore but dubbed "volunteers" by the Japanese. On 5 May 1943, the prisoners sailed from Singapore aboard the 5,000-ton *Thames Maru*. Evidence at the trial indicated that dysentery quickly broke out in the unhygienic conditions on board, and an undetermined number of the prisoners died during the one-month-four-day voyage to the Palau island of Babelthuap.[25]

As characteristic of hellships, *Thames Maru* was grossly overcrowded. In addition to the large number of passengers embarked at Singapore, the ship took on more Japanese troops at Surabaya. Lack of accommodation on the ship meant that there was barely room for the prisoners to sit down.

The latrines included only two lavatory seats, to be shared by the 2,000 prisoners. Despite the outbreak of dysentery, no medical supplies were issued. Much of the food dispensed was infested with maggots, while only small quantities of drinking water were available.[26]

It should be emphasized, however, that conditions on the ship *Thames Maru* made up only a relatively small part of the charges against the defendants in this case. The ten Japanese officers and non-commissioned officers put on trial were accused of mistreating the prisoners from their Singapore departure up until September 1945 when the POWs were liberated by American forces. During their two years and three months captivity, the prisoners claimed they were routinely ill-treated and beaten. From June 1943, the prisoners' rations on Babelthuap progressively diminished to starvation level. At the same time, the prisoners were required to carry out hard labor including the construction of an airstrip.[27]

The senior officer tried was Captain Sadaichi Gozawa, who headed a 61-strong unit known as the "Gozawa Butai."[28] The other defendants, all members of the Imperial Japanese Army, included Lieutenant Kaniyuki Nakamura, Lieutenant Ken Okusawa, Lieutenant Kajino Ryuivchi, Lance-Corporal Masami Chiba, Sergeant-Major Shozo Tanno, Sergeant Jinichiro Yabi, Corporal Makoto Osaki, Sergeant-Major Tadasu Ono and Corporal Tamotsu Ashiya. As characterized by their defense counsel, they were "quite ordinary people."[29] Gozawa, born 14 February 1900, was married with six children. He owned a farm inherited from his parents. Nakamura was born in 1897 and was married. Both men did their original military service in 1919–1920, and then were recalled to the army in 1943.

Most of the other defendants were considerably younger than Gozawa and Nakamura. Ken Okusawa was 29 years old at the time of the trial. He graduated from medical college in September 1942, and then joined the army and was quickly promoted to lieutenant. Shozo Tanno, born 3 February 1910, was married with three children. After an original period of military service in 1929–1931, he was recalled to the army in 1940. Jinichiro Yabi was also born in 1910; he was married with one child. Makoto Osaki, born on 17 November 1911, was married with two daughters. After doing two years of military service from 1931 to 1933, he was recalled in 1941. Masami Chiba was born 24 December 1917 and joined the army in 1940. He was described as a "typical Japanese peasant farmer."[30] On the other hand, Tadasu Ono was 43 years old at the time of his trial. After initial service in the army from 1925 to 1935, he was recalled in 1943. Tamotsu Ashiya, a former farmer, was born 6 January 1906, and was 40 years old at the time of the trial. He was married with two sons. His periods of military service extended from 1926 to 1927, 1938 to 1939, and from 1941 until the end of the war.[31]

The trial was presided over by Lieutenant-Colonel Leon George Coleman, who obtained his law degree from Liverpool University and was appointed President, No. 1 Military Court for the trial of war criminals in November 1945. He was assisted by Major W.M. Gray and Captain R.D. Kohli. The prosecutors were Lieutenant-Colonel Robert Stephen Lazarus and Captain Alan Ashton Hibbert, both from the Allied Land Forces, South East Asia. The defense counsel for the accused were two British officers, Major Alan Fairburn and Lieutenant-Colonel Stuart Colin Sleeman. With only days to prepare for the case, the defense counsel quickly determined that there were no witnesses that could usefully be called. In general terms, the defense argued that the accused acted under superior military orders, which they could not be expected to disobey.[32]

An important element of the defense was the contention that shortages of food, clothing and medicines were the result of Allied air raids and naval blockade, which affected everyone equally. In respect to the *Thames Maru*, Gozawa asserted that he was not in a position of command on the ship and could do nothing to alleviate the conditions. His defense counsel argued that "Gozawa and his officers suffered as much as anyone else on board the *Thames Maru*."[33] In his testimony, Gozawa admitted that conditions on the ship were bad, but insisted that the transportation commander, Major Suzi, was responsible for care, hygiene and supplies on board.[34]

As the first war crime prosecution in Southeast Asia, the eleven-day trial attracted widespread interest. At least one writer suggests that the choice of a case involving Indian victims was primarily political. Particularly given rising Indian nationalism at the time, the trial was calculated to restore some confidence in the equality of Imperial subjects before the law. In any case, the trial attracted throngs of spectators and international press coverage.[35]

One of the defendants, Sergeant-Major Ono, was acquitted. The defense argued that no affidavit evidence applied against him, and there was no evidence that he participated in the alleged abuse of prisoners. Kaniyuki Nakamura was sentenced to death, while Gozawa received a sentence of twelve years imprisonment. The remaining defendants received sentences ranging from two to seven years in prison. The lightest sentence was given to the medical officer Ken Okusawa, the court determining that his crimes were "more of omission than commission."[36] Nakamura, hanged at Changi prison on 14 March 1946, became the first war criminal to be executed in Southeast Asia.[37]

This case, as the first tried in Singapore, set certain precedents and foreshadowed some of the broader problems in conducting war crime trials. Much of the evidence had been deliberately destroyed by the Japanese. Witnesses were widely scattered, so arranging for them to attend court was subject to delays and often impractical. Partly to compensate for these problems, the courts accepted forms of written evidence not usually acceptable in British courts. This meant that the defense was often deprived of the opportunity for cross-examination, while the prosecution lacked the persuasion of powerful first-hand testimony.[38]

One lesson learned from the Gozawa trial was the importance of having a leading witness for the prosecution present at the trial. The prosecution relied in part on the testimony of Colonel O'Dwyer of the Royal Army Medical Corps to explicate the conditions on *Thames Maru* described in prisoners' affidavits.[39] The problems of identifying defendants only from photographs by witnesses not in attendance also became apparent. The defense pointed to discrepancies in witness affidavits and forcibly argued that the courts needed to ensure that they "convict a *man* and not a *photograph.*"[40]

The trial also indicated some of the language problems involved. As the prosecution pointed out in its closing address, "difficulties of language" could make it difficult to assess the evidence of the accused. For example, the terms "beating" and "slapping" were often used interchangeably, and "in many cases the singular of a word was the same as the plural."[41] The various spellings of names created further ambiguities. Nevertheless, defense counsel Colin Sleeman concluded that "the really momentous and optimistic thing" which emerged from the Gozawa trial was "that the Japanese accused of War Crimes are extremely favorably impressed with the kind of trial which they are getting."[42] Given later controversy surrounding the trials, Sleeman almost certainly overstated the case. What was more striking in regard to Australian POWs on hellships was the small numbers of Japanese brought to justice.

CHAPTER 17

Raishin Maru

As it transpired, only one of the Australian trials prosecuted at Singapore involved a hellship and war crimes on the high seas. These charges stemmed from the voyage of *Raishin Maru*, a ship better known to prisoners as "Byoki Maru" or sick ship, a nickname reflecting its pathetic appearance.[1] The only other hellship trial prosecuted by the Australians was held at Hong Kong and involved *Sanuki Maru*; a detailed account of this trial is provided in the following chapter.

Although originally sold to the Japanese as scrap by the British before the war, *Raishin Maru* was still afloat in 1944, if barely. In fact, there were other hellships originally built at British shipyards and sold to the Japanese as "scrap" during the 1930s. One of the ships, re-named *Cho Saki Maru*, carried a thousand prisoners from Surabaya to Haruku in a hold space of only forty feet by fifty feet. As described by one of the POWs, it was a new experience of "disease, despair and death."[2]

By various accounts, *Raishin Maru* was previously known as *Canadian Seigneur*, *Canadian Princess*, and *Potomac* before the Japanese renamed the 5,800-ton ship. In February 1942, Allied aircraft bombed *Rashin Maru* in the Java Sea and the ship was towed to Singapore for repair. In 1944, the damage was still all too obvious. With the entire center section of the ship burned out, including the original bridge, two welded girders held the fore and aft sections together. A "provisional" bridge for steering was rigged at the ship's stern. The ship was so antiquated that its armament included a brass cannon.[3]

Raishin Maru sailed from Singapore on 4 July 1944 with 1,050 prisoners on board. They included 605 Australians, 310 British and 150 Dutch, intended for slave labor in Japan's factories and mines. In addition to the POWs, the ship carried about 30 Korean guards and 135 Japanese personnel including the ship's crew.[4] *Raishin Maru* reached Moji on 8 September, only two days after *Rakuyo Maru* and *Kachidoki Maru* departed Singapore as part of convoy HI-72. *Raishin Maru*'s journey from Singapore to Japan took seventy days, one of the longest hellship voyages of the war. The length of voyages from Singapore to Japan generally became longer as the war progressed. In 1942, ships routinely made the trip in only ten days. By 1944, ships increasingly took circuitous routes, hugging the coastlines and sheltering in ports attempting to avoid submarine attacks. Added to this, *Rashin Maru*'s slow speed contributed to the length of the voyage. The ship had a maximum speed of eight knots, although for most of the journey to Japan it sailed at only six to seven knots.[5]

As part of a convoy of thirteen ships, including three escorts, *Rashin Maru* departed Singapore at the tail end. The convoy stopped at Brunei for several days, picking up an additional six ships and more escorts. *Raishin Maru* arrived at Miri in North Borneo on 8 July, and after remaining there two days, made for Manila. The convoy crawled along the coast of Palawan in the Philippine Islands before anchoring at Manila Bay on 17 July 1944. There the convoy lingered for several weeks, sheltering as the threat of U.S. submarines kept delaying their departure.

Rashin Maru finally left Manila on the evening of 9 August to run a gauntlet of submarines and fierce storms in the South China Sea. Perhaps because it was considered expendable, *Rashin Maru* led the convoy of ships. On the morning of 12 August, submarines attacked the convoy.[6] USS *Puffer* claimed the sinking of two tankers, *Shinpo Maru* and *Teikon Maru*. Following the initial attack, *Puffer*'s commander, Frank Gordon Selby, described the scene as "a mad scramble with ships going in every direction and continuous pop-popping of their guns as they fired into the water."[7] In total, attacks on the convoy resulted in the loss of five ships and damage to three others. According to a story circulated by the prisoners on *Raishin Maru*, the submarines passed up an opportunity to sink their decrepit transport ship because it looked unworthy of a torpedo.[8]

On 13 August, the remnants of the convoy sailed into a typhoon, further scattering the ships that had managed to avoid the submarine attacks.[9] Battling sixty-foot waves, one prisoner claimed that *Raishin Maru* survived only "by a miracle and good seamanship."[10] The ship arrived at Takao, Formosa, on 16 August, but due to fears of an aerial bombardment, it sailed for Keelung where it arrived on 18 August.

At Keelung the ship ran aground, and two tugs were needed to pull it into port. After nine days at Keelung, *Raishin Maru* sailed on 27 August but returned only a few hours later after spotting a submarine. With two other ships, they sailed from Keelung for a second time on 28 August and reached Okinawa on 31 August. *Raishin Maru* next sailed on 1 September and reached Kagoshima at the southern end of Japan on 4 September. The following day the ships sailed again, arriving at Mutsure near Moji on 7 September. At Mutsure, the passengers passed through quarantine before proceeding to Moji where they disembarked on 8 September.[11]

Chapter 17. Raishin Maru

Whereas most of the *Rakuyo Maru* survivors did not give affidavits until 1948, war crime investigators interviewed some of the prisoners from *Raishin Maru* as early as August 1945 while they were still in Japan.[12] This prompt interview of witnesses probably helps to explain why some suspects were prosecuted in relation to *Raishin Maru*. In April 1947, Lieutenant Kishio Uchiyama stood trial with his second in command, Sergeant Major Mitsugu Fukuda, for the prisoners' inhumane treatment on *Raishin Maru*. On the ship, the prosecution alleged, POWs suffered from overcrowding, inadequate food and medical supplies, lack of adequate hygiene and sanitation, as well as repeated beatings by Korean guards. Three prisoners (two Dutch and one Australian) died on board, and another four Australians died shortly after arrival in Japan. Most of the prisoners disembarked at Japan in very poor physical and mental condition.[13]

Uchiyama, a lieutenant in the Imperial Japanese Army, was 37 years old. He served at No. 4 Camp at Tamuan (also known as Tamuang), Thailand, when appointed officer-in-charge of the prisoners to be transported on *Raishin Maru*. A graduate of the "Literary Section" of Kansai University, Uchiyama worked as a manager in a contracting firm before the war. He was married with three children.[14]

Sergeant Major Mitsugu Fukuda, also of the Imperial Japanese Army, was 40 years old and, like Uchiyama, had served at the Tamuan camp in Thailand for three years. At the Thailand camp, Fukuda acted as Uchiyama's subordinate from December 1943 until the end of the war. For a time, he also assisted a Japanese Army doctor there at the hospital. He reportedly spoke fluent English. A graduate from the Political and Economic Department of Waseda University, as a civilian he worked for a company involved in logistics. He was married with two children.[15] In the trial file photos, he appears a handsome man of medium build. Uchiyama and Fukuda were typical of the bulk of those prosecuted for war crimes at sea to the extent that they were drawn from the middling ranks of junior and non-commissioned officers.[16]

The military court proceedings against Uchiyama and Fukuda commenced on 18 April 1947. Lieutenant Colonel S.F. Hodgens acted as president of the court, with members Lieutenant Colonel J.P.H. Mullemeistrer and Captain A.A. Sherlock from the Australian Army Intelligence Corps. Major A. D. MacKay of the First Australian War Crimes Section acted as prosecutor, while Karuhiko Hirose served as the court interpreter. The defense counsel were Fujio Sugimatsu and Takeshi Nakamura, assisted by Captain R.T. Wait of the British Intelligence Corps. Initially, Japanese military lawyers had represented all defendants, but from October 1946 civilian lawyers, as well as additional interpreters, began arriving in Singapore from Japan. The defense called seven witnesses to testify in addition to the defendants.[17]

The prosecution produced only one witness in court—Flight Lieutenant John Hughes Wilkinson, who currently served with the First Australian War Crimes Section. Until recently, he had worked for seven months with the War Crimes Shipping Committee formed to investigate Japanese crimes on transport ships. According to his testimony, he prepared a questionnaire and received affidavits from six men on board *Raishin Maru*. These affidavits, taken between October 1946 and February 1947, made up the bulk of the evidence against the defendants.[18] As previously noted, a reliance on affidavits in war crime trials generally proved to be one of the contentious aspects of the trials. While relying on affidavits avoided some of the costs and other problems of bringing witnesses to court, it meant there was no opportunity to cross-examine their testimony.[19]

The charges against the defendants can be broken down into four main categories: the lack of space afforded prisoners on *Raishin Maru*, inadequate provisions, inadequate medical care and abuse of the prisoners by their guards. The defense, on the other hand, argued that the conditions on board *Raishin Maru* were beyond the defendants' responsibility, largely shifting blame to the Anchorage Command at port and the ship's captain at sea.

As in the case of most Japanese transport ships, *Raishin Maru* was grossly overcrowded. This in turn had consequences which included a shortage of latrines and a greater likelihood of spreading disease. Given the number of prisoners on board, the life-saving equipment was inadequate; there were "very inferior type" kapok life belts available for only about sixty percent of the men on the ship. Under cross-examination, the prosecutor took Uchiyama to task for not allocating adequate space for prisoners, pointing out that they received far less room than the Japanese on board, and less space than required by international law.[20]

According to the defense, No. 3 Army Shipping Transport Command assigned the ships used and the number of prisoners carried, while Anchorage Command and the embarking officer of that command determined the allotment of space for passengers. The defense further emphasized that the defendants were not responsible for the ship's equipment and hygiene, which by their reckoning fell within the purview of the shipping commander. Uchiyama testified that as the draft commander, he was not able to make complaints or ask for improvements because the Shipping Command made such decisions. Somewhat contradictorily, however, he did claim that the original plan was to transport 2,000 prisoners on the ship and that he had helped to reduce this.[21]

A defense witness, 39-year-old Army Captain Takagi Hiroshi, who served as a liaison officer stationed at Singapore, lent some support to Uchiyama's claims. He confirmed that No. 3 Army Shipping Transport

Command determined the number of prisoners carried on *Raishin Maru*. On board the ship, the embarking officer dispatched from Anchorage Command allocated the space for passengers. Further supporting Uchiyama's claim, he testified that 2,000 prisoners originally were intended for the ship, but that authorities reduced this to 1,010 men following a request by Uchiyama and himself.[22]

Evidence submitted by the defense also included a statement by Major General Suketomo Tanabe, taken at Tokyo on 25 February 1947. According to Tanabe, at the end of the war the Japanese systematically burned the records of disembarkation kept at ports. Although he had not seen any regulations on the transportation of prisoners, he believed the orders originated from Imperial General Headquarters. Tanabe pointed out that Japan's general policy was to make maximum use of shipping space. Although military authorities well knew that troop ships were overcrowded, and the issue frequently received discussion at conferences, nothing could be done due to the shortage of shipping.[23] Another former major general of the Japanese Army, Hideitsu Kaji, also testified on the issue of space. According to his evidence, regulations on the allocation of space were set up long before the war. He believed that these allowed one man per three tons, or 3,000 troops for a 9,000-ton vessel. "In effect it was: 'Pack as Many as Possible.'"[24] According to at least one historian, these were in fact conservative estimates. Gavin Daws suggests that with the escalating loss of Japan's shipping capacity, the density of bodies increased from one man per ton to two men per ton.[25]

The evidence taken at other war crime trials tends to support the defense's claim that the central authorities determined which ships were used to transport prisoners and the amount of provisions to be supplied. On the other hand, the Tokyo Tribunal, in addressing the transport of POWs, dismissed the Japanese argument that the transport conditions could not be helped due to the shortage of shipping. The Tokyo Tribunal asserted that the Japanese were not entitled to move prisoners unless they could do it under conditions prescribed by the laws of war.[26]

According to the evidence, due to the conditions on board *Raishin Maru* and the lack of medical supplies, after only two weeks at sea almost all the prisoners suffered from a range of ailments including malaria, beriberi, tropical ulcers, pellagra, dysentery and dengue fever. While it is unclear what killed two Dutch prisoners, the Australian who died on board, identified only as E. Turner, succumbed to dysentery and malaria. By the time the prisoners reached Japan, their condition was bad enough that the Japanese gave them two weeks rest before assigning them to work. Nevertheless, Uchiyama claimed that when the prisoners arrived at Moji they were in better condition than expected. At this stage, there were twenty POWs lying in the ship's "hospital area" and another 60 to 70 receiving medical care. Uchiyama pointed out that he suffered his own health crisis during the voyage, with a bout of dengue fever while at Manila.[27]

From its opening address, the defense emphasized that the accused were not responsible for medical supplies or the treatment of sick POWs. According to their argument, the POW camp commandant was responsible for providing medical supplies, while the shipping commander, anchorage commander and ship's master had responsibility for the rations and other supplies.[28] Another defense witness, 41-year-old Shigeo Muraoka, a medical lieutenant in the army and the medical officer in charge of No. 4 POW camp at Tamuan, Thailand, testified that the medical supplies issued to each draft of prisoners was fixed.[29] In terms of food, the defense asserted that Anchorage Command supplied the provisions, while once on board this became the responsibility of the ship's captain.[30]

Conditions on board for the prisoners deteriorated further after a submarine attacked *Raishin Maru*'s convoy on 11 August 1944. Following the submarine attack, the prisoners were confined below deck for days. Not allowed on deck even to use the latrines, they had to make do with buckets.[31] According to the affidavit of the senior POW officer, Captain Reginald William Newton, the prisoners were denied any exercise on deck for fourteen days.[32]

Much of the case against the defendants hinged on their failure to prevent abuse of the prisoners by the Korean guards on board *Raishin Maru*. There were incessant beatings for trivial offenses. In his affidavit, Captain Richard Parker of the 2/10 Australian Field Ambulance described one of the worst beatings he witnessed, which involved an attack on Lieutenant Rutherford with a wooden clog.[33] According to the affidavit of another former POW, one of the Korean guards named Harimiya beat Lieutenant Rutherford so badly that he had to spend several days in hospital. On another occasion, the defendants allegedly watched without intervening when the Korean guards beat the senior prisoner-of-war officer, Captain Reg Newton. Furthermore, the guards forcibly misappropriated the prisoners' food.[34]

Some prisoners believed that things took a distinct turn for the worse after their convoy suffered a submarine attack following their departure from Manila. According to the affidavit of Lieutenant Ralph Sanderson Forbes, after a submarine sank a tanker only several hundred yards behind their ship, "the treatment became almost intolerable."[35] Australian ex–POW Kenneth Harrison, in a published memoir, reinforced this view. According to Harrison, discipline on the ship was initially "surprisingly mild."[36] He noted that the Japanese allowed many men, including the sick, to sleep on deck. Despite all the hardships, the prisoners considered the ship's captain and the crew as relatively humane. This expansiveness changed, however, once the ship left Manila for the dangerous waters of the South China Sea. As described by Harrison, the honeymoon was over, and the guards bashed anyone trying to access the deck.[37]

At their trial, the defendants denied any knowledge of abuses by the Korean guards. According to Uchiyama's testimony, the 35 Korean guards on board were "practically not necessary," and were mainly employed as lookouts for submarines and aircraft. He further asserted that since he spent time with the prisoners at camps in Thailand, "I was very familiar and took sympathy on them."[38] Indeed, in terms of the prisoners' abuse, the defendants pinned much of their defense on their reputations in Thai POW camps. To support his innocence, Fukuda claimed that while at camp in Thailand, he had strictly forbidden the Korean guards from ill-treating prisoners.[39] One witness for the defense, Captain Zenki Suzuki, testified on the defendants' behalf as their superior officer at No. 4 camp in Thailand. He described both men as "docile" and sympathetic to the prisoners.[40]

At the trial's conclusion, in a statement from the dock, Uchiyama claimed that "it was impossible for me to prevent the bad results" and that "I did my best within the limit of my authority and responsibility."[41] The British officer assisting the defense, Captain R.T. Wait, read their closing address on Tuesday, 29 April 1947. Wait, described in the court records as a law student, had considerable experience working with defense teams, including seven Japanese prosecuted for the mistreatment of prisoners in the notorious F Force on the Thai–Burma railway. He also later worked with the defense of four defendants charged with ill-treatment of prisoners on board *Singapore Maru*.[42]

Wait argued that Uchiyama and Fukuda were "made the scapegoats for the sins of omission and commission of other men in every way more responsible than they but not apparently now available!" The real culprits, "the really Big Men," were "the arm-chair planners of the Army Shipping Transport Unit." Wait also asserted that the ship's captain "was ultimately and actually responsible."[43] In contrast, the defendants were "little men" who were "fundamentally decent men, who were literally In the Same Boat with the Ps.O.W." He described Uchiyama as "a known 'pro–POW commandant.'" Wait underlined the "extraordinary" length of the voyage, as well as the stress of a possible Allied attack, in mitigation of the prisoners' treatment. "No one feels well or happy with submarines below and bombers above at sea."[44] According to Wait, before the submarine scares, the prisoners had been allowed a half-hour for exercise a day.

In effect, the defense blamed the Allied submarines that attacked *Raishin Maru*'s convoy as at least partially culpable for the hardships suffered by the prisoners. The defense specifically blamed potential Allied attacks for extending the length of the voyage to Japan. In any case, the defense could justifiably argue that the accused were not responsible for the length of the voyage. According to evidence, authorities estimated the voyage to take 20 days, while provisioning assumed a voyage of 40 days.

The defendants mainly blamed American submarines for the length of the journey, with the waters between the Philippines and Japan considered especially treacherous. *Raishin Maru*'s delays in several ports, as well as taking a zigzag course and navigating close to land to escape attack, slowed the journey. Because of *Rashin Maru*'s slow speed, the ship spent 26 days at Manila before being allowed to join a convoy by Shipping Command and the escort ship commandant who determined orders to sail. American submarines were blamed not only for the delays of *Rashin Maru*'s journey, but also for the prisoners' low morale. Uchiyama testified that frequent submarine scares kept the prisoners in a nervous and disturbed state.[45]

Given the spirited defense mounted on behalf of Uchiyama and Fukuda, the prosecution had good reason to congratulate the defense team for their "completeness and thoroughness."[46] In his closing address, the prosecutor highlighted the inhumane treatment meted out to the prisoners in terms of accommodation, food, medical supplies, sanitation, facilities for rescue in the event of abandoning ship and physical ill-treatment. He argued that within 14 days of departing Singapore, malnutrition and a very high sick rate were already the direct consequences of the lack of food and medical supplies. The accused not only failed to prevent the physical abuse of prisoners by their guards, but on one occasion witnessed the beating of Captain Newton without intervening.[47]

At the sentencing phase of the trial, Captain Wait pleaded at one stage that the defendants "are men of Education and Culture, not bullet-headed Prussians—remember their good deeds—their comparative youth."[48] The court sentenced Uchiyama to six years imprisonment and Fukuda to three years and six months behind bars. Even before the trial, Uchiyama had spent 11 months in custody at Rangoon and Changi, and Fukuda had spent 19 months in custody. Since sentences were counted from the date of first arrest, Fukuda would spend a relatively short time behind bars.[49]

Although there was no right of appeal, the accused could petition the "Confirming Officer," typically the senior military officer in the region, within fourteen days. In turn, this was referred to the Judge Advocate General or his deputy for a ruling.[50] The defendants petitioned against the findings of the court and sentences on 12 May 1947. In their petition, Uchiyama emphasized his inability to amend arrangements for the voyage as well as the unexpected duration of the trip to Japan. In effect, he largely blamed the enemy threat of submarines and aircraft for the poor conditions on board *Raishin Maru*.[51]

Chapter 17. Raishin Maru

The Judge Advocate General in Canberra reported on 10 July 1947. He confirmed the findings and sentences and dismissed the petition, but recommended mitigation of the sentences. He stated that in his view "the case is not a very bad one." He also asserted that the conditions on board the ship were largely beyond the control of "two relatively junior Japanese."[52] The Judge Advocate was further favorably disposed toward the defendants by a statement from a Captain Woodroffe which claimed that while at a prison camp in Thailand the two men behaved reasonably. Major General W.M. Anderson confirmed these findings on 18 August 1947, and they were promulgated on 8 September 1947.

At least some former prisoners of the Japanese were skeptical of the war crime trials from the outset. One Australian letter writer, who identified himself as a "Burma Road—hellship survivor," claimed, "no one is fool enough to imagine the Nips will serve their full sentence." "They are being saved from the hard time facing Japan and, full fed, will be returned when things are more normal."[53] It is unclear how long the defendants remained incarcerated in Singapore. Largely due to the expense involved in housing convicted war criminals, in July 1949 Singapore and Malaya recommended to Britain the transfer of prisoners to Japan to serve the remainder of their sentences. Despite the Australian government's reluctance to extend clemency and pressure from veteran organizations, few convicted war criminals served their full terms. In 1957, the Australian government agreed to the release of war criminals still in custody. The same year encouraging closer relations with Japan became official policy of the Returned and Services League of Australia (RSL).[54]

The trial of Uchiyama and Fukuda for mistreatment of prisoners on *Raishin Maru* exemplifies the difficulties in prosecuting cases involving hellships. The various hierarchies of command and divided responsibilities enabled defendants to claim they were not responsible or acted only on orders.[55] The fact that those put in charge of prisoners were often relatively junior tended to strengthen their claims that they had no power to alter the prisoners' conditions. The man in charge of prisoners on *Hofuku Maru*, for example, was a sergeant major. At the man's trial for war crimes, his defense team emphasized his lowly status.[56] Neither the POW Information Bureau nor POW Management Office accepted any responsibility for prisoners in transit, leaving their treatment to the discretion of local commands. As in many other war crime trials, the often-divided authority and decision making within the Japanese military made it difficult to assign clear responsibility.[57] Defendants could also appeal to extenuating circumstances beyond their control.

The *Raishin Maru* defendants were not the only ones to emphasize the likelihood of an Allied attack as a mitigating circumstance. When Sergeant

Major Haruyoshi was charged at a British trial for the ill treatment and physical suffering of POWs on the ship *Taian Maru*, his defense raised similar points. The ship departed Ambon for Surabaya on 3 August 1944, with the convoy suffering an air attack only thirty minutes after leaving port. The defendant argued that he had to not only look after the POWs on board but remain vigilant against enemy submarines and aircraft. The prisoners were not allowed an awning for protection from the sun because it might be easily seen by enemy submarines. Because of the danger of attack, prisoners were also prohibited from exercising on deck.[58] Defendants who were charged for the ill-treatment of POWs on *Asaka Maru* claimed that a typhoon encountered off Formosa lengthened the voyage and contributed to the number of deaths on board. They also blamed Japan's "unfavourable situation of the war" by mid–1944, which limited food and equipment.[59]

The *Raishin Maru* trial mainly conforms to the pattern of defendants tried by the British for mistreatment of prisoners at sea. Those trials, too, mainly targeted mid-ranking soldiers who failed to act to ameliorate conditions rather than committing specific crimes. According to research by Cheah, even though the defendants had no control over provisions and accommodation, they faced accusations of being "grossly negligent" and "callously indifferent."[60] Similar to the *Raishin Maru* trial, some defendants were accused of allowing lower-ranking guards under their authority to abuse POWs. Cheah argues that these trials largely fell outside the usual bounds of international criminal law, since criminal law is typically reluctant to penalize failures to act or omissions.[61]

Most commonly, those convicted of committing crimes at sea faced varying prison sentences. While some defendants were accused of directly abusing POWs, most deaths on hellships resulted from the appalling conditions on board. Prosecutors of war crimes generally argued that the defendants failed to perform their duties of reporting and supervision. For example, in a case involving *Takan Maru*, the prosecution accused the defendant of failing to report the need for more latrines and space.[62] A common counter-argument by the Japanese was that they never were instructed on the proper treatment of POWs or the existence of their international rights. As one Japanese veteran put it, instead they were instructed never to be captured and "taught only to die."[63] As for *Raishin Maru*, it shared the fate of most Japanese shipping during the war; on 8 August 1945, the submarine USS *Pargo* sank the ship as it travelled in convoy off Korea.[64]

CHAPTER 18

Sanuki Maru

Apart from the trial involving *Raishin Maru*, the Australians prosecuted only one other case for crimes committed against prisoners at sea, this time at Hong Kong and at the behest of the British.[1] The trial involved the Japanese ship *Sanuki Maru*. The prosecutor in this trial, Major A.D. MacKay, declared the *Sanuki Maru* case "to be without parallel in an Australian Military Court—in that not one Australian is numbered among the victims of this alleged crime."[2] The POW victims on *Sanuki Maru* included three men from the New Zealand navy and another three British merchant seamen. Under the *War Crimes Act*, however, the Australian jurisdiction extended to any "British subjects or citizens of any power allied or associated with His Majesty in war."[3] As such, the prosecutor declared that the case exemplified the unity of the British Commonwealth of Nations.

The trial was held between 23 and 29 June 1948, some four years after the alleged offenses took place. Lieutenant-Colonel N.F. Quinton presided over the military court case as president, with members Major E.J. Gerling and Captain R.Q. Quentin-Baxter. Counsel for the defense was George Kyuzo Sagano of Keiko University, assisted by Major Grant McIntyre, a barrister and solicitor of the Supreme Court of Victoria. The trial record indicates this was the defense counsel's first appearance before an Australian military court.[4] The prosecutor, on the other hand, already had experience with war crimes committed at sea. Major A.D. MacKay, formerly a barrister of the Supreme Court of Western Australia, had prosecuted Uchiyama and Fukuda the previous year for their role in the *Raishin Maru* saga.

Described as a "Naval special transport ship" in the court records, *Sanuki Maru* served as a seaplane tender for much of the war. Originally launched in February 1939, the Imperial Japanese Navy requisitioned the 7,189-ton ship in August 1941.[5] In some ways, the case involving *Sanuki Maru* runs counter to the hellship stereotype. In contrast to the grossly over-crowded conditions on board most Japanese transports, *Sanuki Maru* carried only six prisoners of war who sailed in cabins shared between two men. Indeed, there were about 300 Japanese naval personnel aboard who presumably traveled in less comfort in the hold.⁶ Also uncharacteristic, the prisoners apparently received the same meals as other passengers and crew on board. One of the prisoners, Percy James Green, described their first meal on board as "quite good."⁷ Unfortunately, the standard of food quickly deteriorated as the voyage progressed.

Whereas the worst hellship voyages continued for months, the passage of *Sanuki Maru* was relatively brief, departing Surabaya on 10 June 1944 and arriving at Osaka after nineteen days on 28 June. The ship initially sailed from Surabaya to Bintan Island to load bauxite, before arriving at Singapore on 15 June. *Sanuki Maru* departed Singapore on 17 June as part of the fast convoy HI-66, stopping at Moji and Kure before disembarking the prisoners at Osaka.⁸

The case illustrates the diversity of conditions prisoners might experience on Japanese transports. While the amount of space afforded the prisoners was unusual, it was not unique. At the same time, however, the treatment of prisoners on *Sanuki Maru* shared some depressing similarities with the treatment of POWs on other hellships. As testimony at the trial revealed, the small numbers of prisoners if anything allowed for more focused abuse. The prisoners were required to wear handcuffs the entire voyage. The guards were described as a "bad bunch," and some members of the ship's crew participated in systematic beatings of the POWs along with their guards.⁹

As in most hellship trials, the accused in this case was a relatively low-ranking member of the military who denied any wrongdoing or personal responsibility. Thirty-year-old Petty Officer Tatsuo Yamasaka of the Imperial Japanese Navy stood accused of ill-treatment (i.e., assaults and torture) of prisoners of war "on the high seas" aboard *Sanuki Maru* during the period 10 to 28 June 1944, "causing them bodily injuries and physical and mental sufferings."¹⁰ According to evidence presented at the trial, Yamasaka regularly tightened the handcuffs of the prisoners and forced them to perform "exercises" in awkward positions, inevitably beating them when they failed to sustain these. According to the affidavit of one of the prisoners, Samuel Parker, he was many times beaten unconscious by Yamasaka who used his fists, clubs, bamboo sticks and his bayonet scabbard to hit him.¹¹

In one of Yamasaka's most egregious acts, a British merchant seaman, Captain Percy Green, was nearly hanged to death. With ropes around his neck and waist, Green was kept suspended in his cabin with his toes barely touching the floor for an hour and a half, while the defendant and others beat him. According to Green, he was only able to breathe by forcing his fingers between the rope and his throat.¹² On another occasion, two of the prisoners, Captain Maurice Symons and Lieutenant John Benge, were

Chapter 18. Sanuki Maru

suspended by their thumbs from the roof of their cabin, forced to remain on tip-toe for about five hours in rough seas.[13]

The prisoners' ordeal began on 9 March 1944 when their merchant vessel, *Behar*, was shelled and sunk by the 15,200-ton Japanese heavy cruiser *Tone* off the Cocos Islands in the Indian Ocean. The 7,840-ton *Behar* was making its way from New Zealand to Bombay when attacked. The ship, completed in Scotland in May 1943, attracted the attention of Japanese naval intelligence due to its modern equipment which included Asdic, depth-charge equipment, a rocket launcher and a range of guns. The cruiser *Tone*, commanded by Captain Haruo Mayazumi, initially signaled *Behar* to stop, but opened fire after intercepting a message from *Behar* reporting the attack. *Behar* sank twenty minutes later but not before its lifeboats were successfully launched. Captain Mayazumi picked up about 100 survivors from *Behar*. Many of the survivors were subsequently massacred, but about thirty-five survivors, presumably considered potential intelligence assets, were landed at Batavia on the island of Java.[14]

Six of the survivors were judged to be of high value for the purposes of Japanese interrogation. These prisoners included Captain James Godwin of the New Zealand Military Forces, Captain Maurice Symons (skipper of *Behar*), merchant marine captain Percy Green, *Behar*'s chief radio operator Arthur Walker, Lieutenant Samuel Parker and Lieutenant John Ross Benge. The latter two men, like Godwin, served with the Fleet Air Arm.[15] As described by John Benge, while at Batavia they underwent six weeks of interrogation. At this stage, they were reasonably treated by their interrogator, a man named "Taki."[16]

On about 25 May 1944 the prisoners were transferred to Surabaya by train and housed at a former Dutch naval base for about a month. On 10 June 1944 the men were blindfolded, handcuffed and put on *Sanuki Maru* for Osaka, Japan. The men remained handcuffed until they reached the POW camp at Ofuna, a notorious interrogation center south of Yokohama, on 29 June 1944.[17] The defendant, Yamasaka, was one of the seven men assigned to guard the POWs on *Sanuki Maru*. His testimony revealed that he entered the Sasebo Marine Corps on 30 June 1940. While at Surabaya, he was ordered on 10 June 1944 to join an escort party taking the prisoners to Ofuna. Once in Japan he was to undertake training at the Tateyama Gunnery School. The prisoners nicknamed him "The Snake."[18]

The main evidence for the prosecution was the "live" testimony given by Captain James Godwin, who at the time of the trial was attached to the Second Australian War Crimes Section. Born in New Zealand on 12 March 1923, Godwin served with the Royal New Zealand Naval Volunteer Reserve as a pilot in the Fleet Air Arm. According to Godwin's evidence, typical abuse involved requiring the prisoners to assume awkward positions for extended periods of time, and then beating them with clubs or other objects if they moved. Godwin testified that the ill-treatment of the prisoners escalated as they approached Japan.[19]

Unexpectedly, Captain Percy Green became available as a prosecution witness during the trial. Green, forty-seven years old, was born in Dover, England.[20] At the time *Behar* was attacked by the Japanese cruiser, he was returning from leave in Australia with orders to join a ship in India. He had a spotty record on identifying war crime suspects from photos that the defense tried to capitalize on. On the other hand, he was able to confirm being virtually hung to death in his cabin.[21] Beyond Godwin and Green's testimony, the prosecution relied on affidavits and statements. Statements by John Benge and Samuel Parker had already been used by the IMTFE in Tokyo.[22]

Yamasaka's defense largely focused on trying to uncover minor inconsistencies in Godwin's testimony, such as the size of the cabin where he was confined or the number of guards who were petty officers. The prosecution later concluded, with some justification, that much of the defense was based on red-herrings and irrelevant evidence.[23] To some extent, the defense also attempted to trivialize the abuse the prisoners' received. In their closing address, the defense argued that "In conclusion, a few minor disciplinary physical punishments inflicted upon the Prisoners were carried out on the orders of the Escort Commander and they were not conducted by the Accused voluntarily or on his own initiative."[24]

For the most part, Yamasaka met the allegations against him with outright denial. He denied claims that he whipped prisoners from behind with a rope, when they were taken to the latrine. In relation to the notorious incident in which Captain Green was nearly hanged to death, Yamasaka stated that Green was punished after he refused to do push-ups. He claimed that another petty officer, the senior NCO of the passengers, was the person who tied the ropes. Yamasaka further claimed that the prisoners had their handcuffs removed when required to do exercises. He categorically denied the various accusations of prisoners that he struck them with bamboo poles, bayonet scabbards and his fists.[25] He also denied forcing the prisoners to kneel on wooden gratings or to hold heavy objects for prolonged periods of time. Under cross-examination, he admitted only once beating Lieutenant Parker with his fists, after he was ordered to do so by the Escort Commander. He also admitted hitting Walker and Captain Godwin with a piece of rope.[26]

In a classic case of blaming the victim, the defense argued that "But for their speeches and manners, the Allied Prisoners of War would not have suffered from illtreatment [*sic*] and the Accused would not have become a war criminal."[27] The alleged behavior alluded to was based on a story

Chapter 18. Sanuki Maru   151

that the prisoners taunted their guards, telling them that Japan would be defeated and "disappear" by 1947.[28] According to Yamasaka's testimony, "one of the prisoners on several occasions told the escorts and the crew something like the following—Japan will soon be defeated, the country of Japan will soon disappear, if you treat us well now we will try to save you later on."[29] On this occasion Yamasaka acknowledged punishing the prisoners, but only after being ordered to by one of the ship's officers. Testimony from Captain Green indicated that the incident never happened. Given the admitted language barrier between the prisoners and their guards, it was never fully explained how the prisoners managed to communicate this idea, making such an interchange seem unlikely.[30]

Much of Yamasaka's defense stressed that he was a relatively junior officer with no authority to give orders. According to his testimony, he only became a Petty Officer Third Class in May 1944 and was one of the most junior members of the escort party. The escort commander was Petty Officer First Class Fukuda, who in turn assumed a position below *Sanuki Maru*'s captain and the senior passenger officer in the chain of command on board.[31] The counsel for the defense declared that Yamasaka "did not like to inflict any disciplinary punishment," but that he was "obliged to obey the orders of the Escort Commander." Furthermore, such disciplinary punishment was customary in the Imperial Japanese Navy.[32]

According to Yamasaka's testimony, his instructions were that the prisoners were not to have their handcuffs removed "unless absolutely necessary," and that they were not to be allowed to converse with one another. Along with his denials of wrongdoing, Yamasaka attempted to paint a picture of benevolence toward the prisoners. He claimed that on occasion he gave the prisoners cakes and cigarettes. He also testified that on his own initiative he attempted to keep the prisoners supplied with water during the voyage. At one stage, he also unconvincingly claimed that he didn't have time to beat the prisoners.[33]

As part of Yamasaka's defense, one "character-witness" was examined and one witness to "character and fact." Compared to the *Raishin Maru* trial, the defense for Yamasaka appeared to lack sophistication. After the court pronounced its verdict of guilty, Yamasaka indicated that he wished to call Captain Haruo Mayuzumi as a "character" witness.[34] There was in fact a dark irony in Yamasaka calling Mayuzumi to testify on his behalf. It will be recalled that Mayazumi had commanded the cruiser *Tone* which sank *Behar* and picked up survivors. Mayuzumi later received orders to "dispose" of most of the survivors in line with a more general Japanese directive to eliminate the crews of enemy ships. Evidence confirmed that he in fact ordered seventy of the survivors from *Behar* executed; the men were beheaded with swords and their bodies shoved off the stern of the cruiser. Mayazumi's superior, Vice-Admiral Naomasa Sakonju, was sentenced to death at Hong Kong for originally ordering the massacre in September 1947.[35]

In his testimony, Mayuzumi stated that he knew the defendant from Stanley Prison, where they occupied adjacent cells for five months. Both were navy men who specialized in gunnery. He supported Yamasaka's defense by testifying that there was a naval regulation that prisoners should remain handcuffed.[36] In terms of Yamasaka's character, Mayuzumi characterized him as a person with an "extreme feeling of sympathy." He attributed this partly to his religious feeling as a follower of the Shinshu Sect of Buddhism. He also emphasized that Yamasaka came from a farming family in one of the poorest and most backward prefectures of Japan, with little knowledge of the outside world. Mayuzumi concluded his character reference by asserting that "If a person with such an excellent spirit and soul as Yamasaka had been implicated in war crime acts I think such was because of old naval customs and many complicated circumstances that arose during the War."[37]

In its address for mitigation of Yamasaka's punishment, the defense further emphasized that he was the son of a poor farmer and poorly educated, conscripted by the Japanese Navy in 1940 when he was twenty-two years old. Not only was he naive, but his family depended on him for a livelihood. His brother died during the war, and Yamasaka subsequently married his widow.[38]

On 29 June 1948, the court sentenced Yamasaka to five years imprisonment.[39] As in the case of Uchiyama and Fukuda, sentenced for their role in the sufferings of prisoners on board *Raishin Maru*, many considered Yamasaka's punishment too lenient. Nevertheless, some of those accused of crimes in relation to hellships faced hanging. The U.S. Eighth Army War Crimes Tribunal sentenced two Japanese to execution for their role in the deaths of hundreds of prisoners on *Oryoku Maru*.[40] Despite his relatively low rank, Sergeant Major Kitaichi Jotani was sentenced to hanging for his role on board *Hofuku Maru*. In both physical appearance and behavior, he apparently conformed to the stereotype of the sadistic Japanese. One former prisoner described him as "very strongly and heavily built" with "a bullet head and a few gold teeth ... his expression was stupid and ape-like."[41] If in part a victim of racist perceptions, Jotani nevertheless distinguished himself by his level of brutality to those in his charge and a British court awarded him the ultimate penalty.

In contrast to the *Raishin Maru* trial, Allied submarines barely figured in the evidence at Yamasaka's trial. When questioned whether he had any apprehensions about Allied attacks, Godwin replied "At that stage, I think I was beyond the state of worrying."[42] As in so many cases, however, submarines would eventually sink *Sanuki Maru*. On 21 March 1943, the ship had already suffered a near-death experience when travelling north of Sorol Island in the Caroline group. At about 11 a.m., the submarine USS *Finback* commanded by John Tyree fired three torpedoes at *Sanuki Maru*. Although Tyree claimed two hits, the torpedoes inflicted only minor damage, suggesting they may have been duds.

Sanuki Maru's luck ran out after USS *Spadefish* launched a more successful attack in the Yellow Sea on 28 January 1945. *Spadefish*, along with packmate USS *Pompon*, stalked a three-ship convoy with four escorts northeast of Shanghai. While the Japanese escorts managed to pin down *Pompon*, Commander Gordon Underwood in *Spadefish* positioned for a torpedo attack on *Sanuki Maru* at about 3 a.m. Underwood claimed three torpedo hits on the ship, which sank taking down all but twenty of the 350 troops on board. In the same action, Underwood also sank a *kaibokan*, *Kume*, resulting in the loss of its 89-man crew.[43]

Chapter 19

Yoizuki Incident

Following Japan's surrender, it seemed at times that the Allies treated their enemy prisoners with a contempt not unlike that exemplified by the Japanese during the war. Some clear elements of retribution manifested themselves in addition to the formal processes of war crime trials. In Southeast Asia, the British labeled the Japanese "surrendered personnel" rather than prisoners of war, absolving themselves of responsibility for setting up special camps or following the Geneva Convention. Contrary to the Potsdam Declaration of July 1945, which specified prompt disarmament and repatriation, Japanese troops were employed suppressing nationalist opposition and put to work as laborers.[1] The construction of Paya Lebar Airport in Singapore, commenced by Allied prisoners of war, continued with the forced labor of Japanese. From 1945 to 1947, some 40,000 Japanese "surrendered personnel" remained in camps in Malaya waiting for repatriation and put to work on repairing the war-damaged island of Singapore. In a similar way, the British in Burma employed former Japanese soldiers at hard labor on low rations and in areas with high disease rates.[2] At times, the Australians specifically were criticized for failing to provide enough food for the Japanese under their supervision.[3]

The repatriation of prisoners and internees created another area of potential "pay back." With some 6,000 Japanese civilians waiting to return to Japan from Singapore, the Allies scheduled passengers to sail on the *Daian Maru* with accommodation for only 3,444 people. The Japanese drew lots to see who would board the ship, and then had to walk seventeen miles from Jurong to the harbor. The last Japanese troops did not depart from Singapore until October 1947.[4] Australia became embroiled in its own "hellship" controversy in 1946, after the Japanese destroyer *Yoizuki* embarked from Sydney with former prisoners and internees. The debate surrounding the *Yoizuki* episode highlights some of the conflicting community attitudes at play in the immediate post-war period.

Yoizuki was a relatively new destroyer of the *Akizuki*-class, launched in September 1944—the same month convoy HI-72 sailed from Singapore.

Chapter 19. Yoizuki *Incident*

Completed in January 1945, the ship exemplified Japanese efforts to counter the devastating effects of Allied aircraft and submarines. The 2,744-ton destroyer bristled with eight 100-mm guns and four 25-mm anti-aircraft guns, in addition to 6 depth-charge throwers and 72 depth charges. Although *Yoizuki* saw little action before the war ended, at one stage it sustained light damage after hitting a mine near Kure, Japan.[5] In March 1946, Australia used the "de-militarized" *Yoizuki* to repatriate Formosan and Korean prisoners and internees from Sydney. Those embarked on 6 March included a total of 1,005 people, with 564 Formosan and Korean prisoners from Cowra, 2 Formosans from Liverpool, and 439 Formosan and Koreans from the Victoria No. 4 Internment Camp at Tatura. In addition, the ship carried 180 Japanese crew.[6]

Immediately after the ship departed Sydney on the afternoon of Wednesday, 6 March 1946, controversy over the conditions on board erupted in the press and in the federal parliament. Sydney's *Sun* newspaper headlined its front-page report the same day "Women, Weeping in Fear, Forced on Jap Hell-Ship."[7] According to the report, one young Formosan man tried to commit suicide when being forced to board the overcrowded ship. Numerous photos documented the visible distress of both women and men boarding the ship against their will. A newsreel of the ship's embarkation by Cinesound Review contributed to the public furor. Alerted to the ship's scheduled departure by Army Public Relations, a cameraman filmed what was supposed to be a routine assignment.[8] Scenes screened in cinemas depicted the people boarding the ship, including "Protesting husbands, terrified womenfolk, invalids and children."[9]

Commentators liberally used the term "hellship" to describe *Yoizuki*, making it clear that "hellships" had become part of the Australian vernacular and discourse. In fact, at one stage in 1944 some critics even described the ocean liner *Lurline* as a "hellship" when used to convey Australian war brides and children to the United States.[10] From the beginning of the debate about *Yoizuki*, the experience of Australian prisoners of war and the on-going prosecution of war criminals framed the discussion. A day after the ship's departure, under the leader "A Barbarous Outrage," the *Sydney Morning Herald* asserted that "Just as the Japanese herded Allied prisoners in foetid holds, so these unhappy creatures are jammed beneath a steel deck and huddled in a reeking and ramshackle deckhouse." The same article linked the incident to the war crime trials, asserting that, "Had this been perpetrated by our enemies we should have demanded that those responsible should stand their trial as war criminals."[11]

The *Sydney Morning Herald* drew on the same themes in another article the following day, claiming, "The public conscience is peculiarly sensitive to this matter because of the horrors perpetrated against our own nationals in the late war." The newspaper further asserted, "We are in serious danger of stultifying our position in relation to the prosecution of Japanese when, without even the excuse that there is a war on, we imitate their conduct in one disgraceful respect." At times, hyperbole seemed to be the order of the day. Under the leader "Jap Hell Ship Stirs Sydney," correspondent Russell Atkinson claimed that Sydneysiders were "stirred to a measure of pity and indignation seldom equaled, it is said, in the history of this city."[12] At one stage the *Sydney Morning Herald* claimed "So terrible indeed are the conditions [on *Yoizuki*] that death may seem to many a welcome release before their grim ordeal is over."[13]

Although the most prolific newspaper critic, the *Sydney Morning Herald* was far from alone in denouncing the conditions aboard *Yoizuki*. An editorial in Melbourne's *Advocate* described the incident as an "infamous public offence against humanity" and denounced the way the passengers were "brutally herded, in slave-ship conditions, on board a vessel incapable of accommodating a fraction of them decently."[14] Melbourne's *Herald* declared, "Australian sentiment will not permit a re-creation of the hell-ship and concentration camp conditions for the extirpation of which Australians fought and died."[15] Under the leader "'Yoizuki' A Floating Obscenity," *Smith's Weekly* reported that after a week there was no sign of popular indignation subsiding. It took the government to task for its "shocking indifference" while insisting that public revulsion "was the healthiest manifestation of inherent decency in the people that has been witnessed for many a day."[16] The Australian High Commissioner in Wellington reported that similar press reports and protests reverberated in New Zealand.[17]

As outlined by Australia's Department of External Affairs in a confidential report, charges in the press included the ship's insanitary condition, rough handling of passengers by military provosts, inadequate fitting out of the ship for use as a transport, overcrowding, inadequate medical staff, inadequate provisions for women and children on board, insufficient food and stores. In addition to the inadequacy of the ship, there were concerns about placing the Formosans, recognized as Chinese nationals after the war, under authority of a Japanese captain and crew.[18] Underlying the debate over these issues were in fact myriad others ranging from Australia's international image to U.S.–Australian relations.

While at least some members of the Australian government denounced the publicity surrounding *Yoizuki* as merely a media beat-up, many criticisms of the ship appear well founded. The Australian Journalists' Association insisted on the accuracy of reports and the photographic evidence.[19] Much of the controversy focused on the inclusion of 218 women and children. According to External Affairs, the *Yoizuki* passengers included 97 Formosan women and 112 children. The same documents

Chapter 19. Yoizuki *Incident*

disclose that Colonel Herford, who supervised the loading of the vessel at Sydney, at one stage rang his superior, Brigadier Claude Prior, to state that the ship's accommodation was not suitable for women and children. Their allocated spaces were too crowded, lacked adequate lavatories and required negotiating steep steps to access.[20]

The inclusion of women and children on the ship intertwined with the issue of nationality. The Australian Army as a matter of policy refused to distinguish between Japanese, Formosans and Koreans in prisoner of war compounds and internment camps. Both the government and press often conflated those repatriated as "Japanese," although the passengers on *Yoikuzi* were either Koreans or Formosans (Taiwanese). Many of those embarking on the ship showed distress and some were forced to board against their will, believing they were to be repatriated to Japan. The atmosphere at the embarkation in Sydney reportedly calmed once a Chinese consular representative assured the passengers their destination was Formosa.[21]

Australia's Prime Minister, Ben Chifley, later insisted that only one of the prisoners was forcibly put on the ship. There remained concerns, however, about the treatment of the passengers by *Yoizuki*'s Japanese crew. As early as the evening of 4 March, the Chinese legation in Canberra expressed concerns about the safety of Formosans in the face of a possible attack by *Yoizuki*'s crew. It appears External Affairs simply relayed these concerns to the Americans without taking any further action.[22]

Adequate medical treatment for the passengers was another area of concern. Among the prisoners embarked were ten passengers described in External Affairs documents as "stretcher cases" and another 13 "walking medical cases."[23] Newspapers suggested in fact that the passengers included 32 "stretcher cases" and another six sick women.[24] The Australian government claimed that medical care was entirely the responsibility of the ship's captain and medical officer. It transpired that those embarked included three Formosan doctors, in addition to a Japanese physician on the ship, but this was unknown at the time *Yoizuki* departed Sydney.[25]

In the New South Wales state parliament, the Deputy Opposition Leader, Mr. Treatt, called on the federal government to recall "the hell-ship Yoizuki" to an Australian port.[26] The federal Labor government decided against recalling the ship, ostensibly in the absence of formal passenger complaints to the Army or Chinese representatives. They also attempted to absolve themselves of any responsibility, asserting that *Yoizuki* was entirely under the authority of the Americans who supplied the ship. In federal parliament, the Navy Minister, Norman Makin, claimed that the Commonwealth government was free of any guilt in the issue because the responsibility laid with General Douglas MacArthur as Supreme

Commander for Allied Powers (SCAP), and his headquarters in Tokyo.[27] The Australian Army for its part insisted that inspecting the ship was not part of its responsibility. In a "Top Secret" cablegram on 8 March, Australian Prime Minister Chifley apprised General MacArthur of the situation, noting that since the departure of *Yoizuki* there had been "intense public criticism and agitation," with the press referring to the ship as a "hell ship."[28]

Unfortunately for Chifley's government, MacArthur himself quickly overturned the notion that *Yoizuki* was solely the responsibility of the Americans. In a cablegram dated 11 March, MacArthur wrote to Chifley: "You have apparently been misinformed with reference to the responsibilities involved in loading the Yoizuki." He also quoted from an earlier message of 8 March, requesting that the women, children and related males be taken off at Rabaul or "closer port elected by you" for re-embarkation on *Hikawa Maru* to return via Kiirun, Formosa, to Uraga, Japan.[29] In another cablegram to the Australian prime minister the following day, stamped "Secret" and "Most Immediate," General MacArthur acknowledged receiving a proposed press release. He responded that it was clear "that the division of responsibility in the repatriation programme has not yet been fully presented to you." He emphasized that his headquarters was only to provide shipping as requested; "the responsibility for the actual loading can rest only with the local Australian Authorities."[30]

From Melbourne, Captain G.H. Nickerson, commanding officer of U.S. Army headquarters, publicly reinforced the Americans' position in a statement issued on 11 March. He stated that General Headquarters in Japan "had no responsibility for the repatriation of enemy nationals, prisoners of war or others from the Australian zone other than to furnish the vessels with a designated passenger capacity." MacArthur's command insisted that while supplying a ship for the task, the repatriation process was entirely the responsibility of the Australian Forces. Quoting from radio messages, Nickerson showed that MacArthur twice refused Australian requests to increase the passenger numbers on *Yoizuki* from 948 to 1005. Nickerson also asserted that the Australians made no mention of women and children in their communications.[31] Despite this, the Australian military increased the number above the authorized 948 passengers and included 211 Korean and Formosan women and children.[32]

Given the opposing views put forward, some commentators interpreted the incident as potentially straining Australia's relationship with the United States. Arthur Fadden, leader of the Country Party, asserted that Australians were anxious for good relations with General MacArthur to continue and would not tolerate assigning blame to him for the government's "mishandling of the whole affair."[33] Not surprisingly, Chifley acted to hose down these claims. In a statement intended for the press dated 9

March, Prime Minister Chifley asserted, "I do not propose to enter into any recriminations with the U.S. authorities as to how the present misunderstanding arose."[34] During debate in the House of Representatives days later, Chifley denied any harm to relations with the U.S., claiming that both sides agreed that the incident resulted from bungling at "lower levels."[35] Chifley was in effect following advice forwarded by General MacArthur in his 12 March cablegram, suggesting that any misunderstanding was "on a much lower level than a high Governmental plane." In MacArthur's terms, it was "inappropriate to report the issue as one invoking any clash between your Government and my own or between you and myself."[36]

Attempting to cool down concern over the *Yoizuki* affair, the prime minister formulated the idea for an investigation by "competent Australian representatives."[37] It appears what Chifley originally intended was an inspection of the ship arranged by the Australian Naval Board. He invited MacArthur to send an officer to carry out an inspection with an Australian naval officer.[38] As the plan developed, though, the government decided to dispatch a team of investigators to inspect the ship when it made port at Rabaul on the island of New Britain.

The investigators appointed were Mr. Justice Simpson of the Australian Capital Territory Supreme Court, and Brigadier F.G. Gallaghan, deputy director of the Commonwealth Investigation Branch, New South Wales. They in turn selected two men to assist in the investigation: Adrian Curlewis of the New South Wales Bar and G.P. Mahoney from the Commonwealth Crown Solicitor's Office in Sydney. Curlewis was an especially interesting choice, since he had spent years as a prisoner of the Japanese. As explained by the investigators, Curlewis "had considerable opportunity of seeing the transportation by sea of Japanese Army personnel and of prisoners of war in Japanese hands."[39] A representative of the Chinese legation in Canberra, Vice-Consul Liu Wing-ping, also accompanied the investigators, in part to serve as a translator. The Australian government invited Douglas MacArthur, as Supreme Commander Allied Powers, to send a representative as well, although time constraints made this impossible.[40]

In federal parliament, leader of the opposition Liberal party, Robert Gordon Menzies, criticized the investigation for a lack of transparency in the selection of the investigators and their terms of reference.[41] In fact, this seems borne out by the varying terms used to describe the investigation, which ranged from an "inspection committee" to a "commission." Outside of parliament, the press erupted over the government's refusal to allow newspaper correspondents to accompany the investigators or to be on hand for the inspection of *Yoizuki* at Rabaul. The government refused to allow a Qantas plane chartered by the Australian Newspaper Proprietors' Association to depart from Brisbane.[42] The *Sydney Morning Herald* denounced the move as "a censorship of the Press as effective as any exercised during the war, and rather more absolute in its operation." This was, according to the newspaper, "an abuse of authority and a violation of democratic practice."[43] The *Daily Telegraph* took a similar view, claiming, "Of all the mistakes the Government has made in this sorry affair that was the worst."[44]

As it turned out, the investigators faced their own difficulties with transportation. After departing in a Douglas aircraft, failure of the plane's radio forced them to make an emergency landing at Lae, New Guinea. Bad weather at Lae and more radio trouble further delayed the aircraft. The investigators arrived at Rabaul on the morning of 12 March. They were back in Australia by 16 March when Justice Simpson and Brigadier Galleghan flew to Canberra to brief the prime minister.[45]

The government tabled the investigators' report in federal parliament on 20 March. The report elicited a spectrum of reactions in both the media and community. At one end of the continuum, the *Argus* newspaper trivialized the investigators' findings, noting that while the ship was found to be overcrowded, it "doesn't exactly invite comparisons with the Black Hole of Calcutta." The *Argus* further claimed, "the only unhygienic conditions observed by the commission of inquiry at Rabaul were due to the filthy habits of the Formosans themselves."[46] Melbourne's *Herald*, on the other hand, claimed that "the whole basis of public protest" was the inclusion of women and children , and that the commission's findings "clearly and completely" endorsed this.[47] The president of the New South Wales RSL, K. Bolton, conceded that women and children should not have been put on *Yoizuki*.[48] In a page-one editorial, the *Sun* also saw the report as a vindication, stating that there was no need for the investigation "had the Government acted rightly at its first opportunity."[49]

Sydney's *Daily Telegraph* described the commission's report as appearing "reasonably balanced," but chafed at the government's refusal to allow press correspondents to go to Rabaul. The newspaper emphasized that the investigators found that *Yoikuzi* should have carried no more than 800 passengers, and in fact reduced the number of passengers to 653 before it departed Rabaul.[50] On 12 March, MacArthur's headquarters in Tokyo confirmed the dispatch of a hospital ship to Rabaul, which was sent to take the women and children off the destroyer.[51] At Rabaul, 350 men, women and children were removed from *Yoizuki* to the hospital ship *Hakawa Maru*. As described by Captain Nickerson, the 11,000-ton former liner was "the best passenger vessel, converted to a hospital ship, in the Japanese merchant marine."[52]

The *Sydney Morning Herald* gave the fullest newspaper coverage of the investigators' report, reprinting it in its entirety. The newspaper asserted that the report proved above all "that the removal of the women

Chapter 19. Yoizuki *Incident*

and children and the sick from filthy and crowded conditions was urgently needed in the interests of humanity." The newspaper did shift ground somewhat, but insisted *Yoizuki* was "shockingly overloaded" and "potentially a 'hell-ship' and would literally have become one had her journey not been interrupted at Rabaul."[53] According to a report in the *Sydney Morning Herald*, one of the few Australians able to access *Yoizuki* described the conditions below deck as "vile," adding "He did not think a white man could stand the surroundings for more than 24 hours."[54]

At the same time, the newspaper criticized the report for failing to assign responsibility to anyone. In fact, somewhat reminiscent of the *Raishin Maru* trial, responsibility became a key issue in the *Yoizuki* incident. According to Melbourne's *Herald*, the affair was politicized "by the foolish attempt of some Ministers to deny all responsibility and to pass the whole thing off as a press-inspired outburst of public hysteria."[55] According to the *Sydney Morning Herald*, referring to "suffering human beings confined in the dungeon-like destroyer," some of the Labor Party's own members questioned the cabinet's failure to recall the ship to an Australian port.[56]

In the Australian parliament, the opposition led by Menzies moved a censure motion against the government over the incident, although this was decisively defeated.[57] A lengthy and acrimonious debate erupted in the House of Representatives on Wednesday, 13 March, in which Menzies castigated the Minister of the Army, Frank Forde, for not recalling the ship and for claiming that the American authorities regulated the conditions. Forde insisted that the movement of prisoners of war was made "on a service level" and did not come before ministers.[58] In fact, confidential messages from the Department of Defence disclosed that the same day, 13 March, Forde called for reports on who authorized the additional passengers for transport on *Yoizuki*, as well as reports on conferences held regarding repatriation.[59]

During the debate in the House of Representatives, Arthur Calwell, the government's Minister for Information and Minister for Immigration, took the offensive. He described the whole incident as "nothing but a huge newspaper stunt." He targeted the *Sydney Morning Herald* in particular, claiming that had the Japanese invaded Australia, the newspaper would have come out the next day as the *Sydney Morning Herald Shibun*. Mocking the sincerity of the opposition's concern for the *Yoizuki* passengers, Calwell asserted that a week earlier not one of them knew where Formosa was and that the member for New England "thought it was a new kind of sheep-dip." His most scathing invective focused on opposition leader Robert Menzies, describing him as "one of the most pro–Japanese agents we have had in Australia," and as "a mongrel and cur." According to Calwell, about half of the prisoners on *Yoizuki* "were probably guilty of atrocities against Australian soldiers and nurses."[60]

There is little doubt that the opposition tried to make political capital out of the *Yoizuki* incident in what was an election year, but it is equally clear that the affair generated genuine emotions in a community still processing the legacy of war. Some found it acceptable to apply Japanese standards in repatriating former prisoners and internees from Australia. Particularly telling was the investigators' finding: "We are satisfied that by Japanese Service standards this vessel could accommodate and transport 948 … it would do so at a superior standard to that meted out by the Japanese to Allied prisoners."[61] At least some in the community found such comparisons objectionable. The president of the Methodist Church in New South Wales, the Rev. Richard Piper, reportedly stated that "The attempt to make little of the overloading with the lame excuse that this was no better or worse than what the Japanese would have done is ethically inexcusable."[62]

The debate exposed the conflicting public attitudes toward their former enemies. In an address to the Australian Women's National League in Melbourne, Colonel Kent-Hughes, a prominent member of the Victorian Liberal Party, member of the Legislative Assembly and a former prisoner of the Japanese, described the "typhoon of words" over the *Yoizuki* incident as "of relatively little importance." He added, "The passengers were actually travelling under far better conditions than anything they would experience in their homeland, either in peace or war."[63] Another former prisoner of war, Brigadier Arthur Blackburn, was quoted making a similar point: "The Japanese passengers on the ship would be travelling under conditions which would be like heaven compared with the way they habitually moved Allied prisoners during the war."[64] A number of other high-profile military men weighed in on the debate. Lieutenant-General Vernon Sturdee, Chief of the General Staff, was quoted stating that the public outcry about the *Yoizuki* being a "hell ship" was "more sentimental than sensible." Indeed, he believed the ship might have carried additional passengers. Lieutenant-General Gordon Bennett claimed that the conditions on the ship "demonstrated the difference between the Japanese standard of living and Australia's civilised level."[65]

As might be expected, some of the starkest views and emotions found expression in letters to newspaper editors. A letter writer to the Adelaide *Advertiser* who saw the newsreel of *Yoizuki*'s embarkation described the government's handling of the affair as "political suicide" and dragging Australia's name in the mud. "The injury to our prestige is deep and painful, but the Australian public, by its spontaneous burst of indignation has absolved itself from complicity and show that such an offence is alien to its nature."[66] The damage to Australia's reputation was an often-repeated refrain. Many

Chapter 19. Yoizuki *Incident*   163

letters, however, alluded to the Japanese treatment of Australians during the war as reason not to be overly concerned about the fate of those Asians repatriated. While some writers pointed to the newsreel footage of *Yoizuki*'s departure as an indictment, at least one writer suggested an alternative interpretation. "In every picture of the loading of the Japs, it was clearly shown how well they were looked after. Well dressed and well fed, they are repatriated to their homes not skinny and diseased as ours were."[67]

Numerous writers insisted the conditions on *Yoizuki* were far better than the ex-internees deserved. According to a letter signed "Justice," "The ex-internees should have been crowded into the holds of a cargo vessel which had been three parts or more filled with coal, with no sanitary arrangements, such as our boys had to endure during their passage from Singapore to Japan."[68] It is likely "Justice" was referring to *Raishin Maru*; notoriously some of the prisoners were confined in the ship's coal bunkers.[69] Another writer, apparently an ex-serviceman, criticized such attitudes. "Had they come from a member of the Gestapo or the Black Dragon Society the sentiments expressed by 'Justice' would not have been surprising. To an Australian they are disgusting." The writer concluded, "War all too often necessitates hardships for women and children, but surely no man who claims to be civilised would wish to inflict cruelties on them in times of peace."[70] But then in turn a "Lonely Mother" took this writer to task: "Has 'Ex-TX2162' forgotten the way mothers' sons were crowded in prison hell ships during the war, with no room to move or decent food to eat, that he cries out about a little overcrowding on the Yoizuki? My son lost his life through hunger and cruelty. I, for one, can't forget."[71]

At least some writers identifying themselves as former POWs strongly protested the treatment of the *Yoikuzi* passengers. One, a former chaplain captured in Malaya, recalled the irony of "how often we were pointing out to Japanese guards and Commanders how different were our methods of dealing with prisoners, and how cruel and inhuman were theirs."[72] Another former prisoner identified himself as a medical officer who had witnessed the arrival of *Singapore Maru* in Japan with hundreds of dead POWs. He asserted that the "peace criminals" responsible for *Yoizuki* "are more guilty than the Japanese" who "had the excuse of war."[73]

Many of the letter-writers were in effect debating Australia's future. Those most critical of the conditions on *Yoizuki* tended to fear for Australia's international reputation. They envisioned a nation evincing humanitarian values that contrasted those of recently defeated enemies. On the other side were those who remained focused on the treatment of Australians during the war and the issue of race. A letter-writer, who identified himself as one of the provosts who "roughly forced" passengers on *Yoizuki*, protested, "Surely people don't have to be told that, if the Japanese had dominated Australia, all Orientals would have united and rejoiced in having us as their slaves."[74] Some letter-writers took the opportunity to endorse the White Australia policy and saw those repatriated as future enemies. "They are potential enemies, even though their forces capitulated, and would not hesitate to slit our throats at the first chance."[75] Another letter writer later described the community as "cockeyed" and contrasted the uproar over "a few Japs on the Yoizuki" to the neglect of young Australians, "the very cream of our race," suffering war neurosis.[76]

The responses to the *Yoizuki* incident highlighted some of Australians' conflicting attitudes in the immediate postwar period. On the other hand, it is likely there would have been relatively little outcry had the repatriates included only Japanese males. Melbourne's *Herald* insisted that the protests were mainly about putting women and children on *Yoizuki*, separating this from more general community attitudes. "The protests which were made on behalf of women and children did not display any cheap sentimentality or maudlin sympathy in the people's general attitude towards a brutal enemy. In fact, the same press and public which protested against the treatment of women and children in the Yoizuki have been equally vocal in their protests against the inadequate sentences imposed on some of the Japanese war criminals at Darwin."[77] At this stage, there were relatively few people willing to forgive Japanese atrocities and look towards reconciliation. The main division appeared to be between those who wished to punish their former enemies with a treatment akin to what Australian POWs suffered during the war, and those who were determined that Australia should in no way emulate the behavior of their former enemies.

CHAPTER 20

Hellships in Context

Hellships should be viewed within the wider context of Japan's treatment of prisoners of war to fully appreciate their significance. As described by one writer, the "popular myth" of the Japanese during World War II is that they were "a uniquely cruel people ... an inhuman people from an inhuman culture."[1] The widespread and often systemic mistreatment of Allied prisoners of war by the Japanese is not a "myth," but explanations that attribute this to uniquely Japanese qualities are certainly misleading. At the same time, Japan's treatment of POWs involved a good deal more diversity than usually acknowledged.

Although Japan never ratified the 1929 Geneva Convention, they did ratify the Hague Convention of 1907 which included many prescriptions that were almost identical to the later Geneva Convention. This included undertakings to treat prisoners humanely and not to employ them in work related to the operations of war.[2] The Japanese flagrantly disregarded these provisions. In part this was because the Japanese lacked any sense of reciprocity given that their soldiers were instructed to fight to the death and relatively few soldiers surrendered. As one Japanese historian puts it, since their own soldiers were denied the possibility of surrender as an option, Japan viewed the "time, effort and money spent on the large number of POWs as a one-way burden."[3]

Japan had not anticipated the sudden need to handle large numbers of prisoners. An estimated 210,000 captives were taken by the Japanese within the first three months of the war alone. The Japanese military lacked the administrative and logistical support needed to deal with such large numbers. With the fall of Singapore, the Japanese Imperial Army suddenly became charged with thousands of POWs and with little idea how to manage them. A similar situation arose in the Philippines when the American and Filipino forces surrendered in greater numbers than anticipated. This situation contributed to shortages of food and facilities, including transport.[4]

This does not, of course, excuse the deliberate mistreatment of prisoners. Atrocities committed at sea were all too common. One of the earliest hellships, *Nitta Maru*, was used to transport American prisoners from Wake Island to prison camps in China. Built in 1939, the 17,830-ton ship previously served as part of the Japan Mail Steamship Company, and at one point set a trans-Pacific speed record. The ship departed Wake Island on 12 January 1942 carrying 1,222 POWs in its holds, including some of the same men who had been spared death by Admiral Kajioka after the island's capture. *Nitta Maru* arrived at Yokohama on 20 January, and then sailed on to Shanghai arriving on 23 January. Despite the relatively short duration of *Nitta Maru*'s voyage from Wake Island to Shanghai, junior Japanese officers on the ship killed five of the Americans in horrific circumstances. Three seamen and two soldiers from the U.S. Marine Corps were first beaten and then beheaded with swords. The bodies were used for bayonet practice before being dumped over the side of the ship.[5]

Not surprisingly, stories of the worst hellships are those most often told. Perhaps the most notorious of all is *Oryuko Maru*, where some American prisoners resorted to killing each other to quench their thirsts by drinking blood. One survivor of the ordeal, Major Virgil McCollum, described it as "the most horrible experience imaginable and probably unprecedented in the annals of civilization."[6] Structurally, the ship was far from the worst used to transport prisoners; built in 1937 the vessel served as a first-class passenger ship on the Tokyo–South America run before the war. Before they were forced into three of the ship's holds, the American prisoners assembled at Manila's Pier 7 were favorably impressed by the ship's appearance and anticipated a reasonably comfortable trip to Japan.[7] Yet only a day after the ship was boarded at Manila on 13 December 1944 thirty men were found suffocated in the over-crowded holds.[8]

Hokusen Maru is another notorious hellship where some prisoners reportedly killed each other due to the desperate conditions on board. Sometimes nicknamed the "Benjo Maru" or "Horror Maru," the 2,256-ton ship departed Manila on 1 October 1944 with over a thousand prisoners. The majority were American, but they also included British and Dutch POWs. Lack of water and adequate ventilation resulted in many of the prisoners going insane. As described by one witness, Forrest Knox, the ship quickly became a "madhouse" in which some prisoners were strangled or beaten to death to stop them screaming.[9] Stressed to the limits of their endurance, Knox observed that "It was not unusual to want to kill someone."[10]

Understandably, some writers claim that prisoners on hellships suffered more horribly than any other combatants in the Pacific War.[11] On the other hand, it is misleading to view the hellship experience as a constant collage of cruelty. Although one historian describes the conditions of hellships as "uniformly terrible," those conditions were not uniform even if indeed terrible.[12] As in the case of the Japanese treatment of prisoners generally, it should be recognized that even on hellships there was considerable variation. Even on the same ship, prisoners could experience a range of conditions. A draft of POWs who departed Hong Kong on 19 January 1943 sailed to Nagasaki aboard the high-speed 16,975-ton passenger liner *Tatsuta Maru*. The luxury liner, built at the Mitsubishi shipyard in 1929, had once been the pride of the NYK fleet. The journey took only three days, and some fortunate prisoners were even allocated cabins. On the other hand, many prisoners on *Tatsuta Maru* were crammed into the hold where they could only lie down in turns.[13] Prisoners' fates were influenced by the ships themselves, the numbers of prisoners carried, the length of the voyage and the personnel in charge.

Not surprisingly, the disposition of a ship's crew and guards could have a huge impact on conditions. A prisoner draft of 376 men that sailed from Hong Kong for Osaka on 15 August 1943 aboard the recently-salvaged *Manryu Maru* traveled without serious incident. One prisoner praised the Japanese officers and ship's crew as "quite good to us."[14] Prisoners commonly believed that Japanese naval personnel were more reasonable than their army counterparts. George Patterson of the Royal Artillery concluded that Japanese navy officers "always seem to be a class or two above the Army brutes we met."[15] American prisoner Jack Hawkins reached a similar conclusion, believing that "the Japanese Navy was a superior organization in every way to the Japanese Army."[16] Yet another prisoner, Samuel Grashio, believed that Japanese naval officers were more reasonable than those in the army because they tended to follow more modern Western conventions rather than centuries-old samurai traditions.[17]

On some ships, prisoners were able to negotiate with their captors for improved conditions. On the 4,600-ton *Asaki Maru*, the 750 prisoners who boarded the ship at Singapore on 19 June 1944 were initially herded into only one hold. The Allied officers in this case were able to arrange for 300 prisoners to be kept in the hold while the remaining 450 were allowed on deck.[18]

The guards on ships might on occasion feel sympathetic toward their charges in facing a shared danger of attack. When George Patterson sailed from Formosa to Japan in February 1945, he found the guards "not at all happy about the prospects on the voyage." One of the guards confided that he had lost a brother on a ship that was sunk.[19] In other cases, however, guards might vent their fear on the hapless POWs under their supervision. As described by one prisoner, what made a good guard was predictability and sticking to the rules, whereas a bad guard was likely to erupt into violence at any time.[20]

At least one prisoner, Anthony Cowling, claimed that prisoners were deliberately kept on minimum rations during sea voyages so that they remained too weak and demoralized to stage an uprising.[21] While prisoners were almost inevitably poorly fed, there is little evidence of a deliberate policy to keep them weak. At some camps, an improvement in food presaged the prisoners' transport overseas.[22] Before the *Lisbon Maru* was torpedoed on 1 October 1942 by USS *Grouper*, at least some prisoners believed their diet had improved. One prisoner, Robin Poulter, recorded that "We are a bit of a tight fit with 1800 men on board but at least the food we've had is a little better than we had in the camp."[23] The one thousand prisoners shipped from Manila to Mindanao on board *Erie Maru* in late October 1942 considered the food a great improvement on what they ate at Cabanatuan. Some POWs described their evening meals as "sheer luxury," since they included canned corned beef recovered from the Cavite Naval Yard. For some, it was their first meat since the fall of the Philippines. The more daring prisoners managed to supplement their diet further by pilfering sardines, condensed milk, pork and beans from a storeroom.[24]

Conditions on ships could be dramatically affected by weather and sea states beyond anyone's control. Three days after leaving Manila in August 1944, *Asaki Maru* ran into a typhoon. The storm lasted for three days and washed away the ship's cookhouse and rations.[25] At least some prisoners, however, welcomed rough weather as a deterrent to Allied attacks. As one prisoner caught in a typhoon explained, "This freighter rolled like crazy, but oh, man, were we happy. In a storm like this we knew we didn't have to worry about submarines or bombers. It closed down the shooting gallery."[26]

Among those prisoners who have left a record of their experiences on hellships, perhaps the dominate theme was the inadequacy of the toilet facilities. On the 3,700-ton *Amagi Maru*, for example, over a thousand prisoners were forced to share only two latrines, crude wooden structures built out over the side of the ship.[27] Many prisoner memoirs overflow with scatological descriptions as they faced an "excremental assault" similar to so many prison camps.[28] As dysentery and uncontrollable diarrhea spread on *Enoura Maru*, one American prisoner declared "we were again brought face to face with our greatest obstacle to living—filth."[29] Inadequate sanitary facilities on hellships equated to disease and death. Indeed, as the "filth" problem on *Enoura Maru* became "unmanageable" there was even talk of a prisoner mutiny.[30]

The hellship assault on prisoners' olfactory systems is a ubiquitous element of their memories. Denis Morely, a twenty-three-year-old prisoner on *Lisbon Maru*, professed that "All I can remember is the blackness of the hold and the stink and the stench."[31] On *Noto Maru* the toilet facilities consisted of only a large wooden tub in the center of the hold. Fortunately, in this case the Japanese left the hatch covers open so that there was at least some ventilation.[32]

Ironically, the lining up on deck to use toilet facilities often provided prisoners their only escape from the unbearable stench of the holds and the only opportunity to look at their surroundings. Anthony Cowling, commenting on his 1,100-mile voyage from Surabaya to Ambon in 1943, claimed that "The most enjoyable part of the entire journey was the waiting period during the line up for the latrines."[33] Occasionally the latrine boxes slung over the side of ships could even afford a bit of humor. British private John Tidey recalls, "When the sea was rough enough it hit the box and put you back on deck" which could be "quite funny in some cases."[34]

Contrary to the hellship stereotype, some ships carried only small numbers of prisoners as illustrated by the war crime trial involving *Sanuki Maru* discussed above. Some voyages could also be quite brief. The first American prisoners shipped from the Philippines in August 1942, mainly high-ranking officers, made the trip to Formosa on *Nagara Maru* in only two days.[35] Travelling short distances, however, did not guarantee safe journeys. One of the most dangerous routes for prisoners was the relatively brief voyage from Java to Sumatra. About 5,000 Allied prisoners, in addition to Asian laborers, worked on the 140-mile long Sumatra railway project until its completion the same day the Pacific war ended. Although 673 Allied prisoners died at railway construction sites, an even greater number perished while being shipped from Java to Sumatra. On the afternoon of 26 June 1944, the British submarine HMS *Truculent* torpedoed SS *Van Waerwuyck* carrying 1,190 POWs to work on the railway. Nearly 200 prisoners died. Another ship sunk making its way with laborers to Sumatra proved even more disastrous, after the British submarine HMS *Tradewind* sank *Junyo Maru* just off the west coast of Sumatra on 18 September 1944. The ship carried 2,300 Allied prisoners as well as 4,200 Javanese laborers. The Javanese laborers paid a particularly high price, apparently because most were unable to swim and went down with the ship.[36]

Just as conditions on hellships tended to deteriorate the longer the war continued, so too did the likelihood of being attacked by Allied submarines. During 1942 two hellships, *Montevideo Maru* and *Lisbon Maru*, were sunk by Allied submarines. From 1943 Allied attacks on Japanese transports stepped up considerably, with attacks on those carrying prisoners of war reaching a peak in late 1944. During the eight months between November 1943 and June 1944, the Japanese suffered shipping losses equal to the previous two years. In September 1944 alone, the Allies sank 122 Japanese ships, an unprecedented monthly total that would never be surpassed during the remainder of the war.[37]

The proportion of deaths on Japanese transports that resulted from

Allied attacks is significant given that the death rate of Allied prisoners is often cited as evidence of Japan's barbarity. A frequently cited statistic of the Second World War is that a relatively small 4 percent of Allied prisoners under the Germans and Italians died in captivity, compared to 27 percent of those captured by the Japanese.[38] This differential death rate, however, cannot simply be attributed to the innate cruelty of the Japanese. "Friendly fire," especially the sinking of transports, inflated the death rates of Allied POWs under the Japanese. There were also huge differences in death rates between POW camps. Anthony Cowling claimed that the prisoner death rate on Haruku, a small island in the Moluccas archipelago, was nearly seventy percent. On the other hand, on the island of Amahai during the same period only four out of one thousand prisoners died; all four were executed for trying to escape.[39]

The Japanese government was not oblivious to the ill health and deaths of significant numbers of prisoners on transport ships; from one point of view this represented a loss of potential slave labor. On 10 December 1942, the Ministry of War issued an order acknowledging that "quite a few of them [prisoners] have been incapacitated for further work due to their treatment on the journey, which at times was inadequate." In another order issued in early 1944, the Ministry stated "the average prisoner of war's health is hardly satisfactory. Their high death rate must be brought to your attention." In this case, the order noted not only the loss of potential labor but pointed out that "if the present conditions continue to exist, it will be impossible for us to expect world opinion to be what we would wish for."[40]

The Japanese tended to blame the prisoners' lack of food and medicines on the Americans' submarine and air blockade.[41] There was some truth to this. The same month of the attack on convoy HI-72, September 1944, the future course of the war was being plotted in Quebec, Canada, at the Octagon conference. President Franklin Roosevelt and the British prime minister Winston Churchill agreed to a strategy of strangling Japan through a combination of naval blockade and aerial bombing.[42] The success of American submarines and bombers certainly contributed to prisoners' lack of food.[43] The cutting of Japan's supply lines could also contribute at least indirectly to maritime disasters. The Australian prisoners loaded on *Montevideo Maru* were being shipped to Hainan Island to alleviate Rabaul's food shortages when the ship was sunk by USS *Sturgeon* in 1942.[44]

On the other hand, shortages of food often resulted from Japanese corruption or sheer incompetence. One of the most significant differences between the survival rates of Allied prisoners held by Germany and those under the Japanese was the provision of Red Cross supplies. Allied prisoners held by the Germans were generally issued inadequate rations but were often kept alive by Red Cross parcels.[45] Whereas prisoners in Europe were

Chapter 20. Hellships in Context 171

likely to receive a Red Cross parcel every week, prisoners of the Japanese were lucky to share a parcel once a year.[46] One American prisoner in the Philippines, Samuel Grashio, described a distribution of Red Cross packages as "the best thing that ever happened to me in captivity."[47] Apart from the invaluable contents, the parcels were a reminder that the prisoners had not been forgotten by the outside world. Typically, however, the Japanese confiscated much of the contents or failed to distribute the packages at all.

The Japanese army discouraged any Red Cross interference with their treatment of prisoners of war in Southeast Asia, in some cases killing or torturing Red Cross delegates.[48] Not only did the Japanese reluctantly accept Red Cross materials, they even more reluctantly distributed them to prisoners. As noted above, at many POW camps Red Cross parcels were either pilfered by the Japanese or hoarded as a hedge against starvation in the belief that the war would continue indefinitely. Thomas Hewlett, a medical officer at Fukuoka Camp No. 17, was incensed when soon after liberation they "found several warehouses packed with Red Cross food and medical supplies."[49] These materials apparently reached Japan before August 1943 yet remained stored while prisoners died.

Even as the *Oryuko Maru* sank off the island of Luzon in December 1944, one of the American prisoners on board discovered that the civilian passenger galley of the ship was full of Red Cross supplies. "American Red Cross food was all over the floor—corned beef, Spam, luncheon meat, butter, milk, cheese, sugar—food that would have saved countless American lives, food misappropriated by thieving, selfish Japanese."[50] Only after the Japanese surrendered were they persuaded to release twenty tons of undistributed Red Cross parcels to Allied POWs in Singapore.[51]

In the case of Red Cross supplies, submarines may have unwittingly contributed in part to prisoners' deprivation. At least one historian suggests that the sinking of the Japanese relief ship *Awa Maru* on 1 April 1945 added to the Japanese reluctance to distribute Red Cross parcels.[52] After much negotiation, *Awa Maru* was granted safe passage by the Allies to deliver Red Cross supplies to prisoners of war. In preparation for the mission, the ship's hull and superstructure were painted green with large white crosses, while additional lights were installed for sailing at night. Despite these precautions, the same USS *Queenfish* that helped rescue survivors of *Rakuyo Maru* torpedoed and sank *Awa Maru*. The *Queenfish* crew had missed messages about the ship's passage, while at the time of the attack a dense fog obscured *Awa Maru*'s lights and markings. *Queenfish*'s skipper, Charles Loughlin, was convinced he had sunk a destroyer until they recovered a survivor who confirmed the ship's identity. Loughlin was subsequently court-martialed, and his actions apparently contributed to Japan's rejection of any further Red Cross supplies.[53]

Indirectly, the deaths of prisoners on Japanese transports were symptomatic of Japan's negligence in providing adequate protection for its merchant fleet. Despite Japan's participation in convoy activities during the First World War, including acting as escorts for the Australian Imperial Expeditionary Force in the Indian Ocean, such lessons appeared forgotten by the Second World War.[54] It was not until August 1943 that the Japanese High Command determined that all cargo vessels should be escorted, and it was only in November 1943 that they adopted a general convoy system. The navy's obsession with fighting a decisive battle at sea with the Allies and the low status accorded escort duties left Japanese shipping highly vulnerable.[55]

Nevertheless, overall the single most important factor affecting the survival rate of prisoners on Japanese transports was whether Allied submarines or aircraft attacked them.[56] Allied submarines contributed to POW deaths not only by direct attacks. The mere threat of attack often lengthened voyages and thus added to the misery of prisoners. The longer the war lasted, the more circuitous shipping routes became. Voyages were prolonged not only by hugging the coasts, but often by the practice of anchoring overnight in protected harbors, bays and inlets. Fear of submarines contributed to the often-extended layovers of prisoner transports while they awaited convoys and adequate escorts. These extended periods in port in turn resulted in some of the highest death rates on hellships. Indeed, outbreaks of dysentery appeared to be the inevitable concomitant of delayed departures and long layovers with prisoners crammed into overcrowded holds.[57]

Epilogue

In Singapore, the formal Japanese surrender ceremony took place on 12 September 1945, exactly one year after the submarine attack on convoy HI-72 and the sinking of *Rakuyo Maru*. As emphasized in the above pages, the threat of Allied submarine attacks on Japanese ships created enormous fear and torment for many prisoners of war. The sinking of Japanese transports carrying POWs also left a legacy of suffering for the families and loved ones of those lost at sea. The names of some of those who died are included among the 24,000 inscribed on the Singapore Memorial at Kranji Hill.[1]

One of the most extraordinary stories of the dead would only come to light long after the war. Among those who perished with *Rakuyo Maru* was a Wallabies International rugby union player, Winston Philip James Ide. Taken prisoner after the fall of Singapore, Ide survived the Thai-Burma railway before being drafted to sail to Japan. According to various accounts, Ide heroically assisted the injured after *Rakuyo Maru* sank. Ironically, Ide's father, a Japanese silk merchant, was interned in Australia at the time. Despite having lived in Australia since 1894, being a naturalized British subject, married to a British woman, and with two sons in the AIF, Hideichiroo "Henry" Ide spent most of the war in captivity. Perhaps in deference to his son's death, he was released later the same year.[2]

Those who died with no established place of death, let alone a permanent resting place, left many relatives deeply uncertain about the fates of sons, husbands and brothers. Relatives pressed their respective governments for information about men reported missing, and those governments in turn pressed the Japanese for more information, initially through the International Red Cross and later directly.[3]

The uncertainty continued after the war ended. Had some prisoners survived at sea and washed up on remote islands? As late as April 1946, authorities in Washington, D.C., assured the British War Office "that the whole of the Philippines Area has been thoroughly searched and that although there is little likelihood of further prisoners of war being reported, the search is still being continued."[4]

According to a report in February 1948, the mother of Stanley Raft, one of the Australians missing with the loss of *Rakuyo Maru*, appealed to the Australasian Women's Club in Philadelphia to search for her son in the United States. Mrs. Raft believed he had somehow survived and might be suffering from amnesia.[5] Months later, one of Mrs. Raft's children wrote to the Australian army on her behalf seeking information. After speaking to some of the survivors including Rowley Richards, Mrs. Raft believed that her son was in one of the lifeboats that disappeared. "I emplore [sic] you to trace this Japanese Officer and find out what he did with the other boys, for my Mother's sake, who has never stopped for one day worrying knowing he may be some place waiting for help. The Japanese Officer could have left them on an island."[6]

At least into the 1950s, on the anniversary of *Rakuyo Maru*'s loss, relatives continued to express their palpable grief in newspaper columns usually headed "Heroes of the Empire" or "Roll of Honour." Many of these tributes referred to lives "lost" or "drowned," but at least some relatives still seemed reluctant to concede their loved ones were dead, preferring the phrase "reported missing."[7]

The survivors of *Rakuyo Maru* faced their own demons. Toward the end of his life, Dave Herbert wrote, "There's not a day goes by that I don't remember something about the war."[8] In a letter authored in 1988, John "Jack" Flynn professed that things were still coming back to him 42 years after the loss of *Rakuyo Maru*. He concluded, "I can't forget and I will never forgive."[9]

As historians Lachlan Grant and Christina Twomey point out, the embittered ex-prisoner who fostered anti–Japanese sentiment for decades is a common stereotype. Nevertheless, there was more diversity of opinion toward the Japanese than one might suspect.[10] Especially among those who worked alongside Japanese civilians, they frequently drew a distinction between the "ordinary" Japanese and the Japanese military.[11] While some portrayed the camp commanders and guards as sadistic monsters, their hatred did not flow over to the Japanese in general.[12] Frank McGovern considered that apart from his guards, he held no general animosity toward the Japanese people. Those he had worked with in factories were "all right."[13] Ray Parkin put the case more forcefully: "The fact that we were taken to Japan … lived the last twelve months with the ordinary village people of Japan and they were wonderful. They were sympathetic people. They were good people and had nothing to do with the rest of it … it's the bastards up top that do all the damage."[14]

As already noted, many POWs expressed surprise at how quickly their thirst for vengeance diminished once the Japanese surrendered. Even as Australian prisoners sailed home from Japan on British ships at the end of the war, they impressed crews by the apparent lack of hostility toward the Japanese. Rohan Rivett concluded that "the thing that surprised us most was the entire absence of any desire for revenge or for the humiliation of the wretches from whom we had suffered so much."[15] Stan Arneil commented on the same phenomenon in relation to the Korean guards as well as the Japanese. According to Arneil, "For us they no longer existed, we didn't even want to think of them again, we wanted to resume the business of living as free men."[16] Hugh Clarke expressed similar sentiments, but with an important caveat. "The hatred of the Japanese which had sustained me ... seemed to ebb away, but I didn't want to see another Nip as long as I lived."[17] Even so, he would return to Japan with his wife in August 1983 to visit the sites of his former incarceration.

Other ex-prisoners returned to Japan decades later in the spirit of reconciliation. Rowley Richards vowed that while he might never forgive the individual Japanese who made his life a misery in captivity, he would abstain from blanket prejudice. He returned to Sakata in 1959 to visit the Japanese "friends" who helped him through the horrible winter of 1944–45.[18] Most former prisoners who returned to Japan waited considerably longer. Stan Arneil credited a Marist priest, Samuel Marsden, with convincing him that he should not condemn all Japanese for the treatment he received as a prisoner. He became a secretary of the Japanese Mission League, supporting Catholic missionary activity in Japan.[19] Arneil later visited Thailand with his wife in 1970.[20] In 2002, Neil MacPherson and Owen Heron visited Japan with their sons. In 2004, another party of six Australians returned to Japan and visited the sites of their camps, aided by the POW Research Network of Japan.[21] For some former prisoners, coming to terms with their past involved pilgrimages to the sites of past suffering.

According to some Australian historians there was a palpable shift in popular attitudes toward former prisoners of war by the 1980s. POWs increasingly were integrated into the national narrative of sacrifice in war. It seems prisoners themselves underwent a similar metamorphosis about their own past. Historian E. Bartlett Kerr, writing in 1985, suggested that by this stage the reticence of ex-prisoners was changing into a type of "nostalgia." Most were more willing to talk about their experiences and some of those with the time and money began making pilgrimages to the sites of former camps.[22] Despite vows never to return to Singapore, former British prisoner Jack Morris visited the city-state in January 1984 for the first time since his captivity. During the war his Japanese transport ship was torpedoed off Formosa and he was left drifting in the South China Sea clinging to a plank with a Japanese naval officer. Forty years later, aged 68, he was willing to confront that past.[23]

In 1985, Keith Flanagan, a member of Dunlop Force on the Thai-

Burma railway, organized a trip to Java, Singapore and Thailand. The party included Weary Dunlop and a couple of journalists. This was the first "Quiet Lion Tour" to Thailand, which became an annual pilgrimage and a tribute to Weary Dunlop.[24]

In 1987, Arthur Bancroft and his wife Mirla travelled to Singapore, Bangkok and sites on the Thai-Burma railway. Bancroft made another pilgrimage in 1998 to commemorate Anzac Day. As historian Bruce Scates observes, when ex–prisoners of war return to the places of their incarceration or forced labor they rarely go on their own. Family and other former POWs are likely to accompany them.[25] This time, Arthur's two daughters and son accompanied him as well as Mirla. At one stage, when they visited the railway terminus at Ban Pong, Bancroft posed for a photo wielding a pick.[26] On this trip, the Prime Minister, John Howard, presided over the Anzac Day service and opened the Hellfire Pass Museum, financed by the Australian government. Rowley Richards, then aged 82, was another to attend the service.[27] That year the Quiet Lion Tour included 75 participants, nine of them ex-prisoners who had worked on the railway, including Bancroft. The same year, 1998, the Burma Thailand Railway Memorial Association (BTRMA) formed to perpetuate the memory of those who worked and suffered on the railway. They aspired to acknowledge the dedication of Australian medical personnel, and to educate future generations.[28] Rowley Richards made his last trip to Burma and Thailand in 2003.[29]

In another form of commemoration, in 1979 the publication of Joan and Clay Blair's book *Return from the River Kwai* helped to raise public awareness of the *Rakuyo Maru* episode. Ray Wheeler, among those interviewed for the book, considered it "a pretty accurate account, but it's been embellished a little bit beyond what it should be."[30] There were high expectations for a feature film based on the book, potentially bringing the *Rakuyo Maru* story to a much larger audience. Eventually, in 1989, a British film of the same name appeared, directed by Andrew McLaglen and starring Edward Fox.

Arguably, one reason the story of USS *Indianapolis* remains so well-known is its association with the blockbuster movie *Jaws* (1975). In a central scene of the film, the character Quint (played by Robert Shaw) describes at length the ensuing disaster after a "Japanese submarine slammed two torpedoes into our side." Not only was the *Indianapolis* speech one of the reasons that Shaw accepted the role of Quint, but it is reportedly director Steven Spielberg's favorite scene in the film. According to some writers, Quint's historical references even suggest that the shark in *Jaws* represents the Japanese enemy during the Second World War.[31]

By contrast, any expectations that the film *Return from the River Kwai* might reach a large public soon evaporated. Due to disputes over the title in relation to the 1957 classic movie *The Bridge on the River Kwai*, the film never saw release in the United States. Some might argue this was a small loss. Audiences who expected a sequel to *The Bridge on the River Kwai* were sadly disappointed, while those familiar with the story of *Rakuyo Maru* must have been mystified. Among the film's incongruities, the prisoners are dressed in full uniforms, as opposed to merely shorts or loin cloths in line with the reality in camps on the Thai-Burma railway.

Rather than embarking from Singapore on *Rakuyo Maru*, the filmic prisoners depart from Saigon on *Brazil Maru*. Unlike any documented voyage during the war, the prisoners in the film manage to seize control of the Japanese ship. There were hellship voyages when prisoners at least considered the possibility of mutiny, but there is no evidence of this ever moving beyond the planning stage. Although the prisoners frequently outnumbered the Japanese on board ships, the latter had weapons. Even if the POWs managed to overpower their guards, the ship was likely to get a radio message off before they were subdued.[32] Apart from anything else, racial differences in the Far East rendered the possibility of genuine escape by Western prisoners remote. The only resemblance to the *Rakuyo Maru* incident in the film comes when an American submarine torpedoes the ship. In real life, *Brazil Maru* carried prisoners of war, but submarines never attacked them; the ship's career ended in May 1945 after it hit a mine in the Sea of Japan.[33]

Arthur Bancroft and his fellow survivors in Australia were disappointed after watching the film. Bancroft felt "they spoilt it by bringing fictional stuff into it ... and we thought, well they didn't have to because there was a story there on its own." According to Bancroft, the characters were "half rubbish but to sell the film."[34] Indeed, former prisoners generally were often unimpressed by attempts to represent their experience. Rowley Richards later described the Australian television show *Changi* as "absolutely appalling."[35]

In 1994, the Royal Australian Navy organized a more direct tribute to the victims of *Rakuyo Maru*, inviting the fifty-two survivors still alive to participate in a commemoration service aboard HMAS *Sydney*.[36] A decade later in 2004, another commemoration ceremony took place at Brisbane's Newstead Wharf, where the Australian survivors had returned to their homeland sixty years earlier. The following year, the documentary film *Road to Tokyo* screened in Australia on the ABC in August to commemorate the sixtieth anniversary of the Pacific war's end. Significantly, the film began with footage of the oil-covered and emaciated survivors from *Rakuyo Maru* being pulled from the sea onto an American submarine.[37] The film's writer and director, Graham Shirley, described the rescue as a "key event" of the Pacific war.[38] A press kit for the film went even further, describing the episode as "one of the most dramatic and moving moments in Australia's history."[39] It was at least true that before the recovery of these prisoners, Australians had little idea of the full horror experienced by POWs in Japanese captivity.

For the survivors, dealing with the trauma of the sinking often remained a lifelong ordeal. Many of the survivors continued to experience involuntary commemorations of the events. The wife of one survivor at the 2004 Brisbane ceremony said her husband "still lies awake at night thinking about his experience as a POW."[40] Ray Wheeler, interviewed in 2005, professed that he still relived in nightmares the three days he spent floating in the water after *Rakuyo Maru* sank, seeing the faces of many men who drowned.[41] Roy Cornford believed he still suffered from "nerves" because of his wartime experience.[42]

Many of the men continued to seek solace in each other's company. In Western Australia, Arthur Bancroft did much to keep the bonds of comradeship alive between the men who served on HMAS *Perth*. As early as 1947, he contributed to the "In Memoriam" columns of the *West Australian* newspaper on the anniversary of HMAS *Perth*'s loss. His tribute read: "In Memory of those who lost their lives on H.M.A.S. Perth, March 1, 1942, and later whilst P.O.W. in Japanese hands."[43] Signing the piece as "Blood Bancroft," he also included the lines:

> Happy days we once enjoyed
> When we were all together,
> Happy thoughts of you all
> Will stay with me forever.

At the time of a 2003 interview, Bancroft continued to attend an annual Christmas lunch at Hillary's Boat Harbor for the eight remaining survivors living in Western Australia, as well as their wives and the widows of others. Although at the time there were about forty HMAS *Perth* survivors throughout Australia, Bancroft considered the eight in WA as the most close-knit group. A reunion at the end of February each year commemorated *Perth*'s loss, as well as an annual church service at St John's Church in Fremantle. Perth's mayor hosted an annual dinner for the men, while Bancroft regularly lunched with other survivors at Anzac House. Moving around the state as a bank manager for many years, he served as president of the Returned and Services League of Australia (RSL) in Northam, treasurer of the RSL in Albany and secretary of the RSL in the wheat-belt town of Wongan Hills.[44] Bancroft continued to contribute to the Anzac spirit; he gave talks at local schools and always marched in the Anzac Day parade.

Despite the high mortality rate for many returned prisoners of war, some *Rakuyo Maru* survivors led long lives. Russell Savage, discharged from the army on his birthday, 29 November 1945, died in Brisbane on 18 November 2009, just shy of turning eighty-nine.[45] Arthur Bancroft died on 28 July 2013 at the age of 91. In its obituary, the *Sydney Morning Herald* described him as "A great Australian."[46] Rowley Richards, described by one journalist as "good a man as this country has produced," died aged 98 on 26 February 2015.[47] At the seventy-fifth anniversary of the loss of HMAS *Perth* in 2017, *Rakuyo Maru* survivor Frank McGovern was 98 years old.[48]

Chapter Notes

Abbreviations

AWFA Australians at War Film Archive
AWM Australian War Memorial, Canberra
IWM Imperial War Museum, London
NAA National Archives of Australia, Canberra and Melbourne
NARA National Archives and Records Administration, College Park, Maryland
NIDS National Institute of Defense Studies, Tokyo
SFMNPA San Francisco Maritime National Park Association
SM Submarine Memorabilia
NAS National Archives of Singapore
WMMLA Wisconsin Maritime Museum Library and Archives

Introduction

1. *Daily Post*, undated clipping, Casualties at Sea, War Office 361/733, National Archives of Singapore (hereafter cited as NAS).

2. Doug Stanton, *In Harm's Way* (New York: St. Martin's Paperbacks, 2002), pp. 7, 236; Richard F. Newcomb, *Abandon Ship! The Saga of the U.S.S. Indianapolis, the Navy's Greatest Sea Disaster* (1958; reprint ed., New York: Harper Collins, 2001), pp. xiii, 135–136.

3. Joan Blair and Clay Blair, *Return from the River Kwai* (London: Macdonald General Books, 1979). Parts of the story are also told by Don Wall, *Heroes at Sea* (Mona Vale, NSW: self-published, 1991); Gregory F. Michno, *USS Pampanito: Angel Killer* (Norman, OK.: University of Oklahoma Press, 2000); Gregory F. Michno, *Death on the Hellships: Prisoners at Sea in the Pacific War* (Annapolis: Naval Institute Press, 2001); Aldona Sendzikas, *Lucky 73: USS Pampanito's Unlikely Rescue of Allied POWs in WWII* (Gainesville: University of Florida Press, 2010).

4. Michael McKernan, "Afterword," in Peter J. Dean (ed.), *Australia 1944–45: Victory in the Pacific* (Melbourne: Cambridge University Press, 2016), p. 342.

5. Quoted in Lord Russell, *The Knights of Bushido: A Short History of Japanese War Crimes* (London: Cassell and Company, 1958), pp. 60–61.

6. George Patterson, *A Spoonful of Rice with Salt* (Edinburgh: The Pentland Press, 1993), p. 49.

7. Quoted in Raymond Lamont-Brown, *Ships from Hell: Japanese War Crimes on the High Seas* (Thrupp-Stroud-Gloucestershire: Sutton Publishing, 2002), p. 38.

Chapter 1

1. Andrew Herring, "Farewell Tribute to Arthur Bancroft: A Legend and Inspiration," *Navy Daily*, 4 August 2013; Mike Carlton, *Cruiser: The Life and Loss of HMAS Perth and her Crew* (Sydney: William Heinemann, 2010), p. 354; Rowan Strong, *Chaplains in the Royal Australian Navy:*

1912 to the Vietnam War (Sydney: University of New South Wales Press, 2012), pp. 150, 166–67.

2. Arthur Bancroft (RAN) Reports, series B3856, control symbol 144/1/128 Attachment 9, Melbourne, National Archives of Australia (henceforth cited as NAA).

3. Statement by Abel Seaman Arthur Bancroft, series B6121, control symbol 20S, Melbourne, NAA; Bancroft quoted in Patsy Adam-Smith, *Prisoners of War: From Gallipoli to Korea* (1992; Reprint ed., Melbourne: Penguin, 1997), pp. 339–40.

4. Adam-Smith, *Prisoners of War*, pp. 340–41.

5. Arthur Bancroft with John Harman, *Arthur's War* (Melbourne: Viking, 2010), p. 115.

6. Rohan D. Rivett, *Behind Bamboo* (1946; Ringwood: Penguin Books, 1991), p. 90.

7. Frank McGovern Interview, 8 May 2003, Archive 19, Australians at War Film Archive (henceforth cited as AWFA); A report on war crimes by individual members of the armed forces of the enemy against Australians by Sir William Webb (henceforth cited as Second Webb Report), series A10950, control symbol 1, p. 7, Canberra, NAA; Linda Goetz Holmes, *Four Thousand Bowls of Rice* (Sydney: Allen and Unwin, 1993), p. 22; *Advertiser* (Adelaide), 19 September 1945, p. 6; James D. Hornfischer, *Ship of Ghosts: The Story of the USS Houston, FDR's Legendary Lost Cruiser, and the Epic Saga of Her Survivors* (New York: Bantam Books, 2006), pp. 224–25; *Kenkon Maru*, Combined Fleet, http://www.combinedfleet.com/Kenkon_t.htm (Accessed 20 February 2018); Tony Carter and Neil MacPherson, *The Burma Railway, Hellships and Coalmines* (Laurieton, NSW: Parker Pattison, 2008), p. 41.

8. Kathryn Spurling, *Cruel Conflict: The Triumph and Tragedy of HMAS Perth* (Sydney: New Holland, 2008), p. 224; Lamont-Brown, *Ships from Hell*, pp. 51–52.

9. Holmes, *Four Thousand Bowls of Rice*, p. 22; Michno, *Death on the Hellships*, p. 64; *Advertiser* (Adelaide), 19 September 1945, p. 6; *Maebashi Maru*, Combined Fleet, http://www.combinedfleet.com/Maebashi_t.htm (Accessed 21 February 2018); Carter and MacPherson, *The Burma Railway*, p. 42.

10. A. J. Sweeting, "Prisoners of the Japanese," in Lionel Wigmore, *The Japanese Thrust* (1957; reprint ed. Canberra: Australian War Memorial, 1968) p. 519; Edward Kelk, Affidavit, 24 February 1948, Record Group 331, entry UD1189, box 990, College Park, Maryland, National Archives and Records Administration (henceforth cited as NARA); Second Webb Report, pp. 8, 28, series A10950, control symbol 1, Canberra, NAA. The ship is also sometimes referred to as *Toyahashi Maru*. Even before the fall of Singapore, Australians used the term "hellship" to describe the German tanker *Altmark* that carried POWs. See for example *Advertiser* (Adelaide), 20 February 1940, p. 11.

11. Bancroft (RAN) Reports, series B3856, control symbol 144/1/128 Attachment 9, Melbourne, NAA.

12. Rivett, *Behind Bamboo*, p. 242; Leslie Hall, *The Blue Haze: POWs on the Burma Railway* (Sydney: Kangaroo Press, 1996) p. 179.

13. British and Australian POWs repatriated from the Far East, Secret Minute, 13 January 1945, WO 208/521, NAS; Cameron Forbes, *Hellfire: The Story of Australia, Japan and the Prisoners of War* (Sydney: Pan Macmillan, 2005), p. 366; Clifford Kinvig, *River Kwai Railway: The Story of the Burma-Siam Railway* (1992, reprint ed. London: Conway, 2005), p. 155; Hall, *The Blue Haze*, pp. 178–79.

14. Spurling, *Cruel Conflict*, p. 261.

15. Gavan Daws, *Prisoners of the Japanese: POWs of World War II in the Pacific* (New York: William Morrow and Company, 1994), pp. 18–19, 184.

16. Hall, *The Blue Haze*, p. 281.

17. Spurling, *Cruel Conflict*, p. 267.

18. Lachlan Grant, *Australian Soldiers in Asia-Pacific in World War II* (Sydney: New South, 2014), p. 11; Michno, *Death on the Hellships*, pp. 17, 117; Van Waterford, *Prisoners of the Japanese in World War II: Statistical History, Personal Narratives and Memorials concerning POWs in Camps and on Hellships, Civilian Internees, Asian Slave Labourers and Others Captured in the Pacific Theater* (Jefferson, NC: McFarland, 1994), p. 172; Kyoichi Tachikawa, "The Treatment of Prisoners of War by the Imperial Japanese Army and Navy focusing on the Pacific War," *NIDS Security Reports*, no. 9 (2008), pp. 50, 82; Paul H. Kratoska (ed.),

The Thailand-Burma Railway, 1942–1946: Documents and Selected Writings (London: Routledge, 2006), vol. 1, pp. 3, 13.

19. Carter and Macpherson, *The Burma Railway*, p. 102.

20. Russell J. Savage, *A Guest of the Emperor* (Moorooka, Qld.: Boolarong Press, 1995), p. 44. On Savage's background see *Daily News* (Warwick, Qld.), 17 April 2010, p. 86; *Courier Mail* (Brisbane), 4 February 2010, p. 67.

21. Hall, *The Blue Haze*, p. 132.

22. Rivett, *Behind Bamboo*, p. 254.

23. Arthur Bancroft Interview, 20 November 2003, Archive 1082, AWFA.

24. *Sun* (Sydney), 14 June 1945, p. 4.

25. Bancroft Interview, AWFA; Sweeting, "Prisoners of the Japanese," p. 589; Blair and Blair, *Return from the River Kwai*, p. 36.

26. Akira Hara, "Japan: Guns before Rice," in Mark Harrison (ed.), *The Economics of World War II: Six Great Powers in International Comparison* (Cambridge: Cambridge University Press, 1998), pp. 244–45; Malcolm H. Murfett et al., *Between Two Oceans: A Military History of Singapore from First Settlement to Final British Withdrawal* (New York: Oxford University Press, 1999), p. 256; Greg Huff and Shinobu Majima (ed. and trans.), *World War II Singapore: The Chosabu Reports on Syonan* (Singapore: National University of Singapore Press, 2018), pp. 3–6, 9.

27. H. Sidhu, *The Bamboo Fortress: True Singapore War Stories* (Singapore: Native Publications, 1991), pp. 103, 105; Mamoru Shinozaki, *Syonan My Story: The Japanese Occupation of Singapore* (1975; Singapore: Marshall Cavendish Editions, 2011), pp. 116–119; Paul H. Kratoska, *The Japanese Occupation of Malaya and Singapore, 1942–45: A Social and Economic History* 2nd ed. (Singapore: National University of Singapore Press, 2018), p. 181.

28. Bancroft Interview, AWFA. Other prisoners insist the island was given the same nickname after a brutal Korean guard known as "The Jeep." See for example Carter and Macpherson, *The Burma Railway*, p. 115.

29. Kitchener Loughnan, Affidavit, Record Group 331, entry UD1189, box 990, NARA.

30. Hall, *The Blue Haze*, p. 293.

31. See Daws, *Prisoners of the Japanese*, p. 105.

32. Charles Richards Interview, 4 April 2002, Archive 1144, AWFA; Carter and Macpherson, *The Burma Railway*, p. 66; Michael Caulfield (ed.), *War behind the Wire: Australian Prisoners of War* (Sydney: Hachette Australia, 2008), p. 73; Sandy Macleod, "Psychiatry on the Burma-Thai Railway (1942–1943): Dr. Rowley Richards and Colleagues," *Australasian Psychiatry*, vol. 18, no. 6, 2010, p. 491.

33. Bancroft (RAN) Reports, series B3856, control symbol 144/1/128 Attachment 9, Melbourne, NAA.

34. Hall, *The Blue Haze*, pp. 152, 292–93.

35. Les Cody, *Ghosts in Khaki: The History of the 2/4th Machine Gun Battalion* (Carlisle, WA: Hesperian Press, 1997), p. 309; Michno, *Death on the Hellships*, pp. 171–72, 174; Stan Arneil, *One Man's War* (Sydney: Alternative Publishing Co-operative, 1980), p. 183.

36. Michael Sturma, *Surface and Destroy: The Submarine Gun War in the Pacific* (Annapolis: Naval Institute Press, 2011), pp. 180–81.

37. Arthur Bancroft Interview, 8 October 1990, S04052, Australian War Memorial (henceforth cited as AWM); Bancroft, *Arthur's War*, pp. 127, 217, 227, 287; Bancroft Interview, AWFA; Forbes, *Hellfire*, p. 387; Rowley Richards and Marcia McEwan, *The Survival Factor* (Sydney: Kangaroo Press, 1989), p. 225.

38. W.S. Kent Hughes, *Slaves of the Samurai* (Melbourne: Oxford University Press, 1946), p. 114.

39. David Clark Herbert, "Dave's Way: A POW Memoir," p. 70, MSS 2280, AWM.

40. Arthur Hall, Affidavit, 19 March 1948, Record Group 331, entry EUD1189, box 990, NARA.

41. Second Webb Report, p. 19, series A10950, control symbol 1, Canberra, NAA.

42. Jonathan F. Vance (ed.), *Encyclopedia of Prisoners of War and Internment* (Santa Barbara, CA: ABC-Clio, 2000), p. 412; William C. Braly, *The Hard Way Home* (Washington, DC: Infantry Journal Press, 1947), p. 44; Lizzie Oliver, "Transport Ships in the Far East," London, Imperial War Museum (henceforth cited as IWM), http://www.iwm.org.uk/history/the-sinking-of-prisoner-of-war-transport-ships-in-the-far-east (Accessed 27 February 2016).

43. Thomas Pounder, *Death Camps of the River Kwai* (Cornwall: United Writers, 1977), p. 214.

44. Pounder, *Death Camps of the River Kwai*, pp. 216–17.
45. Sweeting, "Prisoners of the Japanese," p. 611.
46. Pounder, *Death Camps of the River Kwai*, p. 218.
47. Kevin Hyde, Affidavit, 7 April 1948, Record Group 331, entry, EDU1189, box 990, NARA.
48. A. G. Allbury, *Bamboo and Bushido* (London: Robert Hale, 1955), p. 153.
49. Albert Coates and Newman Rosenthal, *The Albert Coates Story: The Will that Found the Way* (1977; Melbourne: Hyland House, 1978), pp. 93–94.
50. Quoted in Lamont-Brown, *Ships from Hell*, p. 20.
51. *Kimikawa Maru*, Combined Fleet, http://www.combinedfleet.com/Kimikawa_t.htm (Accessed 23 February 2016); Robert J. Cressman, *The Official Chronology of the U.S. Navy in World War II* (Annapolis: Naval Institute Press, 2000), p. 265; POW Research Network, http://www.powresearch.jp/en/archive (Accessed 26 November 2015).
52. *Mikura* and *Kurahashi*, Combined Fleet, http://www.combinedfleet.com (Accessed 19 February 2016).
53. Mark Stille, *Imperial Japanese Navy Antisubmarine Escorts, 1941–45* (Oxford: Osprey Publishing, 2017), p. 7.
54. Roydon Cornford Interview, 25 November 2003, Archive 1135, AWFA.
55. Waterford, *Prisoners of the Japanese*, pp. 164–65.
56. Blair and Blair, *Return from the River Kwai*, pp. 66, 72.
57. Gordon Williamson, *U-Boat Tactics in World War II* (Oxford: Osprey Publishing, 2010), pp. 5, 22.
58. See Paul Kennedy, *Engineers of Victory: The Problem Solvers Who Turned the Tide in the Second World War* (London: Penguin, 2014), pp. 12, 46.

Chapter 2

1. Transcript of interview enclosed in Eli Reich to John J. Flynn, 18 July 1988, Records of Sgt. J. J. Flynn, PR88/110, File 419/33/144, AWM. The original *Sealion* was lost when the Japanese bombed Cavite naval base in the Philippines in December 1941. *Sealion II* was commissioned on 8 March 1944, but the submarine will henceforth simply be referred to as *Sealion*.
2. Lamont-Brown, *Ships from Hell*, p. 60.
3. USS *Growler* Tenth War Patrol Report, 12 September 1944 and Torpedo Attack Report, Disc 10, reproduced on DVD by Submarine Memorabilia (hereafter cited as SM).
4. Wrecksite—Hirado Escort Vessel 1943–1944, http://www.wrecksite.edu/wreck.aspx?138706 (Accessed 13 September 2017).
5. Gregory J. W. Urwin, *Victory in Defeat: The Wake Island Defenders in Captivity, 1941–1945* (Annapolis: Naval Institute Press, 2010), pp. 14–17, 33–34, 38; Lamont-Brown, *Ships from Hell*, pp. 31–33.
6. Hirado, Combined Fleet, http://www.combinedfleet.com /Hirado_t.htm (Accessed 17 February 2016).
7. Eugene Fluckey, *Thunder Below! The USS Barb Revolutionizes Submarine Warfare in World War II* (Urbana: University of Illinois Press, 1992), p. 106.
8. Mochitsura Hashimoto, *Sunk: The Story of the Japanese Submarine Fleet 1942–1945*, trans. E. H. M. Colegrave (London: Hamilton and Company, 1955), p. 56; William Bruce Johnson, *The Pacific Campaign in World War II: From Pearl Harbor to Guadalcanal* (London: Routledge, 2006), p. 181; Ian Pfennigwerth, "A Novel Experience: The RAN in 1942, Defending Australian Waters," in Peter J. Dean (ed.), *Australia 1942: In the Shadow of War* (Cambridge: Cambridge University Press, 2013), p. 184.
9. USS *Growler* Tenth War Patrol Report, Remarks.
10. Allbury, *Bamboo and Bushido*, p. 158.
11. Allbury, *Bamboo and Bushido*, p. 151.
12. USS *Growler* Tenth War Patrol Report, 12 September 1944.
13. USS *Sealion* Second War Patrol Report, 12 September 1944, Disc 22, SM.
14. USS *Sealion* Second War Patrol Report, Attack Data; Eli T. Reich, *The Reminiscences of Vice Adm. Eli T. Reich* (Annapolis: U.S. Naval Institute, 1982), vol. 1, p. 201; John D. Alden and Craig R. McDonald, *United States and Allied Submarine Successes in the Pacific and Far East during World War II* (Jefferson, NC: McFarland, 2009), p. 203.
15. USS *Growler* Tenth War Patrol Report, 12 September 1944.

16. USS *Sealion* Second War Patrol Report, 12 September 1944.
17. *Nankai Maru*, Combined Fleet, http://www.combinedfleet.com/Nankai_t.htm (Accessed 22 February 2016); Hiroyuki Shindo, "The IJA, IJN and Japanese Strategy for the South Pacific / SWPA," in Peter Dennis (ed.), *Armies and Maritime Strategy: 2013 Chief of Army History Conference* (Canberra: Big Sky Publishing, 2014), p. 164; Michno, *Death on the Hellships*, p. 211; Alden and McDonald, *Submarine Successes*, p. 203.
18. *Rakuyo Maru*, POW Research Network Japan; E. W. Anderson Interrogation, *Rakuyo Maru* Correspondence, series B3856, control symbol 144/1/128, Melbourne, NAA.
19. Allbury, *Bamboo and Bushido*, p. 161.
20. Quoted in Cody, *Ghosts in Khaki*, p. 311.
21. *Daily News* (Perth), 29 March 1945, p. 12.
22. Flynn to unknown recipient, 6 January 1988, Records of Sgt. J.J. Flynn, PR88/110, File 419/33/44, AWM.
23. Herbert, "Dave's Way," pp. 71–72, MSS 2280, AWM.
24. *The Bulletin*, 18 November 1999, p. 41; Raymond Wheeler Interview, 2003, Archive 944, AWFA.
25. Herbert, "Dave's Way," pp. 71–72.
26. Charles Rowley Richards, Notes prepared for *Reader's Digest* writer Olaf Ruhen, 1966, Rowley Richards Papers, PRO1916, box 6, series 4/8, AWM; Charles Richards Interview, 2002, Archive 1144, AWFA; Wall, *Heroes at Sea*, p. 18.
27. Australian PW Survivors ex *Rakuyo Maru*, Summarized Report of events from 4 Sep 44–18 Oct 44, series MP729/8, control symbol 44/431/73, Melbourne, NAA; Savage, *A Guest of the Emperor*, p. 76; John Wilfred Turner, "A True Autobiography of My Life as a Prisoner of War from 15 February 1942 till 12 September 1944," pp. 88–89, PR00651, AWM.
28. Savage, *Guest of the Emperor*, p. 79.
29. Herbert, "Dave's War," pp. 72–73, MSS 2280, AWM.
30. Quoted in Cody, *Ghosts in Khaki*, p. 312.
31. Cornford Interview, AWFA.
32. Russell Savage, Affidavit, 27 April 1948, Record Group 331, entry EVD1189, box 990, NARA.
33. *Straits Times* (Singapore), 3 November 1946, p. 5.
34. Wheeler Interview, AWFA.
35. Hugh V. Clarke, *Twilight Liberation: Australian Prisoners of War between Hiroshima and Home* (Sydney: Allen and Unwin, 1985), p. 41.
36. Arthur Hall, Affidavit, 19 March 1948; William Hubbard, Affidavit, 20 February 1948; Edward Kelk, Affidavit, 24 February 1948, Record Group 331, entry EUD1189, box 990, NARA; McGovern Interview, AWFA; *Rakuyo Maru*—Japanese Transport, Loss of 1944, Narrative of Events following Sinking by USS "Queenfish" 12/9/44, series B6121, control symbol 20S, Melbourne, NAA.
37. Radio intercept from Mikura, 12 September 1944, Record Group 38, entry A1–344, box 1279, NARA.
38. McGovern Interview, AWM; Rowley Richards, *A Doctor's War* (Sydney: Harper Collins, 2005), p. 230.
39. Rowley Richards transcript for *Reader's Digest* article, no date, Rowley Richards Papers, series 4/10, box 5, PRO1916, AWM.
40. Takashi Nagase, *Crosses and Tigers and the Double-Edged Dagger: The Cowra Incident of 1944*, edited by Gill Goddard (London: Paulownia Press, 2010), p. viii.
41. Yuki Tanaka, *Hidden Horrors: Japanese War Crimes in World War II* (Boulder, CO: Westview Press, 1996), pp. 96–97, 99.
42. Savage, *Guest of the Emperor*, pp. 79–80.
43. Allbury, *Bamboo and Bushido*, p. 162.
44. Arthur Bancroft Interview, 11 December 1982, S02950, AWM.

Chapter 3

1. USS *Growler* Tenth War Patrol Report, 12 September 1944; *Rakuyo Maru*, POW Research Network Japan.
2. Hall, *The Blue Haze*, p. 299.
3. Quoted in Fluckey, *Thunder Below*, p. 112.
4. Matome Ugaki, *Fading Victory: The Diary of Admiral Matome Ugaki 1941–1945*, trans. by Masataka Chihaya (1991; reprint ed. Annapolis: Naval Institute press, 2008), pp. 438–439.
5. *Shikinami*, Combined Fleet, http://www.combinedfleet.com/shikin_t.htm (Accessed 18 February 2016).

6. Radio intercept from *Mikura*, 12 September 1944, Record Group 38, entry A1-344, box 1279, NARA.
7. POW Research Network Japan.
8. Reich, *Reminiscences*, p. 202; USS *Sealion* Second War Patrol Report, 12 September 1944.
9. Quoted in Wall, *Heroes at Sea*, p. 32. Ray Wheeler used very similar terms to describe his feelings in *The Crossing*, a History Channel documentary directed by Nigel Bellis, 2003.
10. Australian PW Survivors ex *Rakuyo Maru*, Summarized report of Events from 4 Sep—18 Oct 44, series MP729/8, control symbol 44/431/73, NAA.
11. Turner, "Autobiography," p. 90, PROO651, AWM.
12. Allbury, *Bamboo and Bushido*, p. 168.
13. Bancroft Interview, 1982, AWM.
14. Quoted in Wall, *Heroes at Sea*, p. 30.
15. Quoted in John M. Wright Jr., *The Men of the Line: Stories of the Thai-Burma Railway Survivors* (Melbourne: The Miegunyah Press, 2008), p. 23.
16. *The Crossing*, 2003.
17. McGovern Interview, AWFA.
18. Rowley Richards to Joan and Clay Blair, 8 January 1980, Rowley Richards Papers, Series 4/12, Box 7, AWM.
19. Bancroft Interview, 1982, AWM.
20. McGovern Interview, AWFA.
21. Herbert, "Dave's War," p. 75, MSS 2280, AWM.
22. Clarke, *Twilight Liberation*, pp. 42–43.
23. Cornford Interview, AWFA.
24. Radio intercept from #16 Maritime Transport Commander, 12 September 1944, Record Group 38, entry A1-344, box 1279, NARA.
25. Radio intercept from #16 Maritime Transport Commander, 12 September 1944, NARA.
26. Radio intercept from Commander 1st Surface Escort Unit, 12 September 1944, NARA.
27. McGovern Interview, AWFA; Richards, *A Doctor's War*, p. 230.
28. Australian PW Survivors ex *Rakuyo Maru*, series B3856, control symbol 144/1/128, NAA.
29. Cornford Interview, AWFA.
30. Bancroft Interview, 1982, AWM.
31. Richards, transcript of interview for Reader's Digest article, AWM.
32. Radio intercept from *Mikura*, 12 September 1944, Record Group 38, entry A1-344, box 1279, NARA.
33. *The Crossing*, 2003.
34. Second Webb Report, p. 12, series A10950, control symbol 1, NAA.
35. Wall, *Heroes at Sea*, pp. 26, 31, 35; *The Crossing*, 2003.
36. Kevin Hyde, Affidavit, 7 April 1948, Record Group 331, entry EDU1189, box 990, NARA.
37. Savage, *Guest of the Emperor*, p. 81.
38. Richards, *A Doctor's War*, p. 222.
39. *Courier-Mail* (Brisbane), 30 June 2005, p. 10; Herbert, "Dave's War," p. 77, MSS 2280, AWM.
40. Richards, *A Doctor's War*, p. 235; Richards Interview, AWFA.
41. USS *Growler* Tenth War Patrol Report, 12 September 1944.
42. Robert Bennett Diary, 12 September 1944, p. 42, San Francisco Maritime National Park Association (hereafter cited as SFMNPA); Charles Lockwood, *Sink 'Em All: Submarine Warfare in the Pacific* (1951; reprint ed., New York: Bantam Books, 1984), p. 216; Clay Blair, Jr., *Silent Victory: The U.S. Submarine War against Japan* (1975; reprint ed., Annapolis: Naval Institute Press, 2001), p. 708; Blair and Blair, *Return from the River Kwai*, p. 157; Michno, USS *Pampanito*, p. 5.
43. *Zuiho Maru*, Combined Fleet, http://www.combinedfleet.com/ZuihoM_t.htm (Accessed 24 February 2016); POW Research Network Japan.
44. *Kachidoki Maru*, Combined Fleet, http://www.combinedfleet.com/Kachidoki_thtm (Accessed 24 February 2016); POW Research Network Japan.
45. Michno, *Death on the Hellships*, pp. 35–36.
46. John Edward Huckins, Unpublished Memoir, p. 12, MSS 1550, AWM.
47. Don LeBlanc, "U.S. Submarine Wolfpack attacks Japanese convoy carrying 2,200 Allied POWs," *The Canadian Press* (Toronto), 1 November 2007; *Kachidoki Maru*, Combined Fleet.
48. Thomas Pounder Interview, 30 April 1981, 4887, Imperial War Museum (hereafter cited as IWM); Pounder, *Death Camps of the River Kwai*, p. 223.
49. *Kachidoki Maru*, Combined Fleet; Alden and McDonald, *Submarine Successes*, p. 203; POW Research Network Japan.

50. Pounder, *Death Camps of the River Kwai*, p. 223.
51. Pounder Interview, IWM.
52. *The Times* (New Brunswick), 10 November 2007, pp. 13, 16.
53. Pounder Interview, IWM; Pounder, *Death Camps of the River Kwai*, pp. 224–26.
54. Huckins, Memoir, p. 13, MSS 1550, AWM.

Chapter 4

1. Allbury, *Bamboo and Bushido*, pp. 175–179.
2. *The Crossing*, 2003.
3. Bennett, "POW Survivor Tales," p. 13, SFMNPA.
4. Bancroft Interview, AWFA; Bancroft Interview, 1982, AWM.
5. *Canberra Times*, 29 November 1944, p. 2. Although not referred to by name in the article, Day was the sole RAAF survivor.
6. Wheeler Interview, AWFA; *The Crossing*, 2003.
7. *Straits Times* (Singapore), 12 February 1967, p. 5.
8. See Macdonald Critchley, *Shipwreck-Survivors: A Medical Study* (London: J. and A. Churchill, 1943), pp. 71–72.
9. Spurling, *Cruel Conflict*, p. 271; Blair and Blair, *Return from the River Kwai*, p. 72.
10. E. W. Anderson interrogation, "Rakuyo Maru" Correspondence concerning the torpedoed Japanese transport carrier, series B3856, control symbol 144/1/128, Melbourne, NAA; Herbert, "Dave's War," p. 77, MSS 2280, AWM; McGovern Interview, AAWFA; Charles Richards, Affidavit, 28 January 1948, Record Group 331, entry EVD1189, box 990, NARA.
11. Henry Sakaida, "The Tragic War of Col. Harry R. Melton Jr.," A War to be Won, http://ww2awartobewon.com/ (Accessed 1 September 2017); Blair and Blair, *Return from the River Kwai*, p. 59; *St. Petersburg Times*, 7 July 1945 (Google News Archive Search); Pacific Wrecks, http://www.pacificwrecks.com/ (Accessed 23 May 2015).
12. Summarized Report, *Rakuyo Maru*, Correspondence, series B3856, control symbol 144/1/128, NAA.
13. Pounder, *Death Camps of the River Kwai*, p. 228; Oliver, "Transport Ships in the Far East," IWM.

14. Pounder Interview, IWM; Pounder, *Death Camps of the River Kwai*, pp. 227–228, 232–233; Huckins, Unpublished Memoir, p. 13, MSS 1550, AWM.
15. Pounder, *Death Camps of the River Kwai*, p. 234.
16. Ray Parkin Interview, 7 June 2000, Archive 2552, AWFA.
17. Pounder, *Death Camps of the River Kwai*, pp. 235–236.
18. Midge Gillies, *The Barbed-Wire University: The Real Lives of Prisoners of War in the Second World War* (London: Aurum Press, 2011), p. 359.
19. CD-11, Combined Fleet, http://www.combinedfleet.com/CD-11_t.htm (Accessed 17 February 2016).
20. *Kurahashi, Mikura*, Combined Fleet.
21. Richards and McEwan, *The Survival Factor*, p. 190.
22. USS Growler Tenth War Patrol Report, 13 September 1944.
23. USS *Sealion* Second War Patrol Report, 13 September 1944; Blair, *Silent Victory*, p. 708.
24. Bancroft Interview, 1982, AWM; Bancroft Interview, 1990, AWM.
25. *Daily News* (Perth), 28 May 1941, p. 15; 18 June 1941, p. 16; *Kalgoorlie Miner*, 13 October 1944, p. 4.
26. Bancroft interview in Tim Bowden, *Prisoners of War: Australians under Nippon*, ABC radio broadcast, 2007.
27. Philip James Beilby Interview, 22 February 2000, 22662, IWM.
28. *The Crossing*, 2003.
29. *Straits Times* (Singapore), 12 February 1967, p. 5.
30. Allbury, *Bamboo and Bushido*, p. 181.
31. McGovern Interview, AWFA.
32. *Weekend West*, 22–23 January 2011, pp. 64–65; E. W. Anderson and L. J. Hock interrogations, Rakuyo Maru Correspondence, series B3856, control symbol 144/1/128, NAA.
33. Radio intercept from CD-10, 14 September 1944, Record Group 38, entry A1–344, box 1279, NARA.
34. Herbert," Dave's War," p. 78, MSS 2280, AWM.
35. Clarke, *Twilight Liberation*, p. 43.
36. Holmes, *Four Thousand Bowls of Rice*, p. 77.
37. Kevin Hyde, Affidavit, 7 April 1948, Record Group 331, entry EUD1189, box 990, NARA.

38. McGovern Interview, 2003, AAWFA.
39. Spurling, *Cruel Conflict*, p. 275.
40. Holmes, *Four Thousand Bowls of Rice*, p. 77.
41. Richards to Joan and Clay Blair, 8 January 1980, box 7, series 4/12, PRO1916, AWM.
42. Stanley Manning, Affidavit, 7 February 1948, Record Group 331, entry EVD1189, box 990, NARA.
43. Research by Hiroyuki Shindo, National Institute of Defense Studies, Shindo to author, 4 November 2017.
44. Richards to Joan and Clay Blair, 21 September 1979, box 7, series 4/12, PRO1916, AWM; *Weekend West Australian*, 22–23 January 2011, pp. 64–65.
45. Shindo to author, 4 November 2017.
46. Wall, *Heroes at Sea*, p. vi; Blair and Blair, *Return from the River Kwai*, p. 207.
47. McGovern Interview, AWFA.
48. See Sturma, *Surface and Destroy*, pp. 50–59.
49. Bennett Diary, 14 September 1944, SFMNPA.
50. Sweeting, "Prisoners of the Japanese," p. 615.
51. Huckins, pp. 10, 14, MSS 1550, AWM.

Chapter 5

1. Interrogations, 1 November 1945, Summary of Interview, *Rakuyo* Correspondence, series B3856, control symbol 144/1/128, NAA; Richards, *A Doctor's War*, pp. 240–42; Harold Ramsey, Affidavit, 13 February 1948, Record Group 331, entry EVD1189, box 990, NARA.
2. *Shincho Maru*, Combined Fleet, http://www.combinedfleet.com/Shincho_t.htm (Accessed 24 February 2016); POW Research Network Japan.
3. Richards, *A Doctor's War*, pp. 240–42.
4. Pounder, *Death Camps of the River Kwai*, pp. 236–37.
5. Huckins, pp. 14–15, MSS 2250, AWM.
6. Richards Interview, AWFA.
7. Charles Richards, Affidavit, 28 January 1948, Record Group, 331, entry EVD1189, box 990, NARA.
8. Quoted in Clarke, *Twilight Liberation*, p. 44.
9. Harold Ramsey, Affidavit, 13 February 1948, Record Group 331, entry EVD1189, box 990, NARA.
10. Pounder, *Death Camps of the River Kwai*, p. 238.
11. POW Research Network Japan.
12. Summary of interview, *Rakuyo Maru* Correspondence, series B3856, control symbol 144/1/128, NAA; *Kibitsu Maru*, Combined Fleet, http://www.combinedfleet.com/Kibitsu_t.htm (Accessed 24 February 2016); Michno, *Death on the Hellships*, p. 223.
13. McGovern Interview, AWFA.
14. *Kibitsu Maru, Mikura*, Combined Fleet; POW Research Network Japan.
15. Summarized Report, *Rakuyo Maru* Correspondence, series B3856, control symbol 144/1/128, NAA.
16. Allbury, *Bamboo and Bushido*, p. 184.
17. Cornford Interview, AWFA.
18. Beilby Interview, IWM.
19. *Daily Telegraph* (Sydney), 19 November 1944, p. 32.
20. *Sun* (Sydney), 14 June 1945, p. 4.
21. USS *Sealion* Second War Patrol Report, 15 September 1944; Blair, *Silent Victory*, pp. 708–709.
22. Blair and Blair, *Return from the River Kwai*, p. 228.
23. Quoted in Sendzikas, *Lucky 73*, p. 218.
24. USS *Pampanito* Third War Patrol Report, 15 September 1944.
25. Wall, *Heroes at Sea*, p. 42; *San Francisco Chronicle*, 18 March 2009, B2.
26. USS *Pampanito* Third War Patrol Report, 15 September 1944.
27. Cornford Interview, AWFA.
28. USS *Pampanito* Third War Patrol Report, 15 September 1944.
29. Blair and Blair, *Return from the River Kwai*, p. 229.
30. Quoted in Bennett, "Survivor Tales," p. 4, SFMNPA.
31. Quoted in Cody, *Ghosts in Khaki*, pp. 313–14.
32. *Straits Times*, 12 February 1967, p. 5.
33. Cornford Interview, AWFA.
34. Statement by Pte. S. Whiley, 22 May 1945, WO 361/733, NAS.
35. Blair and Blair, *Return from the River Kwai*, p. 232.
36. USS *Pampanito* Third War Patrol Report, 15 September 1944.
37. Landon Davis, Oral History, Naval History and Heritage Command, http://www.history.navy.mil/research/library/online/oral_history_davis.htm (Accessed 25 October 2013).

38. Quoted in Michno, *USS Pampanito*, p. 236.
39. USS *Pampanito* Third War Patrol Report, 15 September 1944; USS *Sealion* Second War Patrol Report, 15 September 1944.
40. Reich, *Reminiscences*, p. 203.
41. Turner, Autobiography, p. 90, AWM.
42. Hall, *The Blue Haze*, pp. 138, 166, 168, 213.
43. "U.S. Submarine Rescue of Aussie and British POWs in WW2," narrated by Joe Bates, https://www.youtube.com/watch?y+QFB4bZUJn6A (Accessed 31 October 2017).
44. *The Crossing*, 2003.
45. Summarized Report of events 4 Sep—18 Oct 44, series MP729/8, control symbol 44/431/73, Melbourne, NAA; Michno, *Pampanito*, pp. 244, 246.
46. USS *Sealion* Second War Patrol Report, 15 September 1944.
47. Quoted in *Bulletin*, 18 November 1999, p. 40.
48. "U.S. Submarine Rescue," narrated by Joe Bates.
49. *The Crossing*, 2003.
50. *The Crossing*, 2003.
51. Beilby Interview, IWM.
52. Bancroft Interview, 1982, AWM; Bancroft Interview, 1990, AWM.

Chapter 6

1. Summarized Report, *Rakuyo Maru* Correspondence, series B3856, control symbol 144/1/128, NAA.
2. USS *Sealion* Second War Patrol Report, 16 September 1944.
3. USS *Pampanito*, Rescue of British and Australian Prisoners-of-War, series MP1049/5, control symbol 1951/2/99, Melbourne, NAA; USS *Pampanito* Third War Patrol Report, 16 September 1944.
4. Eli Reich, transcript of interview enclosed in Reich to J.J. Flynn, 18 July 1988, Records of J. J. Flynn, PR88/110, File 419/33/44, AWM.
5. "U.S. Submarine Rescue," narrated by Joe Bates.
6. Allbury, *Bamboo and Bushido*, pp. 185–86.
7. Quoted in Wall, *Heroes at Sea*, p. 80.
8. Bancroft Interview, 1982, AWM.
9. Quoted in Wall, "Heroes at Sea," p. 81.
10. U.S. Naval Institute, http://www.usni.org/navalinstitutepress/loughlin.asp (Accessed 29 January 2017); Blair and Blair, *Return from the River Kwai*, pp. 99–100; Blair, *Silent Victory*, p. 985.
11. USS *Queenfish* First Patrol Report, Endorsements.
12. Charles Elliot Loughlin, *The Reminiscences of Rear Admiral Charles Elliot Loughlin* (Annapolis: U.S. Naval Institute Press, 1982), pp. 93–94, 96.
13. Reich, *Reminiscences*, p. 251.
14. Carl LaVO, *The Galloping Ghost: The Extraordinary Life of Submarine Legend Eugene Fluckey* (Annapolis: Naval Institute Press, 2007), pp. 33–34, 37–38, 42.
15. Loughlin, *Reminiscences*, p. 96.
16. USS *Barb* Ninth War Patrol Report, 16 September 1944; Fluckey, *Thunder Below*, p. 126.
17. POW Research Network Japan; Fluckey, *Thunder Below*, p. 122.
18. See Michael Sturma, *Fremantle's Submarines: How Allied Submariners and Western Australians helped to win the War in the Pacific* (Annapolis: Naval Institute Press, 2015), p. 42.
19. Loughlin, *Reminiscences*, pp. 96–97; Fluckey, *Thunder Below*, pp. 122, 132; Alden and McDonald, *Allied Submarine Successes in the Pacific*, p. 204; Cressman, *Chronology of the U.S. Navy*, p. 255; Blair and Blair, *Return from the River Kwai*, pp. 247–48; Blair, *Silent Victory*, p. 710.
20. Quoted in Fluckey, *Thunder Below*, p. 133.
21. CD-10, CD-20, *Mikura, Asaka Maru, Shincho Maru*, Combined Fleet.
22. POW Research Network Japan.
23. Kevin Hyde, Affidavit, 7 April 1948, Record Group 331, entry EDU1189, box 990, NARA.
24. Pounder, *Death Camps of the River Kwai*, pp. 238–240; Kitchener Loughnan, Affidavit, 14 April 1948, Record Group 331, entry EVD1189, box 990, NARA.
25. Harold Ramsey, Affidavit, 23 February 1948, Record Group 331, entry EVD1189, box 990, NARA.
26. Herbert, "Dave's War," pp. 83–84, MSS 2280, AWM.
27. Pounder, *Death Camps of the River Kwai*, p. 240.
28. Pounder, *Death Camps of the River Kwai*, p. 243.
29. Kitchener Loughnan, Affidavit, 14 April 1948.

30. Holmes, *Four Thousand Bowls of Rice*, p. 78.
31. Fluckey, *Thunder Below*, pp. 124–25, 133, 138.
32. USS *Barb* Ninth War Patrol Report, 17 September 1944.
33. John J. Flynn to unknown recipient, 6 January 1988, Records of Sgt. J. J. Flynn, PR88/110, file 419/33/44, AWM.
34. *Advertiser* (Adelaide), 15 September 2007, p. 82.
35. Fluckey, *Thunder Below*, pp. 141–142.
36. Quoted in Cody, *Ghosts in Khaki*, p. 317.
37. Fluckey, *Thunder Below*, p. 143
38. Quoted in LaVO, *The Galloping Ghost*, p. 86.
39. Allbury, *Bamboo and Bushido*, pp. 187–91.
40. Quoted in LaVO, *The Galloping Ghost*, p. 84.
41. Quoted in LaVO, *The Galloping Ghost*, p. 180.
42. Australian PW Survivors ex *Rakuyo Maru*, Summarized report of events from 4 Sep–18 Oct 44, series MP729/8, control symbol 44/431/73, NAA.
43. Fluckey, *Thunder Below*, p. 142.
44. USS *Queenfish* First War Patrol Report, 17 September 1944.
45. Clifford Leslie Farlow Interview, 8 September 1990, S04058 AWM.
46. Beilby Interview, IWM.
47. *Age* (Melbourne), 13 February 2002, p. 8; *Weekend Australian*, 16 October 2004, p. 4.
48. Wheeler Interview, AWFA.
49. Bancroft Interview, 1982, AWM.
50. See for example *Sydney Morning Herald*, 3 August 2013, p. 16.
51. Bancroft Interview, AWFA.
52. Loughlin, *Reminiscences*, p. 98.
53. Bowden, *Australians under Nippon*, radio broadcast, 2007.
54. *The Crossing*, 2003.
55. Beilby Interview, IWM.
56. Quoted in Wall, *Heroes at Sea*, p. 87.
57. Quoted in *Argus* (Melbourne), 18 November 1944, p. 10.

Chapter 7

1. Fluckey, *Thunder Below*, p. 147.
2. Allbury, *Bamboo and Bushido*, pp. 190, 192.
3. Bancroft Interview, 1982, AWM; *West Australian*, 25 August 2007, p. 9.
4. Bancroft Interview, AWFA.
5. Quoted in Wall, *Heroes at Sea*, p. 87.
6. Beilby Interview, IWM.
7. Beilby Interview, IWM.
8. Bancroft Interview, 1990, AWM.
9. Cornford Interview, AWFA.
10. USS *Pampanito* Third War Patrol Report, 15 September 1944.
11. C.W. Shilling and Jessie W. Kohl, *History of Submarine Medicine in World War II* (New London, CT: U.S. Naval Medical Research Laboratory, 1947), pp. 10–12, 22–23.
12. Blair and Blair, *Return from the River Kwai*, pp. 234, 254.
13. USS *Pampanito*, Rescue of British and Australian Prisoners-of-War, series MP1049/5, control symbol 1951/2/99, NAA.
14. Bennett Diary, 18 September 1944, p. 46, SFMNPA; Cornford Interview, AWFA.
15. *The Crossing*, 2003.
16. USS *Sealion* Second War Patrol Report, 18 September 1944.
17. U.S. Submarine Rescue narrated by Joe Bates; *The Crossing*, 2003.
18. Tim Clayton, *Sea Wolves: The Extraordinary Story of Britain's WW2 Submarines* (London: Little Brown, 2011), p. 369; Michno, *Death on the Hellships*, pp. 235–240; Cressman, *Chronology of the U.S. Navy*, p. 256; Oliver, "Transport Ships in the Far East," IWM.
19. Waterford, *Prisoners of the Japanese*, p. 159.
20. Sinkings of Japanese Ships Carrying Allied Prisoners of War, 29 March 1945, Record Group 38, Entry A1-344, Box 1279, NARA.
21. Table of Japanese Ships Sunk while Transporting Allied Prisoners and Civilian Internees, Record Group 407, Entry A1-1069, box 147, NARA.
22. Lockwood, *Sink 'Em All*, p. 224.
23. USS *Pampanito* Third War Patrol Report, 20 September 1944.
24. Cornford Interview, AWFA.
25. Bennett Diary, 20 September 1944, p. 46, SFMNPA.
26. Thomas B. Buell, *Master of Sea Power: A Biography of Fleet Admiral Ernest J. King* (Boston: Little, Brown and Company, 1980), p. 337.
27. Forbes, *Hellfire*, p. 448; David C.

Earhart, *Certain Victory: Images of World War II in the Japanese Media* (New York: M. D. Sharpe, 2008), p. 399; Dan Van der Vat, *The Pacific Campaign: World War II, The U.S.—Japanese Naval War 1941–1945* (New York: Simon and Schuster, 2006), p. 330.

28. Quoted in Jeffrey M. Moore, *Spies for Nimitz: Joint Military Intelligence in the Pacific War* (Annapolis: Naval Institute Press, 2004), p. 99.

29. Quoted in James D. Hornfischer, *The Fleet at Flood Tide: America at Total War in the Pacific, 1944–1945* (New York: Bantam Books, 2016), p. 259.

30. Fritz Young, USS *Cobia* Reunion, 9–13 September 1992, tape transcription, p. 47, Manitowoc, Wisconsin Maritime Museum and Archives (henceforth cited as WMML).

31. H. Vance Combs, Questionnaire, 1992, WMML.

32. Donald L. Miller, *D-Days in the Pacific* (New York: Simon and Schuster, 2005), p. 147.

33. Fluckey, *Thunder Below*, p. 157.
34. Cornford Interview, AWAF.
35. Reich, *Reminiscences*, p. 204.
36. UK Army personnel rescued but died on board submarines, WO 361/733, NAS.
37. USS *Queenfish* First War Patrol Report, 25 September 1944.
38. Loughlin, *Reminiscences*, p. 101.
39. Fluckey, *Thunder Below*, p. 156.
40. Allbury, *Bamboo and Bushido*, p. 192.
41. Quoted in LaVO, *Galloping Ghost*, p. 88.
42. Turner, Autobiography, pp. 95–97, AWM.
43. Beilby Interview, IWM
44. Wheeler Interview, AWFA.
45. Quoted in Spurling, *Cruel Conflict*, p. 278.
46. *The Crossing*, 2003.
47. Allbury, *Bamboo and Bushido*, p. 192; Beilby Interview, IWM.
48. Wheeler Interview, AWFA.
49. Bennett Diary, 20 September 1944, p. 46, SFMNPA.
50. USS *Sealion* Second War Patrol Report, 21 September 1944; Health, Food and Habitability.
51. Michno, *USS Pampanito*, p. 262.
52. Quoted in LaVO, *Galloping Ghost*, p. 180.

53. Quoted in Blair and Blair, *Return from the River Kwai*, p. 258.
54. Quoted in Michno, *USS Pampanito*, p. 218.
55. Quoted in Walter W. Jaffe, *Steel Shark in the Pacific: USS Pampanito SS-383* (Palo Alto, CA: Glencannon Press, 2001), p. 108.
56. Bennett Diary, 27 September 1944, p. 46, SFMNPA.
57. Fluckey, *Thunder Below*, pp. 150, 152.
58. Quoted in Wall, *Heroes at Sea*, p. 97.
59. Fluckey, *Thunder Below*, p. 146.
60. POW Research Network Japan; *Mikura, Asaka Maru*, CD-10, Combined Fleet.
61. Ray Parkin, *Ray Parkin's Wartime Trilogy* (Melbourne: Melbourne University Press, 2003), p. 796.
62. Pounder, *Death Camps on the River Kwai*, p. 243.
63. POW Research Network Japan; *Kibitsu Maru*, Combined Fleet.
64. CD-10, *Mikura, Asaka Maru*, Combined Fleet.
65. *Shincho Maru*, Combined Fleet.
66. *Kibitsu Maru*, CD-10, CD-20, CD-11, Combined Fleet; POW Research Network Japan.
67. Huckins, pp. 14–15, MSS 2250, AWM.
68. Roy H. Whitecross, *Slaves of the Son of Heaven* (Sydney: Dymock's Book Arcade, 1951), p. 171.
69. Harold Ramsey, Affidavit, 23 February 1948, Record Group 331, entry EVD1189, box 990, NARA.
70. Richards, *A Doctor's War*, p. 245.
71. USS *Plaice* Second War Patrol Report, 24 September 1944, Target Data; Alden and McDonald, *Allied Submarine Successes in the Pacific*, p. 207.
72. USS *Plaice* Second War Patrol Report, 26 September 1944, Target Data, Prologue.
73. USS *Plaice* Second War Patrol Report, 27 September 1944.
74. POW Research Network Japan.
75. USS *Plaice* Second War Patrol Report, 27 September 1944.
76. CD-10, Combined Fleet.
77. McGovern Interview, AWFA; Michno, *Death on the Hellships*, p. 224.
78. Pounder Interview, IWM.
79. USS *Plaice* Second War Patrol Report, 27 September 1944.

Chapter 8

1. *Syonan Shimbun* (Singapore), 9 September 1944, p. 1.
2. Shinshichiro Komamiya, *Senji Yuso-sendan-shi* [History of Wartime Transport Convoys], Kyodo Shuppansha, 1987, pp. 247–248; Shindo, "Japanese Strategy for the South Pacific," p. 164; POW Research Network Japan.
3. Robert Gannon, *Hellions of the Deep: The Development of American Torpedoes in World War II* (University Park: Pennsylvania State University Press, 1996), p. 195.
4. Komamiya, *Senji Yuso-sendan-shi*, pp. 247–249; "Sempaku Yuso-kan ni okeru Sonan (Kaibotsu) (Yukuefumei) Butai (Gunijin Gunzuku) Sieri Shiryo," [Records to Organize Losses (Lost at Sea) (MIA) of Units (Military Personnel and Auxiliaries) during Transport of Ships], Tokyo, National Institute of Defense Studies Library (henceforth cited as NIDSL); Combined Fleet, *Nankai Maru*; Alden and McDonald, *Allied Submarine Successes in the Pacific*, p. 203.
5. Shinozaki, *Syonan My Story*, p. 82.
6. CD-10, Combined Fleet.
7. Atsushi Oi, *Kaijo Goei-sen* [Maritime Protection War] Asahi Sonorama, pp. 392–93.
8. "Showa 19-nen 9-gatsu 27-nichi HI-72 Sendan Hibakugeki Sento Shoho Unso-sen Asaka-Maru" [27 September 1944, Detailed Battle Report of the Bombing of HI-72, Transport Asaka-Maru], NIDSL; 'Showa 19-nen 10-gatsu 12-nichi Asaka-Maru Hi-rai-baku Chinbotsu Sento Shoho Unsosen Asaka-Maru' [12 October 1944, Detailed Battle Report of the Torpedoing, Bombing, and Sinking of the Asaka-Maru, Transport Asaka-Maru], NIDSL; 'Showa 19-nen 10-gatsu Toka Tokusetu Unsosen Nankai-Maru Sento Shoho Showa 19-nen 9-gatsu 12-nichi Minami-shina-kai ni okeru Tai-sensuikan-sen Tokusetu Unsosen Nankai-Maru' [10 October 1944, Detailed Battle Report of Converted Transport Nankai-Maru: Anti-Submarine Battle on September 12, 1944, in the South China Sea, Converted Transport Nankai-Maru], NIDSL.
9. *Asaka Maru* and *Nankai Maru*, Combined Fleet.
10. Robert Dinesch, "Radar and the American Submarine War, 1941–1945: A Reinterpretation," *The Northern Mariner*, vol. 14, no. 3, July 2004, pp. 29, 31–32, 39.
11. Peter Padfield, *War Beneath the Sea: Submarine Conflict 1939–1945* (London: Pimlico, 1997), p. 337.
12. Quoted in Rick Cline, *Final Dive: The Gallant and Tragic Career of the WWII Submarine, USS Snook* (Placentia, CA: R. A. Cline Publishing, 2001), p. 35.
13. Reich, *Reminiscences*, p. 200.
14. USS Growler Tenth War Patrol Report, 12 September 1944.
15. USS *Pampanito* Third War Patrol Report, 12 September 1944.
16. USS Plaice Second War Patrol Report, 26 September 1944.
17. Dinesch, "Radar and the American Submarine War," pp. 31, 33.
18. USS Growler Tenth War Patrol Report, Torpedo Attack Report.
19. Dinesch, "Radar and the American Submarine War," p. 36.
20. Louis Brown, *A Radar History of World War II: Technical and Military Imperatives* (Bristol: Institute of Physics Publishing, 1999), pp. 135–37.
21. Roger I. Wilkinson, "Short Survey of Japanese Radar," *Electrical Engineering*, vol. 65, August-September 1946, pp. 372, 460; Brown, *A Radar History of World War II*, pp. 140, 373.
22. Hashimoto, *Sunk*, pp. 102, 119.
23. Ugaki, *Fading Victory*, p. 439.
24. USS *Pampanito* Third War Patrol Report, 12 September 1944.
25. See Jonathan J. McCullough, *A Tale of Two Subs: An Untold Story of World War II, Two Sister Subs, and Extraordinary Heroism* (New York: Grand Central Publishing, 2008), p. 172; Carl Boyd, *American Command of the Sea: Through Carriers, Codes and the Silent Service* (Newport News, VA: The Mariners' Museum, 1995), p. 36.
26. USS *Pampanito* Third War Patrol Report, 17 August 1944. See also USS Growler Tenth War Patrol Report, 17 August 1944.
27. Stille, *Japanese Navy Antisubmarine Escorts*, p. 6.
28. Reich, *Reminiscences*, p. 200; USS *Sealion* Second War Patrol Report, 11 September 1944; USS Growler Tenth War Patrol Report, 11 September 1944; USS *Pampanito* Third War Patrol Report, 11 September 1944.
29. USS *Sealion* Second War Patrol Report, 15 September 1944; USS *Pampanito* Third War Patrol Report, 15 September 1944.

30. Atsushi Oi, "Why Japan's Anti-Submarine Warfare Failed," *United States Naval Institute Proceedings*, vol. 78, no. 6, June 1952, pp. 596, 598.

31. USS *Plaice* Second War Patrol Report, Anti-Submarine Measures and Evasion Tactics.

32. USS *Growler* Tenth War Patrol Report, 12 September 1944; USS *Sealion* Second War Patrol Report, Attack Data.

33. Mark P. Parillo, *The Japanese Merchant Marine in World War II* (Annapolis: Naval Institute Press, 1993), p. 103.

34. Norman Polmar and Edward Whitman, *Hunters and Killers, Volume 2: Anti-Submarine Warfare from 1943* (Annapolis: Naval Institute Press, 2016), pp. 45–46; Parillo, *Japanese Merchant Marine*, p. 104; Oi, *Kaijo Goei-sen*, pp. 95–96.

35. USS *Sealion* Second War Patrol Report, 12 September 1944.

36. John Ellis, *Brute Force: Allied Strategy and Tactics in the Second World War* (London: Andre Deutsch, 1990), p. 470; J. Rohwer and G. Hummelchen, *Chronology of War at Sea 1939-1945: The Naval History of World War Two* (Annapolis: Naval Institute Press, 1992), p. 260.

37. Joel Ira Holwitt, *"Execute Against Japan": The U.S. Decision to Conduct Unrestricted Submarine Warfare* (College Station: Texas A & M University Press, 2009), pp. 165–166.

38. Y. Horie, "The Failure of the Japanese Convoy Escort," *U.S. Naval Institute Proceedings*, October 1956, p. 595.

39. Stille, *Japanese Navy Antisubmarine Escorts*, p. 5.

40. Boeicho Boeikenshusho Senshishitsu [War History Office, Defence Agency], ed., *Kaijo Goei-sen* [Maritime Protection War], Asagumo Shinbunsha, 1971, pp. 332–35.

41. Stille, *Japanese Navy Antisubmarine Escorts*, p. 6.

42. *Asaka Maru* and *Nankai Maru* Detailed Battle Reports, NIDSL.

43. Parillo, *Japanese Merchant Marine*, p. 98.

44. Reich, *Reminiscences*, p. 199.

45. On the problems of U.S. torpedoes see especially Anthony Newpower, *Iron Men and Tin Fish: The Race to Build a Better Torpedo during World War II* (Westport, CT: Praeger Security International, 2006); Gannon, *Hellions of the Deep*.

46. Oi, "Why Japan's Anti-Submarine Warfare Failed," p. 593; Stille, *Japanese Navy Antisubmarine Escorts*, p. 6.

47. Gannon, *Hellions of the Deep*, p. 140; Reich, *Reminiscences*, p. 170.

48. USS *Sealion* Second War Patrol Report, 6 September 1944.

49. Gannon, *Hellions of the Deep*, p. 140.

50. Reich, *Reminiscences*, pp. 3, 102, 374–375.

51. USS *Sealion* Second War Patrol Report, Major Defects and Damage.

52. Gannon, *Hellions of the Deep*, p. 145; Richard J. Lannigan, *Kangaroo Express: The Epic Story of the Submarine Growler* (Laurel, FL: RJL Express Publications, 1998), p. 40.

53. USS *Growler* Tenth War Patrol Report, Remarks.

54. USS *Plaice* Second War Patrol Report, Major Defects and Damage.

55. Quoted in David C. Evans, *The Japanese Navy in World War II: In the Words of Former Japanese Naval Officers* (Annapolis: Naval Institute Press, 1986), p. 363.

56. Edwin T. Layton with Roger Pineau and John Costello, *"And I was There": Pearl Harbor and Midway—Breaking the Secrets* (1985; Annapolis: Naval Institute Press, 2006), pp. 471–473; McCullough, *A Tale of Two Subs*, pp. 162–163; Padfield, *War Beneath the Sea*, p. 391; Michno, *Death on the Hellships*, p. 140.

57. Fluckey, *Thunder Below*, p. 106.

58. Report of ships joining HI-72 Convoy, 5 September 1944, NARA, Record Group 38, entry 344, box 1279, NARA.

59. Stille, *Japanese Navy Antisubmarine Escorts*, p. 10.

60. USS *Sealion* Second War Patrol Report, 12 September 1944.

61. *Syonan Shimbun* (Singapore), 3 January 1944, p. 1. See also Tom Paine, *The Transpacific Voyage of His Imperial Japanese Majesty's Submarine I-400 (Tom Paine's Journal July–Dec. 1945* (Los Angeles: self-published, 1984), p. 8; Parillo, *Japanese Merchant Ships*, pp. 122–23.

62. Stille, *Japanese Navy Antisubmarine Escorts*, pp. 10, 47; Williamson, *U-Boat Tactics in World War II*, p. 50; Kennedy, *Engineers of Victory*, pp. 55–57.

63. Evan Graham, *Japan's Sea Lane Security, 1940-2004: A Matter of Life and Death?* (London: Routledge, 2006), p. 86.

64. Stille, *Japanese Navy Antisubmarine Escorts*, p. 26.

65. Parillo, *Japanese Merchant Marine*, p. 103.
66. Oi, *Kaijo Goei-sen*, pp. 146–147; Polmar and Whitman, *Hunters and Killers*, vol. 2, p. 61.
67. Boeikenshushp Senshishitsu, *Kaijo Goei-Sen*, p. 306.
68. Carter and MacPherson, *The Burma Railway*, pp. 145–46.
69. Rick Cline, *Submarine Grayback: The Life and Death of the WWII Sub, USS Grayback* (Placentia, CA: R.A. Cline Publishing, 1999), p. 219; Parillo, *Japanese Merchant Ships*, p. 122.
70. Harry Holmes, *The Last Patrol* (Annapolis: Naval Institute Press, 1994), pp. 149–50.
71. Oi, "Why Japan's Anti-Submarine Warfare Failed," p. 601.
72. *Asaka Maru*, Combined Fleet.
73. Braly, *The Hard Way Home*, p. 192.
74. Hara, "Japan: Guns before Rice," p. 251.
75. Cressman, *Chronology of the U.S. Navy*, pp. 263, 265; Ashley Jackson, "Ocean War," in Thomas H. Zeiler with Daniel DuBois (eds.), *A Companion to World War II* (Chichester, West Sussex: Wiley-Blackwell, 2013), vol. 1, p. 246.

Chapter 9

1. Turner, "Autobiography," p. 98, AWM.
2. Blair and Blair, *Return from the River Kwai*, p. 287.
3. Bancroft Interview, 1982, AWM.
4. Casualty Section, 28 September 1944, *Rakuyo Maru* Correspondence, series B3856, control symbol 144/1/128, NAA; Instructions to Captain G. B. Massingham, 29 September 1944, series MP729/6, control symbol 12/402/408, Melbourne, NAA.
5. Draft press release, 17 November 1944, series 54, control symbol 779/10/3, AWM.
6. Report by D. N. C. Tufnell, 3 October 1944, series B6121, control symbol 20S, NAA.
7. Turner, "Autobiography," p. 99, AWM.
8. Bancroft Interview, 1982, AWM.
9. Critchley, *Shipwreck-Survivors*, pp. 63, 72.
10. Turner, "Autobiography," p. 100, AWM.
11. Despatch, 3 October 1944, *Rakuyo Maru* Correspondence, series B3856, control symbol 144/1/128, NAA.
12. Turner, "Autobiography," p. 100, AWM.
13. Holmes, *Four Thousand Bowls of Rice*, p. 76.
14. Turner, "Autobiography," p. 102, AWM.
15. Wheeler Interview, AWFA.
16. Turner, "Autobiography," pp. 103–104, AWM.
17. Turner, "Autobiography," pp. 105–106, AWM.
18. Bancroft Interview, 1982, AWM; Blair and Blair, *Return from the River Kwai*, p. 289.
19. Bancroft Interview, 1990, AWM.
20. Kerrigan to Colonel, 18 October 1944, *Rakuyo Maru* Correspondence, series B3856, control symbol 144/1/128, NAA.
21. Turner, "Autobiography," p. 106, AWM.
22. *Argus* (Melbourne), 18 November 1944, p. 10.
23. Quoted in Christina Twomey, *The Battle Within: POWs in postwar Australia* (Sydney: New South, 2018), p. 16.
24. Turner, "Autobiography," p. 106, AWM.
25. Beilby Interview, IWM.
26. Turner, "Autobiography," pp. 106–107, AWM.
27. *Argus* (Melbourne), 18 November 1944, p. 10.
28. Beilby Interview, IWM.
29. Blair and Blair, *Return from the River Kwai*, p. 291.
30. Draft press release, 17 November 1944, series 54, control symbol 779/10/3, AWM.
31. Turner, "Autobiography," p. 107, AWM.
32. Turner, "Autobiography," p. 108, AWM.
33. Beilby Interview, IWM.
34. "Reception 3," draft press release, undated, series 54, control symbol 779/10/3, AWM.
35. *Argus* (Melbourne), 18 November 1944, p. 10.
36. Richards, *A Doctor's War*, pp. xii, 292, 278, 292; Cody, *Ghosts in Khaki*, p. 189; Michael McKernan, *This War Never Ends: The Pain of Separation and Return* (St Lucia: University of Queensland Press, 2001), pp. 7, 77–78; Savage, *A Guest of the Emperor*, p. 126.
37. Blair and Blair, *Return from the River Kwai*, p. 291.
38. Turner, "Autobiography," p. 108, AWM.
39. Decypher from High Commissioner's Office, London, 14 October 1944, series

MP729/6, control symbol 12/402/408, NAA; *Canberra Times*, 17 October 1944, p. 1.
40. Sibylla Jane Flower, "Memory and the Prisoner of War Experience: The United Kingdom," in Karl Hack and Kevin Blackburn (eds.), *Forgotten Captives in Japanese Occupied Asia* (London: Routledge, 2008), p. 61.
41. Blamey to Prime Minister, 28 September 1944, series MP729/6, control symbol 12/402/408, NAA.
42. Royal Australian Navy to Mr. Bonney, 6 October 1944, series B6121, control symbol 20S, NAA.
43. *West Australian*, 13 October 1944, p. 4.
44. Bancroft Interview, 1982, AWM.
45. Bancroft Interview, AWFA.
46. War Cabinet Minute, 18 October 1944, series A2676, control symbol 3849, Canberra, NAA.
47. *Canberra Times*, 1 November 1944, p. 1.
48. *Sydney Morning Herald*, 18 November 1944, p. 1.
49. Lt. Col. J. H. Russell, 30 October 1944, *Rakuyo Maru* Correspondence, series B3856, control symbol 144/1/128, NAA.
50. Cornford Interview, AWFA.
51. Reginald Hartness Hart Service Record, series B883, control symbol VX23586, Canberra, NAA; Blair and Blair, *Return from the River Kwai*, p. 292.
52. Turner, "Autobiography," p. 108, AWM.
53. Beilby Interview, IWM
54. Bancroft Interview, AWFA.
55. Directorate of Prisoners of War, 4 November 1944, WO 208/521, NAS; Malaya and NEI: Interrogation of survivors from *Rakuyo Maru*, WO 361/435. NAS.
56. *Daily Post*, undated clipping, WO 361/733, NAS.
57. Blair and Blair, *Return from the River Kwai*, p. 296; *The Crossing*, 2003.
58. Allbury, *Bamboo and Bushido*, p. 192.
59. Report on visit of Cas. P.W. representatives to No. 90 Reception Camp, Vache, Bucks—11th & 12th Nov. 1944, WO 361/733, NAS; Superintendent Inter-Service Topographical Department to N.I.D.4, 13 November 1944, WO 208/521, NAS.
60. Directorate of Prisoners of War, 4 November 1944, WO 208/521, NAS.
61. Report of visit of Cas. P.W., 16 November 1944, WO 361/733, NAS.
62. Report of visit of Cas. P.W., 16 November 1944, WO 361/733, NAS.
63. Quoted in Blair and Blair, *Return from the River Kwai*, p. 302.
64. Secret Minute, 30 November 1944, WO 208/521, NAS.
65. Allbury, *Bamboo and Bushido*, p. 192.
66. See for example David Rolf, *Prisoners of the Reich: Germany's Captives 1939–1945* (London: Leo Cooper, 1988), p. 193.
67. Secret Minute, 13 January 1945, WO 208/521, NAS.
68. Secret Minutes, 23 January 1945, WO 208/521, NAS.
69. Report of visit of Cas. P.W., 16 November 1944, WO 361/733, NAS.
70. Interrogation of four British prisoners rescued after sinking of Japanese transport, WO 208/523, NAS.
71. Malaya and NEI: Interrogation of survivors from *Rakuyo Maru*, WO 361/435, NAS.
72. V. Harvey, War Office, to R. C. Cade, Colonial Office, 14 April 1945, WO 361/733, NAS.

Chapter 10

1. War Cabinet minute, 18 October 1944, series A2676, control symbol 3849, NAA.
2. Sandra Wilson, Robert Cribb, Beatrice Trefalt and Dean Aszkielowicz, *Japanese War Criminals: The Politics of Justice after the Second World War* (New York: Columbia University Press, 2017), pp. 42–43; D. C. S. Sissons, "The Australian War Crimes Trials and Investigations (1942–51)," p. 6, https//www.ocf.berkeley.edu/~changmin/documents/Sissons%20Final%20War%20Crimes%20Text%2018-3-06.pdf (Accessed 26 March 2018).
3. Second Webb Report, pp. 6–7, series A10950, control symbol 1, Canberra, NAA.
4. Second Webb Report, p. 7.
5. Second Webb Report, p. 12.
6. Second Webb Report, p. 13.
7. Sissons, "The Australian War Crimes Trials," p. 6.
8. Australian PW Survivors Ex *Rakuyo Maru*, Summarized report of events from 15 Feb 42–4 Sep 44, series MP729/8, control symbol 44/431/73, NAA.

9. Confidential Report, C. E. Loughlin, 25 September 1944, series B6121, control symbol 20S, NAA.
10. *Canberra Times*, 29 January 1944, p. 1 and 31 January 1944, p. 1; *Argus* (Melbourne), 29 January 1944, p. 3; E. Bartlett Kerr, *Surrender and Survival: The Experience of American POWs in the Pacific 1941–1945* (New York: William Morrow and Company, 1985), pp. 7, 163.
11. Robin Rowland, *A River Kwai Story: The Sonkrai Tribunal* (Sydney: Allen and Unwin, 2007), p. 205.
12. Hansard, House of Commons, 28 January 1944, vol. 396, cc 1029–35; Kinvig, *River Kwai Railway*, p. 188.
13. Peter Stanley, "Remembering Captivity: The Prisoner Experience in Literature," in Department of Veteran Affairs, *Stolen Years: Australian Prisoners of War* (Canberra: Commonwealth of Australia, 2002), pp. 100, 104–5; Frances Houghton, "To the Kwai and Back: Myth, Memory and Memoirs of the Death Railway," *Journal of War and Culture Studies*, vol. 7, no. 3, August 2014, p. 227; Sweeting, "Prisoners of the Japanese," pp. 588, 615; McKernan, *This War Never Ends*, p. 49.
14. Nachman Ben-Yehuda, *Atrocity, Deviance and Submarine Warfare: Norms and Practices during the World Wars* (Ann Arbor: University of Michigan Press, 2013), p. 183.
15. Secretary of State, Washington, to American Embassy, London, 11 November 1944, Record Group 59, entry CDF1940, box 3062, NARA.
16. S.P. MacKenzie, "The Treatment of Prisoners of War in World War II," *Journal of Modern History*, vol. 66, no. 3, September 1994, p. 517.
17. Incoming Telegram to Secretary of State, Washington, 13 November 1944, Record Group 59, entry CDF1940, box 3062, NARA.
18. Special Directive: Treatment of Empire Prisoners of War in Burma and Siam, WO 208/521, NAS.
19. Incoming Telegram, Secretary of State, Washington, 14 November 1944, Record Group 59, entry CDF1940, box 3062, NARA.
20. Telegram sent by Department of State, 15 November 1944, NARA.
21. London to Secretary of State, Washington, 20 November 1944, NARA.
22. Communication to the Secretary of State, Washington, 22 November 1944, NARA.
23. Incoming telegram, Secretary of State, Washington, 17 November 1944, NARA.
24. Quoted in *Sydney Morning Herald*, 18 November 1944, p. 1.
25. *Newcastle Morning Herald and Miners' Advocate*, 29 December 1944, p. 2.
26. *Newcastle Morning Herald and Miners' Advocate*, 25 January 1945, p. 3.
27. Parliamentary statement enclosed in British Embassy, Washington, D.C. to Special War Problems Division, 3 January 1945, Record Group 59, entry CDF1945–49, box 4036, NARA.
28. Statement by the Acting Prime Minister, 17 November 1944, series MP1049/5, control symbol 1951/2/99, NAA.
29. Draft cable to Australian High Commissioner, London, series 54, control symbol 799/10/3, AWM.
30. Quoted in *Argus* (Melbourne), 18 November 1944, p. 1.
31. *Argus* (Melbourne), 22 November 1944, p. 3.
32. Swiss Minister to Shigemitsu, 4 December 1944, Record Group 153, entry A1–143, box 1400, NARA.
33. Quoted in *Argus* (Melbourne), 18 November 1944, p. 1.
34. See for example *Sydney Morning Herald*, 18 November 1944, p. 5.
35. Tokyo—Overseas, News in Japanese, 6 December 1944, series MP729/6, control symbol 12/402/408, NAA. The talk was given in English to America in a radio broadcast on 8 December.
36. *Sydney Morning Herald*, 16 December 1944, p. 4; Blair and Blair, *Return from the River Kwai*, p. 294.
37. Confidential Memorandum, 27 January 1945, series MP729/6, control symbol 12/402/408, NAA.
38. Statement by Prime Minister, 15 February 1945, series MP729/6, control symbol 12/402/408, NAA.
39. Casualty Notification, 27 October 1944, *Rakuyo Maru* Correspondence, series B3856, control symbol 144/1/128, NAA.
40. Statement by Arthur Bancroft, series B3856, control symbol 144/1/128 Attachment 9, NAA.
41. Richards, *A Doctor's War*, pp. 240, 284–85.

42. *Age* (Melbourne), 9 November 1945, p. 6.
43. *Cairns Post*, 20 November 1945, p. 4.
44. *Advertiser* (Adelaide), 4 February 1946, p. 5.
45. *Sun* (Sydney), 19 November 1944, p. 4.
46. Holmes, *Four Thousand Bowls of Rice*, pp. 7, 42, 76.
47. See Kate Ariotti, "'At present everything is making us most anxious': Families of Australian Prisoners in Turkey," in Joan Beaumont, Lachlan Grant and Aaron Pegram (eds.), *Beyond Surrender: Australian Prisoners of War in the Twentieth Century* (Melbourne: Melbourne University Press, 2015), p. 61.
48. See, for example, Clifford Kinvig, "Allied POWs and the Burma-Thailand Railway" in Philip Towle, Margaret Kosuge and Yoichi Kibata (eds.), *Japanese Prisoners of War* (London: Hambledon and London, 2000), p. 56.
49. Tom Wade, *Prisoner of the Japanese: From Changi to Tokyo* (Sydney: Kangaroo Press, 1994), p. 53.
50. R. P. W. Havers, *Reassessing the Japanese Prisoner of War Experience: The Changi POW Camp, Singapore, 1942–45* (London: Routledge Curzon, 2003), pp. 49, 111; Sweeting, 'Prisoners of the Japanese,' p. 525.
51. Arneil, *One Man's War*, p. 60.
52. Parkin, *Wartime Trilogy*, p. 543.
53. Rivett, *Behind Bamboo*, p. 376. See also Kratoska, *The Thailand-Burma Railway*, vol. 3, p. 69; Hall, *The Blue Haze*, p. 324.
54. See for example Kinvig, *River Kwai Railway*, p. 86.
55. Rivett, *Behind Bamboo*, pp. 318–319. See also for example Betty Jeffrey, *White Coolies* (1954; Sydney: Angus and Robertson, 1976), pp. 121–22.
56. Braly, *The Hard Way Home*, p. 137.
57. McKernan, *This War Never Ends*, p. 27.
58. Hall, *The Blue Haze*, p. 308.
59. Roy Bulcock, *Of Death but Once* (Melbourne: F.W. Cheshire, 1947), p. 165.
60. Wheeler Interview, AWFA.
61. Beilby Interview, IWM.
62. Hall, *The Blue Haze*, p. 308.
63. Adam-Smith, *Prisoners of War*, p. 685.
64. Winifred J. Meagher to L/Sgt Cornelius, 7 November 1944, *Rakuyo Maru* Correspondence, series B3856, control symbol 144/1/128, NAA.
65. *Daily News* (Perth), 15 November 1944, p. 7.
66. *Argus* (Melbourne), 1 December 1944, p. 6.
67. Quoted in McKernan, *This War Never Ends*, p. 56.
68. Bancroft Interview, 1990, AWM.
69. Report on visit of Cas. P.W., 16 November 1944, WO 361/733, NAS.
70. Farlow Interview, AWM.
71. Quoted in Holmes, *Four Thousand Bowls of Rice*, p. 43.
72. Cornford Interview, AWFA.
73. Carter and MacPherson, *The Burma Railway*, p. 140.

Chapter 11

1. Clarke, *Twilight Liberation*, p. 10.
2. Nagase, *Crosses and Tigers*, p. 42; Ryoko Adachi and Andrew McKay (eds.), *Echoes of War: Australians voice their feelings about Japan* (Carnegie, VIC: Mirai Books, 2009), p. 268; Jim Brigginshaw, *Shimpu-San Healer of Hate: The Life of Father Tony Glynn* (Lismore, NSW: Marist Fathers' Province of Australia, 1996), p. 95; Charles G. Roland, *Long Night's Journey into Day: Prisoners of War in Hong Kong and Japan, 1941–1945* (Waterloo, ON: Wilfred Laurier University Press, 2001), pp. 209, 225.
3. Sweeting, "Prisoners of the Japanese," p. 616; Rosalind Hearder, *Keep the Men Alive: Australian POW Doctors in Japanese Captivity* (Sydney: Allen and Unwin, 2009), pp. 75, 80; Spurling, *Cruel Conflict*, p. 209.
4. Clarke, *Twilight Liberation*, p. 12; *England Maru*, Combined Fleet.
5. Spurling, *Cruel Conflict*, p. 223.
6. Forbes, *Hellfire*, p. 306; Hugh V. Clarke, *Last Stop Nagasaki* (London: George Allen and Unwin, 1984), p. xii.
7. Alden and McDonald, *Allied Submarine Successes in the Pacific*, p. 169.
8. Lance Gibson, Report on Draft, 1 October 1945; Affidavit, 16 September 1946, Record Group 331, entry EUD1189, box 990, NARA.
9. *Tamahoka Maru*, Combined Fleet, http://www.combinedfleet.com/Tamahoko_t.htm (Accessed 20 February 2020).
10. Gibson, Report on Draft, 1 October 1945.

11. Hugh V. Clarke and Colin Burgess, *Barbed Wire and Bamboo: Australian POWs in Europe, North Africa, Singapore, Thailand and Japan* (Sydney: Allen and Unwin, 1992), p. 137.
12. Kenneth Harrison, *Road to Hiroshima* (1966; Adelaide: Rigby, 1983), p. 217.
13. Quoted in Clarke and Burgess, *Barbed Wire and Bamboo*, p. 138.
14. Parkin Interview, AWFA.
15. Harrison, *Road to Hiroshima*, p. 220.
16. Adachi and McKay, *Echoes of War*, pp. 37–38.
17. Hugh Clarke, Affidavit, War Crimes Tribunal, p. 178, series A471, control symbol 81642, Canberra, NAA.
18. Lance Gibson, Report on Draft, 1 October 1945, Record Group 331, entry EUD1189, box 990, NARA.
19. Harrison, *Road to Hiroshima*, p. 239.
20. Adachi and McKay, *Echoes of War*, p. 268; Brigginshaw, *Shimpu-San Healer of Hate*, pp. 95–96.
21. Hearder, *Keep the Men Alive*, p. 120.
22. Peter Withycombe, Affidavit, War Crimes Tribunal, p. 167, series A471, control symbol 81642, NAA.
23. Thomas Martz, Affidavit, War Crimes Tribunal, p. 198, series A471, control symbol 81642, NAA.
24. Linda Goetz Holmes, "Mitsui: 'We Will Send You to Omuta,'" in Peter Li (ed.), *Japanese War Crimes: The Search for Justice* (New Brunswick, NJ: Transaction Publishers, 2003). 110–111; Donald Knox, *Death March: The Survivors of Bataan* (New York: Harcourt Brace Jovanovich, 1981), p. 364.
25. Quoted in Miller, *D-Days in the Pacific*, p. 322.
26. Roland, *Long Night's Journey into Day*, pp. 219–220; Miller, *D-Days in the Pacific*, pp. 323–24; Hearder, *Keep the Men Alive*, p. 82.
27. Knox, *Death March*, p. 377.
28. Roland, *Long Night's Journey into Day*, p. 209.
29. Daws, *Prisoners of the Japanese*, p. 301.
30. Sweeting, "Prisoners of the Japanese," p. 615.
31. Kitchener Loughnan, Affidavit, 14 April 1948, Record Group 331, entry EVD1189, box 990, NARA.
32. McGovern Interview, AAWFA.
33. Russell Savage, Affidavit, 27 April 1948; Kevin Hyde, Affidavit, 7 April 1948, Record Group 331, entry EVD1189, box 990, NARA.
34. Blair and Blair, *Return from the River Kwai*, p. 273.
35. McGovern Interview, AWFA.
36. McGovern Interview, AWFA; Holmes, *Four Thousand Bowls of Rice*, pp. 78–80.
37. Quoted in Holmes, *Four Thousand Bowls of Rice*, p. 78.
38. McGovern Interview, AWFA.
39. Quoted in Adachi and McKay, *Echoes of War*, p. 37.
40. Parkin, *Wartime Trilogy*, pp. 849–50.
41. Quoted in Adam-Smith, *Prisoners of War*, p. 550.
42. Clarke, *Last Stop Nagasaki*, p. 30.
43. Roland, *Long Night's Journey into Day*, p. 218.
44. John Lane, *Summer Will Come Again: The Story of Australian POWs Fight for Survival in Japan* (Fremantle: Fremantle Arts Centre Press, 1987), pp. 108, 148.
45. Richards Interview, AWFA.
46. Clarke, *Twilight Liberation*, p. 45; Sweeting, "Prisoners of the Japanese," p. 627.
47. Edward Kelk, Affidavit, 24 February 1948, Record Group 331, entry EUD1189, box 990, NARA.
48. Pounder, *Death Camps of the River Kwai*, pp. 245–46, 252, 256.
49. Adachi and McKay, *Echoes of War*, pp. 185–86.
50. Pounder Interview, IWM.
51. Hearder, *Keep the Men Alive*, p. 75.
52. Charles G. Roland, "Allied POWs, Japanese Captors and the Geneva Convention," *War and Society*, vol. 9, no. 2, 1991, p. 93.
53. Adachi and McKay, *Echoes of War*, pp. 185–186.
54. Knox, *Death March*, p. 414.
55. Tachikawa, "The Treatment of Prisoners of War," pp. 54–55; Kerr, *Surrender and Survival*, p. 257; Edward Kelk, Affidavit, 24 February 1948, Record Group 331, entry EUD1189, box 990, NARA.
56. McGovern Interview, AWFA.
57. Adam-Smith, *Prisoners of War*, p. 639.
58. Hearder, *Keep the Men Alive*, p. 74.
59. Knox, *Death March*, pp. 445–446.
60. Pounder Interview, IWM; Pounder, *Death Camps of the River Kwai*, p. 260.
61. McGovern Interview, AWFA; *Daily*

Telegraph (Sydney), 27 February 2003, p. 47; Spurling, *Cruel Conflict*, p. 285.
62. Gillies, *The Barbed-Wire University*, pp. 393–94.
63. Tachikawa, "The Treatment of Prisoners of War," pp. 53, 56, 57; David Aquila, "A Deeper Level of Hell," *MHQ: The Quarterly Journal of Military History*, vol. 24, no. 1, Autumn 2011, p. 104.
64. Quoted in Adachi and McKay, *Echoes of War*, p. 132.
65. Roland, *Long Night's Journey into Day*, p. 244.
66. Wade, *Prisoner of the Japanese*, p. 141.
67. Quoted in Clarke, *Twilight Liberation*, p. 27.
68. Quoted in Clarke, *Twilight Liberation*, p. 83.
69. Robert Holman, *On Paths of Ash: The Extraordinary Story of an Australian Prisoner of War*, edited by Peter Thomson (Sydney: Pier 9, 2009), p. 188.

Chapter 12

1. Clarke, *Twilight Liberation*, p. 16.
2. Holman, *On Paths of Ash*, p. 167.
3. Holman, *On Paths of Ash*, pp. 169, 175.
4. Carter and MacPherson, *The Burma Railway*, p. 225.
5. Miller, *D-Days in the Pacific*, pp. 367–68.
6. Gillies, *The Barbed-Wire University*, pp. 396–97.
7. Pounder Interview, IWM.
8. McGovern Interview, AWFA.
9. Holman, *On Paths of Ash*, p. 189. See also for example Clarke, *Twilight Liberation*, p. 61; Lane, *Summer Will Come Again*, p. 179; Wade, *Prisoner of the Japanese*, p. 65.
10. Pounder, *Death Camps on the River Kwai*, p. 262.
11. Quoted in Clarke, *Twilight Liberation*, p. 87.
12. Quoted in Clarke, *Twilight Liberation*, p. 106.
13. Harrison, *Road to Hiroshima*, p. 280.
14. Hall, *The Blue Haze*, p. 324; Lane, *Summer Will Come Again*, p. 180; Clarke, *Twilight Liberation*, p. 91.
15. Roland, *Long Night's Journey into Day*, pp. 222, 264, 268.
16. Quoted in Adam-Smith, *Prisoners of War*, p. 703.
17. Quoted in Clarke, *Twilight Liberation*, p. 65.
18. Quoted in Clarke, *Twilight Liberation*, p. 91.
19. Harrison, *Road to Hiroshima*, p. 272.
20. Hornfischer, *The Fleet at Flood Tide*, p. 467.
21. Holmes, *Four Thousand Bowls of Rice*, p. 84.
22. Quoted in Adam-Smith, *Prisoners of War*, p. 555.
23. Adachi and McKay, *Echoes of War*, p. 186.
24. Harrison, *Road to Hiroshima*, p. 256.
25. Quoted in Tony Banham, *We Shall Suffer There: Hong Kong's Defenders Imprisoned* (Hong Kong: Hong Kong University Press, 2009), p. 217.
26. McGovern Interview, AWFA.
27. Parkin, *Wartime Trilogy*, p. 933.
28. McGovern Interview, AWFA.
29. John Dower, *Embracing Defeat: Japan in the Aftermath of World War II* (London: Penguin Books, 1999), p. 54.
30. Quoted in Adachi and McKay, *Echoes of War*, p. 78.
31. Quoted in Holmes, *Four Thousand Bowls of Rice*, p. 86.
32. Parkin Interview, AWFA.
33. Holman, *On Paths of Ash*, pp. 194, 200; Hornfischer, *The Fleet at Flood Tide*, p. 474.
34. Carter and MacPherson, *The Burma Railway*, p. 209.
35. Quoted in Adachi and McKay, *Echoes of War*, p. 186.
36. Quoted in Clarke, *Twilight Liberation*, p. 70.
37. Clarke, *Twilight Liberation*, pp. 70–73; Clarke, *Last Stop Nagasaki*, p. 124.
38. Richards and McEwan, *The Survival Factor*, pp. 221, 225; Pounder, *Death Camps of the River Kwai*, p. 262; Richards Interview, AWFA.
39. McGovern Interview, AWFA.
40. Kerr, *Surrender and Survival*, p. 291; Sweeting, "Prisoners of the Japanese," p. 642.
41. Quoted in Clarke, *Twilight Liberation* p. 74.
42. Carter and MacPherson, *The Burma Railway*, p. 220.
43. Parkin, *Wartime Trilogy*, pp. 639, 939; Parkin Interview, AWFA; Spurling, *Cruel Conflict*, p. 290.
44. Harrison, *Road to Hiroshima*, p. 274.

45. Arneil, *One Man's War*, p. 247.
46. Arneil, *One Man's War*, pp. 264, 267, 269.
47. Holmes, *Four Thousand Bowls of Rice*, p. 87.
48. Lane, *Summer Will Come Again*, pp. 208–15.
49. Holmes, *Four Thousand Bowls of Rice*, p. 142.
50. Lane, *Summer Will Come Again*, pp. 206–207.
51. Wade, *Prisoner of the Japanese*, p. 180.
52. See for example Parkin, *Wartime Trilogy*, p. 939.
53. Quoted in Ben Shephard, *A War of Nerves: Soldiers and Psychiatrists in the Twentieth Century* (Cambridge, MA: Harvard University Press, 2001), p. 319.
54. See for example Knox, *Death March*, p. 477.

Chapter 13

1. Quoted in Kelly E. Crager, *Hell under the Rising Sun: Texan POWs and the Building of the Burma-Thailand Death Railway* (College Station: Texas A&M University Press, 2008), p. 46.
2. Quoted in Hearder, *Keep the Men Alive*, p. 141.
3. Rivett, *Behind Bamboo*, p. 221.
4. Rivett, *Behind Bamboo*, p. 348.
5. Special Directive: Treatment of Empire Prisoners of War in Burma and Siam, November 1944, WO 208/521, NAS.
6. Statement to House of Commons on Japanese Atrocities in Connection with British and Australian Prisoners of War in Siam, enclosed in Communication by Special Messenger, British Embassy, Washington, D.C., 18 November 1944, Record Group 59, entry CDF1940, box 3062, NARA.
7. Department of External Affairs, Canberra, to American Minister, 21 November 1944, Record Group 313, entry P-50, box 7, NARA.
8. Acting Secretary of State to the Secretary of the Navy, 22 February 1945, 313-P-50-7, NARA.
9. *Syonan Shimbun* (Singapore), 24 October 1942, p. 1.
10. Talk in English to America (Radio Broadcast), 8 December 1944, series MP729/6, control symbol 12/402/408, NAA.
11. Quoted in Banham, *We Shall Suffer There*, p. 61.
12. Australian PW Survivors ex *Rakuyo Maru*, Summarized report of Events from 4 Sep 1944–18 Oct 1944, series MP729, control symbol 44/431/73, NAA.
13. Sendzikas, *Lucky 73*, pp. 113, 124.
14. Arthur Bancroft and R. G. Roberts, *The Mikado's Guests* (Perth: Paterson's Printing Press, 1945), p. 171.
15. Cody, *Ghosts in Khaki*, pp. vi, 66, 72; 2/4th Machine Gun Battalion, Australian War Memorial, https://www.awm.gov.au/unit/U56173/ (Accessed 31 August 2015).
16. Quoted in Blair and Blair, *Return from the River Kwai*, p. 284.
17. Michno, *USS Pampanito*, pp. 305–307.
18. Marshall Roberts, Tape Transcript, USS *Cobia* Reunion, 9–13 September 1992, p. 50, WMML.
19. Michno, *USS Pampanito*, p. 388.
20. Michno, *Pampanito*, p. 371.
21. Cornford Interview, AWFA.
22. *Sunday Mail* (Brisbane), 28 January 2007, p. 42; Wall, *Heroes at Sea*, pp. 176–77, 211.
23. Cornford Interview, AWFA.
24. Spurling, *Cruel Conflict*, p. 269.
25. McGovern Interview, AWFA.
26. See for example Wall, *Heroes at Sea*, pp. 18, 139; Blair and Blair, *Return from the River Kwai*, pp. 61, 86–87; Lamont-Brown, *Ships from Hell*, p. 58; Aquila, "A Deeper Level of Hell," p. 101; *The Crossing*, 2003; Gillies, *The Barbed-Wire University*, p. 357.
27. Richards, *A Doctor's War*, p. 221.
28. David Miller, *Mercy Ships* (London: Continuum, 2008), pp. 133, 165–73; Michno, *Death on the Hellships*, pp. 87–88; Lachlan Grant, "Hellships, prisoner transport and unrestricted submarine warfare in World War II," in Joan Beaumont, Lachlan Grant and Aaron Pegram (eds.), *Beyond Surrender Australian Prisoners of War in the Twentieth Century* (Melbourne: Melbourne University Press, 2015), pp. 198, 200.
29. *Hansard*, House of Commons, 28 January 1944, vol. 396, cc1029–35; Tony Banham, *The Sinking of the Lisbon Maru: Britain's Forgotten Wartime Tragedy* (Hong Kong: Hong Kong University Press, 2006), pp. 90–91, 97, 112, 186; Daws, *Prisoners of the Japanese*, p. 287; John Lane, *Summer*

Will Come Again, pp. 60–62; Meg Parkes and Geoff Gill, *Captive Memories* (Lancaster: Palatine Books, 2015), p. 32.
30. Brayly, *The Hard Way Home*, p. 235.
31. W. J. Holmes, *Undersea Victory: The Influence of Submarine Operations on the War in the Pacific* (New York: Doubleday and Company, 1966), p. 370; Lee A. Gladwin, "American POWs on Japanese Ships take a Voyage into Hell," Prologue: *Quarterly of the National Archives and Records Administration*, vol. 35, no. 4, Winter 2003, p. 34; Mark Felton, *Slaughter at Sea: The Story of Japan's Naval War Crimes* (Annapolis: Naval Institute Press, 2007), p. 7; Kerr, *Surrender and Survival*, pp. 199–200; Daws, *Prisoners of the Japanese*, pp. 286–287; Alan J. Levine, *Captivity, Flight and Survival in World War II* (Westport, CT: Praeger, 2000), p. 165; John D. Lukacs, *Escape from Davao: The Forgotten Story of the Most Daring Prison Break of the Pacific War* (New York: Simon and Schuster, 2010), pp. 343–344.
32. Levine, *Captivity*, p. 165; Blair, *Silent Victory*, p. 737.
33. Kerr, *Surrender and Survival*, pp. 206–7; Levine, *Captivity*, p. 166; Gladwin, "American POWs on Japanese Ships," p. 34; Felton, *Slaughter at Sea*, p. 7.
34. Parkes and Gill, *Captive Memories*, pp. 34–35.
35. Telegram from Australian Government, 18 November 1944, WO 208/521, NAS.
36. Gladwin, "American POWs on Japanese Ships," p. 38.
37. Michno, *Death on the Hellships*, pp. 293–94.
38. Gladwin, "American POWs on Japanese Ships," pp. 33–34.
39. Intercepted Enemy Radio Traffic and Related Documentation, Office of Naval Intelligence, Record Group 38, entry A1–344, box 1279, NARA.
40. Lee A. Gladwin, "Did Signit Seal the Fates of 19,000 POWs?," *Cryptologia*, vol. 30, no. 3, July-September 2006, pp. 199, 203.
41. Lamont-Brown, *Ships from Hell*, p. 58.
42. Adrian R. Martin, *Brothers from Bataan: POWs, 1942–1945* (Manhattan, Kansas: Sunflower University Press, 1992), pp. 186–87, 194–95; *Noto Maru*, Combined Fleet, http://www.combinefleet.com/Noto_t.htm (Accessed 10 February 2020).

43. Quoted in Martin, *Brothers from Bataan*, pp. 192–93.
44. Quoted in *Times* (New Brunswick), 10 November 2007, p. 13.
45. Quoted in Wall, *Heroes at Sea*, p. 81.
46. Aquila, "A Deeper Level of Hell," p. 104.
47. Harrison, *Road to Hiroshima*, p. 217.

Chapter 14

1. Waterford, *Prisoners of the Japanese*, p. 151.
2. Lamont-Brown, *Ships from Hell*, p. 118. The lower death rate is due mainly to Lamont-Brown's higher estimate for the total number of prisoners transported by sea, which he puts at 123,779 men.
3. Michno, *Death on the Hellships*, p. 317. Similar estimates for the numbers of Allied POW deaths at sea are given by Daws, *Prisoners of the Japanese*, p. 297; Gladwin, "American POWs on Japanese Ships," p. 31; Wall, *Heroes at Sea*, p. iv.
4. Michno, *Death on the Hellships*, p. 292.
5. Michno, *Death on the Hellships*, pp. 238–40, 316.
6. Michno, *Death on the Hellships*, pp. 314, 316; *Junyo Maru*, *Tango Maru* and *Koshu Maru*, Combined Fleet (Accessed 17 October 2018); Lamont-Brown, *Ships from Hell*, p. 115.
7. Clarke, *Twilight Liberation*, p. 11.
8. Brian MacArthur, *Surviving the Sword: Prisoners of the Japanese 1942–45* (London: Abacus, 2005), p. 325. See also Miller, *D-Days in the Pacific*, p. 317.
9. Memorandum for British Army Staff, Washington, DC, 22 November 1945, WO 361/752, NAS.
10. Memorandum for Imperial Japanese Government, General Headquarters, Supreme Commander of the Allied Forces, 26 November 1945, WO 361/752, NAS.
11. Summary enclosed in Allied Land Forces SEA to Under Secretary of State for War, London, 19 March 1946, Record Group 407, entry A1–1069, box 147, NARA.
12. Lists of missing and dead from 14 sunk Japanese transports carrying British POW, WO 361/1741, NAS.
13. Holmes, *The Last Patrol*, pp. 81–82; *Chuyo*, Combined Fleet, http://www.

combinedfleet.com/chuyo.htm (Accessed 25 October 2018); Felton, *Slaughter at Sea*, pp. 77–78.

14. A Report indicating Japanese vessels sunk while carrying Allied prisoners of war or internees, WO 361/1741, NAS.

15. Lamont-Brown, *Ships from Hell*, p. 39.

16. Colin Sleeman (ed.), *Trial of Gozawa Sadaichi and Nine Others* (London: William Hodge and Company, 1948), pp. xxxi-xxxiv, xli, 12–13, 32; Lamont-Brown, *Ships from Hell*, pp. 40–41; Russell, *The Knights of Bushido*, pp. 171–72.

17. Lamont-Brown, *Ships from Hell*, p. 115; *Ikoma Maru*, Combined Fleet, http://www.combinedfleet.com/Ikoma_t.htm (Accessed 16 October 2018).

18. James F. DeRose, *Unrestricted Warfare: How a New Breed of Officers led the Submarine Force to Victory in World War II* (New York: John Wiley and Sons, 2000), pp. 65–66, 77, 94, 287; Sturma, *Surface and Destroy*, pp. 45–46.

19. Lamont-Brown, *Ships from Hell*, p. 116.

20. Lamont-Brown, *Ships from Hell*, pp. 116–117; John Toland, *The Rising Sun: The Decline and Fall of the Japanese Empire 1936–1945* (London: Cassell and Company, 1971), p. 599.

21. Quoted in Miller, *D-Days in the Pacific*, p. 319.

22. Quoted in Knox, *Death March*, p. 350.

23. Betty B. Jones, *The December Ship: A Story of Lt. Col. Arden R. Boellner's Capture in the Philippines, Imprisonment and Death on a World War II Japanese Hellship* (Jefferson, NC: McFarland, 1992), pp. 100, 102–106; Wright, *Captured on Corregidor*, p. 87; Toland, *The Rising Sun*, pp. 599–602; *Oryoku Maru*, Combined Fleet, http://www.combinedfleet.com/Oryoku_t.htm (Accessed 24 October 2018).

24. John C. Shively, *Profiles in Survival: The Experiences of American POWs in the Philippines during World War II* (Indianapolis, IN: Indiana Historical Society Press, 2012), 153.

25. Wright, *Captured on Corregidor*, p. 113.

26. Wright, *Captured on Corregidor*, pp. 113, 115.

27. Wright, *Captured on Corregidor*, p. 117.

28. Alden and McDonald, *Allied Submarine Successes*, pp. 251–2.

29. Toland, *The Rising Sun*, p. 631; Miller, *D-Days in the Pacific*, p. 321.

30. Quoted in Toland, *The Rising Sun*, p. 631.

31. Wright, *Captured on Corregidor*, p. 127; Toland, *The Rising Sun*, p. 632; Miller, *D-Days in the Pacific*, p. 322; Knox, *Death March*, p. 356.

32. Wright, *Captured on Corregidor*, pp. 131–32.

33. *Chicago Daily News*, 20 November 1945; Gladwin, "American POWs on Japanese Ships," p. 37; Russell, *The Knights of Bushido*, p. 188; Wright, *Captured on Corregidor*, p. 33; Toland, *The Rising Sun*, p. 633; *Brazil Maru*, Combined Fleet, http://www.combinedfleet.com/Brazil_t.htm (Accessed 9 October 2018).

34. Lamont-Brown, *Ships from Hell*, p. 117; Knox, *Death March*, p. 348.

35. Quoted in Parkes and Gill, *Captive Memories*, p. 33.

36. Lamont-Brown, *Ships from Hell*, pp. 49–50.

37. *Straits Times* (Singapore), 15 December 1946, p. 6.

38. Quoted in Parkes and Gill, *Captive Memories*, p. 30.

39. *Straits Times* (Singapore), 3 May 1947, p. 3; Judge Advocate General's Office, British War Crime Trial, Defendants Nishimi, Yoshinari; Ogasawara, Makoto; Maruyama, Naosuke; Uchida, Yoichi, WO235/1043, NAS.

40. Judge Advocate General's Office, War Crimes Case Files, Defendant Kaneoka Kiko, WO 235/910, NAS; *Straits Times*, 18 October 1946, p. 3; Russell, *The Knights of Bushido*, pp. 132–33.

41. Judge Advocate General's Office, British War Crime Trial, Defendant Jotani Kitaichi, WO 235/995, NAS; *Singapore Free Press*, 28 May 1947, p. 1.

42. Lamont-Brown, *Ships from Hell*, pp. 36–37; Alden and McDonald, *Allied Submarine Successes*, p. 109.

43. Lamont-Brown, *Ships from Hell*, p. 39; Alden and McDonald, *Allied Submarine Successes*, p. 290.

44. *Clyde Maru*, Combined Fleet, http://www.combinedfleet.com/Clyde_t.htm (Accessed 4 November 2019).

45. *Tatsuta Maru*, Combined Fleet, http://www.combinedfleet.com/Tatsuta_t.htm (Accessed 4 November 2019).

46. *Kurahashi*, Combined Fleet, http://www.combinedfleet.com/Kurahashi_t.htm (Accessed 19 February 2016).

Chapter 15

1. See Rolf, *Prisoners of the Reich*, p. 190.
2. *West Australian*, 31 October 1944, p. 2; *Daily News* (Perth), 10 March 1945, p. 24.
3. *Sunday Times* (Perth), 15 April 1945, p. 14; *West Australian*, 11 April 1944, p. 4.
4. *Daily News* (Perth), 14 April 1945, p. 14.
5. Arthur Bancroft, Service Records, series A6770, service number F3239, NAA; Bancroft Interview, AWFA; Bancroft Interview, 1982, AWM; Bowden, *Australians under Nippon*, radio broadcast.
6. Beilby Interview, IWM.
7. *Courier-Mail* (Brisbane), 23 November 1944, p. 1.
8. Twomey, *The Battle Within*, pp. 21, 37, 40, 68.
9. Quoted in Hearder, *Keep the Men Alive*, p. 185.
10. *Courier-Mail* (Brisbane), 1 December 1944, p. 3.
11. *Courier-Mail*, 26 April 1945, p. 3.
12. McGovern Interview, AWFA.
13. Quoted in Holmes, *Four Thousand Bowls of Rice*, p. 146.
14. Bowden, *Australians under Nippon*, radio broadcast.
15. Shephard, *A War of Nerves*, pp. 320–21.
16. McGovern Interview, AWFA.
17. Cornford Interview, AWFA.
18. Beilby Interview, IWM.
19. Wheeler Interview, AWFA.
20. Quoted in Adam-Smith, *Prisoners of War*, p. 704.
21. Richards and McEwan, *The Survival Factor*, pp. 178, 225.
22. Richards Interview, AWFA; Richards, *A Doctor's War*, p. 289.
23. *Sun* (Sydney), 27 May 1945, p. 8.
24. Bowden, *Australians under Nippon*, radio broadcast.
25. Holman, *On Paths of Ash*, p. 207.
26. Quoted in Shephard, *A War of Nerves*, p. 316.
27. See John Nichol and Tony Rennell, *The Last Escape: The Untold Story of Allied Prisoners of War in Europe 1944–45* (New York: Viking, 2002), p. 428; Rolf, *Prisoners of the Reich*, pp. 190, 194; Bowden, *Australians under Nippon*, radio broadcast.
28. Bancroft Interview, AWFA.
29. Beilby Interview, IWM.
30. Russell Braddon, *The Naked Island* (1951; Melbourne: Penguin Books, 1993), p. 263.
31. Coates and Rosenthal, *The Albert Coates Story*, pp. 160–61.
32. Herbert, "Dave's Way," pp. 96–97, AWM.
33. See for example Richards, *A Doctor's War*, p. 287; Savage, *A Guest of the Emperor*, pp. 130–31; Betty Peters, "The Life Experience of Partners of ex-POWs of the Japanese," *Journal of the Australian War Memorial*, no. 28, April 1996, p. 2.
34. Ronald Williams, Affidavit, War Crimes Tribunal, p. 212, series A471, control symbol 81642, NAA.
35. See Bowden, *Australians under Nippon*, radio broadcast; Michno, *Death on the Hellships*, p. vii; John Wyatt with Cecil Lowry, *No Mercy from the Japanese: A Survivor's Account of the Burma Railway and the Hellships 1942–1945* (Barnesly, South Yorkshire: Pen and Sword, 2008), p. 88; Carter and MacPherson, *The Burma Railway*, p. 154.
36. Quoted in Havers, *Reassessing the Japanese Prisoner of War Experience*, p. 17.
37. Bancroft, *Arthur's War*, p. 139.
38. Bancroft Interview, AWFA.
39. Bancroft and Roberts, *The Mikado's Guests*, p. 5.
40. Margaret Mogan, "Prison Camp Life in Burma," *The Mail* (Adelaide), 25 August 1945, p. 6.
41. Stephen Garton, "Changi as Television: Myth, Memory, Narrative and History," *Journal of Australian Studies*, vol. 26, no. 73, 2002, p. 85.
42. Robin Gerster, "The rise of the Prisoner-of-War Writers," *Australian Literary Studies*, vol. 12, no. 2, October 1985, p. 271.
43. See Joan Beaumont, "Prisoners of War in Australian National Memory," in Bob Moore and Barbara Hatley-Broad (eds.), *Prisoners of War, Prisoners of Peace: Captivity, Home coming and Memory in World War II* (Oxford: Berg, 2005), pp. 187–88, 191; Joan Beaumont, "Officers and Men: Rank and survival on the Thai-Burma Railway," in Beaumont et al., *Beyond Surrender*, p. 174; Joan Beaumont, "The Long Silence: Australian Prisoners of the Japanese," in Peter J. Dean (ed.), *Australia*

1944–45: Victory in the Pacific (Melbourne: Cambridge University Press, 2016), pp. 80, 91.

44. See Grant, *Australian Soldiers in Asia-Pacific*, p. 150; Garton, "Changi as Television," p. 82.

45. Bancroft and Roberts, *The Mikado's Guests*, pp. 79–84.

46. Bancroft Interview, 1982, AWM.

47. Richards, *A Doctor's War*, p. 208.

48. Richards and McEwan, *The Survival Factor*, p. 216.

49. Savage, *A Guest of the Emperor*, pp. ix, 76.

50. Richards to Blair, 21 September 1979, series 4/12, box 7, PRO1916, AWM.

51. Richards to Blair, 22 April 1980, AWM.

52. Clay Blair to Richards, 18 April 1978, AWM.

53. Richards and McEwan, *The Survival Factor*, p. 226.

54. Stephen Garton, *The Cost of War: Australians Return* (Melbourne: Oxford University Press, 1996), p. 226.

55. Quoted in Pamela Ballinger, "The Culture of Survivors," *History and Memory*, vol. 10, no. 1, 1998, p. 99.

56. Hearder, *Keep the Men Alive*, p. 200.

57. Didier Fassin and Richard Rechtman, *The Empire of Trauma: An Inquiry into the Condition of Victimhood*, trans. Rachel Gomme (Princeton: Princeton University Press, 2009), pp. 88, 95–96, 284.

58. Ballinger, "Culture of Survivors," p. 101; Garton, *The Cost of War*, p. 226; Edgar Jones and Simon Wessely, *Shell Shock to PTSD: Military Psychiatry from 1900 to the Gulf War* (New York: Psychology Press, 2005), p. 212.

59. Peter Monteath, *P.O.W.: Australian Prisoners of War in Hitler's Reich* (Sydney: Macmillan, 2011), p. 419.

60. MacLeod, "Psychiatry on the Burma-Thai Railway," p. 495.

61. Kinvig, *River Kwai Railway*, p. xiii.

62. Daws, *Prisoners of the Japanese*, p. 384.

63. Shephard, *A War of Nerves*, p. 323.

64. Christopher Tennant, Kerry Goulston and Owen Dent, "Australian Prisoners of War of the Japanese: Post-War Psychiatric Hospitalisation and Psychological Morbidity," *Australian and New Zealand Journal of Psychiatry*, vol. 20, no. 3, 1986, pp. 334–340.

65. Robert J. Ursano, "Prisoners of War: Long-term Health Outcomes," *The Lancet*, vol. 362, December 2003, Supplement, p. 23.

66. Gerald F. Linderman, *The World Within War: American Combat Experience in World War II* (New York: The Free Press, 1997), p. 361.

67. Christina Twomey, "POWs of the Japanese: Race and Trauma in Australia, 1970–2005," *Journal of War and Culture Studies*, vol. 7, no. 3, August 2014, p. 202; Christina Twomey, "Trauma and the Reinvigoration of Anzac: An Argument," *History Australia*, vol. 10, no. 3, December 2013, p. 85; Twomey, *The Battle Within*, pp. 220–21.

68. Bancroft Interview, 1982, AWM.

69. John Harman to author, 2 November 2017.

70. Bancroft and Harman, *Arthur's War*, p.106.

71. Bancroft and Harman, *Arthur's War*, pp. 3, 280.

72. George Fink, *Stress of War, Conflict and Disaster* (San Diego: Academic Press, 2010), p. 623; Fassin and Rechtman, *The Empire of Trauma*, p. 75; Samuel Hynes, *The Soldiers' Tale: Bearing Witness to Modern War* (New York: Penguin Books, 1997), p. 218.

73. Bancroft and Harman, *Arthur's War*, pp. 244–45.

74. Bancroft and Harman, *Arthur's War*, p. 266.

75. Bancroft and Harman, *Arthur's War*, p. 279.

76. See Mary Chamberlain, "Narrative Theory," in Thomas A. Charlton, Lois E. Myers and Rebecca Sharpless (eds.), *Thinking About Oral History: Theories and Applications* (New York: Alta Mira Press, 2008), pp. 151, 162.

Chapter 16

1. Dean Aszkielowicz, "Repatriation and the Limits of Resolve: Japanese War Criminals in Australian Custody," *Japanese Studies*, vol. 31, no. 2, September 2011, p. 215.

2. Yuma Totani, *Justice in Asia and the Pacific Region, 1945–1952: Allied War Crimes Prosecutions* (New York: Cambridge University Press, 2015), pp. 3, 9.

3. Russell, *The Knights of Bushido*, p. 308.

4. McGovern Interview, AWFA.

5. Adam-Smith, *Prisoners of War*, p. 698; Twomey, *The Battle Within*, p. 161.
6. Quoted in Hearder, *Keep the Men Alive*, pp. 125-126.
7. Coates and Rosenthal, *The Albert Coates Story*, pp. 91, 93-95, 116.
8. Coates and Rosenthal, *The Albert Coates Story*, pp. 161, 166.
9. Twomey, *The Battle Within*, p. 172.
10. World War II war crimes—Fact sheet 61, NAA, http://www.naa.gov.au/collection/fact-sheets/fs61.aspx (Accessed 27 March 2018); Georgina Fitzpatrick, Tim McCormack and Narelle Morris, *Australia's War Crime Trials 1945-51* (Leiden: Brill Nijhoff, 2016), pp. xi, 19; Rowland, *A River Kwai Story*, p. 12.
11. Rowland, *A River Kwai Story*, p. 262; Dower, *Embracing Defeat*, p. 448.
12. Fitzpatrick et al., *Australia's War Crimes Trials*, p. 581.
13. Allied Land Forces South East Asia, War Crimes Instructions, BMA 42/46, NAS.
14. Fitzpatrick et al., *Australia's War Crimes Trials*, pp. 568, 574, 576.
15. Russell, *The Knights of Bushido*, pp. 68-69.
16. *Straits Times* (Singapore), 18 May 1945, p. 3; Aszkielowicz, "Repatriation and the Limits of Resolve," p. 211; Fitzpatrick et al., *Australia's War Crimes Trials*, pp. 602-3.
17. Richards, *A Doctor's War*, p. 288; Charles Richards, Affidavit, 28 January 1948, Record Group 331, entry EVD1189, box 990, NARA.
18. *Straits Times* (Singapore), 28 July 1948, p. 4; *Canberra Times*, 9 December 1948, p. 1.
19. See for example Harold Ramsey, Affidavit, 13 February 1948; Keith Martin, Affidavit, 10 February 1948, Record Group 331, entry EVD1189, box 990, NARA.
20. See for example Sleeman, *Trial of Gozawa*, p. 207.
21. Russell Savage, Affidavit, 27 April 1948, Record Group 331, entry EVD1189, box 990, NARA.
22. Kitchener Loughnan, Affidavit, 14 April 1948, Record Group 331, entry EVD1189, box 990, NARA. See also affidavits of Raymond Burridge, 11 March 1948 and Keith Martin, 10 February 1948.
23. Japanese Camp Commandants and Guards, *Rakuyo Maru*—Japanese Transport, series B6121, control symbol 20S, NAA.
24. Parkin, *Wartime Trilogy*, pp. 348, 754; Clarke, *Twilight Liberation*, p. 14.
25. Sleeman, *Trial of Gozawa*, pp. xxxi-xxxiv, xli, 12-13, 32; Lamont-Brown, *Ships from Hell*, pp. 40-41; Russell, *The Knights of Bushido*, pp. 171-172. Babelthuap is also known as Babeldaob.
26. Sleeman, *Trial of Gozawa*, pp. xxxiii, 12-13, 32-33.
27. Sleeman, *Trial of Gozawa*, pp. xxxiv-xxxv.
28. Sleeman, *Trial of Gozawa*, pp. xxxi-xxxii.
29. Sleeman, *Trial of Gozawa*, p. lvii.
30. Sleeman, *Trial of Gozawa*, p. lxi.
31. Sleeman, *Trial of Gozawa*, pp. lix, lxi.
32. Sleeman, *Trial of Gozawa*, pp. lii-lii, 88, 242.
33. Sleeman, *Trial of Gozawa*, p. 222.
34. Sleeman, *Trial of Gozawa*, p. 183.
35. Sleeman, *Trial of Gozawa*, p. xlv-xlii.
36. Sleeman, *Trial of Gozawa*, pp. xlv, 83, 230-231.
37. Sleeman, *Trial of Gozawa*, p. xlvi.
38. Sleeman, *Trial of Gozawa*, p. 213.
39. Sleeman, *Trial of Gozawa*, pp. 32-33.
40. Sleeman, *Trial of Gozawa*, pp. lxvi-lxvii, 206-208. Italics in original.
41. Sleeman, *Trial of Gozawa*, p. 200.
42. Sleeman, *Trial of Gozawa*, p. lxviii.

Chapter 17

1. Parkin, *Wartime Trilogy*, pp. 348, 754; Clarke, *Twilight Liberation*, p. 14. The ship is also variously referred to as *Byoke Maru*, *Beyoke Maru*, and *Bioki Maru*.
2. Quoted in Lamont-Brown, *Ships from Hell*, p. 24.
3. War Crimes—Military Tribunal, series A471, control symbol 81642, Canberra, NAA [henceforth cited as Trial of Uchiyama and Fukuda]; Harrison, *Road to Hiroshima*, p. 208; Bowden, *Australians under Nippon*, radio broadcast; *Rashin Maru*, https://wrecksite.edu/wreck.aspx?136393 (Accessed 23 March 2018).
4. Trial of Uchiyama and Fukuda, pp. 29, 47, 74, 150.
5. Sweeting, "Prisoners of the Japanese," p. 612; Trial of Uchiyama and Fukuda, pp. 47-49.
6. Trial of Uchiyama and Fukuda, pp. 28, 204; Harrison, *Road to Hiroshima*, pp. 208, 210-211; Adam-Smith, *Prisoners of War*,

pp. 545-48; Alden and McDonald, *Allied Submarine Successes*, p. 189.

7. Quoted in Craig R. McDonald, *The USS Puffer in World War II: A History of the Submarine and Its Wartime Crew* (Jefferson, NC: McFarland and Company, 2008), p. 158.

8. Forbes, *Hellfire*, pp. 384-386; Clarke, *Last Stop Nagasaki*, p. 1.

9. Ralph Everett, Affidavit, Trial of Uchiyama and Fukuda, p. 150; Spurling, *Cruel Conflict*, p. 268.

10. Richard Parker, Affidavit, Trial of Uchiyama and Fukuda, p. 205.

11. Thomas Martz, Affidavit, Trial of Uchiyama and Fukuda, pp. 197-198; Harrison, *Road to Hiroshima*, p. 215.

12. John Inglis Jennings, Affidavit, 30 August 1945; Geoffrey Arthur Worland, Affidavit, 30 August 1945; George Colevas, Affidavit, 31 August 1945, Record Group 331, EVD1189, box 990, NARA.

13. Trial of Uchiyama and Fukuda, pp. 2, 31, 135; Fitzpatrick et al., *Australia's War Crimes Trials*, p. 595.

14. Trial of Uchiyama and Fukuda, pp. 47, 59, 228.

15. Trial of Uchiyama and Fukuda, pp. 79, 83, 90, 98, 103, 229.

16. Sandra Wilson, "Koreans in the Trials of Japanese War Crimes Suspects," in Kerstin von Lingen (ed.), *Debating Collaboration and Complicity in War Crimes Trials in Asia, 1945-1956* (New York: Palgrave Macmillan, 2017), p. 22.

17. Trial of Uchiyama and Fukuda, pp. 20, 22, 46; *Straits Times* (Singapore), 23 October 1946, p. 4.

18. Trial of Uchiyama and Fukuda, pp. 36-37, 40-41.

19. Cribb, "The Life and Trial of Cho Un-kuk, Korean War Criminal," *Critical Asian Studies*, vol. 50, no. 3, 2018, p. 344.

20. Trial of Uchiyama and Fukuda, pp. 61, 64.

21. Trial of Uchiyama and Fukuda, pp. 45, 49, 100.

22. Trial of Uchiyama and Fudkuda, pp. 108-109.

23. Trial of Uchiyama and Fukuda, p. 142.

24. Trial of Uchiyama and Fukuda, pp. 146-47.

25. Daws, *Prisoners of the Japanese*, p. 284.

26. Wu Ling Cheah, "Post-World War II British 'Hell-Ship' Trials in Singapore: Omissions and the Attribution of Responsibility," *Journal of International Criminal Justice*, vol. 8, no. 4, 2010, pp. 1036, 1038.

27. Trial of Uchiyama and Fukuda, pp. 50, 58, 151, 203-204.

28. Trial of Uchiyama and Fukuda, p. 45.

29. Trial of Uchiyama and Fukuda, pp. 116-117.

30. Trial of Uchiyama and Fukuda, p. 53.

31. Ralph Forbes, Affidavit, Trial of Uchiyama and Fukuda, p. 151.

32. Reginald Newton, Affidavit, Trial of Uchiyama and Fukuda, p. 188.

33. Richard Parker, Affidavit, Trial of Uchiyama and Fukuda, pp. 203-204.

34. Trial of Uchiyama and Fukuda, pp. 30, 78.

35. Ralph Forbes, Affidavit, Trial of Uchiyama and Fukuda, p. 152.

36. Harrison, *Road to Hiroshima*, p. 209.

37. Harrison, *Road to Hiroshima*, p. 210; Bowden, *Australians under Nippon*, radio broadcast.

38. Trial of Uchiyama and Fukuda, pp. 55-56.

39. Trial of Uchiyama and Fukuda, p. 86.

40. Trial of Uchiyama and Fukuda, pp. 102-103.

41. Trial of Uchiyama and Fukuda, p. 137.

42. Judge Advocate General's Office, British War Crime Trial, Defendants Nishimi, Yoshinari; Ogasawara, Makoto; Mauryama, Naosuke,; Uchida, Yoichi, War Office, WO235/1043, NAS; Rowland, *A River Kwai Story*, p. 251.

43. Trial of Uchiyama and Fukuda, p. 123.

44. Trial of Uchiyama and Fukuda, pp. 124-26.

45. Trial of Uchiyama and Fukuda, pp. 50, 59.

46. Trial of Uchiyama and Fukuda, p. 128.

47. Trial of Uchiyama and Fukuda, pp. 132-34.

48. Trial of Uchiyama and Fukuda, pp. 138-39.

49. Trial of Uchiyama and Fukuda, pp. 5, 137; Wilson, "Koreans in the Trials of Japanese War Crimes Suspects," p. 32.

50. Rowland, *A River Kwai Story*, p. 13; Trial of Uchiyama and Fukuda, p. 139.

51. Petition of Uchiyama and Fukuda, 12 May 1947, Trial of Uchiyama and Fukuda, p. 6.

52. Adjutant-General / Judge Advocate General, Canberra, 10 July 1947, Trial of Uchiyama and Fukuda, p. 5.
53. A. G. Wright to Editor, *Daily Telegraph* (Sydney), 20 February 1946, p. 10.
54. Wilson et al., *Japanese War Criminals*, p. 141; Aszkielowicz, "Repatriation and the Limits of Resolve," pp. 212, 224; Twomey, *The Battle Within*, pp. 182, 185.
55. Wilson et al., *Japanese War Criminals*, p. 85.
56. Judge Advocate General, War Crimes Trials, Defendant: Jotani Kitaichi, WO235/995, NAS.
57. See Totani, *Justice in Asia and the Pacific Region*, p. 183
58. Judge Advocate General, War Crimes Trials, Defendant: Nakanishim, Haruyoshi, WO235/1006, NAS.
59. Judge Advocate General, War Crimes Trials, Defendants: Odake, Bunji; Ino, Takeo, WO235/1052, NAS.
60. Cheah, "Post-World War II British 'Hell-Ship' Trials in Singapore," pp. 1037, 1053.
61. Cheah, "Post-World War II British 'Hell-Ship' Trials in Singapore," pp. 1042–43, 1057–58.
62. Cheah, "Post-World War II British 'Hell Ship' Trials in Singapore," p. 1046.
63. Nagase, *Crosses and Tigers*, p. 86.
64. Alden and McDonald, *Allied Submarine Successes*, p. 331; *Rashin Maru*, wrecksite.

Chapter 18

1. War Crimes—Military Tribunal—Yamasaka Tatsuo (Petty Officer)—Hong Kong, 23 and 29 June 1948, series A471, control symbol 81636, Canberra, NAA [henceforth cited as Trial of Yamasaka].
2. Prosecutor's opening address, Trial of Yamasaka, p. 116.
3. Trial of Yamasaka, p. 179.
4. Trial of Yamasaka, p. 124.
5. Trial of Yamasaka, p. 52; *Sanuki Maru*, Combined Fleet (Accessed 23 September 2019).
6. Trial of Yamasaka, pp. 52, 56.
7. Percy Green, Affidavit, 26 February 1947, Trial of Yamasaka, p. 127.
8. *Sanuki Maru*, Combined Fleet.
9. Percy Green, Affidavit, p. 127.
10. Trial of Yamasaka, p.3.
11. Samuel Parker, Affidavit, Trial of Yamasaka, p. 145.
12. Evidence of Percy Green, Trial of Yamasaka, p. 132.
13. Trial of Yamasaka, p. 125; John Benge, Affidavit, p. 139.
14. Evidence of Mayuzumi, Trial of Yamasaka, p. 79; Lamont-Brown, *Ships from Hell*, pp. 110–111; Felton, *Slaughter at Sea*, p. 115.
15. Trial of Yamasaka, p. 14.
16. John Benge, Affidavit, p. 138.
17. Trial of Yamasaka, p. 15.
18. Trial of Yamasaka, pp. 16, 48.
19. Evidence of James Godwin, Trial of Yamasaka, pp. 20–23.
20. Evidence of Percy Green, p. 131.
21. Evidence of Percy Green, pp. 65–67.
22. Trial of Yamasaka, pp. 45–46.
23. Trial of Yamasaka , p. 183.
24. Trial of Yamasaka, p. 178.
25. Evidence of Yamasaka, pp. 87–88, 91–93, 98.
26. Evidence of Yamasaka, p. 100.
27. Trial of Yamasaka, p. 185.
28. Trial of Yamasaka, p. 173.
29. Evidence of Yamasaka, p. 59.
30. Evidence of Green, pp. 72–73.
31. Evidence of Yamasaka, pp. 48, 51–52.
32. Trial of Yamasaka, p. 177.
33. Evidence of Yamasaka, pp. 54, 57, 99.
34. Trial of Yamasaka, p. 112.
35. Felton, *Slaughter at Sea*, pp. 116–117; Lamont-Brown, *Ships from Hell*, pp. 112–114, 146; *Courier Mail* (Brisbane), 26 April 2008; Russell, *The Knights of Bushido*, pp. 230–232.
36. Evidence of Mayuzumi, p. 77.
37. Evidence of Mayuzumi, pp. 113–114.
38. Trial of Yamasaka, p. 185.
39. Trial of Yamasaka, p. 115.
40. *Advertiser* (Adelaide), 10 May 1947, p. 1.
41. Captain James Gibson, Affidavit, Judge Advocate General, War Crimes Trial, Defendant Jotani Kaitaichi, WO235/995, NAS.
42. Evidence of James Godwin, Trial of Yamasaka, p. 31.
43. *Sanuki Maru*, Combined Fleet.

Chapter 19

1. Romen Bose, *Singapore at War: Secrets from the Fall, Liberation and*

Aftermath of WWII (Singapore: Marshall Cavendish, 2012), p. 136; Stephen Connor, "Side-stepping Geneva: Japanese Troops under British Control, 1945–7," *Journal of Contemporary History*, vol. 42, no. 2, 2010, pp. 390–91.

2. Shinozaki, *Syonan My Story*, p. 175; Romen Bose, *Kranji: The Commonwealth War Cemetery and the Politics of the Dead* (Singapore: Marshall Canvendish, 2006), p. 53; Kazuo Tamayama, *Railwaymen in the War: Tales by Japanese Railway Soldiers in Burma and Thailand 1941–47* (New York: Palgrave Macmillan, 2005), pp. xii, 15, 275–76.

3. See Stephen B. Connor, *Mountbatten's Samurai: Imperial Japanese Army and Navy Forces under British Control in Southeast Asia, 1945–1948* (London: Seventh Citadel, 2015, pp. 148–49.

4. Connor, "Side-stepping Geneva," p. 404.

5. Yoizuki, Combined Fleet, http://www.combinedfleet.com/yoizuk_t.htm (Accessed 15 August 2018).

6. External Affairs papers, 26 February 1946, series A1067, control symbol P146/11/7/1, Canberra, NAA; *Sydney Morning Herald*, 21 January 1946, clipping in series A5954, control symbol 2170/1, Canberra, NAA.

7. *Sun* (Sydney), 6 March 1946, p. 1.

8. *Sydney Morning Herald*, 15 March 1946, p. 3.

9. *Canberra Times*, 8 March 1945, p. 1.

10. *Sun* (Sydney), 10 November 1944, p. 2.

11. *Sydney Morning Herald*, 7 March 1946, clipping in series A5954, control symbol 2170/1, NAA. Subsequent newspaper references cited without page numbers refer to clippings in this record group.

12. *Sydney Morning Herald*, 8 March 1946.

13. *Sydney Morning Herald*, 7 March 1946.

14. *Advocate* (Melbourne), 13 March 1946, p. 6.

15. *Herald* (Melbourne), 7 March 1946, p. 4.

16. *Smith's Weekly* (Sydney), 16 March 1946, p. 3.

17. Australian High Commissioner, Wellington, 9 March 1946, series A1067, control symbol P146/11/7/1, Canberra, NAA.

18. External Affairs statement, 11 March 1946, series A1067, control symbol P146/11/7/1, NAA.

19. *Sun* (Sydney), 11 March 1945, p. 2.

20. External Affairs confidential background, series A1067, control symbol P146/11/7/1, Canberra, NAA.

21. External Affairs confidential background, series A1067, control symbol P146/11/7/1, Canberra, NAA.

22. Message to Secretary, Department of External Affairs, 11 March 1946, series A5954, control symbol 1654/5, NAA.

23. External Affairs communication, 2 March 1946, series A1067, control symbol P146/11/7/1, NAA.

24. *Daily Telegraph* (Sydney), 21 March 1946, clipping.

25. External Affairs, series A1067, control symbol P146/11/7/1, NAA; *Telegraph* (Brisbane), 12 March 1946, p. 2.

26. *Sydney Morning Herald*, 8 March 1946.

27. *Argus* (Melbourne), 8 March 1946.

28. Prime Minister to General MacArthur, 8 March 1946, series A5954, control symbol 1654/5, NAA.

29. MacArthur to Prime Minister, 11 March 1946, series A5954, control symbol 1654/5, NAA.

30. MacArthur to Prime Minister, 12 March 1946, series A5954, control symbol 1654/5, NAA.

31. *Daily Telegraph* (Sydney), 12 March 1946, p. 2; *Melbourne Herald*, 12 March 1946.

32. *Sydney Morning Herald*, 12 March 1946, p. 1.

33. *Telegraph* (Brisbane), 12 March 1946, p. 2.

34. Statement by Prime Minister for Press, 9 March 1946, series A5954, control symbol 1654/5, NAA.

35. *Sydney Morning Herald*, 14 March 1946.

36. MacArthur to Prime Minister, 12 March 1946, series A5954, control symbol 1654/5, NAA.

37. Statement by Prime Minister for Press, 10 March 1946, series A5954, control symbol 1654/5, NAA.

38. Prime Minister to General MacArthur, 8 March 1946, series A5954, control symbol 1654/5, NAA.

39. Quoted in *Sydney Morning Herald*, 21 March 1946.

40. External Affairs confidential

background, series A1067, control symbol P146/11/7/1, NAA; *Sydney Morning Herald*, 21 March 1946.
41. House of Representatives, 13 March 1946, extract in series A5954, control symbol 2170/1, NAA.
42. *Sydney Morning Herald*, 11 March 1946; *Daily Telegraph*, 11 March 1946.
43. *Sydney Morning Herald*, 12 March 1946.
44. *Daily Telegraph* (Sydney), 12 March 1946.
45. *Herald* (Melbourne), 12 March 1946; *Sydney Morning Herald*, 12 March 1946, p. 1; *Sydney Morning Herald*, 21 March 1946; *Daily Telegraph* (Sydney), 17 March 1946, p. 12.
46. *Argus* (Melbourne), 22 March 1946.
47. *Herald* (Melbourne), 21 March 1946, p. 4.
48. *Daily Telegraph* (Sydney), 21 March 1946.
49. *Sun* (Sydney), 21 March 1946, p. 1.
50. *Daily Telegraph* (Sydney), 21 March 1946.
51. *Age* (Melbourne), 15 March 1946.
52. *Daily Telegraph* (Sydney), 12 March 1946.
53. *Sydney Morning Herald*, 21 March 1946.
54. *Sydney Morning Herald*, 15 March 1946.
55. *Herald* (Melbourne), 21 March 1946.
56. *Sydney Morning Herald*, 11 March 1946.
57. *Sydney Morning Herald*, 12 March 1946, p. 1.
58. House of Representatives, 13 March 1946, extract in series A5954, control symbol 2170/1, NAA.
59. Confidential message from Minister for the Army to Adjutant-General, Victoria Barracks, 13 March 1946, series A5954, control symbol 1654/5, NAA.
60. House of Representatives, 13 March 1946, extract in series A5954, control symbol 2170/1, NAA.
61. Quoted in *Sydney Morning Herald*, 21 March 1946.
62. Quoted in *Daily Telegraph* (Sydney), 21 March 1946.
63. *Herald* (Melbourne), 13 March 1946.
64. House of Representatives, 13 March 1946, extract in series A5954, control symbol 2170/1, NAA.
65. *Herald* (Melbourne), 9 March 1946.
66. M. M. Evans to Editor, *Advertiser* (Adelaide), 13 March 1946, p. 10.
67. No Protest to Editor, *Newcastle Morning Herald and Miners' Advocate*, 15 March 1946, p. 5.
68. Justice to Editor, *Mercury* (Hobart), 15 March 1946, p. 13.
69. John Inglis Jennings and Geoffrey Arthur Worland, Affidavits, 30 August 1945, Record Group 331, entry EVD1189. Box 990, NARA.
70. EX-TX2162 to Editor, *Mercury* (Hobart), 19 March 1946, p. 15.
71. Lonely Mother to Editor, *Mercury* (Hobart), 20 March 1946, p. 3.
72. M. K. Jones to Editor, *Sydney Morning Herald*, 8 March 1946, p. 2.
73. Ex-P.O.W. Medical Officer to Editor, *Sydney Morning Herald*, 9 March 1946, p. 2.
74. Obedient to Editor, *Sydney Morning Herald*, 14 March 1946, p. 2.
75. Justice to Editor, *Mercury* (Hobart), 15 March 1946, p. 13.
76. John Allen to Editor, *Daily Telegraph* (Sydney), 9 December 1946, p. 8.
77. *Herald* (Melbourne), 21 March 1946, p. 4.

Chapter 20

1. Laurence Rees, *Horror in the East: Japan and the Atrocities of World War II* (Cambridge, MA: Da Capo Press, 2001), p. 13.
2. Maria Hsia Chang and Robert P. Barker, "Victor's Justice and Japan's Amnesia: The Tokyo War Crimes Trial Reconsidered," in Peter Li, *Japanese War Crimes: The Search for Justice* (New Brunswick, NJ: Transaction Publishers, 2003), p. 44; Sleeman, *Trial of Gozawa*, p. 198.
3. Ikuhiko Hata, "From Consideration to Contempt: The Changing Nature of Japanese Military and Popular Perceptions of Prisoners of War through the Ages," in Bob Moore and Kent Fedorowich (eds.), *Prisoners of War and their Captors in World War II* (Oxford: Berg, 1996), p. 266.
4. Tanaka, *Hidden Horrors*, p. 2; Havers, *Reassessing the Japanese Prisoner of War Experience*, pp. 5–6; Tachikawa, "The Treatment of Prisoners of War," p. 47.
5. Felton, *Slaughter at Sea*, p. 66; Lamont-Brown, *Ships from Hell*, pp. 33–36.

6. Quoted in Toland, *The Rising Sun*, p. 600.
7. Wright, *Captured at Corregidor*, p. 87.
8. Shively, *Profiles in Survival*, pp. 87, 145–48.
9. Quoted in Miller, *D-Days in the Pacific*, pp. 318–19.
10. Quoted in Knox, *Death March*, p. 342.
11. See for example Miller, *D-Days in the Pacific*, p. 317.
12. Shively, *Profiles in Survival*, p. 87.
13. Roland, *Long Night's Journey into Day*, pp. 211–12, 265; Banham, *They Shall Suffer There*, p. 112. The ship was also known as *Tatuta Maru*.
14. Quoted in Roland, *Long Night's Journey into Day*, p. 213.
15. Patterson, *A Spoonful of Rice*, p. 49.
16. Quoted in Lukacs, *Escape from Davao*, p. 113.
17. Samuel C. Grashio and Bernard Norling, *Escape to Freedom: The War Memoirs of Col. Samuel C. Grashio USAF* (Tulsa, OK: MCN Press, 1982), p. 94.
18. *Straits Times*, 15 December 1946, p. 6.
19. Patterson, *A Spoonful of Rice*, p. 87.
20. Knox, *Death March*, p. 380.
21. Anthony Cowling, *My Life with the Samurai* (Sydney: Kangaroo Press, 1996), pp. 86, 141.
22. Toland, *The Rising Sun*, p. 599.
23. Quoted in Banham, *We Shall Suffer There*, p. 60.
24. Lukacs, *Escape from Davao*, pp. 111, 113; Grashio and Norling, *Escape to Freedom*, pp. 79–80; Shively, *Profiles in Survival*, p. 357.
25. *Straits Times* (Singapore), 15 December 1946, p. 6.
26. Quoted in Knox, *Death March*, p. 347.
27. Cowling, *My Life with the Samurai*, p. 80.
28. I am borrowing the phrase of Levine, *Captivity*, p. 186.
29. Wright, *Captured at Corregidor*, p. 115.
30. Wright, *Captured on Corregidor*, p. 119.
31. Quoted in Parkes and Gill, *Captive Memories*, p. 31.
32. Martin, *Brothers from Bataan*, p. 189.
33. Cowling, *My Life with the Samurai*, p. 81.
34. Quoted in Parkes and Gill, *Captive Memories*, 33.
35. Shively, *Profiles in Survival*, p. 86.
36. Lizzie Oliver, *Prisoners of the Sumatra Railway: Narratives of History and Memory* (London: Bloomsbury Academic, 2019), pp. 2, 12, 15–16.
37. H. P. Wilmott, *The Battle of Leyte Gulf: The Last Fleet Action* (Bloomington: Indiana University Press, 2005) pp. 10, 32–33.
38. See for example Russell, *The Knights of Bushido*, p. 57; Rees, *Horror in the East*, p. 91; Cowling, *My Life with the Samurai*, p. 83; MacArthur, *Surviving the Sword*, p. 2.
39. Cowling, *My Life with the Samurai*, p. 83.
40. Quoted in Russell, *The Knights of Bushido*, pp. 128–29; Lamont-Brown, *Ships from Hell*, pp. 42–43.
41. See for example Cowling, *My Life with the Samurai*, p. 83; Sleeman, *Trial of Gozawa*, p. liv.
42. Hornfischer, *The Fleet at Floodtide*, p. 340; Cressman, *Chronology of the U.S. Navy*, p. 253.
43. See for example Banham, *They Shall Suffer There*, p. 154.
44. Bruce Gamble, *Darkest Hour: The True Story of Lark Force at Rabaul* (St. Paul, Minn.: Zenith Press, 2006), p. 233.
45. Levine, *Captivity*, pp. 84–85.
46. Roland, *Long Night's Journey into Day*, p. 246.
47. Grashio and Norling, *Escape to Freedom*, p. 87.
48. Henry Frei, "Surrendering Syonan," in Akashi Yoji and Yoshimura Mako (eds.), *New Perspectives on the Japanese Occupation of Malaya and Singapore, 1941–1945* (Singapore: National University of Singapore Press, 2008), pp. 223–24.
49. Quoted in Knox, *Death March*, p. 446.
50. Wright, *Captured on Corregidor*, p. 95.
51. Frei, "Surrendering Syonan," p. 223.
52. Roland, *Long Night's Journey into Day*, p. 264.
53. Miller, *Mercy Ships*, pp. 133–136, 139, 141; Roland, *Long Night's Journey into Day*, p. 264.
54. Graham, *Japan's Sea Lane Security*, p. 73.
55. See Shindo, "Japanese Strategy for

the South Pacific," p. 155; Douglas Ford, *The Pacific War: Clash of Empires in World War II* (London: Continuum, 2012), pp. 61, 108.

56. See Shively, *Profiles in Survival*, p. 587.

57. See for example Patterson, *A Spoonful of Rice*, p. 48.

Epilogue

1. Bose, *Kranji*, p. 12.
2. *Weekend Australian*, 24 March 2012, p. 22; *Sun Herald* (Sydney), 22 April 2007, p. 82; 24 April 2011, p. 51; Yuriko Nagata, *Unwanted Aliens: Japanese Internment in Australia* (St. Lucia: University of Queensland Press, 1996, p. 116.
3. See for example H. A. Dawkins to Madame Morrieur, 10 August 1945, WO 361/733, NAS.
4. G. D. Loup, Brigadier, PW Branch, Washington, to War Office, 2 April 1946, WO 361/733, NAS.
5. *West Australian*, 7 February 1948, p. 5.
6. Mrs. A. Raft, 31 August 1948, *Rakuyo Maru* Correspondence, series B3856, control symbol 144/1/128, NAA.
7. See for example *Courier-Mail*, 12 September 1951, p. 12; 12 September 1952, p. 12.
8. Herbert, *Dave's War*, p. 104, AWM.
9. John J. Flynn to unknown recipient, 6 January 1988, Records of Sgt. J. J. Flynn, PR88/110, file 419/33/44, AWM.
10. Grant, *Australian Soldiers in Asia-Pacific*, pp. 6, 159, 201; Twomey, *The Battle Within*, pp. 159–160.
11. Grant, *Australian Soldiers in Asia-Pacific*, pp. 103, 163–164, 166.
12. See for example John Winton, *The Forgotten Fleet: The British Navy in the Pacific 1944–1945* (New York: Coward-McCann, 1970), p. 358.
13. McGovern Interview, AWFA.
14. Parkin Interview, AWFA.
15. Rivett, *Behind Bamboo*, p. 378.
16. Arneil, *One Man's War*, p. 247.
17. Clarke, *Last Stop Nagasaki*, p. 124.
18. Richards, *A Doctor's War*, pp. 268, 286, 299.
19. Brigginshaw, *Shimpu-San Healer of Hate*, p. 15.
20. Arneil, *One Man's War*, p. 272.
21. Carter and MacPherson, *The Burma Railway*, pp. 227, 231.
22. Kerr, *Surrender and Survival*, p. 299.
23. *Straits Times* (Singapore), 16 January 1984, p. 2.
24. Carter and MacPherson, *The Burma Railway*, pp. 232–33.
25. Bruce Scates, Catherine Tiernan and Rebecca Wheatley, "The Railway Men: Prisoner Journeys through the Traumascapes of World War II," *Journal of War and Cultural Studies*, vol. 7, no. 3, August 2014, p. 211.
26. Bancroft Interview, AWFA.
27. Richards, *A Doctor's War*, p. 301.
28. Carter and MacPherson, *The Burma Railway*, pp. 5–6, 233.
29. Richards, *A Doctor's War*, p. 302.
30. Wheeler Interview, AWFA.
31. David Sutton and Peter Wogan, *Hollywood Blockbusters: The Anthropology of Popular Movies* (Oxford: Berg, 2009), pp. 118–119.
32. See for example Grashio and Norling, *Escape to Freedom*, pp. 80–81; Shively, *Profiles in Survival*, p. 359.
33. *Brazil Maru*, Combined Fleet.
34. Bancroft Interview, AWFA.
35. Richards Interview, AWFA.
36. Savage, *A Guest of the Emperor*, p. 137.
37. *Road to Tokyo*, Film Australia, writer / director Graham Shirley, 2005.
38. *Age* (Melbourne), 11 August 2005, p. 16.
39. *Road to Tokyo* press kit, National Film and Sound Archive.
40. *Weekend Australian*, 16 October 2004, p. 4.
41. *Road to Tokyo*, 2005.
42. *Illawarra Mercury* (Woolongong), 11 September 2004, p. 36.
43. *West Australian*, 1 March 1947, p. 1.
44. Bancroft Interview, AWFA.
45. *Daily News* (Warwick, Queensland), 17 April 2010, p. 86; *Courier Mail* (Brisbane), 4 February 2010, p. 67.
46. *Sydney Morning Herald*, 3 August 2013, p. 16.
47. *Sydney Morning Herald*, 27 March 2015, online.
48. Nicole Chettle, "HMAS Perth Survivors share stories of hardship on 75th anniversary of disaster," ABC News, 7 October 2017, https://www.abc.net.au/news/2017-10-07/hmas-perth-survivors-share-stories-75-anniversary/9023970 (Accessed 5 February 2019).

Bibliography

Archival Materials

Australians at War Film Archive (AWFA) (Australiansatwarfilmarchive.unsw.edu.au)

Bancroft, Arthur. Interview (audio-visual and transcript). 20 November 2003. Archive 1082.
Cornford, Roydon. Interview (audio-visual and transcript). 25 November 2003. Archive 1135.
McGovern, Frank. Interview (audio-visual and transcript). 8 May 2003. Archive 19.
Parkin, Ray. Interview (audio-visual and transcript). 7 June 2000. Archive 2552.
Richards, Charles. Interview (audio-visual and transcript). 4 April 2002. Archive 1144.
Wheeler, Raymond. Interview (audio-visual and transcript). 15 September 2003. Archive 944.

Australian War Memorial, Canberra (AWM)

Brief stories told by prisoners of war rescued by U.S.A. submarines, series 54, control symbol 779/10/3.
Consolidated interrogation report of ninety-one Australian prisoners of war recovered from torpedoed Japanese transport in China Sea Sept 1944, series 54, control symbol 779/3/45.

INTERVIEWS

Bancroft, Arthur. Interview (audio recording). 8 October 1990. S04052.
Bancroft, Arthur. Interview (audio recording). 11 December 1982. S02950.
Farlow, Clifford Leslie. Interview (audio recording). 8 September 1990. S04058.
McGovern, Francis Joseph. Interview (audio recording). 24 October 1990. S04089.

PRIVATE PAPERS

Bancroft, Arthur. HMAS *Perth* Survivors Prisoners of War 1942–45. Naval Historical Society of Australia. File F359.009 N318.
Flynn, John J. Records. PR88/110.
Herbert, David Clark. "Dave's Way: A POW Memoir." Compiled by Cherie Lawton. 2014. MSS 2280.
Huckins, John Edward. Unpublished memoir. 1994. MSS 1550.
Murphy, Thomas Francis. War Diary. PR87/029.
Richards, Rowley. Papers. 1942–1984. PR01916.
Turner, John Wilfred. "A True Autobiography of My Life as a Prisoner of War from 15 February 1942 till 12 September 1944. Also of my experience from 12 September 1944 till arrival in Australia." PR00651.

Bibliography

Imperial War Museum, London (IWM)

Beilby, Philip James. Interview. 22 February 2000. 22662.
Pounder, Thomas. Interview. 30 April 1981. 4887.

National Archives of Australia (NAA)

Canberra

War Cabinet Minute No 3849—Prisoners of war recovered from Japanese vessel torpedoed by US submarine, series A2676, control symbol 3849.
War Cabinet Minute No 3912—Prisoners of war rescued from torpedoed Japanese transport, series A2676, control symbol 3912.
A Report on Japanese atrocities and breaches of the rules of warfare, Sir William Webb, series A10943, control symbol 1.
A report on war crimes by individual members of the armed forces of the enemy against Australians by Sir William Webb, series A10950, control symbol 1. [Second Webb Report]
Japanese Destroyer "Yoizuki," series A1067, control symbol P146/11/7/1.
Japanese vessel "Yoizuki," series A5954, control symbol 1654/5.
Repatriation of Formosans on Japanese destroyer "Yoizuki," series A5954, control symbol 2170/1.
War Crimes—Military Tribunal—Yamasaka Tatsuo (Petty Officer)—Hong Kong, 23 and 29 June 1948, series A471, control symbol 81636.
War Crimes—Military Tribunal—Uchiyama Kishio (Lieutenant); Fukuda Mitsugu (Sergeant)—Singapore, 18, 22, 23, 24 and 29 April 1947, series A471, control symbol 81642.

Melbourne

Rakuyo Maru—Japanese Transport. Loss of 1944. Narrative of Events following Sinking by USS "Queenfish" 12/9/44, series B6121, control symbol 20S.
"Rakuyo Maru," Correspondence concerning the torpedoed Japanese transport carrier, related newspaper cuttings and some statements of interrogation by rescued POWs, series B3856, control symbol 144/1/128.
Searchers Reports, "Rakuyo Maru," Arthur Bancroft (RAN) Reports, series B3856, control symbol 144/1/128 Attachment 9.
Australian PW Survivors ex *Rakuyo Maru*, Summarised report of Events from 4 Sep 44–18 Oct 44, series MP729/8, control symbol 44/431/73.
Rescued PsW ex "Rakuyo Maru," series MP720/6, control symbol 12/401/408.
Ex-Prisoners of War rescued from Japanese Transport "Ryuko [sic] Maru," series MP1049/5, control symbol 1951/2/72.
USS *Pampanito*, Rescue of British and Australian Prisoners-of-War, series MP1049/5, control symbol 1951/2/99.

Service Records

Anderson, Edward William. Series B883, control symbol QX22678.
Antrill, Frank. Series B883, control symbol VX41477.
Bancroft, Arthur. Series A6770, control symbol F3239.
Boulter, James Leo. Series B883, control symbol VX43375.
Cook, Harold Oliver. Series A9300, control symbol 280229.
Cross, Frederick Victor. Series B883, control symbol WX7268.
Cornford, Roydon Charles. Series B883, control symbol NX44955.
Day, Noel Charles Ephraim. Series A9301, control symbol 35423.
Hart, Reginald Hartness. Series B883, control symbol VX23586.
Hinchy, George Frederick. Series B883, control symbol NX31557.
Leithhead, Vivian Charles. Series A9300, control symbol 406858.
Nagle, Harry Lionel. Series A6770, control symbol F3060.
Renton, Kenneth Clive. Series B883, control symbol VX22728.

Smith, William George. Series B883, control symbol QX4556.
Thomson, Murray Andrew. Series B883, control symbol SX8776.

National Archives and Records Administration, College Park, Maryland (NARA)

Records of the Office of the Chief of Naval Operations, Office of Naval Intelligence, Intercepted Enemy Radio Traffic and Related Documentation, 1940–1956, Record Group 38, entry A1–344, box 1279.
Department of State Central Decimal File 1940–1944, Record Group 59, entry CDF1940–1944, box 3062.
Department of State Central Decimal File 1945–49, Record Group 59, entry CDF1945–1949, box 4036.
Records of the Office of the Judge Advocate General (Army), War Crimes Branch, Case Files 1944–1949, Record Group 153, entry A1–143, box 1400.
Record of the War Department General and Special Staffs, Military Intelligence Division, S-C Intelligence Reference Pubs ("P" File) 1940–1945, Record Group 165, entry NM84–79, box 1981.
Naval Operating Force (Blue 443), Commander, Submarine Force U.S. Pacific Fleet Confidential, Restricted and Unclassified Administrative Files, 1942–1945, Record Group 313, entry P-50, box 7.
SCAP Legal Section Administrative Area Case File 1945–1948, Record Group 331, entry UD1189, box 990.
Philippine Archives Collection POWS / Civilian Internees Sunken POW Transport *Arisan Maru*, Record Group 407, entry A1–1069, boxes 146–147.

National Archives of Singapore (NAS)

War Crimes Investigations: Allied Land Forces South East Asia Instructions, British Military Administration (BMA), 42/46.
British and Australian POWs repatriated from the Far East: Interrogation Reports 1944–45, War Office (WO) 208/521.
Far East Report on Interrogation of four British prisoners rescued after sinking of a Japanese transport 1945, WO 208/523.
Judge Advocate General's Office: War Crimes Case Files, Kaneoka Kiko, WO 235/910.
Judge Advocate General's Office: War Crimes Case Files, Jotani Kitaichi, WO 235/995.
Judge Advocate General's Office: War Crimes Case Files, Nakanishi Haruyoshi, WO 235/1006.
Judge Advocate General's Office: War Crimes Case Files, Nishimi, Yoshinari (Captain) and Ogasawara, Makoto (Lieutenant), WO 235/1043.
Judge Advocate General's Office: War Crimes Case Files, Odake, Bunji (Captain) and Ino, Takeo (Lieutenant), WO 235/1052.
Malaya and NEI: Interrogation of survivors from *Rakuyo Maru*, WO 361/435.
Casualties at sea, China Sea, POWs aboard Japanese transport ship *Rakuyo Maru*, WO 361/733.
Casualties at sea, Far East. Japanese POW transport ships sunk: presumption of death, WO 361/752.
Lists of missing and dead from 14 sunk Japanese transports carrying British POWs, WO 361/1741.

National Institute of Defense Studies Library, Tokyo (NIDSL)

(Materials translated by Hiroyuki Shindo)
Boeicho Boeikenshusho Senshishitsu [War History Office, Defence Agency] (ed.), *Kaijo Goei-sen* [Maritime Protection War], Asagumo Shinbunsha, 1971.
Komamiya, Shinshichiro. *Senji Yuso-sendan-shi* [History of Wartime Transport Convoys]. Kyodo Shuppansha, 1987.

Oi, Atushi. *Kaijo Goei-sen* [Maritime Protection War]. Asahi Sonorama.
"Senpaku Yuso-kan ni okeru Sonan (Kaibotsu) (Yukueflumei) Butai (Gunijin) Sieri Shiryo" [Records to Organize Losses (Lost at Sea) (MIA) of Units (Military Personnel and Auxiliaries) during Transport of Ships].
"Showa 19-nen 9-gatsu 27-nichi HI-72 Sendan Hibakugeki Sento Shoho Unso-sen *Asaka-Maru*" [27 September 1944, Detailed Battle Report of Bombing of HI-72, Transport *Asaka-Maru*].
"Showa 19-nen 10-gatsu 12-nichi *Asaka-Maru* Hi-rai-baku Chinbotsu Sento Shoho Unsosen *Asaka-Maru*" [12 October 1944, Detailed Battle Report of the Torpedoing, Bombing, and Sinking of the *Asaka-Maru*, Transport *Asaka-Maru*].
"Showa 19-nen 10-gatsu Toka Tokusetu Unsosen *Nankai-Maru* Sento Shoho Showa 19-nen 9-gatsu 12-nichi Minami-shina-kai ni okeru Tai-sensuikan-sen Tokusetu Unsosen *Nankai-Maru*" [10 October 1944, Detailed Battle Report of Converted Transport *Nankai-Maru*: Anti-Submarine Battle on September 12, 1944, in the South China Sea, Converted Transport *Nankai-Maru*].

San Francisco Maritime National Park Association (SFMNP)

Bennett, Robert. POW Survivor Tales and Robert Bennett Diary.

Wisconsin Maritime Museum Library and Archives, Manitowoc (WMML)

Combs, H. Vance. Interview. October 1992.
Roberts, Marshall. Tape transcription, USS *Cobia* Reunion. 9–13 September 1992.
Spivy, Carl. Questionnaire. 24 November 1992.

U.S. Submarine Patrol Reports

(Originally held by the U.S. National Archives and Records Administration, College Park, Maryland; the following reports were accessed on DVDs produced by Submarine Memorabilia.)
USS *Growler* Tenth War Patrol Report, disc 10.
USS *Pampanito* Third and Fourth War Patrol Reports, disc 25.
USS *Plaice* Second War Patrol Report, disc 26.
USS *Sealion* Second War Patrol Report, disc 22.

Newspapers

Advertiser (Adelaide)
Age (Melbourne)
Argus (Melbourne)
Bulletin (Sydney)
Cairns Post (Queensland)
Canadian Press (Toronto)
Canberra Times
Chicago Daily News
Courier-Mail (Brisbane)
Daily Mail (UK)
Daily News (Perth)
Daily News (Warwick, Queensland)
Daily Telegraph (Sydney)
Herald (Melbourne)
Indian Daily Mail (Singapore)
Kalgoorlie Miner
Mail (Adelaide)
Newcastle Morning Herald and Miners' Advocate
St. Petersburg Times
Singapore Free Press
Straits Times (Singapore)
Sun (Sydney)
Sydney Morning Herald
Syonan Shimbun (Singapore)
Telegraph (Brisbane)
Times (New Brunswick)
West Australian (Perth)

Personal Communications

John Harman to author, 2 November 2017.
Hiroyuki Shindo to author, 4 November 2017.

Books and Articles

Adachi, Ryoko, and Andrew McKay, eds. *Echoes of War: Australians Voice their Feelings About Japan*. Carnegie, Victoria: Mirai Books, 2009.
Adam-Smith, Patsy. *Prisoners of War: From Gallipoli to Korea*. 1992. Reprint ed., Melbourne: Penguin, 1997.
Alden, John D., and Craig R. McDonald. *United States and Allied Submarine Successes in the Pacific and Far East during World War II*. Jefferson, NC: McFarland, 2009.
Allbury, A.G. *Bamboo and Bushido*. London: Robert Hale Limited, 1955.
Aquila, David. "A Deeper Level of Hell." *MHQ: The Quarterly Journal of Military History*, vol. 24, no. 1, Autumn 2011, pp. 98–104.
Ariotti, Kate. "'At present everything is making us most anxious': Families of Australian Prisoners in Turkey," pp. 57–74. In Joan Beaumont, Lachlan Grant and Aaron Pegram, eds., *Beyond Surrender: Australian Prisoners of War in the Twentieth Century*. Melbourne: Melbourne University Press, 2015.
Arneil, Stan. *One Man's War*. Sydney: Alternative Publishing Co-operative, 1980.
Aszkielowicz, Dean. "Repatriation and the Limits of Resolve: Japanese War Criminals in Australian Custody." *Japanese Studies*, vol. 31, no. 2, September 2011, pp. 211–228.
Ballinger, Pamela. "The Culture of Survivors," *History and Memory*, vol. 10, no. 1, 1998, pp. 99–108.
Bancroft, Arthur, and R. G. Roberts. *The Mikado's Guests*. Perth: Patersons Printing Press, 1945.
Bancroft, Arthur, with John Harman. *Arthur's War*. Melbourne: Viking, 2010.
Banham, Tony. *The Sinking of the Lisbon Maru: Britain's Forgotten Wartime Tragedy*. Hong Kong: Hong Kong University Press, 2006.
_____. *We Shall Suffer There: Hong Kong's Defenders Imprisoned*. Hong Kong: Hong Kong University Press, 2009.
Beaumont, Joan. "The Long Silence: Australian Prisoners of the Japanese," pp. 79–97, in Peter J. Dean, ed. *Australia 1944–45: Victory in the Pacific*. Melbourne: Cambridge University Press, 2016.
_____. "Officers and Men: Rank and survival on the Thai-Burma Railway," pp. 174–195. In Joan Beaumont, Lachlan Grant and Aaron Pegram, eds. *Beyond Surrender: Australian Prisoners of War in the Twentieth Century*. Melbourne: Melbourne University Press, 2015.
_____. "Prisoners of War in Australian National Memory," pp. 185–194. In Bob Moore and Barbara Hatley-Broad, eds. *Prisoners of War, Prisoners of Peace: Captivity, Home Coming and Memory in World War II*. Oxford: Berg, 2005.
_____. "Protecting Prisoners of War, 1939–95," pp. 277–297. In Bob Moore and Kent Fedorowich, eds. *Prisoners of War and their Captors in World War II*. Oxford: Berg, 1996.
_____. "Victims of War: The Allies and the Transport of Prisoners-of-War by Sea, 1939–1945." *Journal of the Australian War Memorial*, no. 2, April 1983, pp. 1–7.
_____, Lachlan Grant, and Aaron Pegram, eds. *Beyond Surrender: Australian Prisoners of War in the Twentieth Century*. Melbourne: Melbourne University Press, 2015.
Ben-Yehuda, Nachman. *Atrocity, Deviance and Submarine Warfare: Norms and Practices during the World Wars*. Ann Arbor: University of Michigan Press, 2013.
Blair, Clay Jr. *Silent Victory: The U.S. Submarine War against Japan*. 1975. Reprint ed., Annapolis: Naval Institute Press, 2001.
Blair, Joan, and Clay Blair. *Return from the River Kwai*. London: Macdonald General Books, 1979.
Bose, Romen. *Kranji: The Commonwealth War Cemetery and the Politics of the Dead*. Singapore: Marshall Cavendish, 2006.
Bose, Romen. *Singapore at War: Secrets from the Fall, Liberation and Aftermath of WWII*. Singapore: Marshall Cavendish, 2012.

Bibliography

Bourke, Roger. *Prisoners of the Japanese: Literary Imagination and the Prisoner-of-War Experience.* St. Lucia: University of Queensland Press, 2006.

Boyd, Carl. *American Command of the Sea: Through Carriers, Codes and the Silent Service.* Newport News, VA: The Mariners' Museum, 1995.

Braddon, Russell. *The Naked Island.* 1951. Melbourne: Penguin Books, 1993.

_____. "Statement." *Australian Literary Studies,* vol. 12, no. 2, October 1985, pp. 261–263.

Braly, William C. *The Hard Way Home.* Washington, D.C.: Infantry Journal Press, 1947.

Bridgland, Tony. *Waves of Hate: Naval Atrocities of the Second World War.* Annapolis: Naval Institute Press, 2002.

Brigginshaw, Jim. *Shimpu-San Healer of Hate: The Life of Father Tony Glynn.* Lismore, NSW: Marist Fathers' Province of Australia, 1996.

Brown, Louis. *A Radar History of World War II: Technical and Military Imperatives.* Bristol: Institute of Physics Publishing, 1999.

Brune, Peter. *Descent into Hell: The Fall of Singapore—Pudu and Changi—the Thai-Burma Railway.* Sydney: Allen and Unwin, 2014.

Buell, Thomas B. *Master of Sea Power: A Biography of Fleet Admiral Ernest J. King.* Boston: Little, Brown and Company, 1980.

Bulcock, Roy. *Of Death but Once.* Melbourne: F. W. Cheshire, 1947.

Carlton, Mike. *Cruiser: The Life and Loss of HMAS Perth and Her Crew.* Sydney: William Heinemann, 2010.

Carter, Tony, and Neil MacPherson. *The Burma Railway, Hellships and Coalmines.* Laurieton, NSW: Parker Pattison, 2008.

Caulfield, Michael, ed. *War behind the Wire: Australian Prisoners of War.* Sydney: Hachette Australia, 2008.

Chamberlain, Mary. "Narrative Theory," pp. 142–165, in Thomas A. Charlton, Lois E. Myers and Rebecca Sharpless, eds. *Thinking About Oral History: Theories and Applications.* New York: Alta Mira Press, 2008.

Chang, Maria Hsia, and Robert P. Barker. "Victor's Justice and Japan's Amnesia: The Tokyo War Crimes Trial Reconsidered," pp. 33–58, in Peter Li, ed. *Japanese War Crimes: The Search for Justice.* New Brunswick, NJ: Transaction Publishers, 2003.

Cheah, Wui Ling. "Post-World War II British 'Hell-ship' Trials in Singapore: Omissions and the Attribution of Responsibility." *Journal of International Criminal Justice,* vol. 8, no. 4 (2010), pp. 1035–1058.

Clarke, Hugh V. *Last Stop Nagasaki!* London: George Allen and Unwin, 1984.

_____. *Twilight Liberation: Australian prisoners of war between Hiroshima and home.* Sydney: Allen and Unwin, 1985.

_____, and Colin Burgess. *Barbed Wire and Bamboo: Australian POWs in Europe, North Africa, Singapore, Thailand and Japan.* Sydney: Allen and Unwin, 1992.

Clayton, Tim. *Sea Wolves: The Extraordinary Story of Britain's WW2 Submarines.* London: Little Brown, 2011.

Cline, Rick. *Final Dive: The Gallant and Tragic Career of the WWII Submarine, USS Snook.* Placentia, CA: R. A. Cline Publishing, 2001.

_____. *Submarine Grayback: The Life and Death of the WWII Sub, USS Grayback.* Placentia, CA: R. A. Cline Publishing, 1999.

Coates, Albert, and Newman Rosenthal. *The Albert Coates Story: The Will That Found the Way.* 1977, reprint ed. Melbourne: Hyland House, 1978.

Cody, Les. *Ghosts in Khaki: The History of the 2/4th Machine Gun Battalion.* Carlisle, W.A.: Hesperian Press, 1997.

Connor, Stephen. "Side-stepping Geneva: Japanese Troops under British Control, 1945–7." *Journal of Contemporary History,* Vol. 45, no. 2, 2010, pp. 389–405.

Connor, Stephen B. *Mountbatten's Samurai: Imperial Japanese Army and Navy Forces Under British Control in Southeast Asia, 1945–1948.* London: Seventh Citadel, 2015.

Cowling, Anthony. *My Life with the Samurai.* Sydney: Kangaroo Press, 1996.

Crager, Kelly E. *Hell Under the Rising Sun: Texan POWs and the Building of the Burma-Thailand Death Railway.* College Station: Texas A&M University Press, 2008.

Cressman, Robert J. *The Official Chronology of the U.S. Navy in World War II*. Annapolis: Naval Institute Press, 2000.
Cribb, Robert. "The Life and Trial of Cho Un-kuk, Korean War Criminal." *Critical Asian Studies*, vol. 50, no. 3, pp. 329–352.
Critchley, Macdonald. *Shipwreck-Survivors: A Medical Study*. London: J. and A. Churchill, 1943.
Cunningham, Michael. "Prisoners of the Japanese and the Politics of Apology: A Battle over History and Memory." *Journal of Contemporary History*, vol. 39, no. 4, Special Issue: Collective Memory (October 2004), pp. 561–574.
Davis, Landon. Oral History, Naval History and Heritage Command. http://www.history.navy.mil/research/library/online/oral_history_davis.htm (Accessed 25 October 2013).
Daws, Gavan. *Prisoners of the Japanese: POWs of World War II in the Pacific*. New York: William Morrow and Company, 1994.
Dean, Peter J., ed. *Australia 1942: In the Shadow of War*. Cambridge: Cambridge University Press, 2013.
_____. *Australia 1944–45: Victory in the Pacific*. Melbourne: Cambridge University Press, 2016.
Department of Veterans' Affairs. *Stolen Years: Australian Prisoners of War*. Canberra: Commonwealth of Australia, 2002.
DeRose, James F. *Unrestricted Warfare: How a New Breed of Officers led the Submarine Force to Victory in World War II*. New York: John Wiley and Sons, 2000.
Dienesch, Robert. "Radar and the American Submarine War, 1941–1945: A Reinterpretation." *The Northern Mariner*, vol. 14, no. 3, July 2004, pp. 27–40.
Dingman, Roger. *Ghost of War: The Sinking of the Awa Maru and Japanese American Relations, 1945–1995*. Annapolis: Naval Institute Press, 1997.
Dower, John. *Embracing Defeat: Japan in the Aftermath of World War II*. London: Penguin Books, 1999.
Dower, John W. *War Without Mercy: Race and Power in the Pacific War*. New York: Pantheon Books, 1986.
Duffy, James P. *The Sinking of the Laconia and the U-Boat War: Disaster in the Mid-Atlantic*. Lincoln: University of Nebraska Press, 2013.
Dunlop, E. E. *The War Diaries of Weary Dunlop: Java and the Burma-Thailand Railway 1942–1945*. 1986. Reprint, Ringwood: Penguin Books, 1990.
Earhart, David C. *Certain Victory: Images of World War II in the Japanese Media*. New York: M. S. Sharpe, 2008.
Ellis, John. *Brute Force: Allied Strategy and Tactics in the Second World War*. London: Andre Deutsch, 1990.
_____. *The World War II Databook: The Essential Facts and Figures for All the Combatants*. London: BCA, 1993.
Evans, David C., ed. *The Japanese Navy in World War II: In the Words of Former Japanese Naval Officers*. Annapolis: Naval Institute Press, 1986.
Fassin, Didier, and Richard Rechtman. *The Empire of Trauma: An Inquiry into the Condition of Victimhood*. Translated by Rachel Gomme. Princeton: Princeton University Press, 2009.
Felton, Mark. *Slaughter at Sea: The Story of Japan's Naval War Crimes*. Annapolis: Naval Institute Press, 2007.
Fink, George, ed. *Stress of War, Conflict and Disaster*. San Diego: Academic Press, 2010.
Fitzpatrick, Georgina, Tim McCormack and Narelle Morris. *Australia's War Crimes Trials 1945–51*. Leiden: Brill Nijhoff, 2016.
Flower, Sibylla Jane. "Memory and the Prisoner of War Experience: The United Kingdom," pp. 57–72, in Karl Hack and Kevin Blackburn, eds. *Forgotten Captives in Japanese Occupied Asia*. London: Routledge, 2008.
Fluckey, Eugene. *Thunder Below! The USS Barb Revolutionizes Submarine Warfare in World War II*. Urbana: University of Illinois Press, 1992.
Forbes, Cameron. *Hellfire: The Story of Australia, Japan and the Prisoners of War*. Sydney: Pan Macmillan, 2005.
Ford, Douglas. *The Pacific War: Clash of Empires in World War II*. London: Continuum, 2012.

Frei, Henry. "Surrendering Syonan," pp. 217–33, in Akashi Yogi and Yoshimura Mako eds. *New Perspectives on the Japanese Occupation of Malaya and Singapore, 1941–1945*. Singapore: National University of Singapore Press, 2008.

Gamble, Bruce. *Darkest Hour: The True Story of Lark Force at Rabaul*. St. Paul, MN: Zenith Press, 2006.

Gannon, Robert. *Hellions of the Deep: The Development of American Torpedoes in World War II*. University Park: Pennsylvania State University Press, 1996.

Garton, Stephen. "Changi as Television: Myth, Memory, Narrative and History." *Journal of Australian Studies*, vol. 26, no. 73, 2002, pp. 79–88.

_____. *The Cost of War: Australians Return*. Melbourne: Oxford University Press, 1996.

Gerster, Robin. "The Rise of the Prisoner-of-War Writers." *Australian Literary Studies*, vol. 12, no. 2, October 1985, pp. 270–274.

Gillies, Midge. *The Barbed-Wire University: The Real Lives of Prisoners of War in the Second World War*. London: Aurum Press, 2011.

Gladwin, Lee A. "American POWs on Japanese Ships take a Voyage into Hell." *Prologue: Quarterly of the National Archives and Records Administration*, vol. 35, no. 4, Winter 2003, pp. 30–39.

_____. "Did Sigint Seal the Fates of 19,000 Pows?" *Cryptologia*, vol. 30, no. 3, July–September 2006, pp. 199–211.

Graham, Evan. *Japan's Sea Lane Security, 1940–2004: A Matter of Life and Death?* London: Routledge, 2006.

Grant, Lachlan. *Australian Soldiers in Asia-Pacific in World War II*. Sydney: New South, 2014.

_____. "Hellships, prisoner transport and unrestricted submarine warfare in World War II," pp. 196–217. In Joan Beaumont, Lachlan Grant and Aaron Pegram, eds. *Beyond Surrender: Australian Prisoners of War in the Twentieth Century*. Melbourne: Melbourne University Press, 2015.

_____. "They Called them 'Hellships': Prisoners at Sea faced an Uncertain Fate." *Wartime: Official Magazine of the Australian War Memorial*, no. 63, Winter 2013, pp. 30–36.

Grashio, Samuel C., and Bernard Norling. *Escape to Freedom: The War Memoirs of Col. Samuel C. Grashio USAF (Ret)*. Tulsa, OK: MCN Press, 1982.

Hack, Karl, and Kevin Blackburn, eds. *Forgotten Captives in Japanese-Occupied Asia*. London: Routledge, 2008.

Hall, Leslie. *The Blue Haze: POWs on the Burma Railway*. Sydney: Kangaroo Press, 1996.

Hara, Akira. "Japan: Guns before Rice," pp. 224–267. In Mark Harrison, ed. *The Economics of World War II: Six Great Powers in International Comparison*. Cambridge: Cambridge University Press, 1998.

Hardie, Robert. *The Burma-Siam Railway: The Secret Diary of Dr Robert Hardie 1942–1945*. Sydney: Collins, 1983.

Harrison, Kenneth. *Road to Hiroshima*. 1966. Reprint, Adelaide: Rigby, 1983.

Harrison, Mark, ed. *The Economics of World War II: Six Great Powers in International Comparison*. Cambridge: Cambridge University Press, 1998.

Hashimoto, Mochitsura. *Sunk: The Story of the Japanese Submarine Fleet 1942–1945*. Trans. E. H. M. Colegrave. London: Hamilton and Company, 1955.

Hastings, Max. *Retribution: The Battle for Japan, 1944–45*. New York: Alfred A. Knopf, 2008.

Hata, Ikuhiko. "From Consideration to Contempt: The Changing Nature of Japanese Military and Popular Perceptions of Prisoners of War through the Ages," pp. 253–276. In Bob Moore and Kent Fedorowich, eds. *Prisoners of War and their Captors in World War II*. Oxford: Berg, 1996.

Havers, R.P.W. *Reassessing the Japanese Prisoner of War Experience: The Changi POW Camp, Singapore, 1942–5*. London: Routledge Curzon, 2003.

Hearder, Rosalind. *Keep the Men Alive: Australian POW Doctors in Japanese captivity*. Sydney: Allen and Unwin, 2009.

Herring, Andrew. "Farewell Tribute to Arthur Bancroft: A Legend and Inspiration." *Navy Daily*, 4 August 2013.

Holman, Robert. *On Paths of Ash: The Extraordinary Story of an Australian Prisoner of War*. Edited by Peter Thomson. Sydney: Pier 9, 2009.

Holmes, Harry. *The Last Patrol*. Annapolis: Naval Institute Press, 1994.
Holmes, Linda Goetz. *Four Thousand Bowls of Rice*. Sydney: Allen and Unwin, 1993.
_____. "Mitsui: 'We Will Send You to Omuta,'" pp. 107–116, in Peter Li, ed. *Japanese War Crimes: The Search for Justice*. New Brunswick, NJ: Transaction Publishers, 2003.
Holmes, W. J. *Undersea Victory: The Influence of Submarine Operations on the War in the Pacific*. New York: Doubleday and Company, 1966.
Holwitt, Joel. *"Execute Against Japan": The U.S. Decision to Conduct Unrestricted Submarine Warfare*. College Station: Texas A&M University Press, 2009.
_____. "Unrestricted Submarine Victory: The U.S. Submarine Campaign against Japan," pp. 225–238. In Bruce A. Elleman and S.C.M. Paine, eds. *Commerce Raiding: Historical Case Studies, 1755–2009*. Newport: RI: Naval War College Press, 2013.
Horie, Y. "The Failure of the Japanese Escort Convoy." *U.S. Naval Institute Proceedings*, October 1956, pp. 1073–1081.
Hornfischer, James D. *The Fleet at Flood Tide: America at Total War in the Pacific, 1944–1945*. New York: Bantam Books, 2016.
_____. *Ship of Ghosts: The Story of the USS Houston, FDR's Legendary Lost Cruiser, and the Epic Saga of Her Survivors*. New York: Bantam Books, 2006.
Hosty, Kieran, James Hunter and Shinatria Adhiyatama. "Wreck of HMAS Perth (1): International Maritime Archaeology Team Assessment." *AAMH Quarterly Newsletter*, issue 146, December 2017, pp. 5–8.
Houghton, Frances. "'To the Kwai and Back': Myth, Memory and Memoirs of the Death Railway." *Journal of War and Culture Studies*, vol. 7, no. 3, August 2014, pp. 223–235.
Huff, Greg, and Shinobu Majima, ed. and trans. *World War II Singapore: The Chosabu Reports on Syonan*. Singapore: National University of Singapore Press, 2018.
Hughes, Geraint. "A 'Post-War' War: The British Occupation of French-Indochina, September 1945—March 1946." *Small Wars and Insurgencies*, vol. 17, no. 3, 2006, pp. 263–286.
Hughes, W.S. Kent. *Slaves of the Samurai*. Melbourne: Geoffrey Cumberlege Oxford University Press, 1946.
Hynes, Samuel. *The Soldiers' Tale: Bearing Witness to Modern War*. New York: Penguin Books, 1997.
Jackson, Asley. "Ocean War," pp. 243–261. In Thomas H. Zeiler with Daniel M. Dubois, eds. *A Companion to World War II*. Chichester, West Sussex: Wiley-Blackwell, 2013.
Jaffe, Walter W. *Steel Shark in the Pacific: USS Pampanito SS-383*. Palo Alto, CA: Glencannon Press, 2001.
Jeffrey, Betty. *White Coolies*. 1954. Reprint ed., Sydney: Angus and Robertson, 1976.
Johnson, William Bruce. *The Pacific Campaign in World War II: From Pearl Harbor to Guadalcanal*. London: Routledge, 2006.
Johnston, Mark. *Fighting the Enemy: Australian Soldiers and their Adversaries in World War II*. Cambridge: Cambridge University Press, 2000.
Jones, Betty B. *The December Ship: A Story of Lt. Col. Arden R. Boellner's Capture in the Philippines, Imprisonment and Death on a World War II Japanese Hellship*. Jefferson, NC: McFarland, 1992.
Jones, Edgar, and Simon Wessely. *Shell Shock to PTSD: Military Psychiatry from 1900 to the Gulf War*. New York: Psychology Press, 2005.
Kennedy, Paul. *Engineers of Victory: The Problem Solvers Who Turned the Tide in the Second World War*. London: Penguin, 2014.
Kerr, E. Bartlett. *Surrender and Survival: The Experience of American POWs in the Pacific 1941–1945*. New York: William Morrow and Company, 1985.
Kinvig, Clifford. "Allied POWs and the Burma-Thailand Railway," pp. 37–57. In Philip Towle, Margaret Kosuge and Yoichi Kibata, eds. *Japanese Prisoners of War*. London: Hambledon and London, 2000.
Kinvig, Clifford. *River Kwai Railway: The Story of the Burma-Siam Railroad*. 1992. Reprint ed., London: Conway, 2005.
Knox, Donald. *Death March: The Survivors of Bataan*. New York: Harcourt Brace Jovanovich, 1981.
Kratoska, Paul H. *The Japanese Occupation of Malaya and Singapore, 1942–45: A Social and Economic History*. 2nd ed. Singapore: National University of Singapore Press, 2018.

Kratoska, Paul H., ed. *The Thailand-Burma Railway, 1942–1946: Documents and Selected Writings*. London: Routledge, 2006.
Lamont-Brown, Raymond. *Ships from Hell: Japanese War Crimes on the High Seas*. Thrupp-Stroud-Gloucestershire: Sutton Publishing, 2002.
Lane, John. *Summer Will Come Again: The Story of Australian POW's Fight for Survival in Japan*. Fremantle: Fremantle Arts Centre Press, 1987.
Lanigan, Richard J. *Kangaroo Express: The Epic Story of the Submarine Growler*. Laurel, FL: RJL Express Publications, 1998.
LaVO, Carl. *The Galloping Ghost: The Extraordinary Life of Submarine Legend Eugene Fluckey*. Annapolis: Naval Institute Press, 2007.
Layton, Edwin T., with Roger Pineau and John Costello. *"And I was There": Pearl Harbor and Midway—Breaking the Secrets*. 1985. Reprint, Annapolis: Naval Institute Press, 2006.
Levine, Alan J. *Captivity, Flight and Survival in World War II*. Westport, CT: Praeger, 2000.
Li, Peter, ed. *Japanese War Crimes: The Search for Justice*. New Brunswick, NJ: Transaction Publishers, 2003.
Linderman, Gerald F. *The World Within War: American Combat Experience in World War II*. New York: The Free Press, 1997.
Lockwood, Charles. *Sink 'Em All: Submarine Warfare in the Pacific*. 1951. Reprint ed., New York: Bantam Books, 1984.
Loughlin, Charles Elliot. *The Reminiscences of Rear Admiral Charles Elliot Loughlin*. Annapolis: U.S. Naval Institute Press, 1982.
Lukacs, John D. *Escape from Davao: The Forgotten Story of the Most Daring Prison Break of the Pacific War*. New York: Simon & Schuster, 2010.
MacArthur, Brian. *Surviving the Sword: Prisoners of the Japanese 1942–45*. London: Abacus, 2005.
MacKenzie, S.P. "The Treatment of Prisoners of War in World War II." *Journal of Modern History*, vol. 66, no. 3, September 1994, pp. 487–520.
MacLeod, Sandy. "Psychiatry On the Burma-Thai Railway (1942–1943): Dr Rowley Richards and Colleagues." *Australasian Psychiatry*, vol. 18, no. 6, 2010, pp. 491–495.
Martin, Adrian R. *Brothers from Bataan: POWs, 1942–1945*. Manhattan, KS: Sunflower University Press, 1992.
Mazza, Eugene A. "The Rescue of Australian and British Prisoners of War by Four USS Submarines September 1944." http://www.submarinesailor.com/history/pow/AussieBritRescue/
McCormack, Gavin, and Hank Nelson, eds. *The Burma-Thailand Railway: Memory and History*. Sydney: Allen and Unwin, 1993.
McCullough, Jonathan J. *A Tale of Two Subs: An Untold Story of World War II, Two Sister Subs, and Extraordinary Heroism*. New York: Grand Central Publishing, 2008.
McDonald, Craig R. *The USS Puffer in World War II: A History of the Submarine and Its Wartime Crew*. Jefferson, NC: McFarland, 2008.
McKernan, Michael. "Afterward," pp. 341–344. In Peter J. Dean, *Australia 1944–45: Victory in the Pacific*. Melbourne: Cambridge University Press, 2016.
_____. *This War Never Ends: The Pain of Separation and Return*. St. Lucia: University of Queensland Press, 2001.
McNitt, Robert W. "U.S. Naval Institute 1873–1998: The Sea Service forum." *Proceedings*, 124.1, January 1998, p. 4.
Michno, Gregory F. *Death on the Hellships: Prisoners at Sea in the Pacific War*. Annapolis: Naval Institute Press, 2001.
_____. *USS Pampanito: Angel Killer*. Norman: University of Oklahoma Press, 2000.
Miller, David. *Mercy Ships*. London: Continuum, 2008.
Miller, Donald L. *D-Days in the Pacific*. New York: Simon & Schuster, 2005.
Monteath, Peter. *P.O.W.: Australian Prisoners of War in Hitler's Reich*. Sydney: Macmillan, 2011.
Moore, Bob, and Barbara Hatley-Broad, eds. *Prisoners of War, Prisoners of Peace: Captivity, Homecoming and Memory in World War II*. Oxford: Berg, 2005.
Moore, Bob, and Kent Fedorowich, eds. *Prisoners of War and their Captors in World War II*. Oxford: Berg, 1996.

Moore, Jeffrey M. *Spies for Nimitz: Joint Military Intelligence in the Pacific War.* Annapolis: Naval Institute Press, 2004.
Murfett, Malcolm H., John M. Miksic, Brian P. Farrell and Chiang Ming Shun. *Between Two Oceans: A Military History of Singapore from First Settlement to Final British Withdrawal.* New York: Oxford University Press, 1999.
Nagase, Takashi. *Crosses and Tigers and the Double-Edged Dagger: The Cowra Incident of 1944.* Edited by Gill Goddard. 1990. London: Paulownia Press, 2010.
Nagata, Yuriko. *Unwanted Aliens: Japanese Internment in Australia.* St. Lucia: University of Queensland Press, 1996.
Nelson, Hank. "A Bowl of Rice for Seven Camels." *Journal of the Australian War Memorial,* issue 14, 1989, pp. 33–42.
_____. "Travelling in Memories: Australian Prisoners of the Japanese." *Journal of the Australian War Memorial,* issue 3, 1983, pp. 13–24.
Newcomb, Richard F. *Abandon Ship! The Saga of the U.S.S. Indianapolis, the Navy's Greatest Sea Disaster.* 1958. Reprint, New York: HarperCollins, 2001.
Newpower, Anthony. *Iron Men and Tin Fish: The Race to Build a Better Torpedo during World War II.* Westport, CT: Praeger Security International, 2006.
Nichol, John, and Tony Rennell. *The Last Escape: The Untold Story of Allied Prisoners of War in Europe 1944–45.* New York: Viking, 2002.
Oi, Atsushi. "Why Japan's Anti-Submarine Warfare Failed." *United States Naval Institute Proceedings,* vol. 78, no. 6, June 1952, pp. 587–601.
Oliver, Lizzie. *Prisoners of the Sumatra Railway: Narratives of History and Memory.* London: Bloomsbury Academic, 2019.
_____. "Transport Ships in the Far East." Imperial War Museum, http://www.iwm.org.uk/history/the-sinking-of-prisoner-of-war-transport-ships-in-the-far-east
Padfield, Peter. *War Beneath the Sea: Submarine Conflict 1939–1945.* London: Pimlico, 1997.
Paine, Tom. *The Transpacific Voyage of His Imperial Japanese Majesty's Submarine I-400 (Tom Paine's Journal July-Dec. 1945).* Los Angeles: self-published, 1984.
Parillo, Mark P. *The Japanese Merchant Marine in World War II.* Annapolis: Naval Institute Press, 1993.
Parkes, Meg, and Geoff Gill. *Captive Memories.* Lancaster: Palatine Books, 2015.
Parkin, Ray. *A POW's Survival.* Melbourne: Melbourne University Press, 2005.
_____. *Ray Parkin's Wartime Trilogy.* Melbourne: Melbourne University Press, 2003.
Patterson, George. *A Spoonful of Rice with Salt.* Edinburgh: The Pentland Press, 1993.
Peek, Ian Denys. *One Fourteenth of an Elephant: A Memoir of Life and Death on the Burma-Thailand Railway.* Sydney: Pan Macmillan, 2003.
Peters, Betty. "The life experience of partners of ex-POWs of the Japanese." *Journal of the Australian War Memorial,* issue 28, April 1996, pp. 1–6.
Pfennigwerth, Ian. "A Novel Experience: The RAN in 1942, Defending Australian Waters," pp. 179–198. In Peter J. Dean, ed. *Australia 1942: In the Shadow of War.* Cambridge: Cambridge University Press, 2013.
Polmar, Norman, and Edward Whitman. *Hunters and Killers. Volume 2: Anti-Submarine Warfare from 1943.* Annapolis: Naval Institute Press, 2016.
Poolman, Kenneth. *The Winning Edge: Naval Technology in Action, 1939–1945.* Annapolis: Naval Institute Press, 1997.
Pounder, Thomas. *Death Camps of the River Kwai.* Cornwall: United Writers, 1977.
Rees, Laurence. *Horror in the East: Japan and the Atrocities of World War II.* Cambridge, MA: Da Capo Press, 2001.
Reich, Eli T. *The Reminiscences of Vice Adm. Eli T. Reich, USN.* Vol. 1. Annapolis: U.S. Naval Institute, 1982.
Richards, Rowley. *A Doctor's War.* Sydney: HarperCollins, 2005.
_____, and Marcia McEwan. *The Survival Factor.* Sydney: Kangaroo Press, 1989.
Rivett, Rohan D. *Behind Bamboo.* 1946. Ringwood: Penguin Books, 1991.
Rohwer, J., and G. Hummelchen. *Chronology of the War at Sea 1939–1945: The Naval History of World War Two.* Annapolis: Naval Institute Press, 1992.

Roland, Charles G. "Allied POWs, Japanese Captors and the Geneva Convention." *War and Society*, vol. 9, no. 2, 1991, pp. 83–101.

_____. *Long Night's Journey into Day: Prisoners of War in Hong Kong and Japan, 1941–1945*. Waterloo, ON: Wilfred Laurier University Press, 2001.

Rolf, David. *Prisoners of the Reich: Germany's Captives 1939–1945*. London: Leo Cooper, 1988.

Rowland, Robin. *A River Kwai Story: The Sonkrai Tribunal*. Sydney: Allen and Unwin, 2007.

Russell, Lord of Liverpool. *The Knights of Bushido: A Short History of Japanese War Crimes*. London: Casssell and Company, 1958.

Sakaida, Henry. "The Tragic War of Col. Harry R. Melton Jr." A War to be Won. http://ww2awartobewon.com/

Savage, J. Russell. *A Guest of the Emperor*. Moorooka, QLD: Boolarong Press, 1995.

Scates, Bruce, Catherine Tiernan and Rebecca Wheatley. "The Railway Men: Prisoner Journeys through the Traumascapes of World War II." *Journal of War and Cultural Studies*, vol. 7, no. 3, August 2014, pp. 206–222.

Sendzikas, Aldona. *Lucky 73: USS Pampanito's Unlikely Rescue of Allied POWs in WWII*. Gainesville: University of Florida Press, 2010.

Shephard, Ben. *A War of Nerves: Soldiers and Psychiatrists in the Twentieth Century*. Cambridge, MA: Harvard University Press, 2001.

Sherwin, Hiroko. *Japan's World War II Legacy*. London: Quartet Books, 2015.

Shilling, C.W., and Jessie W. Kohl. *History of Submarine Medicine in World War II*. New London, CT: U.S. Naval Medical Research Laboratory, 1947.

Shindo, Hiroyuki. "The IJA, IJN and Japanese Strategy for the South Pacific / SWPA," pp. 145–166. In Peter Dennis, ed. *Armies and Maritime Strategy: 2013 Chief of Army History Conference*. Canberra: Big Sky Publishing, 2014.

Shinozaki, Mamoru. *Syonan My Story: The Japanese Occupation of Singapore*. 1975. Reprint ed, Singapore: Marshall Cavendish Editions, 2011.

Shively, John C. *Profiles in Survival: The Experiences of American POWs in the Philippines during World War II*. Indianapolis: Indiana Historical Society Press, 2012.

Sidhu, H. *The Bamboo Fortress: True Singapore War Stories*. Singapore: Native Publications, 1991.

Sissons, D.C.S. The Australian War Crimes Trials and Investigations (1942–51). https://www.ocf.berkeley.edu/~changmin/documents/Sissons%20Final%20War%20Crimes%20Text%2018-3-06.pdf

Sleeman, Colin, ed. *Trial of Gozawa Sadaichi and Nine Others*. London: William Hodge and Company, 1948.

Spurling, Kathryn. *Cruel Conflict: The Triumph and Tragedy of HMAS Perth*. Sydney: New Holland, 2008.

Stanley, Peter. "Remembering Captivity: The Prisoner Experience as Literature," pp. 91–108. In Department of Veterans' Affairs, *Stolen Years: Australian Prisoners of War*. Canberra: Commonwealth of Australia, 2002.

Stanton, Doug. *In Harm's Way*. New York: St. Martin's Paperbacks, 2002.

Stille, Mark. *Imperial Japanese Navy Antisubmarine Escorts 1941–45*. Oxford: Osprey Publishing, 2017.

Strong, Rowan. *Chaplains in the Royal Australian Navy: 1912 to the Vietnam War*. Sydney: University of New South Wales Press, 2012.

Sturma, Michael. *Fremantle's Submarines: How Allied Submariners and Western Australians Helped to Win the War in the Pacific*. Annapolis: Naval Institute Press, 2015.

_____. *Surface and Destroy: The Submarine Gun War in the Pacific*. Lexington: University Press of Kentucky, 2011.

Sutton, David, and Peter Wogan. *Hollywood Blockbusters: The Anthropology of Popular Movies*. Oxford: Berg, 2009.

Sweeting, A.J. "Prisoners of the Japanese," pp. 509–642. In Lionel Wigmore, *The Japanese Thrust*. 1957. Reprint ed., Canberra: Australian War Memorial, 1968.

Tachikawa, Kyoichi. "The Treatment of Prisoners of War by the Imperial Japanese Army and Navy focusing on the Pacific War." *NIDS Security Reports*, no. 9 (2008), pp. 45–90.

Tamayama, Kazuo. *Railwaymen in the War: Tales by Japanese Railway Soldiers in Burma and Thailand 1941–47*. New York: Palgrave Macmillan, 2005.

Tanaka, Yuki. *Hidden Horrors: Japanese War Crimes in World War II*. Boulder, CO: Westview Press, 1996.
Tennant, Christopher, Kerry Goulston and Owen Dent. "Australian Prisoners of War of the Japanese: Post-War Psychiatric Hospitalisation and Psychological Morbidity." *Australian and New Zealand Journal of Psychiatry*, vol. 20, no. 3, 1986, pp. 334–340.
Thomson, Alistair. *Anzac Memories: Living with the Legend*. New edition. Clayton: Monash University Publishing, 2013.
Toland, John. *The Rising Sun: The Decline and Fall of the Japanese Empire 1936–1945*. London: Cassell and Company, 1971.
Totani, Yuma. *Justice in Asia and the Pacific Region, 1945–1952: Allied War Crimes Prosecutions*. New York: Cambridge University Press, 2015.
Towle, Philip, Margaret Kosuge and Yoichi Kibata, eds. *Japanese Prisoners of War*. London: Hambledon and London, 2000.
Twomey, Christina. *The Battle Within: POWs in Postwar Australia*. Sydney: New South, 2018.
_____. "POWs of the Japanese: Race and Trauma in Australia, 1970–2005." *Journal of War & Culture Studies*, vol. 7, no. 3, August 2014, pp. 191–205.
_____. "Trauma and the Reinvigoration of Anzac: An Argument." *History Australia*, vol. 10, no. 3, December 2013, pp. 85–108.
Ugaki, Matome. *Fading Victory: The Diary of Admiral Matome Ugaki 1941–1945*. Trans. Masataka Chihaya. 1991. Reprint ed., Annapolis: Naval Institute Press, 2008.
Ursano, Robert J. "Prisoners of War: Long-Term Health Outcomes." *The Lancet*, vol. 362, December 2003, Supplement, pp. 22–23.
Urwin, Gregory J.W. *Victory in Defeat: The Wake Island Defenders in Captivity, 1941–1945*. Annapolis: Naval Institute Press, 2010.
Vance, Jonathan F., ed. *Encyclopedia of Prisoners of War and Internment*. Santa Barbara, CA: ABC-Clio, 2000.
Van der Vat, Dan. *The Pacific Campaign: World War II, The U.S.–Japanese Naval War 1941–1945*. New York: Simon & Schuster, 2006.
Wade, Tom Henling. *Prisoner of the Japanese: From Changi to Tokyo*. Sydney: Kangaroo Press, 1994.
Wall, Don. *Heroes at Sea*. Mona Vale, NSW: self-published, 1991.
Waterford, Van. *Prisoners of the Japanese in World War II: Statistical History, Personal Narratives and Memorials concerning POWs in Camps and on Hellships, Civilian Internees, Asian Slave Laborers and Others Captured in the Pacific Theater*. Jefferson, NC: McFarland, 1994.
"When U.S. Subs Sank Our POWs." *Parade* (Melbourne), no. 263, October 1972, pp. 20–21.
Whitecross, Roy H. *Slaves of the Son of Heaven*. Sydney: Dymock's Book Arcade, 1951.
Wigmore, Lionel. *The Japanese Thrust*. 1957. Reprint ed., Canberra: Australian War Memorial, 1968.
Wilkinson, Roger I. "Short Survey of Japanese Radar." *Electrical Engineering*, vol. 65, August-September 1946, pp. 370–377, 455–463.
Williamson, Gordon. *U-Boat Tactics in World War II*. Oxford: Osprey Publishing, 2010.
Willmot, H.P. *The Battle of Leyte Gulf: The Last Fleet Action*. Bloomington: Indiana University Press, 2005.
Wilson, Sandra. "Koreans in the Trials of Japanese War Crimes Suspects." In Kerstin von Lingen, ed. *Debating Collaboration and Complicity in War Crimes Trials in Asia, 1945–1956*. New York: Palgrave Macmillan, 2017.
Wilson, Sandra, Robert Cribb, Beatrice Trefalt and Dean Aszkielowicz,. *Japanese War Criminals: The Politics of Justice after the Second World War*. New York: Columbia University, 2017.
Wright, John M. Jr. *Captured on Corregidor: Diary of an American P.O.W. in World War II*. Jefferson, NC: McFarland, 1988.
Wright, Pattie. *The Men of the Line: Stories of the Thai-Burma Railway Survivors*. Melbourne: The Miegunyah Press, 2008.
Wyatt, John, with Cecil Lowry. *No Mercy from the Japanese: A Survivor's Account of the Burma Railway and the Hellships 1942–1945*. Barnesly, South Yorkshire: Pen and Sword, 2008.
Yoji, Akashi, and Yoshimura Mako, eds. *New Perspectives on the Japanese Occupation of*

Malaya and Singapore, 1941–1945. Singapore: National University of Singapore Press, 2008.

Zeiler, Thomas H., with Daniel M. DuBois, eds. *A Companion to World War II.* Volume I. Chichester, West Sussex: Wiley-Blackwell, 2013.

Internet Sources

Australian War Memorial. https://www.awm.gov.au
Combined Fleet. http://www.combinedfleet.com/
Pacific Wrecks, http://www.pacificwrecks.com/
POW Research Network Japan. http://www.powresearch.jp/en/archive/html
US Naval Institute. http://www.usni.org

Audio-Visual

Allam, Lorena. "The History of Forgetting, from shell shock to PTSD." *Hindsight*, ABC Radio National. 15 September 2014.

Bowden, Tim. *Prisoners of War: Australians under Nippon.* ABC, 2007.

Return from the River Kwai. Director Andrew McLaglen. Roadshow Productions, 1989.

Road to Tokyo. Writer/Director Graham Shirley. Film Australia, 2005.

The Crossing. Director Nigel Bellis. History Channel, 2003.

"The Great Survivor." *60 Minutes.* Broadcast 13 April 2008. Story transcript. http://sixtyminutes.ninemsn.com.au/stories/lizhayes/441581/the-great-survivor

"US Submarine Rescue of Aussie and British POWs in WW2." Narrated by Joe Bates. https://www.youtube.com/watch?v=QFB4bZUJn6A

Index

Numbers in ***bold italics*** indicate pages with illustrations

Aki Maru 15
SS *Alcon Polaris* 72–73
Allbury, Alfred 14, 19, 21, 23–25, 31, 35, 39, 45, 50, 53, 58, 59, 78–79
Amagi Maru 168
HMS *Amphion* 8
Anderson, Cyril 79
Anderson, Edward 32
Anderson, W.M. 145
Anzac Day 121, 123, 176
Aquila, Andrew 110–111
Arisan Maru 109, 112, 114–115
Arneil, Stan 102, 175
Asaka Maru 15, 25, 48, 60, 64–68, 70, 146
Asaki Maru 167–168
Ashiya, Tamotsu 134
Atkinson, Russell 156
atomic bomb 95, 97
atrocities 37, 40, 81–83, 108, 130, 151–152, 162, 164, 166
Australia: army 121, 125, 155, 157–158; attitudes toward Japanese 6, 162–164, 174–175; navy 76–77, 88, 120, 177; prosecution of war crimes 5, 130–133, 137, 145, 147, 156, 164; relations with allies 5–6, 27, 83, 100, 104–107, 156–159; repatriation of enemy prisoners 155–164
Awa Maru 70, 97, 171
Azusa Maru 48

Bancroft, Arthur 5, 8, 10–11, 23, ***58***, 59, 76–77, 176; post-war adjustment 120–121, 123–128; survivor of *Perth* 8–9, 26, 31, 34, 74, 88, 120, 178; survivor of *Rakuyo Maru* 25, 26, 31, 34–35, 44, 46, 51–53, 86, 88, 105–106, 110, 120, 177–179
USS *Barb* 17, 46, 48–50, 53, 57, 58, 60
Barber, Syd 90
Barnett, Wilfrred 31
Barton, Peter 117
Bassett, James 132
Bates, Joseph 43, 44, 45, 55

Battle of Leyte Gulf 36, 70
Battle of Ormoc Bay 36
Battle of Sunda Strait 8, 24, 26, 74, 76
Battle of the Coral Sea 18
SS *Behar* 149–151
Beilby, James 35, 39, 44, 51–53, 74–75, 78, 87, 121–123
USS *Benevolence* 99
Benge, John 148–150
Bennett, Gordon 162
Bennett, John 57
Bennett, Robert 40, 41, 56, 107
Bicycle Camp 9, 104
Black, C.M. 9
Blackburn, Arthur 162
Blair, Clay, Jr. 3–4, 36, 125–126, 176
Blair, Joan 3–4, 36, 125, 176
Blamey, Thomas 74, 76
Bolger, Les 88
Bolton, K. 160
Bonney, Edmund 76
Boulter, James 77
Bowden, Tim 125, 127
Braddon, Russell 123, 125
Brazil Maru 109, 116–117, 177
Britain 102, 113–114, 154; prosecution of war crimes 130–131, 136, 145–147; and *Rakuyo Maru* survivors 74, 78–80, 82–84, 88, 103–104; relations with allies 83, 104–105
Brown, Fred 88
Brown, Tara 127
Buerckner, Ted 89
Bunker, Harold 21
Burridge, Raymond 132
Buyo Maru 115

Calwell, Arthur 161
Campbell, Hugh 36
Campbell, Jim 50
Campbell, John 45, 57
SS *Cape Douglas* 78
USS *Cape Gloucester* 100

227

Index

Carr, Thomas 50
Carroll, George 35, 36, 49, 93, 99, 102
USS *Case* 54–55
Case, Harold 59
USS *Cavalla* 56
CD-10 39, 48, 61–63
CD-11 33, 36, 61–62
CD-13 47
CD-15 91
CD-18 39, 48, 61
CD-19 47
CD-20 61
CD-21 47, 61
CD-26 39, 48, 61
CD-27 47
CH-19 48
Changi 10, 87, 118–119, 135, 144
Cheah, Wui Ling 146
Chiba, Masami 134
Chiburi 47
Chifley, Ben 157–159
Chivers, Harry 31, 105
Cho Saki Maru 137
Churchill, Winston 170
Chuyo 114
Circassia 102
Clark, David 94–95, 99–100
Clark, Edwin 13
Clarke, Hugh 91, 94, 112, 175
Clifford, Vic 86
Clive, Tony 43
Clyde Maru 92, 119
Coates, Albert 130–131
USS *Cobia* 56
Cocking, Alfred 106–107
Coleman, Leon 135
Collins, Bob 74
Collins, John 124
comfort women 22–23
USS *Consolation* 102
convoy HI-66 148
convoy HI-68 110
convoy HI-72 2–5, 15, 23, 38, 63, 70, 173; attack on 17–20, 24, 33–34, 48, 60–70, 110; composition of 15–16, 38–39, 48, 66; escorts 15–16, 19, 20, 39, 62, 66, 67, 69, 70, 119
convoy HI-74 46–48
convoy HI-84 70
convoy MAMO-02 110
convoy MAMO-73 15–16
convoy protection 15–16, 47, 48, 66, 69–70, 172
Cornelius, Leo 50, 86, 89
Cornford, Roy 15, 22, 26, 39, 41, 55, 72, 77–78, 89, 107, 121–122, 178
Cowling, Anthony 168–170
Cross, Frederick 76
Cumstock, W.A. 54
Curlewis, Adrian 159
Curtin, John 76
Curtis, Owen 132
Cutter, Slade 115, 119

Dai Ichi Maru 117
Daian Maru 154
Dandie, Alex 96
Davis, Ezra 50
Davis, Landon, Jr. 42
Daws, Gavin 11, 141
Day, Noel 32
Dean, Roly 96
Demers, Maurice 54, 106
Dickson, Cecil 86, 102
Dickson, Freda 86
Donnelly, William 50
Downes, M.M. 86
Dunbar, Ross 132
Duncan, Victor 22, 32, 36
Dunlop, Edward 123, 130, 176

Eden, Anthony 82
Eiko Maru 107
England Maru 90, 130
Enoura Maru 109, 114, 116–117, 168
Erie Maru 168
Etorofu 39, 48
Evatt, Herbert 81, 84

Fadden, Arthur 158
Fairburn, Alan 135
Farlow, Cliff 50
Farmer, Frank 41, 107
Fassin, Didier 126
Feiner, Harold 92
Fenno, Mike 106
Ferguson, David 107
Fieldhouse, Ernest 32, 35, 41
USS *Finback* 153
Finkemeyer, Colin 96
Fisk, William 59
Flanagan, Keith 175–176
Fluckey, Eugene 46, 48–*51*, 58, 60
Flynn, John 21, 50, 174
Forde, Francis 77, 84, 85, 161
HMS *Formidable* 102
Fox, Edward 176
friendly fire 1, 10, 95–96, 112–119, 170
Fukkai Maru 5, 90
Fukuda, Mitsugu 139, 143–145, 147, 152
Fukuoka camps 91–92, 95, 97, 171
Fuller, Augustus 50, 78
Fuller, William 79
USS *Fulton* 55, 56, 68

Gallaghan, F.G. 159–160
Garton, Stephen 124
Gebhardt, Reginald 86
Geneva Convention 1, 4, 108, 154, 165
Gerling, E.J. 147
Germany 56, 65, 170
Gibson, Lance 90–91
Gladwin, Lee 109–110
Godwin, James 149–150, 153
Gokoku Maru 16, 24, 39, 48, 60

Index

Gooch, Colin 98
Gozawa, Sadaichi 134–136
Grant, Lachlan 174
Grashio, Samuel 167, 170
Gray, W.M. 135
Green, Percy 148–151
Grice, Cyril 57
Grigg, James 76, 105
USS *Grouper* 108, 168
USS *Growler* 17, 18, 19, 20, 24, 27, 34, 46, 64–66, 68, 70
Guadalcanal 24, 72–73

USS *Haddock* 64
Hague Convention 165
Hakawa Maru 160
Hakko Maru 47
Hakusan Maru 117
Halfhide, Eric 79
Hall, Arthur 22, 132
Hall, Les 87–88
USS *Hammerhead* 119
Hampson, Robert 50
Harima Maru 47
Harrison, Kenneth 91–92, 98–99, 102, 111, 142–143
Harman, John 127
Hart, Reginald 78
Harugiku Maru 13, 113, 115
Haruyoshi Maru 118
Hashimoto, Mochitsura 65
Hauptman, Tony 40
Hawkins, Jack 167
Hayate 18
hellships 2, 165–172; conditions on 6, 14–15, 117, 133–134, 137–138, 140–148, 166–169; definitions of 1, 5, 10, 155
Herbert, David 13, 21, 22, 26, 27, 35, 123–124, 174
Heron, Owen 175
Hewlett, Thomas 95, 171
Hibbert, Alan 135
Hinchy, George 77
Hirado 15, 18, 19, 29, 30, 68
SS *Hiram Bingham* 100
Hirose, Karuhiko 139
Hiroshi, Takagi 140
Hocking, Jack 86
Hodgens, S.F. 139
Hodgson, Alec 124
Hofuku Maru 118–119, 145, 152
Hokusen Maru 166
Hole, Frank 99
Holman, Robert 96–98, 100, 123
Hopper, Gordon 40, 59
USS *Hornet* 116
Hosoya, Sukehiko 30
Houghton, Jack 74, 78
USS *Houston* 8, 9, 24, 74
Howard, John 176
Hubbard, William 22, 132

Huckins, John 30, 37, 61
Hutchinson, Cecil 50
Hyde, Kevin 27, 36, 48, 132

I-158 65
I-365 114
Ichinose, Shiro 62
Ide, Hideichiroo 173
Ide, Winston 173
Ikoma Maru 115
USS *Indianapolis* 3, 176
International Military Tribunal of the Far East 125, 130, 141, 150
Iskov, Ken 99
Itagaki, Seishiro 4

James, Bert 103
James, Clive 103
Japan: navy 18, 33, 64, 66–67, 69, 70, 152, 167; POW camps 90–97, 99, 100; surrender of 87, 97–100, 154; treatment of POWs 82–87, 92, 94–95, 97, 118, 144, 148–150, 163, 165–171; *see also* Fukuoka camps; Kawasaki camp; Naoetsu camp; Ofuna camp; Sakata camp
Jeep Island 12, 31
Johnson, Jimmy 50
Johnston, Tommy 36
Jones, Harry 22, 79
Jordan, G.S. 80
Jotani, Kitaichi 119, 152
Junyo Maru 55, 109, 112–113, 169

Kachidoki Maru 3–5, 14, 25–26, 28–29, 63, 113; and rescue efforts 34, 36–37; sinking of 28–30, 55, 64; survivors of 30, 33, 38, 62, 92, 110
Kagu Maru 16, 24, 26, 39, 48, 60–63
kaibokan 15, 18, 37, 66–67, 69
Kainan Maru 39, 48
Kaiyo 70
Kaji, Hideitsu 141
Kajioka, Sadamichi 18, 166
Kakko Maru 29
Kaneoka, Kioshi 118
Kashii 47
Kasuga Maru 33
Kawasaki camp 93, 95
Kelk, Edward 22, 94, 132
Ken-yo Maru 114
Kenkon Maru 9, 10
Kerr, E. Bartlett 175
Kibitsu Maru 16, 24, 39, 48–49, 60–63, 72, 93
Kimikawa Maru 15
Kisaragi 18
Knox, Forrest 166
Kohli, R.D. 135
Kokai Maru 114
Koshu Maru 112
Kosinski, Julian 50
Koyanagi, Tomiji 68

230 Index

Kume 153
Kurahashi 15, 26, 33, 119
Kuramasan Maru 114

Laconia 1
Lamont-Brown, Raymond 1, 110, 112
Lane, John 102
Lansdowne, Jim 40
USS *Lapon* 68
Lasslett, Fred 93–94
Latham, Colin 87
Lawton, Marion 116
Lazarus, Robert 135
Linderman, Gerald 127
Lisbon Maru 105, 108, 113, 168–169
Liu, Wing-ping 159
Loughlin, Charles 46, 48, 52, 57, 74, 132, 171
Loughnan, Kitchener 22, 26, 35, 38, 49, 94, 98, 100, 102, 133
SS *Lurline* 155

MacArthur, Brian 112
MacArthur, Douglas 98, 113, 157–160
MacDiarmid, Ian 27
MacKay, A.D. 139, 147
MacPherson, Neil 97, 175
Maebashi Maru 10
Mahoney, G.P. 159
Major, Pat 36
Makin, Norman 157
Manning, Stanley 36, 132
Manryu Maru 167
Marks, Bill 30, 110
Maros Maru 118
Marsden, Samuel 175
Martin, David 40
Martin, Keith 132
Martz, Thomas 92
Massingham, G.B. 72–74
Matsen, Syd 36
Mayazumi, Haruo 149, 151–152
Maydon, Stephen 55
Mayne, Bill 99
McCabe, Graeme 98
McCarthy, Mick 89, 97, 100, 102
McCollum, Virgil 166
McEwan, Marcia 126
McGovern, Francis 22, 25, 26, 35–37, 93, 95, 97, 99, 101, 107, 121, 130, 174, 179
McGrath, Frank 25
McIntyre, Grant 147
McKenchnie, Charlie 25
McKernan, Michael 4, 87
McLaglen, Andrew 176
McNitt, Robert 49, 50
Mellish, Cedric 91, 107
Melton, Harry, Jr. 32–33, 37
Menzies, Robert 159, 161
Michno, Gregory 1, 109, 112, 115
Mikura 15, 22, 24, 26, 27, 33, 39, 48, 60–61
Miller, Don 50, 59, 60

Mills, Keith 36
Miyo Maru 90–91
Moe, T.I. 118
Mokuto 36
USS *Monadnock* 73–74
Montevideo Maru 113, 169–170
Moore, Don 91
Morley, Denis 108, 168
Morris, Jack 175
Morton, Dudley 115
Mullemeistrer, J.P.H. 139
Mullins, Jim 27
Munro, Darby 74
Munro, Lloyd 50
Muraoka, Shigeo 142

Nagahashi, Kimata 36–37
Nagano, Osami 70
Nagara Maru 169
Nagasaki Maru 29
Nagle, Harry 31, 128
Nakamura, Kaniyuki 134–135
Nakamura, Takeshi 139
Nankai Maru 15, 19, 20, 24, 27, 63–68
Naoetsu camp 92, 98
USS *Narwhal* 109
New Syonan 12
New Zealand 147, 149, 156
Newton, Reginald 91, 142
Nickerson, G.H. 158, 160
Nighimei Maru 113
Niishio Maru 33
Nimitz, Chester 3, 78
Nippon Maru 114
Nissyo Maru 110
Nitta Maru 166
Noto Maru 110, 168

Oakley, Ben 17, 19, 68
Octagon conference 170
Ofuna camp 90, 149
Okusawa, Ken 134–135
Omuroyama Maru 47
Ono, Tadsu 134–135
Oryoku Maru 70, 108–109, 114–117, 152, 166, 171
Osaki, Makoto 134
Otoriyama Maru 110
Otowa Maru 36
Otowayama Maru 47

USS *Paddle* 15, 108–109
Palmer, Mike 93
USS *Pampanito* 17, 19, 25, 27–29, 34, 37, 40–46, 54–**57**, 59, 60, 64–66, 105–107
Panama Maru 115
Pappas, Paul 41–42
USS *Pargo* 146
Parker, Richard 142
Parker, Samuel 148–150
Parkes, Jerry 26

Index 231

Parkin, Ray 33, 60, 87, 91, 94, 100, 102, 174
Patterson, George 5, 167
Pearson, Jack 105
HMAS *Perth* 5, 8–9, 11; survivors 22, 26, 27, 32–34, 36, 50, 53, 74, 76, 86, 88, 90–91, 93–95, 102, 107, 120, 122, 127, 178–179
Pickett, Harry 21, 41, 106
USS *Picuda* 119
Piper, Richard 162
USS *Plaice* 61–64, 66, 68
USS *Pogy* 10
USS *Pompon* 153
Post-Traumatic Stress Disorder 126–128
Potsdam Declaration 154
Poulter, Robin 105, 168
Pounder, Thomas 14, 29, 30, 33, 38, 49, 94–95, 97–98, 100
SS *President Harrison* 28–29
Prior, Claude 157
Prisoner of War Relatives' Association 84, 88, 120, 123
prisoners of war 82, 87, 98, 114, 115, 126, 133, 175; death toll 82, 84–85, 90, 95, 103, 108, 113–118, 127; diaries 13, 122–124; and Korean guards 94, 137, 139, 142–143, 175; trauma 103, 126–128, 178; *see also* Japan
USS *Puffer* 138

Queen Mary 78
USS *Queenfish* 17, 46, 48–53, 57, 74, 82, 105, 171
Quenton-Baxter, R.Q. 147
Quinton, N.F. 147

Raft, Stanley 174
Raishin Maru 5, 60, 91–92, 124, 133, 137–147, 151–152, 161, 163
Rakuyo Maru 3–5, 13–14, 20, 23, 113, 173–174; and rescue efforts 26, 34–38, 81, 85, 90, 105, 109; sinking of 20–22, 27, 55, 66; survivors in Australia 81, 106, 120–128, 178–179; survivors in water 25, 31, 32, 34, 39–46, 51; survivors on Saipan 56–59, 72; and war crime trials 132–133, 139
Ramsey, Harold 25, 49, 61, 132
USS *Rasher* 112
USS *Raton* 90–91
USS *Ray* 112
USS *Razorback* 116
Rechtman, Richard 126
Red Cross 1, 73, 77, 83, 92, 94, 97–99, 102, 108–109, 113, 170–171, 173
Reich, Eli 17, 19, 20, 25, 34, 42, 44–46, 56, 68
Reid, C.R. 74
Renton, Kenneth 41
USS *Rescue* 100
Return from the River Kwai (film) 176–177
Returned and Services League 122, 145, 160, 178
Richards, Charles 5, 12, 22–23, **101**, 122–126; and Japan 94–95, 100–101, 130, 175–176;

survivor of *Rakuyo Maru* 25–27, 32, 34–38, 49, 61, 86, 107–108, 132, 174, 177, 179
River Valley Road camp 10, 12, 13, 115
Rivett, Rohan 9, 11, 87, 104, 125, 175
Road to Tokyo (film) 177–178
Roberts, Marshall 106
Roberts, Rowland 124
Rodger, T.F. 103
Roediger, Claude 99
Rogers, G.T.H. 78
Rolph, Douglas 57
Roosevelt, Franklin 82, 170
Rosen, Melvin 116
Ryuivchi, Kajino 134

S-14 46
Sagano, George 147
USS *Sailfish* 114
Saipan 17, 44, 54–60, 67, 72, 77, 78
Sakata camp 94–95, 99, 100–101
Sakonju, Naomasa 152
Sanderson, Ralph 98
Sanuki Maru 5, 133, 147–153, 169
Savage, Russell 11, 21–23, 26, 125–126, 132, 133, 178–179
USS *Sawfish* 15, 119
SC-19 33
USS *Scabbardfish* 114
Scates, Bruce 176
Schiff, G.H. 54
USS *Sculpin* 114
USS *Seahorse* 115, 119
USS *Sealion II* 17, 19–21, 25, 27, 34, 40, **42**–46, 54–60, 64–69, 89
Selby, Frank 138
sharks 32, 39, 43, 45, 51
Shaw, Robert 176
Sherlock, A.A. 139
Sherwood, H.W. 95
Shigeru, Kyoda 108
Shikinami 15, 24, 25, 27, 63, 68
Shincho Maru 15, 25, 38, 39, 48, 61
Shinpo Maru 138
Shinyo Maru 15, 55, 108–109, 113
Shirley, Graham 177
Singapore 5, 10–12, 14, 154, 165, 171, 173; and war crime trials 131–**132**, 133, 135, 137, 145; *see also* Changi; River Valley Road camp
Singapore Maru 117, 163
SJ surface radar 18, 27, 61, 64
Skeels, Fred 9, 122
Sleeman, Stuart 135–136
Smith, Ross 50
Smith, Sydney 123
Smith, William 31, 74
USS *Snook* 64, 115
Somerville, James 83
South China Sea 13, 17, **28**, 61, 70, 138, 143
USS *Spadefish* 153
HMS *Speaker* 99, 102
Spielberg, Steven 176

Index

Stark, Edith 73
Starkey, Ed 79
Steele, R.E. 75
Stening, Samuel 90, 92
Stevens, Clyde, Jr. 61–62, 66, 68
Stille, Mark 69
Stuartholme 75, 78, 81
Sturdee, Vernon 162
USS *Sturgeon* 170
submarines 13, 17, 19, 46, 65, 67–70, 119, 146, 153; and rescue of POWs 40–53, 59, 60, 77, 105; success against Japan 64–70, 119, 144, 170; toll on POWs 1–2, 55, 107–119, 168–172
Suez Maru 113
Sugimatsu, Fujio 139
Sumatra railway 169
Summers, Paul 17, 27, 42, 54, 106
Sumner, Arthur 21
Suzuki, Zenki 143
Swinburne, Edwin 48
HMAS *Sydney* 177
Symons, Maurice 148–149

Taian Maru 146
Takahashi, Tatsuhiko 24
Takan Maru 146
Taksuke, Oda 15
Tamahoko Maru 90–91, 113
Tamuan camp 139, 142
Tanabe, Suketomo 141
USS *Tang* 90
Tangney, Dorothy 76–77
Tango Maru 112
Tanno, Shozo 134
USS *Tarpon* 119
Tatsuta Maru 119, 167
Teikon Maru 138
Tenney, Lester 97
Thai-Burma railway 3, 4, 10–11, 43, 79, 81–82, 84–85, 91, 100, 104, 120, 125, 143, 175–177
Thames Maru 115, 133–136
Thams, Neville 50
Thomas, Alf 36
Thomas, Neville 45
Thompson, Murray 50, 77
Tidey, John 169
Tojuki Maru 90
Tomczyk, Charles 48
Tone 149, 151
Tottori Maru 119
Toyashi Maru 10
Toyofuku Maru 55, 113
HMS *Tradewind* 55, 112 , 169
Triebel, Charles 64
HMS *Truculent* 13, 115, 169
Tufnell, Desmond 72
USS *Tunny* 46
Turner, John 42, 58, 72–75, 78

Twomey, Christina 127, 174
Tyree, John 153

U-boats 1, 16
Uchiyama, Kishio 139–145, 147, 152
Ugaki, Matome 65
Underwood, Gordon 153
Ultra 18, 68–69
United States 83, 113, 155, 166, 174; navy 102, 104, 109–110; relations with allies 83, 104–107, 156–160; *see also* submarines
Unyo 47, 48

SS *Van Waerwuyck* 13, 169
Varley, Arthur 10, 12, 13, 32–33, 37
Vietnam War 126–128
Voge, Richard 17
Voisey, Rouse 109

Wade, Ernest 24
Wade, John 24
Wade, Thomas 96, 103
USS *Wahoo* 115
Wait, R.T. 139, 143–144
Wake Island 18, 166
HMS *Wakeful* 101
Walker, Arthur 149
Wall, Herbert 132
Waller, Hector 8
war crime trials 5, 92, 108, 115, 118, 130–155
War Graves Commission 123
Waterford, Van 55, 112
Webb, William 81, 84, 130
Wheeler, Ray 21, 22, 25, 27, 32, 44, 51, 52, 59, 87, 176, 178
Whelan, Alan 94
Whiley, Samuel 41
White, Strachan 40
Whitecross, Roy 61
Wilkinson, John 140
Wilkinson, Mirla 77, 120, 176
Williams, John 11
Williams, Ronald 124
Williams, Roy 54
Winter, Alfred 22, 59
Winter, Walter 106
Wright, John 116
Wylie, A. 78

Yabi, Jinichiro 134
Yamagumo 114
Yamasaka, Tatsuo 148–152
Yoizuki 5, 6, 154–164
Yonai, Mitsusa 63
Yubari 18

Zamaria, Joe 50
Zuiho Maru 15, 25, 28, 34